LISTE EVERY[...]E

DATE

A Personal and Professional Approach

Second Edition

Edited by

Michael Purdy
and
Deborah Borisoff

University Press of America, Inc.
Lanham • New York • London

Copyright © 1997 by
University Press of America,® Inc.
4720 Boston Way
Lanham, Maryland 20706

t
ngland

d
of America
formation Available

Library of Congress Cataloging-in-Publication Data

Listening in everyday life : a personal and professional approach /
edited by Michael Purdy, Deborah Borisoff.--2nd ed.
p. cm.
Includes index.
1. Listening. 2. Oral communication. I. Purdy, Michael. II. Borisoff,
Deborah.
P95.46.L57 1996   302.2'242--dc20   96-9654 CIP

ISBN 0-7618-0460-9 (cloth: alk. ppr.)
ISBN 0-7618-0461-7 (pbk: alk. ppr.)

CONTENTS

Foreword
Ralph Nichols   v

Preface
Deborah Borisoff & Michael Purdy   ix

Introduction: Why Listening?
Deborah Borisoff & Michael Purdy   xiii

Part I

Processes and Contexts of Listening

1. What is Listening?
   Michael Purdy   1

2. Intrapersonal and Interpersonal Listening:
   Self Listening and Conscious Action
   Michael Purdy   21

3. Gender and Listening: Values Revalued
   Deborah Borisoff & Dan Hahn   55

4. Intercultural Listening
   Dean Thomlison   79

5. Managing Interpersonal and Team Conflict:
   Listening Strategies
   Patrice Johnson, & Kittie Watson   121

6. The New Digital Presence: Listening, Access,
   and Computer-Mediated Life
   Rob Anderson   139

7. Listening as an Indiscreet Public Act, or,
   Eavesdropping Can Be Fun
   Gary Gumpert and Susan J. Drucker   163

Part II

Listening in the Professions

8. **Listening in the Educational Environment**
    Carolyn Coakley & Andrew Wolvin   179

9. **Listening Training:**
    The Key to Success in Today's Organizations
    Lyman K. Steil   213

10. **Listening in the Service Industries:**
    It Makes Good Cents
    Judi Brownell   239

11. **Listening and the Helping Professions**
    William Arnold   267

12. **The Lawyer–Client Encounter:**
    Listening for Facts and Relationship
    David A. Victor & Cindy Rhodes Victor   285

13. **Listening: A Crucial Competency for Effective**
    Health Care Delivery
    Gary Kreps, Ellen Bonaguro, & Jim Query   295

14. **Listening in Journalism: All the**
    News We've Heard About That's Fit to Print
    Rob Anderson & Mike Killenberg   *311*

Part III

Conclusion

15. **Steps to Strengthen Listening Ability**
    Deborah Borisoff & Michael Purdy   333

    About the Contributors   341

FOREWORD

Ralph G. Nichols

Because the listening factor in human communication has been a central focus of study and concern throughout my professional life, it is extremely stimulating to discover a new book which reveals the pervasive role of that factor in the lives of a wide variety of people now commonly recognized as "professionals"?

Immediately a question arises. What is meant by "professional"? For centuries the three occupations most frequently granted the respect of being considered professional were those of the lawyer, doctor, and the priest. Occasionally school teachers and college professors were included. But with the arrival of the industrial revolution and its many highly specialized training programs, along with a rapid and impressive growth of public education, vastly expanded numbers of vocations have become similarly honored. Engineers, chemists, dentists, managers, executives, surveyors, accountants, nurses, astronomers—the list seems endless. Now the term "learned professionals" has attained common usage, and it does much to clarify the issue.

Today we readily accept as professional any occupation that requires a stipulated and completed training procedure before the trainee may become a practitioner. Thus, all college and university students automatically become "would-be" professionals. If they attain that goal, they leave behind them lives of repetitive work and effort, and enter lives of decision-making, problem-solving, and creativity. Their search for appropriate answers is unending.

Listening in Everyday Life: A Personal and Professional Approach, carefully analyzes basic principles which can assure increased success for the practicing professional. It opens doors and vastly expands the importance of a long-neglected skill. In recent decades more and more educational leaders have recognized the significance of the listening factor in a learning economy. These leaders are suggesting that listening skills are at least as important as those of reading, writing, and speaking. Hundreds of schools and colleges now offer courses or training units in effective listening. In recent decades, business and industrial management have definitely come to recognize the dollar value of perceptive listening. The concept that "when customers make decisions, they make them for their reasons, not those of the salesman," is now widely recognized. "Customer satisfaction" has now become the hallmark of the trading place. "Quality listening circles" are but one of many devices now employed by industrial management to avert waste, managerial error, and decision-making based upon inadequate communication.

Now, with this book's new approach, specific questions are raised and answered. Effective listening is conceived to be an active and dynamic process, with clearly identifiable rewards for energy expended. Step by step procedures and performance are delineated. The routines presented are based upon careful analysis and basic principles which can assure success to the practitioner. One key point is repeatedly emphasized: our professional lives are an outgrowth of our personal lives. The listening habits we develop in our youth carry over into adulthood and directly influence our ability to be open and receptive to the ideas and feelings of co-workers. Often they directly affect our professional relationships; often, too, they are the determining factor in spelling success or failure for our careers.

Curiously, human beings are deemed to be the only animal life form capable of controlling the direction of their thoughts. Many other animals have better developed sensory mechanisms than we possess; many see, hear, touch, taste, or smell far beyond our natural capabilities. Computers and other machinery can outperform us in calculation and other simple tasks. But through our ability to control thought direction, we have produced tools, machinery, methods of measuring and computing, an alphabet and a vocabulary; above all else we have attained communicative processes which permit a broad sharing of feelings, information, and ideas. It is now widely recognized that the most basic of all human needs is to understand others, and to be understood by them. This precept provides the underlying foundation of this very valuable book.

The authors contributing to this book are among the most productive in the field of listening improvement, including some of the best that the field of listening has produced. They are recognized for their research on listening, the books and articles they have written, their experience in listening-training programs applied to business, industry, government, and social organizations, and for the roles they have played in developing the field of listening through significant organizations such as the International Listening Association, the Speech Communication Association, and the International Communication Association. To bring them together in this text,

with each writing in their own area of expertise, is a valuable contribution to the theory and practice of listening throughout our
personal and professional lives.

PREFACE

The importance of listening in college classrooms and corporate training continues to grow at a rapid pace. At the same time the dynamic expansion of interpersonal communications via the Internet, World Wide Web, internet phones and personal videoconferencing continue to challenge our abilities to adapt as listeners. People are seeing an ever greater need to be able to listen effectively in every part of their lives.

This book addresses the role listening plays in both our personal and our professional lives, and provides steps to strengthen our listening skills. Each chapter was written specifically for this book with the intention of introducing the reader to the major theories that affect the processes of listening, and to the impact of listening on our ability to be effective communicators.

The phenomenal growth and increased awareness of new technologies, public communication and health care have called out for new chapters in this second edition to address these issues. The postmodern awareness of the critical interpretive role media play in our communication lives has prompted the introduction of a chapter on the role of listening for journalists and other information filters in society. This is a major step toward improving media literacy skills for listeners.

The Chapters within the book are self-contained, and hence may be arranged in any sequence to fit the needs of individual readers, classes, or seminars. Exercises designed to enhance listening ability are included at the end of the chapters.

Part One considers the process and contexts of listening. The first two chapters help us understand what listening is, the role listening plays in our personal and professional lives, the different kinds of listening that exist, and the factors that affect our ability to listen intrapersonally and interpersonally. Specifically, Chapter 1 explores the importance of listening, defines listening, and presents the kinds of listening that we use daily. In Chapter 2, the psychological factors that affect our ability to listen intra- and inter-personally are examined.

Chapter 3 examines how gender-based listening behavior is acquired, displayed and interpreted, as well as the social forces that contribute to stereotypes and misunderstandings due to gender-based listening. Acknowledging and understanding these differences can hopefully dispel some of the communication difficulties men and women experience in our culture. Similarly, as our interaction with other countries expands, our need to engage in productive listening with individuals from different cultures becomes a mater of moral, economic, social, and political survival. The fourth chapter places effective listening prominently in the process of crosscultural and intercultural communication and demonstrates how listening is critical to improving relations with people from other countries. The fifth chapter considers the process of listening behavior in the context of conflict. By understanding the powerful role listening plays in the social process, the reader will gain greater insight into how effective listening can be used productively to manage interpersonal and group conflict. Chapters six and seven explore the impact of technology on our ability to listen to one another. Specifically, Chapter 6 looks at how new technologies inform our ability to listen and considers barriers to listening created by computer-mediated life. The interactivity of the Internet means the skills we use in our personal and professional relationships need to adapt as we adopt these new media—especially listening. In Chapter 7, some of the legal and ethical issues about listening—especially eavesdropping on the internet and in other public arenas are addressed. The significance of listening in public places takes on new meaning and in turn stretches our understanding of listening in all contexts.

Part Two applies the listening processes and contexts provided in Part One to the professional arena and looks at listening skills in specific professions—professions with which we have frequent contact. The importance of listening in the educational system, the organizational structure, the service industry, and the helping professions are the foci of Chapters 8 through 11. These chapters examine the financial and emotional costs of ineffective listening in each of these contexts. In addition, steps to maximize productive listening are provided.

One primary professional arena is that of education. The foundation of much of our success in adulthood is laid during our early educational experiences. Chapter 8 points to the critical role listening plays in the educational process and provides practical steps to enhance effective listening in the school setting. The chapter explores the critical role that students, parents, teachers and administrators must play as effective listeners. How we apply the listening behavior acquired at home and at school will have an enormous impact on how we listen and how we are perceived as listeners in our professional encounters. We are all too familiar with costly errors, including loss of life, money, and satisfaction that occur when interactants fail to listen accurately. Chapters 7 through 14 provide in-depth understanding of the role of listening within organizations (including training) and within specific professions, and explores strategies to improve listening behavior in the professional setting. Whether one is studying to be a medical doctor, a lawyer, a business executive, or a journalist, the professional and the client or customer must share equally in the responsibility for effective listening in the relationship.

Chapters 12, 13 and 14 address the responsibility of the medical practitioner and the patient, the attorney and the client, and the journalist and his/her subject to listen and be listened to. In the past, it was often-times assumed that the lawyer or physician would talk; the client or patient would listen. Recently, however, there has been a greater recognition that the responsibility for managing the communication exchange lies with both the practitioner and the consumer. These two professions merely typify the growing awareness of the increased role listening plays in numerous contemporary professions. In the case of journalism, how effectively and accurately the practitioner gathers, interprets and reports information can have far-reaching implications in society: from creating fear, to influencing public perceptions about policy issues, global affairs, and political candidates. Actually, individuals pursuing any career where communication is a matter of concern can incorporate the techniques provided in these three chapters into their own work.

In the final analysis, we all hope to become better listeners. Often in our haste to convey our own ideas, or as a result of distractions, or when we cannot immediately discern how something can directly benefit us, we become ineffective listeners. The last chapter of this book attempts to integrate the techniques and strategies presented in Parts One and Two of this book in order to provide a practical framework to enhance our ability to listen. Only through truly effective listening can mutual understanding be achieved.

Ralph Nichols has indicated that the ability to "understand others and to be understood by others" is crucial to us all. The authors anticipate that the reader of this book will gain an awareness of and a mastery of active listening. The attainment of this knowledge will move us all closer to allowing for the mutual understanding that Nichols so strongly advocates in the Foreword.

Deborah Borisoff and Michael Purdy

INTRODUCTION
Why Listening?

Deborah Borisoff & Michael Purdy

> The natural human being is not a writer or a reader, but a speaker and a listener. This must be as true of us today . . . as it was 7,000 years ago. Literacy at any stage of its development is in terms of evolutionary time a mere upstart, and to this day it is in our spoken communication with each other that we reveal and operate our biological inheritance. (Eric Havelock, interviewed by David Cayley for a CBC Radio series on "Orality and Literacy," in *Listen: The Newsletter of the Listening Centre*, Winter 1989/90, Toronto, Ontario.)

We have all heard the old adage that children should be seen and not heard. Only as adults are we afforded the opportunity to speak and be listened to. The ability to speak and control speech, therefore, becomes a source of power in American culture. The child learns that the parent has the last word and often cannot speak until spoken to. The young student can speak out only when called upon by the teacher; the rest of the time, he or she is expected to listen.

Our culture has learned its lessons only too well. We listen to the voice of authority—be that authority a medical or legal practitioner, a manager, an officer of the law, or a religious leader. Listening has, consequently, come to be associated with passivity, often times with weakness. As a result of this attitude which trivializes listening, listening training has been largely ignored in the classroom, as well as in business and industry.

In recent years, a growing awareness of the important role listening plays in our personal and professional lives has shaped a more informed attitude toward listening. Largely due to the efforts of a pioneering researcher in listening, Ralph Nichols, we have become keenly aware of the results of effective listening. Some of these positive effects include enhanced mutual understanding among friends and family members, increased productivity and performance in organizations, greater learning and retention of material, and productive understanding among peoples of different race, nationality, age, and gender.

Through the works of Nichols and many other researchers, several of whom are contributors to this edition and many others of whom are cited, we have learned that listening is not a passive skill that shows weakness. Rather, it is a highly active and demanding art. Moreover, through practice, we can strengthen our ability to listen more efficiently, effectively, and accurately. This text focuses on how we can become a more accomplished listener.

We are fortunate to have some of the most prominent names in the field of listening as contributing authors to this text. While we have provided editorial guidelines regarding the tone, approach and scope of each chapter, we invite you to listen to each author's unique voice.

Chapter 1

WHAT IS LISTENING?

Michael Purdy

Points to be Addressed:

- The neglect of listening.
- The importance of listening in personal and professional life.
- The predominance of communication time spent listening.
- Listening Definitions and listening standards
- The components of listening.
- Types of listening and their use in everyday situations.
- Ethical Listening

Communication has two dimensions: speaking (expression), and listening (reception). For most of Western Civilization, speaking has been the form of communication regarded as most important. The first books on communication were about how to be an effective speaker. Listeners were recognized, but only as they were important to the purposes of the speaker. In fact, speaking has been championed as the way to success throughout Western history. We give honors and awards to great speakers, but how may people do you know who have been recognized for their listening talents? There is even a popular speaking course that purports to teach "how to win friends and influence people." The road to success is not through listening, they suggest.

The Primacy Of (Conscious) Listening

Today we know differently. In the chapters that follow you will discover how much power listening can provide in interacting with others in personal and professional situations. But the listening that has power must be a conscious listening, listening with self-conscious awareness. We all learn to listen naturally with little striving as we mature, but learning to listen consciously takes extra effort. Becoming a conscious listener will make you more sensitive to the needs of the listener (audience) and hence, improve your competence as a speaker. It will also make you more sensitive to the needs of people in general.

As Paul Tournier, Swiss Psychiatrist and author has expressed:

> It is impossible to overemphasize the immense need humans have to be really listened to, to be taken seriously, to be understood. Listen to all the conversations of our world, between nations as well as those between couples. They are for the most part dialogues of the deaf." (Powell, p. 5)

Thankfully, an awareness of the importance of listening has been growing and with it recognition of the need for conscious listening. There has been increased publication of books and journal articles[1] about listening, but, also one cannot help noticing, articles in popular magazines and newspapers.

The importance of listening has been recognized by many professional organizations and influential individuals. Coakley and Wolvin cite no less than 12 major research studies by organizations which found listening to be one of the most important skills (in many cases *the* most important skill) for employees at every level of the organization (1988, p. 28). Another study cited in Wolvin and Coakley and conducted by the Speech Communication Association, surveyed 194 community college Career Advisory Board members (representing a wide range of occupations) to determine the members' perceptions as to the relative importance of forty-nine selected communication skills in the performance of career duties. Survey results showed that listening skills were consistently ranked as the most important communication skills for career competence (p. 28) *In Academic Preparation for the World of Work* the College Board indicated listening and speaking as the primary form of communication in business and industry, "yet one in which many students receive little or no instruction" (1984, p. 3).

---

[1] For example, *The International Journal of Listening* published by the International Listening Association, and journal articles and books from a discourse perspective, such as *Speakers, listeners and communication*, by Brown.

Individuals from diverse occupations have praised listening. Lee Iacocca, in his autobiography, cannot say enough about the value of good speaking. However, he also says:

> I only wish I could find an institute that teaches people how to listen. After all, a good manager needs to listen at least as much as he needs to talk. Too many people fail to realize that good communication goes in both directions. (1984, p. 54)

Tom Peters, the recognized authority on quality service declared in his 1982 book, *In Search of Excellence*, that "the excellent companies are not only better on service, quality, reliability, and finding a niche. They are better listeners" (p. 196). These companies are strong on service because they pay attention to their customers; they listen. In his 1988 book *Thriving on Chaos* Peters devotes three major sections of the book to listening: Customer Responsiveness, "becoming obsessed with listening;" Empowering People, "listen, celebrate, recognize;" and Leadership, "pay attention! (more listening)." In Peter's 1994 book, *The Pursuit of Wow*, he is still extolling the virtues of listening to customers and clients, "just [to] check in . . . see if there's anything they want to talk about" (262).

Listening is one important ingredient to success in personal and professional life. Those who master the art of listening will at the very least be regarded positively.

Merrill and Borisoff (1987) have written on the importance of listening in the legal profession. Davis (1984) has written an excellent book, *Listening and Responding*, about listening in the helping professions, and Arnold, in *Crisis Communication*, stresses that listening is vital to crisis intervention (1980, p. 56). In the book *Communicating With Medical Patients*, Weston and Lipkin state that "Skill in communicating with patients is the single most important skill the student physician learns" (1989, p. 54). Judging from the most important activities involved, such as taking a history and interviewing, listening would be the most important communication skill. Similar sources could be cited for each of the major professions. Clearly, the ability to listen effectively is a skill essential for professional success.

Not only is listening a valuable skill, it is also conducive to good health. Studies have shown that when we talk our blood pressure goes up; when we listen it goes down (Lynch, 1985, p. 160). Sometimes we talk to control people and/or situations. Sometimes we talk so we will not have to listen to ourselves. Regardless, when we talk to another person our whole system becomes more excited. When we listen we are more relaxed. It would seem best, then, for optimum health to balance our listening and talking.

From this it would follow that it is vital for hospital staff to listen to individual patients who are ill. Additionally, Wahlers (1989) in a presentation on listening to the dying (as well as others in institutional situations) has stressed the importance of good listening skills for hospice volunteers and medical professionals working with the terminally ill.

As essential as our physical health is to each of us it is equally important to recognize how crucial good communication is to the health of our interpersonal relationships; to our roles as parents, children, friends and lovers. Listening is especially important in the family where in the long run it strengthens both individuals and communities. Maintaining good relationships leads to a healthier and happier life. As Stewart says *"The quality of your life is directly linked to the quality of your communication"* (1986, p. 7). In personal life, as well as in the business and professional world we can only benefit from the constructive role of effective listening.

Among the basic skills we need for success in life, listening is primary—there is no meaningful communication without listening. Developmentally, we listen before we learn to speak, read, or write. Brown, one of the pioneers of listening research has noted that "Of foremost importance is the role of listening in language acquisition, [itself] the basis of all subsequent communication, the foundation of all life-long reading, writing, speaking and listening activities" (1987, p. 5). Heidegger, considered one of the 20th century's greatest philosophers, recognized the primacy of listening in creating meaning and in developing our relationships with one another (1962, p. 204). Listening establishes us in our life situation and enables us to maintain meaningful relations with family, friends, and professional associates.

Time Spent Listening

Studies, beginning with Rankin's famous work (1928) reporting the amount of time adults spent in various forms of communication, have indicated that of the four basic communication skills (reading, writing, speaking, listening) we use the skill of listening most. From 42 to 60% (or more) of our communication time is spent listening, depending on whether we are students, managerial trainees, doctors, counselors, lawyers, or nurses. Cotton (1986) found that attorneys spent more time listening than any of the other skills, and that listening was especially important in legal interviewing and counseling, and to a lesser degree in oral argument. A 1980 study found that college students spend 52.5% of their time listening (Barker, Edwards, Gaines, Gladney, & Holley). Studies of dieticians indicated they spent three times as much time listening as any other verbal communication skill, and similar results were found for housewives, and technical employees (Barker, et al., 1980, pp. 101–102). Gilbert notes that students in grades K–12 "are captive and are expected to listen

65-90% of the time, . . . [and yet] language arts instruction is focused upon reading and writing" (1988, p. 122).[2]

Studies—particularly those such as Barker, et al.—have shown a trend, beginning with Rankin, toward increased time spent listening. This trend has definitely been reinforced by the continued increase in mediated communication. Many of us in the listening field have observed that as we watch more television, movies, videos; listen to the radio, CDs or the internet, increasingly more demands are being made on our ability to listen.

Obviously it is important to learn to be more effective listeners, and early studies have shown that our listening comprehension may be only about 25%, with little change even if the speaker is an excellent presenter. (Nichols & Lewis, 1954, p. 4). Yet, we must conclude that although listening is our most used skill, rarely do we receive formal listening training in the home or at school.

Both editors have, as an assignment, had students interview professionals in the field they were pursuing. Doctors, lawyers, hotel managers, teachers, counselors, executives, administrators, and nurses were interviewed. Each interviewee was asked to estimate the percentage of their time they spent in their jobs speaking, reading, writing, and listening. With few exceptions, every professional indicated that they listened the most. The interviewees were also asked to rank which skills they felt were most important. Unanimously, they rated listening the highest.

Listening Definition and Standards

The process of listening is often contrasted with hearing. Lundsteen considered hearing a physical act and listening a mental act. Hearing she said had to do with our physiological capacity to receive and process sounds (1979, p. xv). Problems with our ability to hear could hinder our listening. Hence, it behooves each of us to have our hearing checked if we think it could be affecting our ability to listen. In contrast to hearing, listening has to do with assigning meaning to the stimuli received by our brain. To listen, according to Nichols and Lewis, in one of the first books on listening, is to attach "meaning to the aural symbols perceived" (p. 1).

We will maintain this defined distinction between hearing and listening, here, even though in our day-to-day usage the words may be used interchangeably. We may say "I did not hear you." But we did hear, we just were *not fully attending* and hence were not listening. (Sometimes, if we quickly focus our mind on what was said we can still remember what was said. The words remain in short term memory for a brief period of time and can be recalled.)   There is also

---

2 See Gilbert, & Barker, et al., for reference to the studies on amount of time spent listening and time allocated to teaching listening.

confusion in our everyday usage because parents tell their children "you're not listening." What the parent often means is "you are not obeying." In the Germanic roots of the Anglo–Saxon language there is a sense in which "to listen" means "to obey". Hearing and listening will have precise meanings in this text.

There are several distinct definitions of listening, and there is little agreement about which is the best; nor should there be. Each definition represents a different perspective of listening, and with the many approaches to listening there are bound to be a number of definitions. Ethel Glenn (1989) in the *Journal of the International Listening Association*[3] lists fifty different ways of describing listening. This list is not exhaustive. It indicates, however, that listening is conceived differently depending upon how people intend to *apply* the definition. For example, researchers who seek to *predict* listening behavior, versus those who *interpret* listening, versus consultants who provide listening *skills training* in the workplace may each employ a viable, albeit different definition of the term listening. Glenn's content analysis of the fifty definitions found that the concepts most often included in the definition of listening were: perception, attention, interpretation, response, and spoken and visual cues.

Since Glenn's study, the International Listening Association[4] (ILA) has adopted an official definition of listening:

> Listening: the process of receiving, constructing meaning from, and responding to spoken and/or nonverbal messages (Emmert, 1996, p. 2).

At the same time the Speech Communication Association was developing new standards for communication education: *Speaking, Listening, and Media Literacy Standards for K through 12 Education* (1996) and immediately incorporated the ILA definition in the listening standard. This definition includes all of the essential elements from Glenn's study and those mentioned in our definition (below).

It was ironic that when *USA Today* covered news of the report, published by the Speech Communication Association, the title of the article on the front page of the Life section of the newspaper was "Helping Youth to *Speak*" [my emphasis]. We could be generous and suggest that *Speaking* implied listening (although it would be a stretch to suggest it also included media literacy), but this is one more case of the unthinking neglect of listening, supported by the fact that listening was only given one short phrase in the article.

Throughout Western history we have assumed listening was natural and automatic. Listening needed no special attention. We did not concern ourselves with study and training in the art of listening. Lis-

---

[3] Now the *International Journal of Listening.*
[4] Contact the ILA at Box 25324, Overland park, KS 66225-5324; phone (913) 685-9228 or 1-800-ILA-4505.

tening, however, is not automatic, it requires our full and conscious attention. To be better listeners we need to understand, and work with the components of the listening process.

For our purposes, whatever definition of listening we choose we must know that listening is based on several premises. Listening:

- Can be *learned*,

- Is a *dynamic* process,

- Is an *active* process,

- Involves mind and body, with *verbal* and *nonverbal* processes working together, and

- Allows us to be *receptive* to the needs, concerns, and information of others, as well as the environment around us.

It seems trivial to say that listening can be *learned*, but unless we perceive and know listening to be a behavior that can be improved any study of listening would be wasted effort. Indeed, studies of listening beginning with Nichols and Lewis in the 50's indicate that we can change how we listen in very significant ways. Tests such as the *Watson-Barker Listening Test* and *the Kentucky Listening Test* have two parts that measure changes in listening before and after instruction and use of the tests does indicate improvements from learning and practicing listening.

That listening is *dynamic* means that while there may be essential listening components the act of listening itself is never the same twice. We must be constantly alert and open to improvisation as the elements of the listening situation change. Like a jazz musician's spontaneous and unrehearsed play, we must adapt to the communication of the other members of our social group, always conscious and alert for changing meanings in the situation.

Listening is also *active* as opposed to passive. It is something that we consciously *do*; it does not simply happen. Rogers and Farson, in a classic article on active listening define "active" as meaning:

> the listener has a very definite responsibility. He does not passively absorb the words which are spoken, but he actively tries to grasp the facts and feelings in what he hears, to help the speaker work out his own problems. (p. 149)

The above components of the listening process focus not only upon the speaker's *verbal* message, but also upon the *nonverbal* message, involving both mind and body. The meaning may be grasped from what is said, as well as, what is unsaid. Birdwhistell's work in the early seventies, in fact, argued that perhaps the majority of a message derives from the nonverbal dimension (1970). Thus the listener must attend not only to *what* the speaker says, but also to *how* he or she says it (e.g., tone of voice, pitch, rate of speaking, etc.), and to the *context* in which the message is delivered (e.g., a formal auditorium, an informal gathering, a classroom, etc.). The *how* of what the speaker says includes feelings; for if we just listen to denotative meaning we miss the *emotional* content. Listening to feelings in a situation may tell us what is motivating the speaker, as well as other pertinent information. The listener who attends to both the verbal and the nonverbal communication will likely listen more accurately than the individual who is oblivious to these important cues.

Finally, through conscious listening we can be *receptive* to other human beings as well as to our environment. I think except in rare cases good listening never hurt anyone. On the positive side effective listening can be extremely helpful in knowing what is in the heart of another human being. Through listening we can learn to know another human being better and on that basis be more receptive to them. We cannot *receive* another's words unless we understand them, and we cannot understand them without listening.

Listening to the world around us can also make us more receptive to out environment. If we listen to the bird's songs, the rustle of the grass and the leaves, the howl of the wind, the crashing of the ocean waves, we cannot help but appreciate natural environment a little more.

With these premises as a foundation, our definition of listening reads as follows:

> Listening is the active and dynamic process of attending, perceiving, interpreting, remembering, and responding to the expressed (verbal and nonverbal) needs, concerns, and information offered by other human beings.

This is a definition that encompasses the official definitions of the SCA and the ILA and is at the same time more specific, emphasizing the need for attention, perceiving *and* interpreting, and remembering. In addition it focuses our attention on the all important needs and concerns of real people.

The Components of Effective Listening

Having defined listening we can then discuss the important components of the listening process which are summarized in the seven steps for becoming an effective listener.

Steps to Becoming an Effective Listener
1.   Want to listen
2.   Focus your attention
3.   Be aware (perceptive) as you listen

4. Keep in mind that the listening process involves interpretation (including both verbal and nonverbal cues)
5. Consciously work to remember what you hear
6. Make a habit of responding with feedback
7. Care about the relationship as you listen

These seven components are an integral part of the dynamic and active process of listening.

First, for an individual to be able to listen, he or she must *want* or desire to listen. Thus, *volition*, or the will to listen is the initial component of effective listening. Even having willed ourselves to attend to the ideas of another, it sometimes takes courage to listen fully to another human being. To listen fully may mean we may have to change our beliefs or attitudes based upon what we hear. Nichols and Stevens recognized the difficulty in their 1957 book, *Are You Listening?*: "Whenever we listen thoroughly to another person's ideas we open ourselves up to the possibility that some of our own ideas are wrong" (p. 51–52).

Second, good listening requires *focused attention*. If our minds are wandering, or, if we are jumping ahead anticipating what we *think* the speaker might say, we are apt to miss important information. The third component of the listening process is *perception*. We need to be aware of all of the elements of message, speaker, and context. This also implies that we must be open and receptive to the messages of others. A critical part of communication is lost when individuals are unwilling to listen to others because of, for example, prejudicial or opposing viewpoints.

The fourth component of the listening process is the capacity to *interpret* the messages and meanings of the others. The process of interpretation includes understanding. In interpreting a message we naturally make sense of that message in terms of our own experience. This means each message understood is a creative process; it also implies we are limited by our experience. For example, listening to someone's story of divorce when we've never experienced divorce means we must creatively stretch to understand something beyond our immediate ken. A person may be highly motivated to listen to a message, for instance on contemporary physics. However, if the message is especially complex or technical beyond the listener's ability, then the likelihood for an accurate interpretation is greatly diminished.

Fifth, competent listening includes *remembering*. Often we remember without exerting any effort. In many critical listening situations, however, we need to consciously and actively include listening skills that help us retain what we have heard. Some basic skills for enhancing memory will be covered in the next chapter. A sixth component is the need for *response* as essential to completing the process of good listening. Sometimes our response is internal as we integrate what we have understood and internally comment upon it.

Usually after understanding a complete thought it is important that we give feedback to the speaker, or respond in such a way that the speaker has an idea of how we have understood and interpreted what he or she has said. Unless we do give the speaker meaningful and useful feedback (preferably both verbal and nonverbal), the speaker is in the dark and must imagine what her/his impact on us has been.

The seventh and last component is the *human being*. In listening we must always be receptive to the personal element. In both our personal and business lives people are the most important resource. Listening should validate and empower people, thus enhancing relationships. We also listen for information, but we must keep in mind that information is colored and given meaning by a person's needs and concerns (the listener's as well as the speaker's). As students, doctors, lawyers, law enforcement officers, etc., we cannot "manage" without good information. Information is the lifeblood of our professions. Today organizations cannot function without a continuous flow of information. All information, however, is only meaningful as it describes and relates to a human condition.

How We Use Listening

Definition is one way to describe our most powerful communication skill. Equally significant are the functions or uses of listening. The functions Dance and Larson offer for communication, in general, also work well for listening. In responding to the question, "What are the functions of human communication?," Dance and Larson reply:

> regardless of the intent, purpose or goal of an individual engaged in any level of human communication—there are always three functions ... (1) the linking of the individual with the environment, (2) the development of higher mental processes, and (3) the regulation of human behavior (1976, p. 49).

Listening as a linking function serves to build relationships. We build strong links with others by listening to who they are and what they mean. Listening is also our primary means of growth and intellectual development. We impart knowledge when we speak; we learn when we listen. Finally, through speaking we manipulate and control our environment, but we could not do so effectively unless we had listened first to know how to direct our speaking for maximum results. This has traditionally been know as audience analysis. Listening, therefore, functions to serve our basic human needs. More specifically, listening serves the purposes of learning; establishing and maintaining friendships; getting good grades; making a sale; building relationships; finding out about our clients' needs, concerns, or objections; and is crucial in many other important activities each day.

Listening Situations And Types Of Listening

There are many different types of listening or different situations in which we use listening. Some of the different situations might include social/conversational, in relationships, at work, listening to the media. Each situation is different and each may require a different kind of listening.

In studies where adult students were asked to indicate how their listening differed in work, social, and family situations, Purdy (1982) found that the majority of students said they listened more concertedly at work, because they were required to listen at work. They did not put forth as much effort at home or in social situations. Why do we make such distinctions regarding how and where we expend our listening effort? Should not listening at home with our families, or in social situations deserve as much attention as work? Perhaps it does for you.

Another way to look at listening is in terms of the type of listening required in different situations. Barker (1971) divides listening into active–passive and serious–social. Barker maintains that active listening is "involved listening with a purpose." Passive listening, in contrast, is "barely more than hearing" (pp. 9–13). For our purposes passive listening can be considered hearing; active listening as defined above is our primary concern.

Other authors distinguish among, (1) discriminative, (2) comprehensive, (3) critical (evaluative), (4) therapeutic (empathic), and 5) appreciative listening.[5] Nichols and Lewis combined comprehensive under the heading of discriminative and found it "so basic that it is actually a controlling factor in the other two [appreciative and critical]" (2). Wolvin and Coakley consider discriminative and comprehensive listening to be fundamental to the other three types of listening.

Discriminative listening is "listening to distinguish the aural stimuli" (Wolvin & Coakley, p. 141). This type of listening involves the basic skill of noticing the aspects or details of the message itself (both verbal and nonverbal). It is essentially our ability to be aware of the features of a message, rather than the content. For example, if a speaker's message is tough but his or her voice is cracking slightly, this could tell us that the speaker may have a subtext, or hidden motive that is not being expressed. Some of President Nixon's messages denying any knowledge of Watergate, for example, had this quality.

---

5 See Wolvin & Coakley, Wolf, et al., and Nichols & Lewis for three different ways of breaking out the types of listening.

We should be able to discriminate verbal and nonverbal cues that will help us to understand the full meaning of a message.

Comprehensive listening is listening for an understanding of a message. It goes beyond discrimination to include comprehension of the message's content. This is essentially listening without being critical or evaluating the message, but listening simply to learn. Listening to a classroom lecture on the state of the economy, or on organic chemistry are obvious examples of comprehensive listening. An interpersonal example might involve listening to know more about a friend's financial situation or love life. There are many techniques that will help us to understand messages better, from focusing our attention, to improving our memory, sensitivity to language, note-taking skills, to expanding our underlying experience of life. Each strategy will enable us to understand people and situations better.

Critical-evaluative listening is the intelligent response to persuasive or propagandistic messages. Critical listening assumes discriminative and comprehensive listening have taken place so we already understand the message. In our personal lives we must critically evaluate people's intentions; in our professional lives we must do the same. In both fields of experience we must be able to distinguish the sales pitch from the word of the true believer. A friend asks her roommate to invest a substantial amount of her savings in a great deal. A director of research and development in a major corporation attempts to persuade his colleagues that his division rather than marketing needs to hire a new manager. In both personal and professional circumstances, it is crucial that the roommate and the director of marketing listen closely, and carefully scrutinize the request and the rationale behind it.

To be an effective critical listener, we must be able to consider the influence of a speaker's packaged image, demonstrate the ability to detect whether a proposition is logical and supported with reasonable arguments, and be able to assess when our own psychological needs or weaknesses are being unfairly played upon.

Therapeutic listening is listening which lends a non-judgmental, healing ear to family, friends, and professional associates. It is listening with the interests of the other in mind. The person who understands fully a friend's loss, the parent who can empathize with a child's anxiety, the employee who understands a colleague's special concern, or the therapist who helps a patient work out a particular problem are all demonstrating therapeutic listening. Because in each instance the listener attempts to *feel with* the other person rather than attempting to change his or her behavior, we call this type of listening *empathic* listening. The final goal of empathic listening is therapeutic—to help the other person feel better and understand themselves through the attentive ear of a caring other. To be an effective therapeutic listener, it is essential to set aside our own interests and focus primarily on the needs and concerns of the other. Therapeutic listening implies, as Wolvin and Coakley state, an ability to listen discriminatively and comprehensively.

Appreciative listening is enjoyment of messages for their own sake. In personal and professional life it may involve listening to the nuances of a voice, an artistic performance, or television, radio, internet, and film productions. Wolf, Marsnik, Tacey, and Nichols in their book *Perceptive Listening* suggest that "we listen appreciatively when we listen to aural symbols in order to gain pleasure through their reception" (1983, p. 59). Appreciative listening is purposeful in our personal and professional lives as we learn to enjoy our listening and take delight in our relationships, as well as thinking of them in terms of accomplishments. Listening appreciatively relaxes us and puts us more in tune with ourselves and our environment.

Thus, the student who turns on the radio after a full day of classes, the executive who plays a personal stereo while jogging, or the parent who finds a welcome respite by watching television are all experiencing appreciative listening.

All of us engage in the five types of listening behavior. How well we listen, however, depends on a variety of factors that are influenced by our backgrounds and experiences. In Chapter Two we examine the various factors that affect our intra- and inter–personal listening skills.

Regardless of the *type* of listening we are engaged in, there are rules of behavior we must learn in order to be an effective listener. By way of illustration, how good would a friend be at therapeutic listening if he provided no feedback, or a doctor if she were to look away when discussing a diagnosis with a patient?[6] Similarly, a college student may contend that he can listen simultaneously to a teacher's lecture and to a football game. Appropriate comprehensive listening, however, suggests that such distractions severely limit comprehension.

How do we learn to demonstrate proper behavior for discriminative, critical, comprehensive, therapeutic, and appreciative listening? As with all of our behavior, appropriate communication is a function of cultural norms and of group expectations. Sociologists Stockard and Johnson (1980) contend that the familial, educational, religious, and institutional systems we are immersed in serve to influence our behavior. Additionally, our personal backgrounds (i.e., intelligence, psychological make–up, gender, ethnicity, religion, etc.) shape our interest and willingness to listen to others. We may, therefore, share in the belief that we should listen quietly to an orchestral symphony or to a dramatic performance. Yet individuals may be perplexed by

---

6 Admittedly, there are instances when limited feedback is appropriate. For example, a psychoanalyst may not look at a patient. However, such behavior is generally in response to the patient's needs.

the affective display of listening by a member of the opposite sex or a different country.

Subsequent chapters in this book will address the impact of gender, ethnicity, and specific professional roles on listening behavior. Despite the different focus of these chapters, each one acknowledges that through listening we empower people. In all of our relationships—both personal and professional—our ultimate goal is to empower individuals so that they may creatively function at their best. Issues such as these naturally lead to the discussion of ethics.

Ethical Listening

Ethics is about decision-making and behavior—what is the proper thing to do in any situation. What we should do involves action; and listening, as much as any aspect of communication, is action. As an action, listening (or not listening) has real consequences for people and messages. If we ignore—or do not listen—to a friend the result can be very hurtful. So a basic principle might be: "Listen first and ask questions later!"

As a start, we can state that listening ethics has to do with to whom and to what we listen. Ultimately, it comes down to why. Why do we listen to certain people and certain messages differently than other people and messages. The key word here is differently, because being an ethical listener we wouldn't want to not listen when listening is appropriate. If we are an ethical listener we don't reject any person or message wholesale without first understanding what we are missing by not listening. Having not listened to a person or message we may cause consequences for ourselves and others that are difficult or impossible to change.

Some authors suggest that when and where we listen are also important (Brownell, 1996, p. 368), but they are secondary to people and messages. For instance, we might decide to schedule meetings, classes or training in the morning knowing that we are at our listening best in the first hours of the day. Or me might put off listening to a friend's problem until we can listen in a quiet, secluded place where we won't be interrupted. These are some decisions about where and when we listen, but they usually are of secondary importance to people and messages.

We might also say, "I have a right to not listen." That is true. We all have a right to turn off other people or messages like we turn off the radio or the television. One women in a listening training session actually said this. The difficulty is that it is easy to exercise our rights and a real challenge to exercise our responsibility. Not listening is a simple act of "turning a deaf ear," "tuning out," or pretending to listen. Listening, on the other hand, involves attention, conscious effort to remember, awareness of how we interpret and distort messages through our culture and personal filters, sustained empathy, and a concerted effort to respond to the speaker in meaningful ways. So the ethics of listening depends on all of the skills and understandings we have covered in this chapter. Ethical listening will also depend on the skills and understandings in all of the contexts and professional situations which will be discussed in the coming chapters of this book. Watch for the ethical principles implicit within each of these chapters.

In this book we do not want to set down any unalterable rules about ethical listening, but rather present one guiding principle. That principle is: "that we put forth the effort to listen as much as we are able, and with as much openness and empathy as we can muster" (Purdy, 1995, p. 9). There are many qualifications that go along with this principle: sometimes we are physically sick or tired, sometimes people rub us the wrong way, sometimes we just don't like people, or the environment may make it difficult to listen. The message itself may be difficult to listen to for a number of reasons: we may dislike the subject, we might not know anything about the topic, or maybe we strongly disagree with the opinion expressed. There can be many reasons for not listening to a person or a message.

The prime compelling reason to listen to a person or message is that only through listening, and communication in general, do we have any hope of working together and accomplishing our personal and professional goals. Only through listening can we learn anything about people and situations in order to make sound ethical decisions and take action. An ethical decision made without careful listening to the people and messages in a situation is suspect.

We conclude with two examples (stripped down and simplified to be sure) as a basis for discussion of listening ethics. We leave it to the reader to continue to analyze some of the issues involved in listening ethics through examples in the exercises at the end of this chapter.

First, let's take an example which is all too common in our lives—rumor. Our friend/spouse (whomever) tells us about a mutual friend who is cheating on her/his partner. We want to listen, out of interest, if for no other reason. We also need to listen to discriminate what might be fact from fiction, and to comprehend what is happening in our friend's relationship, as well as to understand why our friend/spouse is presenting this situation as she/he is; i.e., what is motivating them? If someone continually spreads baseless rumors or talks about people with injurious motives, we should consider whether it is necessary to listen at all. If the rumors help us to understand our friend/spouse who is telling the tale, or our friend who is having the relationship problems, we need to listen critically and evaluatively, weighing the facts and the personalities involved and making a decision about what to pass on to others. With rumor it is more than a simple matter of listening or not listening, but also of how to listen, what to listen for, what to make of what we hear and

what to tell others based upon our critical understanding (Purdy, p. 8).
     Second is the challenge of listening to ideas and issues that are controversial. This challenge cuts both ways: it may be easy to naively accept an issue we think we agree with but it may also be too easy to reject out-of-hand an issue we disagree with. Both are problematic—issues do not come in only two flavors, but have as many nuances of taste as there are people presenting them. If someone presents a stance on abortion, for example, we have a responsibility to listen carefully to their unique stance on the issue—whether we agree or not. Controversial issues, or differences of opinion, then, involve more than listening and not listening, they may also involve our relationship to the particular person presenting the idea.
     Controversial issues also involve our commitment to ideas or ideology (a body of doctrine or thought forming a political or social program). We must be aware of our own position on the issue and be sure to bracket it (or put it out of play) while we openly listen to the other person. We cannot listen openly to another's ideas if our own ideas are in the way. Based upon our comprehension of a unique person and message we can move forward to critically evaluate the position we heard.
     So, listening ethics is making decisions about how we listen. That decision includes several important concerns. We have discussed a few of them here. Ethics, however, is complex, depending upon delicate considerations of people and messages before acting. Those considerations rest upon effective listening. An old carpenter once said: "measure twice, cut once." We would say: "Listen twice, act once."

Summary

     In this chapter we have discussed the importance of listening in our personal and professional lives. We have admitted the difficulty we confront when attempting to define listening and have proposed one definition that takes into account the individual's desire to listen, and the importance of focused attention, awareness, remembering, and the ability to interpret verbal and nonverbal communication. In addition, we have reviewed the concise definition of the ILA, meant to be useful for a broad range of people trying to work with the concept of listening. We also recognized the importance of listening to the needs and concerns of each individual. The five kinds of listening that we all engage in—discriminative, critical, evaluative, therapeutic, appreciative—are also explained as useful in our everyday living. Finally, this chapter introduced concepts describing how we acquire listening behavior and the appropriate ethical approach to listening.

Exercises

1. For the duration of this class keep a listening journal in which you record observations of listening behavior in your classes/seminars, at home (where you live), at work, and in your relationships. Begin your journal with observations of effective and ineffective listening. For a five day period find examples of effective and ineffective listening, and compare and contrast the differences between the two. Report on your findings to the group.

2. At the beginning of the class/seminar, have each individual introduce him- or her-self to the rest of the group and mention a few things about him- her-self. Once the self-introductions are complete, ask each participant to take out a sheet of paper and write down what they remember about each individual. Group discussion should follow on how effectively each person recalled what was said and to what extent effective listening was or was not impaired, and why.

3. Break up the class/seminar into several small groups. Assign each group a professional role to discuss (i.e., nurse, teacher, surgeon, lawyer, police officer, mother, business executive, journalist, secretary, etc.). Have each group generate a list of verbal and nonverbal cues that a member of this profession would need to display that would indicate to others that they were listening. Would the communication change if the individual were trying to listen discriminatively versus critically? How?

4. Ask each class/group participant to interact with a friend or family member but to refrain from providing feedback (verbal or nonverbal). What kind of reactions did they receive from the other party? How did they feel when they were not allowed to respond? What role does feedback play in listening?

5. Read Ethel Glenn's short article on the content analysis of fifty definitions of listening (see references). Consider the strengths and weaknesses of each group of definitions for your professional area. Then either write your own definition, or choose one of those listed and defend you choice (or your created definition) in 250-300 words. Compare your definition with the official definition of the ILA. For example, you might consider what makes listening in your profession special or different, and hence requires a unique definition of listening.

6. Discuss how you would listen ethically in each of the following situations:

    One of your siblings (friends if you are an only child) is talking disparagingly about another sibling (friend).

You hear a colleague at work telling racist jokes.

A religious extremist is presenting their position on campus.

Your child, or a friend's, talks incessantly.

Why would you make certain listening decisions and not others?

References

Arnold, W. E. (1980). *Crisis communication.* Dubuque, IA: Gorsuch Scarisbrick.

Barker, L. L. (1971). *Listening behavior.* Englewood Cliffs, NJ: Prentice-Hall.

Barker, L., Edwards, R., Gaines, C., Gladney, K., & Holley, F. (1980). An investigation of proportional time spent in various communication activities by college students. *Journal of Applied Communication Research.* 8, 101–110.

Birdwhistell, R. L. (1970). *Kinesics & context: Essays on body motion communication.* Philadelphia: U. of PA.

Brown, G. (1995). *Speakers, listeners and communication: Explorations in discourse analysis.* Cambridge: Cambridge University Press.

Brown, J. I. (1987). Listening—Ubiquitous yet obscure. *Journal of the International Listening Association.* 1 (1), 3–14.

Brownell, J. (1996). *Listening: Attitudes, principles, and skills.* Boston: Allyn and Bacon.

Cotton, S. M. (1986). An assessment of time spent in various communication activities by attorneys. Thesis. Auburn U.

Dance, F. E. X., & Larson, C. E. (1976). *The functions of human communication.* New York: Holt, Rinehart & Winston.

Davis, A. J. (1984). *Listening and responding.* St. Louis: C.V. Mosby Co.

Emmert, P. (1996, Spring). President's Perspective. *ILA Listening Post.* 56, 2-3.

Iacocca, L. (with W. Novak). (1984). *Iacocca: An autobiography.* New York: Bantam.

Gilbert, M. B. (1988). Listening in school: I know you can hear me—But are you listening? *Journal of the International Listening Association.* 2, 121–132.

Glenn, E. C. (1989). A content analysis of fifty definitions of listening. *Journal of the International Listening Association.* 3, 21–31.

Heidegger, M. (1962). *Being and time.* Trans. J. Macquarrie & E. Robinson. New York: Harper & Row.

Kelly, D. (1996, June 4). Helping youth to speak: Standards offered to improve skills. *USA Today.* Sec. D (Life), 1.

Lundsteen, S. (1979). Listening: Its impact on reading and the other language arts. Urbana, IL: ERIC Clearing House on Reading and Communication Skills.

Lynch, J. J. (1985). *The language of the heart: The body's response to human dialogue.* New York: Basic Books.

Merrill, L., & Borisoff, D. (March, 1987). Effective listening for lawyers. *The Champion.* 12 (2), 16–19.

Mindell, A. (1985). *Working with the dreaming body.* London: Routledge & Kegan Paul.

Nichols, R. G., & Lewis, T. R. (1954). *Listening and speaking: A guide to effective oral communication.* Dubuque, Iowa: Wm. C. Brown.

Nichols, R. G., & Stevens, L. A. (1957). *Are you listening.* New York: McGraw-Hill.

Peters, T. J. (1982). *In search of excellence: Lessons from America's best-run companies.* New York: Harper & Row.

Peters, T. J. (1994). *The pursuit of wow: Every person's guide to topsy-turvy times.* New York: Vintage Books.

Peters, T. J. (1988). *Thriving on chaos: Handbook for a management revolution.* New York: Harper & Row.

Powell, J. (1969). *why am i afraid to tell you who i am?.* Niles, IL: Argus.

Purdy, M. (1982, March). Listening and consciousness: Research in progress, presented at the International Listening Association conference, St. Paul, MN.

Purdy, M. (1995, November). Ethics in listening: What's to say? Paper presented at the Speech Communication Association, San Antonio, Texas.

Rankin, P. T. (1928). The importance of listening ability. *English Journal* (College Edition). 17, 623–30.

Rogers, C. R., & Farson, E. F. (1986). *Active listening.* In W. Haney, *Communication and interpersonal relations* (pp. 149–163). Homewood, IL: Irwin.

Speech Communication Association. (1996). *Speaking, listening, and media literacy standards for K through 12 education.* Annandale, VA: Speech Communication Association.

Stewart, J. (1986). Introduction to the editor and the assumptions behind this book. In J. Stewart (Ed.), *Bridges not walls: A book about interpersonal communication* (pp. 3–11). 4th ed. New York: Random House.

Stockard, J., & Johnson, M. M. (1980). *Sex roles: Sex inequality and sex role development.* Englewood Cliffs, N. J.: Prentice-Hall.

Weston, W. W., & Lipkin, M. Jr. (1989). Doctors learning communication skills: Developmental issues." In M. Stewart & D. Roter (Eds.), *Communicating with medical patients* (pp. 43–57). Newbury Park, CA: Sage.

Wahlers, K. J. (1989, March). Therapeutic listening: Listening to the terminally ill. Paper presented at the International Listening Association conference, Atlanta.

Wolf, F. I., Marsnik, N. C., Tacey, W. S., & Nichols, R. G. (1983). *Perceptive listening*. New York: Holt, Rinehart & Winston.

Wolvin, A., & Coakley, C. G. (1988). *Listening*. 3rd ed. Dubuque, IA: Wm. C. Brown.

Chapter 2

INTRAPERSONAL/ INTERPERSONAL LISTENING: Self-Listening and Conscious Action

Michael Purdy

Points to be Addressed:

- The nature of intrapersonal listening.
- Skills for effective intrapersonal listening.
- The nature of interpersonal listening.
- A model for personal and professional listening.
- Developing and using questioning skills.
- Barriers to interpersonal listening.

An effective listener in interpersonal and professional contexts is self-aware. As a listener he or she is attuned to the thoughts and feelings of others. However, without being conscious of our own inner voice, it is difficult to improve listening ability. By becoming aware of our intrapersonal communication, defined as "the physiological and psychological processing of messages that happens within individuals at conscious and non-conscious levels" (Roberts, Edwards, and Barker, 1987, p. 2); that is by listening to this internal voice, we can observe our positive and negative habits that are barriers to good listening. Then by making a sincere effort we can take steps to overcome them when we listen. What we do to change our listening behavior will affect directly our interpersonal relationships and affect the lives of friends, family, and professional colleagues.

Our approach to listening in this chapter is based upon the proposition that listening is a 90–90 proposition—that both the speaker and the listener must take responsibility for effective and accurate communication. Furthermore, it is important to realize that improving our listening skills is an ongoing process. Each new person or new situation presents a challenge to our ability to listen and fully understand another individual's message. Toward this end we should set specific goals for improving our listening behavior. (The exercises at the end of this chapter provide strategies for goal-setting and listening improvement.)

Five aspects of intra-personal listening are addressed in the first part of this chapter:

1. the nature of intrapersonal communication

2. decoding, a technical word for how we interpret messages

3. the role of memory in the listening process

4. self-listening (to our bodies, dreams, and self-talk)

5. the interrelationship between intra- and inter-personal listening.

The second part of this chapter discusses a model of interpersonal listening for personal and professional application. The relationship of self disclosure to receptivity, empathy, questioning, and barriers to effective listening are included as important components of interpersonal listening.

Self-listening becomes an integral extension of our inter-personal communication and influences our inter-personal relationships. Intra-personal communication is not limited in its consequences to what we do in communication with ourselves.

THE NATURE OF INTRAPERSONAL LISTENING

Only those voices from without are effective which can speak in the language of the voice within (Kenneth Burke, 1950, p. 39).

Burke's comment is generally true in all spheres of our lives. As we listen to others, everything they say is interpreted in terms of our own internal "voice." That is to say, when we listen we make sense of messages in terms of our own experience. Do we have any other choice? We can only know our own experience. How can we be someone, or something we are not? In a very real sense we cannot (though we may act and pose) because we are shaped by such factors as personal history, intelligence, gender, age, and culture. We are who we are. In another light we are constantly changing and growing to meet our own needs and expectations (as well as those of others) and to cope in the changing world around us. As we experience more, we can better understand and listen to "those voices from without" because our voice within has become a larger, more universal voice.

Although when we listen we interpret "those voices from without" with respect to our own experience, that experience (our experience as expressed by the "voice within") is not wholly unique. We share so much of who and what we are with every human being, but especially with members of our own group and (sub)culture. We share with every human being the need to eat, sleep, procreate, socialize, be creative, and the desire to feel good about ourselves and what we do and produce. With those of our own culture we share a common verbal and nonverbal language, styles of dress and grooming, habits of shopping, eating, recreating, working/making a living; as well as the commonalties of our major institutions of government, religion, education, business, and commerce. In spite of these many shared experiences each of us is still unique.

If we are to become more effective listeners in our personal and professional lives we need to first understand the voice within—who we are—and the extent of our personal experience. We need to know our likes and dislikes, our prejudices and biases, our own limitations, the basic beliefs and ethical principles upon which we act. As the ancient Greeks proclaimed "know thyself." By knowing ourselves we will be receptive to and able to interpret and understand what others communicate to us.

In short if we are to communicate more effectively with others we need to become better listeners, first to self (intrapersonal listening), but also to others (interpersonal listening). Since the process of listening to ourselves is integrally linked with the process of listening to others, we begin to realize that to have meaningful relationships with those with whom we live and work we need to know ourselves better.

How do we begin to listen to ourselves? Where do we start? We can begin in many ways, but essentially we first must become conscious of our inner dialogue as we are listening. An exercise, such as the one that follows, can help make us aware of the inner listening process as we listen.

Exercise

(This can be done in a class/seminar session, or on your own.)

Engage in a conversation with someone you know and gradually turn the conversation to a controversial issue. Once you begin to discuss the controversial issue your assignment is to try to help the speaker talk about his or her point of view. You must not make any statements about any of your own views. Ask questions and acknowledge what the speaker says with nonverbal and short verbal responses. While you are listening, notice what is going through your mind. Observe your feelings, attitudes, and self-talk while you are listening.

If you are honest with yourself, you should find this exercise a challenge. You should find it difficult to listen without expressing your own opinions, or at least commenting upon what the speaker has said. Why? In an article about the power of speech, Meerloo gives us a hint of what might be happening: "In conversation the listener is to some extent enslaved, for every speaker experiments with the imperialistic weapon of his mind. He seeks to colonize his ideas . . ." (Stewart, 1973, p. 143).

Speaking and listening reflect different aspects of our desire to communicate with others and are, hence, two sides of the same process. As speakers we have a "missionary zeal," an often less-than-conscious desire to propagate our ideas in the mind of another. We want to express our own point of view and we want others to agree with us. When our communication role changes from speaker to listener we often find it difficult to stop imposing our own ideas long enough to listen. We need to ask ourselves if we are listening to hear something that will confirm our own ideas, or if we are listening to share an experience with a friend or colleague. It is difficult to not impose and to just help the speaker talk about his or her feelings and ideas; however, if we do listen we may learn and grow.

The first thing to notice about our intrapersonal communication, therefore, is how it can interfere with the process of listening effectively to others. We need to quiet our inner voice, as well as our outer voice, if we are to fully comprehend what others have to tell us. We cannot fill a full cup. If we are to truly listen to friends and colleagues we must first empty our own cup (our mind) of thoughts so we have room for the ideas of the speaker. The process of quieting the mind takes personal effort and discipline. Practices that discipline the attention, concentration, and awareness of the mind, such as meditation or martial arts, can be very helpful in making us better listeners.[1]

---

1 For suggestions on meditation and inner listening, see such books as: Crum (1975), *The Art of Inner Listening*, and, Ram Dass and Gorman (1985), *How Can I Help? Stories and Reflections on Service*, especially chapter 4, "The Listening Mind."

So, in order to have a place for the message of the speaker in our consciousness we need to set aside our own thoughts through a disciplined effort. The ego which wants to talk on and on in our head must be temporarily silenced in order to hear the other. Peck has discussed this practice in his best selling book, *The Road Less Traveled*:

An essential part of true listening is the discipline of bracketing, the temporary giving up or setting aside of one's own prejudices, frames of reference and desires so as to experience as far as possible the speaker's world from the inside, stepping inside his or her shoes (1978, pp. 127–8).

Bracketing, making room in our mind for the speaker's feelings and thoughts, is the prerequisite for empathy. (We will discuss empathy more in the next section on interpersonal listening.) Here we must appreciate that effective communication in the home or at the office begins with understanding and the ability to manage our inner communication. Becoming conscious of what is taking place in our own head through inner listening is the beginning of a productive interaction with others.

Ralph Nichols and Leonard Stevens offer a second way to learn more about our selves in their 1957 book *Are You Listening?* They suggest that people learn about themselves when they have a good listener to talk with. A friend, or just someone who is understanding, can help us to talk about what is inside us and bring it out into the open where we can listen to ourselves. We can serve the same function for others. First, however, we must become good listeners and/or know how to identify a good listener. Our model for effective interpersonal listening later in this chapter will give concrete suggestions for interpersonal listening. The discussion of the elements of intrapersonal listening that follows will prepare the way to better understand that model.

Decoding

Decoding is literally the process of taking words coded in sounds and making sense of them. DeVito in *The Communication Handbook* defines decoding as: "The process of extracting a message by changing it from one form to another, for example, transforming speech sounds into nerve impulses" (1986, p. 91). As a speaker we express, and hence, share our view of the world. We tell stories about our family, our profession, or company. We express opinions about anything and everything. When we listen, we organize and structure our perceptions of the world in terms of the familiarity of our own experience. We experience, to some degree, what we *expect* to experience. Our personal experience is idiosyncratic and unique but is also the general experience of our culture, social group, gender, profession, and work place. When we hear (and decode) the talk of other speakers we give their words a slightly different interpretation from the interpretation anyone else would give, while at the same time reflecting all the things we have in common with them.

In considering decoding we must examine two general, overlapping categories of influence that have an effect on how we interpret what we perceive: (1) *immediate*, here–and–now influences, and (2) *long–term*, fundamental influences. Immediate influences have to do with our attitudes, thoughts and feelings due to the current role(s) we are playing, who we are interacting with, the social occasion, and physical setting. Fundamental influences, working less consciously and more in the background of social interactions, are a result of personal history and the basic values this background has instilled within us. Each category of influences contributes to establishing different expectations in each situation, expectations that filter our perceptions and color our meanings. Typically, we can become aware of immediate influences more easily, and being aware of these influences we can use that awareness to improve our listening effectiveness. Fundamental influences are ingrained, having accumulated over years of living, and may be more difficult to alter or control.

We are not always aware of the effect of immediate influences on decoding, but they are the obvious stuff of each interaction in a personal or professional situation. The role we are playing has a very strong impact on our decoding. As a professional we often interpret situations in a wholly different light. A woman may be a psychologist, spouse, lover, mother, friend, and daughter. Each of these roles demands different behaviors. For example, if a marriage counselor's relative is in the midst of a divorce, the counselor's family experience helps her understand and identify with the hardship of the relative. Yet, from her professional experience as a counselor she would recognize as well that every relationship is a two–way street; with the implication that both parties in the marriage bear some responsibility. Consequently, the personal and professional roles we play shape our understanding of and attitudes toward events.

Similarly, the other people involved in any situation (and the roles they are playing), the social occasion, and the physical setting (in the office or a restaurant) also make a contribution to how we decode the messages communicated. For example, our perceptions of bosses and co–workers certainly differ. If the occasion is formal our expectations are quite distinct from what they might be for an informal occasion. We "see" things differently at a formal office function than we would at a lunch meeting planned to be informal. In each of these examples, the factors of setting can be equally important in how we interpret perceptions. Is the lighting soft, does the furniture arrangement invite intimate conversation, are the colors conducive to a cheerful disposition?

Long-term, fundamental influences are equally important to how we decode perceptions. The influence of the familiar on perception is a basic principle of psychology. Who we are, the history we have lived, shaped by the values of our family and friends, has a powerful influence on how we listen (Goss, 1982, p. 7). Hence, our interpretation of events and ideas are normally similar to other members of our family, who share similar values, and who have provided role models for development. Thus a child who grows up in a family of social activists may be predisposed to become involved in such activities as an adult. Sadly, at the other extreme, children of alcoholics are more likely than children of non-drinkers to resort to alcohol to escape from or solve their problems.

As another example, look at the effect of values in the workplace. We may favor quality possessions because our background has taught us to value things that endure long enough to become familiar and cherished. Yet as a salesperson we could be talking with a customer who is primarily interested in price. Our values may cause us to filter out parts of the customer's message, and hence fail to understand his or her needs and not make a sale. We need to be cognizant of our values if we are to decode our customer's interests clearly.

Language

Most problems with listening have to do with wrong assumptions we have made. We make wrong assumptions quite naturally. They stem from the fact that we assume that our experience is the same as anyone else's, and hence that the words we hear mean the same thing. Yet, we have different values, our experience is based upon different social and cultural situations, and we generally think and operate uniquely to some degree from everyone else we will ever meet. These differences are most obviously realized in the different words we use and the meaning we have for those words. There are four common sources of language-based listening problems: (1) personal or unique language usage; (2) divergent meanings for the same word ; (3) distortion; and (4) vocabulary.

Personal or Unique Language Usage

Because we have a particular personal history we have, to a degree, our own meanings for many words. In your house the bathroom may have been referred to as the "washroom," the "toilet," the "lavatory," or some other variant. At work it may be referred to as the "restroom." As another example, consider members of a family, or friends, for whom the concept of "making a deal" is probably understood without formalities like drafted contracts involving lawyers. On the other hand, in professional life meanings are clearly codified in a legal document because individuals do not trust their individual listening skills to assure them of the same meanings for the same words. Often, in professional situations, even if we believe we have clearly heard those we are working with, we may want to reinforce the message by following up with a clearly written memo or e-mail.

Divergent Meanings for the Same Word

We must remember meanings change with time, with the situation, and with different individuals and subcultural groups. For instance, words like "cool" have changed meanings several times in our life time. We need, therefore, to strive to listen to the other individual's meaning; for what we assume the other has said may not be exactly what was meant. The identical   word may convey diverse ideas or hold alternate meanings for different people. Thus, when a vice-president tells one of her directors that his work is "fine," the director should clarify the term "fine." Does it mean "I'm pleased with your work," or, "Your work is okay, but could stand some improvement"?

Distortion of the Message

In everyday communication messages often get passed serially from one speaker to another, passing through several listeners before we receive the message. As the listener gets further away from the source of a message the potential for distortion increases proportionally. There are several reasons for distortion some of which were covered already like different life experiences and meanings for words.

The telephone (or rumor) game illustrates how distortion occurs. In the game, a story is whispered to another person who privately repeats all that he or she remembers to the next person in the chain, and so on until the message started has serially been passed through four, five, or more people. We all know that to begin with details get left out of the message. After that the message gets distorted, and in order to continue to make sense of the distorted message new information is added. One factor that causes the listener to leave out details of the story is memory—which leads to errors of omission. If an individual is overwhelmed with too many details, certain aspect of the message may be forgotten. A second, and perhaps more significant reason why listeners in serial communication distort the message is the result of errors of commission. If, due to errors of omission, many significant details of the message are left out, individuals are apt to lose the sense of the original message and transmitted meaning deteriorates quickly. To make sense of what is heard, the listener may imbue the message with details that, in fact, were never part of the initial communication.[2]

Vocabulary

Another factor of language that affects our ability to listen, is our vocabulary, and of course the vocabulary of the speaker. The larger our vocabulary the more likely we are to understand a speaker. Thus, if messages such as "The new equipment will obviate the need for more staff," "The new mission statement is fraught with possibilities," or "Her actions militated against the strike" are articulated, the listener will be better able to understanding the messages fully if he or she is familiar with the words obviate, fraught, and militate. Although we are often required to ascertain meaning through the context in which a word or phrase is used, the greater our vocabulary, the less likely the possibility of miscommunication.

We may conclude that vocabulary is especially critical when we are listening to a "technical" message. In many fields there is a specialized vocabulary that must be learned. When we listen to experts or professionals outside our field different words may be common. It behooves us to improve our working vocabulary and be familiar with vocabulary used by those with whom we regularly associate.

Sometimes, despite our best intentions we miss the theme of the message. What do we do when we lose the meaning of the message? If the speaker is still available, the answer is easy, we can ask clarifying questions, or ask the speaker to repeat what they said. We can also give extra attention to the message if the speaker is still holding forth. We may yet recover the theme of the message since there is a lot of redundancy built into speech patterns. A better solution is to listen to the meaning as someone speaks so we do not have to say to ourselves: "Now I wonder what they meant by that?"

Some guiding rules for listening to language would include:

- focus on the meaning, as determined by the people speaking and by the situation

- stress the point of view or theme over the words themselves

- ask questions when something "doesn't compute"

- build a vocabulary of words typically used in your profession.

---

2 Goss (1982), in *Processing Communication*, cites research by Black, Turner, and Bower (1979), which "tells us that listeners look for a point of view or a theme through which they can make sense out of a message. They are able to respond meaningfully when they apply an underlying point of view to the message" (p. 92).

Situation/Context

As Erving Goffman (1959) so aptly noted, the context of a situation can be important in determining the meaning of a message. Many variables of the context are important. Who is present? What value do we place on this occasion? What is our attitude toward those present; toward the occasion? What do we have to lose or gain by the situation? Each of these factors can effect how we decode a message. A message is determined by everything that enters our awareness, consciously or unconsciously. Listening to a colleague talk about office politics over coffee has a different meaning than the same person discussing the same problems at an open departmental meeting.

So, first, observe who is present in the listening situation. How does the mix of status levels of individuals affect the messages? Do we respect the person to whom we are listening? What sort of personal attachments do we have for the people present? Each can have an affect on how we interpret the meanings in the situation.

Suppose our boss, who is also our friend, presents a plan for listening training for all of the frontline employees in our hotel. Another department manager suggests that all of the hotel's management should take part in the training with the frontline employees. Our boss does not agree, she does not feel she needs more training. Will we be able to listen for the facts in this situation and filter out the weight of opinion? Can we set aside the roles and status of the individuals involved? Would we want everyone to receive the training?

What is our stake in this situation? What is our attitude? What do we have to gain or lose? Will our boss still like us if we listen carefully and decide to disagree with her? Can we listen as objectively if our status in the group may rise or fall with how we respond? Emotions and attitudes can and do affect our processing of messages. We have the saying that "love is blind." Actually, any strong emotion can distort perception and make the job of accurate listening more difficult.

Memory

Memory is included as an important component in most listening models because there are many situations where just understanding the message is not enough. It is often essential to be able to recall information. When discussing some of the principles and techniques for effective memory. It is crucial to keep in mind Loftus' warning, gleaned from nearly a century of experimental research, "that our memories are continually being altered, transformed, and distorted"

(1980, p. xiii). We cannot expect what we remember to remain permanently unaltered in our minds. Memory can be very malleable, changing due to time, situation, and intensity of intervening experience. This is both a caution and a challenge to work at retaining what we hear.

You can recall anything if you remember, as Lorayne declares, "There is no such thing as a poor memory! There are only trained and untrained memories" (1985, p. 56). That is to say, we have control over our memory. In personal and professional relationships a good memory will help insure success in many of our endeavors. When we meet new people it is critical to the relationship to remember names and a few essential facts. People always respond more positively when they feel that we care enough about them to remember important personal details. One way to remember names is to associate a name with a unique physical detail of the person and see that visual image when you say the name (big ears, mustache, red hair).

Goss, in Communication Processing, provides two general principles for improving listening perception. These principles also facilitate memory:

1. Somehow [a] message must stand out from the array of messages coming at you at once. It is easier to recall information that you have successfully isolated than it is to recall messages that were blended into the background of all the other messages.

2. [L]ook for structure and ideas, not for words. Sometimes people get so anxious about remembering "all this information" that they try to memorize the exact wording [and end up forgetting the main point of the message] (pp. 95–96).

These suggestions can be implemented by noting the unique features of what the listener wants to extract from the message.

If, for example, a director tells her colleague, "I just came from a meeting with the vice–president and have some important information on next years budget," her colleague may anticipate obtaining critical information and prepare to focus his attention on her message. More than attending to his director's message, however, as a listener he will need to prevent initially extraneous details from interfering with the message. Thus, if the director begins her account with "well, we were supposed to begin the meeting at 10 AM in the Boardroom, but Alec and Jessica were delayed in traffic, so we ended up moving to Mr. Alcot's office . . . ." her colleague may be well advised to concentrate his listening efforts on the main points of the message: "Next year we will have a 15% increase in salaries, a 5% decrease in our travel and entertainment account, and a 30% increase in our advertising budget." Arguably, it is often the case that little details may be extremely important for assessing a message—for example who was invited or excluded from a meeting. In any situation it is experience which enables individuals to determine the import and relative value of the details of a message.

Remembering according to Lorayne, is a process of association. If we can associate the thing we want to remember with an interesting image (which may require some ingenuity) we can recall anything (pp. 3-20). Considerable research exists to show that "pictures [images] are remembered better than their corresponding verbal labels" (p. 153). So, associating what we want to retain with vivid images can be one effective method to assist our memory as we listen. Like listening, however, all the associating and imaging will be to no avail if we have not first paid careful attention. Bentley (1989) suggests the ARC model as a guide to specific techniques for improving memory. The acronym itself is an aid for remembering the model. The "A" is for attention, for being alert when listening to remember. "R" is rephrasing, or putting the message into words that make sense to the listener. The "C" is for connecting or organizing the new material into a logical framework or pattern (p. 3).

Return to the previous example of the director and her colleague. If he is in a rush and does not have time to take notes, he may "rephrase" the message by thinking to himself, "this means salary increases are 50% greater than they were last year; we are losing 30% of our travel and entertainment, and gaining 100% in advertising." In his mind, he is already "connecting" or organizing this information by making a mental note to meet with his assistant to prepare next year's budget plan; moreover, he may visualize details of arranging the upcoming meeting and associate them with a vivid image, reinforcing his director's message even more.

Note how the director's colleague organized the information in terms of percentages, a pattern that made sense to him. Master chess players can reproduce an entire chess board from an actual game of chess, but arrange the pieces at random and master players are no better than novices at remembering the placement of pieces (Seamon, 1980, pp. 76-77). So not only is the pattern of the information important but also familiarity with the ways the information can be organized. Master chess players are extremely familiar with the patterns of action in a chess game; professionals may be familiar with statistics, reports, clinical cases, etc.

We have observed the significance of effective listening, and explored factors that can enhance individual listening ability. However, before we can listen to others (interpersonal listening), we must first be able to listen to ourselves (intrapersonal listening). The section that follows examines specific instances of what we mean by listening to self, and demonstrates how listening to our body, dreams, and self-talk can make us better communicators.

Ways to Listen to Self

Our body affects how we listen. If we are "down" we may be unable to attend to what is happening with situations and people around us. A headache, a touch of flu, depression, or exhaustion may distract us. Our attention may be more self-absorbed with our own feelings and discomfort than with the individuals around us. On these days we are not our usual selves. We have all had intense weekends where we packed in too much activity. We come into work on Monday wanting to take it easy and hoping we do not have to interact with too many people. On days like this we may be more introverted and find it more demanding to be an astute listener.

Similarly, mood can also affect attention and color the messages we hear. We might just be having a "blue Monday," or have had a fight with our friend (spouse/lover) the night before. We will, no doubt, be self-absorbed and unaware of the interaction around us; moreover, we may find ourselves not wanting to be involved. If we have had relationship problems, perhaps we are going over the previous night's episode in our mind, and again are not very much in touch with our colleagues. On these days we will need to exert extra effort to function effectively.

Listening To Our Body

One way to proceed on these days is to actually listen to our bodies—to our aches, pains, mood—and acknowledge our state of being. What am I feeling? Why am I feeling this way? We might not be able to get in touch with some of our feelings. Nor will we always understand exactly what our moods are about. The first step, however, is to become aware of as much of what is going on within us as possible. (This may become material for one of the journal exercises at the end of the chapter.) Just listening to our self will usually help us to feel a little better. Then we need to ask what we can do to help orient ourselves externally.

These are steps we can take to listen effectively whether we have responsibilities at home on Monday morning or we are at work waiting to see a client. Generally, we need to set aside time to listen to our self, to understand our bodily feelings and moods, and to respond to them. Maybe our bodies are telling us to take better care of ourselves; maybe our moods are saying we have interpersonal relationships that need attention.

By learning to "listen" to our body we may also understand better how we are communicating nonverbally. For instance, in conversation with a colleague about a problem with another faculty (or staff) member, I became aware that the communication was awkward and I felt uncomfortable. I was having a hard time listening to my colleague. As I listened to my body, I noticed the tension, and, more obviously, under the table my whole lower body was oriented away from the speaker. I had several options. I could ask my body why it was experiencing tension and turning away from the speaker, or I could talk with the speaker about the source of my uncomfortableness. If we listen, our body will give us obvious signs about the effectiveness of our listening.

The above example illustrates what is called in the nonverbal literature, a lack of congruence between speaker and listener (Mehrabian, 1972). Typically, when two communicators are attuned, their body orientations will be similar. Both speaker and listener, or several members of a group such as those at a meeting, will show similar body posture such as, legs crossed, hand under chin, arms crossed, or leaning on the table. When there is congruence, that is when speaker and listener are attuned, there will be a confluence or synchrony of interaction: speech will flow, the listener will be caught up in the flow, and the body action of the interactants will be similar. Becoming aware of body congruence when we feel that communication is not flowing can be helpful to the process of effective listening. We can become aware of our body orientation and by listening to what that orientation is telling us alter our nonverbal behavior. Our body awareness can positively influence the quality of the communication.

Listening to Our Dreams

There are many theories and approaches to understanding our dream experience (Faraday, 1972; Freud, 1965; Jung, 1973; Perls, 1975). Essentially, all suggest that sleep–time dreams (as well as, fantasies, daydreams, and personal imagery in general) are a direct reflection of secondary, less–conscious processes of our lives. Listening, literally listening to the content of our dreams, as well as, remembering the imagery, the word–associations, and the characters, can be a helpful way to understand the less–conscious communication of our lives. Klinger, author of *Daydreaming*, that daydreams are equally deserving of our attention, "They reveal the state of our soul. If we listen to them closely, they tell us what's missing from our lives, what we need to be happy and fulfilled" (1996). Faraday, a recognized expert in the area of dream research, integrates the theory of American psychologists who took the subject of dreams out of the consulting room "and made dream interpretation a possibility for all of us in everyday life" (p. 137). She recommends that "anyone who becomes seriously disturbed by the things he finds in dreams, or . . . has reason to suspect they are connected with mental instability, to seek professional advice" (p. 156). For most of us however, dreams are a source of inspiration and knowledge.

Our approach will consider dreams as form of a self-communication. By listening to our dreams we can discover words, images, and their meanings which will help us to communicate with our self (and others). Dreams have helped people solve problems, they have been sources of creative material, they can provide guidance for relationships at home, in our social life, and at work. This may at first seem to be unrelated to effective listening; but to the contrary, for those with the diligence to pursue this self-communication, the rewards are self-knowledge and a more creatively productive personal and professional life.

The processing of dreams is in a way the reverse of remembering during the act of listening. In remembering we try to make associations that will organize ideas so they will lodge in our memory. In dreams we try to unpack the strange associations we have created in the less-conscious mental processing of sleep. The less-conscious mind seems to relish creating colorful associations to communicate with the conscious mind. We need only pay attention to our dreams to begin to understand the unique symbols we use to communicate with our self. In turn, our dreams will reveal unnoticed (or blocked) feelings and experiences from not only the day's activities, but from the collected salient events of our lives.

The place to begin to listen to our dreams is with the desire to communicate with our self. Some people claim they never dream. Research indicates everyone dreams, because everyone has REM (rapid eye movement) sleep associated with dreaming. If we want to listen to our self we will begin to remember dreams.[3] (There are people who do not recall dreams well; if you are one see exercise three at the end of the chapter.) The essential tools for remembering dreams are a notebook or tape recorder kept by the bed. When you wake try not to move, or if you must, sit up very gently, and review the dream until you have recalled all of the details you can remember. As soon as you move you lose the details. The process of remembering immediately upon awakening moves the dream from a "short-term" memory where it disappears quickly, to our permanent memory so we can dictate or write down the dream.

The second phase of dream communication involves noting on paper (or recording) all of the stories, themes, images, characters, emotions, words, objects you can remember. After you get down what you can remember be sure to date the entry and try to fill in more details. Sometimes pieces of the dream will come to you throughout the day. Add them to your dream notations (always leave an extra page or so after writing down each dream; you will need it for further processing of the dream). Jung and others have typically suggested that dreams be looked at in series, rather than strictly individually, though each dream can offer insight on its own.

There are many techniques for making sense of dream communication. We will offer two methods here which can get you started.

---

3 For hints for recalling and recording dreams, see appendix A in Faraday (1972), *Dream Power.*

Morris (1985) recommends keeping a dream journal and using a series of questions to direct self listening and elicit insights from the dream. The questions (to be answered as soon after writing down the details as possible) include: What are your feelings upon awakening? What real–life memories or prior dreams does this dream remind you of? What are the settings, colors, events of the day that might be related? What are the key symbols and phrases and your associations to them? What traits do the characters have "that might be parts of yourself you're disowning?" (pp. 16–17). After answering these questions, look at the whole response and see what relationships there are to your waking life. What problems and concerns have you had? What light does this dream (or series of dreams) shed on your worries? Morris, Faraday, and Steele, provide many examples to guide you through dream analysis step-by-step.

A second method suggested by Fritz Perls, the renowned Gestalt therapist, helps us to go beyond the immediate relevance of the dream to the day's events to illuminate symbolic associations which may be present. Perls contends that every part of your dream is part of you, since it is your creation and the material for the dream arose out of your life situation: "Dream work calls attention to those needs in the individual which have not been met because they have not been recognized" (Fantz, 1987, p. 193). The dream is like a movie, or television screen, where we can explore our needs and recognize parts of ourselves that have not been recognized before. Perls' technique has the dreamer identify with the significant characters or objects in the dream and have them talk to you, as if you were the character or object. Or the dialogue could take place with you taking the part of two characters, or objects in the dream. In one example a woman dreams of standing on the shore of a lake as an eight year old child. Perls says to the dreamer, Madeline: "Y[es]. Let me work on the dream a bit. Be the lake. And Lake, tell me your story" (p. 188). We would carry on the same dialogue, only with ourselves, in the journal described above.

Of course, aside from simply recording your dreams, you can also program your dreams. Go to sleep thinking of a relationship you wish you could improve or a problem that needs solving. With practice you may get answers from your dreams. The answers may not be literal, but as you learn to decode your dream communication you will find the solutions presented there. Some relationships and problems which have persisted for a long time may not give way to simple solutions so it is important to persevere.

Listening To Self-talk

The major part of listening to self-talk, like listening in general, is attention; becoming aware of what is going on in our conscious and less-conscious life. We all "chatter" continuously inside our head as we go through the day. To some extent, this chatter helps us maintain our personal identity. It may also get in the way of effective interpersonal communication, as William Howell (1982) suggests, if we are attending to our "internal monologue" rather than listening to the other person. So our reference here is to listening to yourself when not engaged in active interpersonal communication.

Listening to how we talk to our self can be helpful in understanding how we relate to our self, and also to others. What we say to our self is, ultimately, an extension of how we feel and think about our self. We project this experience into our relationships, and it influences how we interpret what others say to us. Essentially, it is important that we develop an understanding of how we listen to our emotional feelings, and also, some comprehension of how we listen to our thoughts. We may consider emotions the "color" of our thoughts; feelings and thoughts are not really two separate processes.

Emotions in and of themselves are never a problem. Everyone feels and everyone needs to be in touch with this human process. What is problematic is how we behave as a result of the emotions we feel. John Powell has said this does not mean we surrender to emotions. "Though it is necessary to `report' our emotions, it is not at all necessary that we 'act on' them" (1969, p. 87). We might think that the best response to felt emotions is to express them. However, the immediate expression of emotions may not always be the best recourse. In general, it is more important that we control our emotions and not be controlled by them.

Therefore, we propose a process by which emotions are recognized and expressed, including:

- listening to and acknowledging feelings

- owning our emotions

- noticing the situations which give rise to emotions

- learning from an awareness of our emotional experiences.

The first step is to listen to our feelings and acknowledge them as our own. It does no good for us to blame our emotions on someone else as the only person we really have control over and can change is our self. Getting a grasp on our emotions may be accomplished with the general semantics tool of "delayed reaction" (Haney, 1986, pp. 520–50). Very few exchanges require us to respond immediately; the consequences of "undelayed reactions" may be dire indeed. A few words said in heated communication have ruined many family, social, and work relationships. When situations arouse strong emotions, we advise individuals to take a short break, and to listen to how they are feeling.

Second, admit that we have emotions and find out how they are linked to thoughts and feelings. Listening to our thoughts can give us the key to working with our emotions, and ultimately to bringing our behavior into harmony with our thoughts and feelings for a healthier and more productive self. As Burns has discovered through extensive clinical research, and reported in the book *Feeling Good*, "You feel the way you do right now because of the thoughts you are thinking at this moment" (1981, p. 11). Report what you are feeling to yourself and others. For example, you might say to your office project leader, "Look, your criticism of my report is irritating me, what are some of its strengths?" Put your feelings on paper (for example, in your journal) to help make them more objective and to clarify them.

Third, if we can catch emotions as they are building we have a chance to talk about them and alter their direction and intensity. A good example to begin with is anger. Actually, anger is not a basic emotion. We say we *get* angry. The first emotion we experience is irritation, frustration, anxiety, or perhaps fear. We bring anger into play as we *decide* to escalate this feeling of irritation to exert more power in the relationship. People "listen" to us immediately when they see that we are getting angry. The object of working with emotions is to become more attentive to our emotions, to delay hasty responses and to listen inside for what we are feeling. Knowing (listening to) what we are feeling, we may change our response to a more supportive comment; one more conducive to a productive relationship. Listening to our communication partner will, of course, give us an opportunity to reflect on how we are feeling. (See exercise 4 at the end of this chapter.)

Finally, we need to learn from listening to our emotions. If we keep our emotions bottled up they will still be there the next time someone criticizes our work. Admitting and reporting how we are feeling is the beginning. Learning from what we discover about how we react emotionally is the start of a solution. Having listened to how we react we can develop new strategies for coping in emotion-provoking situations. "Listen boss, next time we talk about my report can we go over the shortcomings and then list all of its strengths as well?"

Our intent is not to present a self-help manual here; there are many books that can be very beneficial for personal growth in local bookstores. However, realizing that listening to your self-talk can help you to use more of your human potential at home and at work can be a worthwhile start. Thoughts and feelings do shape our actions. Paying attention to our thoughts and actions can bring them into line with the way we want to perform, and help us to be more effective in personal and professional encounters. We should ultimately, "forgive and forget;" emotions not dealt with only fester inside of us.

This is not simply a positive thinking approach. As Newman and Berkowitz, two psychoanalysts, have written in the book *How to Be Your Own Best Friend*: "You do need determination, but good things don't come out of forcing your self. When you try to do it all out of will power, you are not treating your self with respect" (1971, p. 21). Your actions must begin to come into harmony with your thoughts, and vice versa. You must listen to your self-talk, discover what it is you would like to do, and coordinate your thoughts to bring these results to fruition. Nothing is gained by the will of positive thinking alone. The results we desire must flow from a merging of thought, feeling, and action. This implies that we must allow our authentic self to emerge. If we are real, as Carl Rogers indicates, we are satisfied with ourselves and we are better able to help the other person (1980, p. 19).

In the book *What To Say When You Talk To Your Self*, Helmstetter (1986) suggests that most of us are held back from reaching our full potential because we program our minds with negative self-talk. If we are to be successful, we must do more than think positively. He says we must also replace our negative self-talk with positive self-talk. For example, we need to say "I can be open and listen to opinions different from my own," rather than "I really ought to listen to opinions different from my own." The road to effective behavior, then, is reprogramming ourselves with positive self-talk. Most of Helmstetter's book is devoted to recognizing self-talk and redirecting our programming in positive directions. The process of redirecting our self-talk, and our lives, however, begins with listening to our self-talk. He suggests that we start by listening to not only our own self-talk, but equally important, that we listen to our family, friends, and the media, to discover the sources of our negative self-talk.

"As we think, so we become," are the words of one sage[4]. And if we are to be successful in personal and professional life we need to listen to our emotions and our thoughts; to find the roots of our action. If we are to operate more effectively, we need to acknowledge our feelings and thoughts and direct them in ways that match our desired behavior. When body, mind, and spirit are in harmony, we can do our best.

INTERPERSONAL LISTENING

Intrapersonal listening, knowing our self, provides a solid foundation for listening to those who are significant in our lives. As Hillel has said in Sayings of the Fathers (1:14) "If I am not for myself, who will be for me? And if I am only for myself, what am I? And if not

---

[4] Kirpal Singh. See works such as *Morning Talks*.

now—when?" (Rosten, 1972, p. 459). Our lives have little meaning without relationships. These relationships, both personal and professional, give meaning to our lives; they help define who we are and what we do. Nor do we learn about ourselves by withdrawing from the world to a cave. We learn about our selves through interaction and relationship with others. Others are a mirror for us. They give us feedback if we would only listen. To listen, we must trust.

Elements of Interpersonal Listening

Some of the essential elements of interpersonal listening include:

- awareness of the other

- other–centeredness or empathy

- trust

- self–disclosure

- a supportive environment that confirms the other.

First, we must become aware of the other as a distinct individual. That means recognizing the unique experience of this person. Listening is a tremendous asset for heightening awareness of another. We haven't grown up in the same family, shared all of the same friends, walked the same streets, or generally, seen the world from within the same body as this person. As we have suggested above, this person has a unique meaning for everything he or she perceives. At the same time, we need to keep in mind that no human being is completely alien, there are many human experiences we share with any individual which provide a basis for genuine interpersonal communication; we need to listen for similarities as well as differences.

Second, every human relationship that has any pretension to being meaningful and productive must arise out of empathy, or the ability of each to become other–centered and understand the world from the other's perspective. It means literally, the ability to feel with the other and imagine what it would be like to experience from that person's place in life. The experience of empathy is built upon a sensitive awareness of the other person gathered through listening.

Third, and some say the most critical element of interpersonal communication, is trust. "The development of trust allows for greater risk-taking" (Brownell, 1996, p. 9). How do we develop trust? For sure by disclosing important aspects of who we are to the important people in our lives. As much, however, as expression (speaking) builds trust, listening is equally as important. People trust us if they feel we are open to them, if we receive their ideas and feelings without judgment, if we accept who and what they are without reservation. Building trust through listening lays a groundwork for a relationship that allows us to depend upon that relationship to meet our needs and to get things done both personally and professionally.

Fourth, when we speak about ourselves, or self-disclose, we feel like we are doing something—like we are taking action. Speaking is associated with *giving*. Listening is thought of as *receiving*, but it also *giving*. When we listen we self-disclose as well. We show that we are actively receptive, we disclose that we are open and actively attentive. When we listen we allow others to express themselves. We give them the space to tell us things, that is, to provide us with information that may be important to our relationship or to our business. Listening also permits others to communicate their needs and concerns. Thus, we can see, as defined in Chapter One, listening is an active process. It is not only receiving; it is an act of selfless giving. When we give the gift of paying careful attention—listening—we give a rare gift that will build trust and goodwill in our relationships.

Last, Jack Gibb's article on "defensive communication" discusses the qualities that make for a defensive environment for communication, and contrasts it with the qualities that make for a supportive environment. According to Gibb, "Defense arousal prevents the listener from concentrating upon the message" (1961, pp. 141-142). *Defensive climates,* he goes on to say, are created by:

- evaluation of the other or their ideas

- attempts to control the conversation (or situation)

- use of strategy or concealed motivations

- being neutral (uninvolved)

- an attitude of superiority

- being certain or dogmatic

A supportive climate is indicated by the contrasting behaviors of:

- non-judgemental description

- a problem orientation that is not imposing

- spontaneity or non-calculating behavior

- empathy or identification with the speaker

- equality with mutual trust and respect

- provisionalism, shared openness to explore the relationship

The supportive environment reflects the overall qualities that describe the style of interpersonal listening we are advocating. A supportive environment confirms people and helps them to feel good about themselves. These are attitudes and skills that empower people.

Empowered friends, family, and colleagues are healthy and productive. They feel affirmed and supported.

Being able to change the defensive climate of an interpersonal situation to a supportive climate is very important in working with people in any personal or professional setting. Let's look at some of the elements of a defensive climate in a work setting and how they might be changed to create a supportive climate.

Suppose, for instance, that you are a project leader of a group in an ad agency working on a television advertising project for a major fast food restaurant chain. The group's productivity has been satisfactory but you know it could be excellent if you could turn around the defensive climate that exists in the group. As you get private feedback from trusted group members, and listen to and observe your own behavior in the group, you discover that you are defensive toward certain members of the group because they seem to be dogmatic in their approach to the client's account. They have set ideas of what has worked before and want to use the same techniques again. You have negatively evaluated these previously used advertising techniques (and the members who espouse them), and, further, you have concealed your strategy to control the group's conversation toward the end of getting your own plans accepted. What can you do?

In this situation building a supportive climate calls for listening and non-judgemental response with a problem orientation. Rather than you being negative toward ideas you perceive as not useful you will need to trust and respect other group members and give descriptive feedback in a non-calculating way. If one of the members suggests a technique that has worked in the past, you need to listen to be sure that what you are hearing is indeed merely the same idea. You might respond with: "Rachel, I hear you saying that we should develop this ad campaign in the same manner as the Better Burger campaign, is that right?" You might find if you are more receptive that Rachel had intended something else: "No, I thought there were similarities between the two and we should build on those similarities, but actually I see this as calling for a unique solution. Let me tell you how I see it. . . ." Shifting from a defensive climate to a supportive one is not always so simple. The changes in attitude and behavior called for demand that we take risks by trying new behaviors.

Building a supportive environment is the last element of interpersonal listening, but it is also the culmination of the other four. To build a supportive environment demands an awareness of others, empathy for those with whom we have personal or work relationships, trust, and a willingness to honestly self-disclose. With these as elements, the structure of a model of interpersonal listening can now take shape.

A Model For Interpersonal Listening

Let us then, describe a model of listening for both personal and professional life. This is a helping or customer/client-oriented model which is collegial in nature. It is also a service model that considers the frontline worker, or the customer as the most important component of any organization. To review, listening is the primary way we have of knowing about, understanding, and helping those we live with, work with, and/or serve. It is a broad-based skill of receptivity which includes both verbal and nonverbal messages. As we have said, listening is hearing and more. Effective listening includes the ability to attend carefully, be aware of our active receptivity, critically interpret messages, understand and remember, and provide appropriate feedback/response to another human being.

Listening Objectives, Attitudes, and Skills

To be proficient listeners, we must first believe that listening can be influential. We must believe that we can affect people by listening. We need to acknowledge that listening empowers us to relate to, help, and/or work with friends, family, and professional colleagues.

Outcomes of Good Listening

By listening we achieve the following:

- *Building and Maintaining Relationships.* Careful listening says you and your needs are important to me—I respect you. Listening to another person makes that person feel good about themselves; it enhances their self esteem and feeling of personal worth.

- *Learning.* We find out about friends, family members, clients, and co-workers. We discover their unique needs, concerns, desires, fears, and objections. A wise person picks up information about a great many subjects by being receptive and open to learning.

- *Understanding.* We realize what it is to experience from another person's point of view. Each person is different. What we may think is quite simple may be difficult for another; what seems routine for us can be quite foreign to another. By active, empathic listening we see what it's like to wear the shoes of another. First, however, we must get out of our own shoes. As one of our students commented, "we are doing well if we can get one of our shoes off and one of their shoes on."

The Competent Listener

How do we listen interpersonally? What constitutes good listening? We must start with the premise that a competent communicator perceives listening as receiving with nothing to prove. With this in mind a competent listener needs the following skills and attitudes:

- *A desire to listen.* Enter the listening situation prepared and ready to listen;

- *A willingness to help.* Listening is not problem solving. If we help our friend, client, or colleague to solve their own problems they will want our relationship and resources;

- *Patience.* Devote undivided attention; do not interrupt; being silent can be helpful;

- *The ability to attend to communication cues.* Recognize the central themes, emotions, needs, and concerns of communicators, and accept them without reservation or argument;

- *Self monitoring.* Self monitoring is the ability to monitor ourselves as we listen, and to observe our own nonverbal reactions, as well as self-talk or inner reactions that could interfere with listening perceptively (such as getting angry, becoming neutral or indifferent, day-dreaming, or becoming involved in our own thoughts);

- *Respect.* Respect is the capacity to listen with consideration, recognizing a friend or colleague's expertise in their own affairs;

- *Non-judgemental response.* Non-judgemental responding is the ability to listen openly without responding critically (internally or externally).

The Listening Cycle

These seven attitudes/skills are fundamental for effective interpersonal listening. They are applied as part of an on-going process of communication interaction which is quite different when considered from the listener's perspective. As a speaker we talk and wait for a response, and then make adjustments to our message and perhaps try again. As a listener we have what may be a more complex set of skills and attitudes to master.

The Listening Cycle. The skills and attitudes listed above operate as part of the communication cycle from the listener's perspective. The cycle consists of:

- Attending, while at the same time demonstrating interest in the speaker through short affirmations and nonverbal gestures that acknowledge and recognize the speaker;

- Asking questions and inserting short focusing comments that seek to help the speaker present his or her ideas;

- Responding, first with feedback to let the speaker know how we have interpreted and understood their message, and then with a reply that genuinely advances the conversation in a way that is in the best interest of both parties.

As we noted in the first chapter, our main work as a listener is to "empty our own cup," to remove our self, so that we can help the speaker articulate his or her feelings and ideas. If we have a need to challenge or argue with the speaker there is plenty of time for that, and it will be more effective after we have truly listened and know better what the speaker has said. Good debaters are good listeners, since if they have not listened they are arguing with what they think the speaker has said; not with what the speaker has actually said.

An important part of the work of listening is to encourage the speaker through short statements and paralinguistic cues ("yes," "uh huh," "I hear you"), and nonverbal gestures (leaning toward the speaker, and especially, having good eye contact). We may have had experiences similar to that of the speaker, but we should never assume we know exactly what the speaker is saying. By asking open, empathic questions we can help the speaker to express her/his feelings and ideas more fully and clearly. By asking questions we may find out if the speaker (who may be a client, friend or colleague) needs more information, if he/she understands our common goals and objectives, if there are objections. By asking questions we may discover if we have been understood, or if we are even talking about the same things. Short comments to the speaker are sometimes useful too, but they should help the speaker focus on her/his message and not advance our own views.

Feedback

Finally, the process of listening is not complete until we provide feedback that lets the speaker know *how* we have heard them. The feedback we provide should adhere to Gibb's guidelines for constructing a supportive communication climate. When we have allowed speakers to acknowledge and incorporate the feedback into their talk, we may respond in such a way as to continue the interaction (which may be simply sharing and enjoying each other's company). As a proficient listener we do not need to follow the cycle rigidly; rather, it is more the spirit of the process that proves effective in personal and professional relationships. In a paper discussing the failures in management at NASA leading to the Challenger shuttle disaster, Hyatt and Kernisky (1989) indicate that the problem was caused by a lack of feedback in the communication systems. Critical information did not reach top management who had to make the final decisions. Distortion and interference with the free–flow of information resulting from lack of feedback was the result. Feedback, Hyatt and Kernisky (1989) wrote, "is the key to most effective listening behavior. . . . If the sender of the message anticipates that the feedback will be negative or that no feedback will be forthcoming, a distortion of the message may occur, or for that matter, the information may not be sent" (p. 6).

This is what happened at NASA. The model of listening we have described prescribes that feedback with a minimum of distortion needs to occur because it is part of sensitive and perceptive listening.

Questioning: Adjunct to Effective Listening

Asking questions is an active component of our listening model. If done empathically and used cautiously, it elicits from others what we need to know; but more importantly, it helps our client or colleague communicate their needs. As communicators, we have an agenda (which we are aware of if we listen to ourselves), however, it should not get in the way of serving a client or professional colleague. Questioning, if done sensitively, takes the focus of the conversation away from ourselves and puts it on the speaker.

We should be cautious in our questioning, however, that we do not fall into the all too frequent pattern in our culture of using questioning to manipulate, challenge and control what the speaker says. Use questioning in moderation, especially if you notice you are controlling the conversation with questions. Bolton observes that "we often rely on questions excessively and use them poorly. Questions usually focus on the intent, perspective, and concerns of the listener rather than on the speaker's orientation" (1979, p. 170). If a person is experiencing a problem or is emotionally distraught, it may be best to ask questions only after offering an empathic and supportive response. This is not an excuse for avoiding questions; it only alerts us to the need to use questions to facilitate healthy communication and not to control the conversation.

The tone of voice used in asking the question has a lot to do with how the question is received, as illustrated by the question "Are you kidding?" asked as a point of information verses in a sarcastic or condescending manner. Our purpose in using questioning as an important element of good listening is to help speakers express themselves more fully. Hence, we need to describe the various questions we may use and their impact on the relationship we are building. The following five kinds of questions may be used singly, or in combinations to facilitate understanding between speaker and listener.

Clarifying questions. In the process of listening we should typically begin with questions that clarify what has been said or which seek more information to understand the speaker. We might ask for examples, illustrations ("could you paint me a picture?", "describe it for me?"), facts, definitions. This would include the five journalistic questions: who, what why, where, when, and how. Care should be exercised with "why" questions. People's typically response to "why?" is to feel they are being asked to justify their behavior; that is not the response we are seeking. If our tone of voice sounds interested we can encourage the speaker to tell us more. A related type of question requests expansion of meaning, "tell me the whole story," "is there more to this incident?" In the same sense that we can ask for details and clarification, we can also ask about feelings. We must be careful not to probe; but a well-phrased question can help speakers talk about their feelings. We might ask: "How did you feel when she criticized you for being late?", or "What were you feeling as you told them you had to quit?"

Paraphrasing questions. A second type of question that follows up on the first, is the paraphrase, where we repeat in our own words what the speaker has said, and follow the statement with a question mark. We use the paraphrase to check for accuracy of facts and feelings. We want to check to see if what we heard is what the speaker said. "Did you say you wanted to quit the operation?" Or we might phrase it in such a way that we repeat what the speaker said first: "You said . . . did I hear you correctly?" A simpler form of the paraphrase question is the mirror question, where we reflect back to the speaker exactly what the speaker has said to us. This helps speakers to be more conscious of what they have said. The paraphrase question is generally a good question to use as a check to see if we are being empathic and identifying with the speaker.

Summarizing questions. A third type of question seeks to establish the accuracy of our interpretation of the speaker's message. It builds upon the first two questions, with one addition. We try to synthesize, summarize, or interpret what the speaker has said. Like the paraphrase question, we follow it with a question mark to check that we have not made any unwarranted assumptions about the intended message. However, at this level of questioning assumptions naturally creep in as we speculate about what we think the speaker has in mind. We may check our assumptions with properly phrased questions: "So what you have said so far adds up to . . . , is that correct?" If the question is not phrased delicately, and/or does not reflect what the speaker actually said, it could divert the speaker from the intended message. Therefore, we try to ask questions based pretty much on what the speaker has offered in his or her remarks.

Exploratory Questions. A fourth type of question is used to encourage the speaker to explore the possibilities inherent in a situation. We judiciously challenge speakers to extend their thinking and evaluate their limitations. This is the mode of questioning typically used by competent teachers or coaches, or managers. "Are there any other ways to approach this problem?" "Have you looked at this relationship from your spouse's (child's) point of view?" "How would you feel if your proposal was not chosen?" The pitfall in this type of questioning is that of the teacher who already knows the answer to the question when they ask. A proficient listener (teacher, coach) must be humble; to understand we must literally "stand under." We ask questions to encourage, to learn, not to confirm what we already know. We can learn a great deal by helping others to explore the potential of their thoughts and experience.

Supportive questions. The final type of question seeks to support speakers while exploring the values and/or criteria upon which they have made a decision, or to evaluate the consequences of their behavior. This might be thought of as a constructive parent (or coach) role, in which we non-judgmentally help speakers to evaluate their thoughts and behavior. In this role the listener works to help a colleague, a client, or perhaps a child, to examine their behavior and its possible outcomes or consequences. Again, the intent is not to be directive, but to be an empathic, concerned, co-communicator, helping the other express themselves. We might ask: "Do you feel that what you did was in your best interest?", or "Have you weighed the alternatives?" Teenagers, for example, will soon be leaving the family nest to make decisions for themselves. Through non-judgmental questions we may help them to grow in the ability to form their own considered decisions. The same could be true of a worker, or a client.

It may not be obvious but there is an escalation of commitment assumed in the relationship of listener to speaker as the questioning roles progress. To ask questions for clarification is typically less demanding of a relationship than to play a supportive or parental role. There is also an escalation of the assumptions made by the listener. We do not make assumptions when we are seeking clarification, but when we begin to synthesize we could be interpreting statements entirely out of the context of the other's discourse. Being open-minded and non-judgmental are the most productive strategies to assure that true communication has occurred.

Blocks to Effective Listening

According to Jann Davis (1984) in the book *Listening and Responding* there are several blocks to smoothly flowing communication between listener and speaker. Questions we ask, feedback and/or responses we give may short-circuit effective communication making relationships at home or at work difficult. Using Davis as a guide we can suggest seven typical blocks to effective listening.

Using Silence

Sometimes the very act of questioning and giving feedback can get in the way of supportive and helpful listening. At times such as these silence may be the best way to listen. By being silent we communicate that we are not going to interrupt and are ready and willing to be receptive.

Avoid Leading Questions

Beware of questions that make the interaction more questioner-oriented. The object of questioning is to create a speaker-orientation; to avoid "leading" questions which may be fine in the courtroom, but are counter productive in other situations.

Avoid Giving Advice

Avoid any desire you may have to give advice. Your advice originates from *your* experience and is seldom appropriate for anyone else. Giving advice makes the client or family member dependent upon you for answers. We should rather seek to empower people; let them find their own solutions arising out of their own experience. Guidance is sometimes appropriate, but it must be based on careful, empathic listening.

Approval or Disapproval

When listening be careful of approving or disapproving of the speaker's stated values, opinions, and goals. Understanding (listening) has nothing to do with whether we approve or disapprove. For example, to empower the people we are working with we want their goals to come from them. They will be more likely to work toward goals they helped create.

Agreeing or Disagreeing

The same holds true for agreeing or disagreeing with the speaker. Once the listener agrees or disagrees with the client or colleague, for instance, it may be difficult for them to change, especially if you have a higher perceived status. If you disagree it may also make the client defensive because you have not identified with him or her. Again, good listening is not a matter of agreeing or disagreeing, but rather of understanding without regard for politics or point of view.

Defensiveness

If the speaker puts you on the defensive, try to put any contentious or retaliatory response aside. Just acknowledge such comments without excuse. To respond in kind would simply escalate the defensive climate and spoil the possibility of a supportive climate.

Cliches

Finally, avoid inappropriate phrases like generalizations and cliches. "Everything will be alright, you'll see." "Every one has these problems." Such empty reassurances ignore the uniqueness of a situation, and may tend to trivialize one's feelings. People need a personal response from us.

Summary

The above are listening strategies that may be helpful in all personal and professional situations. The skills involved need to be practiced and applied on a daily basis if we are to grow more skillful in their use. Listening is an art as Dominick Barbara stressed in his book, *The Art of Listening*, and "as an art then, it requires knowledge and effort" (1958, p. 1). Our book provides the knowledge; you, the reader, must contribute the effort.

Exercises

1. Goal setting. Goals are long term changes we desire. "I want to listen better to friends or colleagues." Objectives are the specific actions we can perform to accomplish the goal. "I will practice talking less and listening more." "I will try to listen, question, and understand, rather than challenge, when I get into an argument." Write our two or three listening goals you would like to accomplish. Set a time period for accomplishing the goals and the amount of improvement you would like to see. List two or more specific actions that will help you reach each goal.

   At the beginning of each new chapter revise these goals or set new goals. At the end of the book review your intrapersonal goals to see how much progress you have made and how far you still have to go.

2. Using the journal you began in chapter 1, keep a running record of the negative self-talk you hear as you listen to your self. Take note of how we all have an "inner critic" which tells us we may fail. Suggest some positive phrases you can substitute for negative

phrases. Pick phrases which will be constructive and will not sabotage your desire to succeed.

3 Use your journal to keep a log of your daily dreams. If you are someone who does not recall dreams well, you may build a story around any fragment of a dream you remember, or just write a story upon awakening, and use the story as dream material. Use one of the two methods suggested in this chapter to work with your dream. If some of this material gets too personal you may want to keep it in a separate journal from your class journal.

4. Pick three or four people with whom your relationship is liable to involve more emotion (love, jealousy, anger, hate). During the process of communication listen inside periodically and make note of what you are feeling and how your emotions are manifesting. Pay attention to your body. Do you feel a tightness in your stomach? Is some part of your body turned away from your partner? What emotions are associated with these bodily reactions? Record three or four experiences and discuss them in your journal, or in a short assignment to present and discuss in class.

References

Barbara, D. (1958). *The art of listening.* Springfield, IL: Thomas.

Bentley, S. (March, 1989). Building memory power. International Listening Association Conference. Atlanta.

Bolton, R. (1979). *People skills.* Englewood Cliffs, NJ: Prentice-Hall.

Burke, K. (1950). *A rhetoric of motives.* Englewood Cliffs, NJ: Prentice Hall.

Burns, D. D. (1981). *Feeling good: The new mood therapy.* New York: New American Library.

Brownell, J. (1996). Listening: Attitudes, principles, and skills. Boston: Allyn and Bacon.

Crum J. K. (1975). *The art of inner listening.* Wheaton, Illinois: Re-Quest Books.

Davis, A. J. (1984). *Listening and responding.* St. Louis: C.V. Mosby Co.

DeVito, J. A. (1986). *The communication handbook: A dictionary.* New York: Harper and Row.

Fantz, R. E. (1987). Gestalt approach." In J. L. Fosshage and C.A. Loew, (Eds.). *Dream interpretation: A comparative study* (pp. 191–241). Rev. ed. New York: PMA.

Faraday, A. (1972). *Dream power.* New York: Berkley.

Freud, S. (1965). *The interpretation of dreams.* Trans. James Strachey. New York: Avon.

Gibb, J. R. (1961). Defensive communication. *Journal of Communication.* 11, 141–148.

Goffman, E. (1959). *Presentation of self in everyday life.* Garden City, NY: Anchor.

Goss, B. (1982). *Communication processing: Information processing in intrapersonal communication.* Belmont, CA: Wadsworth.

Haney, W. V. (1986). *Communication and interpersonal relations: Text and cases.* 5th ed. Homewood, IL: Irwin.

Helmstetter, S. (1986). *What to say when you talk to yourself.* New York: Pocket Books.

Howell, W. S. (1982). *The empathic communicator.* Prospect Heights, IL: Waveland.

Hyatt, D. A., and I. F. Kernisky. (March, 1989). From challenger 'disaster' to 'flawless' mission: A new way of listening at NASA. Paper presented at the International Listening Association Conference, Atlanta.

Jung, C. (1973). *Dreams.* Trans. R. F. Hull. Bollingen Series 20. Princeton, N.J.: Princeton.

Klinger, E (1996). *Daydreaming* Minneapolis, MN: UMM Books..

Krishnamurti, J. (1964). *Think on these things.* New York: Perennial Library–Harper and Row.

Loftus, E. (1980). *Memory: Surprising new insights into how we remember and why we forget.* Reading, MA: Addison–Wesley.

Lorayne, H. (1985). *Page-a-minute memory book.* New York: Holt, Rinehart and Winston.

Meerloo, J. A. M. (1973). The word tyrannizes us or is our slave. In John Stewart, (Ed.). *Bridges not walls: A book about interpersonal communication.* 1st ed. Reading, MA: Addison–Wesley.

Mehrabian, A. (1972). *Silent messages.* 2nd ed. Belmont, CA: Wadsworth.

Morris, J. (1985). *The dream workbook: Discover the knowledge and power hidden in your dreams.* Boston: Little, Brown and Company.

Nichols, R. G., and L. A. Stevens. (1957). *Are you listening?* New York: McGraw-Hill.

Newman, M., and B. Berkowitz (with J. Owen). (1971). *How to be your own best friend.* New York: Random House.

Peck, M. S. (1978). *The road less traveled: A new psychology of love, traditional values and spiritual growth.* New York: Touchstone–Simon and Schuster.

Perls, F. (1973). *The gestalt approach & eye witness to therapy.* Palo Alto: Science and Behavior Books.

Powell, J. (1969). *why am i afraid to tell you who i am?.* Niles, IL: Argus.

Ram Dass, and P. Gorman. (1985). *How can i help? Stories and reflections on service.* New York: Knopf.

Roberts, C., R. Edwards, and L. Barker. (1987). *Intrapersonal communication processes.* Scottsdale, AZ: Gorsuch, Scarisbrick.

Rosten, L. (1972). *Leo Rosten's treasury of jewish quotations.* New York: McGraw-Hill.

Rogers, C. R. (1980). *A way of becoming.* Boston: Houghton Mifflin.

Seamon, J. G. (1980). *Memory & cognition: An introduction.* New York: Oxford University Press.

Singh, Kirpal. (1992, 1970). *Morning Talks.* Bowling Green, VA: Sawan Kirpal Publications.

Steele, M. A. (with R. M. Armstrong). (1971). "I had the craziest dream last night.": *A psychiatrist helps you interpret your dreams.* Chicago: Nelson-Hall.

Chapter 3

LISTENING AND GENDER: Values Revalued

Deborah Borisoff and Dan F. Hahn

Points to be Addressed:

- Listening Communities
- Speech versus Listening: A Reflection of Bipolar Spheres
- Listening Traits: A Reflection of the Feminine Stereotype
- Acceptance and Valuation in the Listening Process: Reflections of Sex-Role and Sex-Trait Expectations

> Listening is the active and dynamic process of attending, perceiving, interpreting, remembering, and responding to the expressed (verbal and nonverbal) needs, concerns, and information offered by other human beings.(Purdy, 1991, p. 11)

Purdy's definition conforms to the salient aspects of the more than fifty definitions for listening that appear in the extant literature (Brownell, 1986; Glenn, 1989; Nichols, 1948; Steil et al, 1983; Wolvin and Coakley, 1988, etc.).Implicit in this definition is that by actively engaging in the "dynamic process of attending, perceiving, interpreting, remembering, and responding" to others, listening may be achieved. Also implied is that those who embrace this definition presumably share certain commonalties in how they attend and respond to others; in what they perceive, interpret and remember from such interactions.

Listening Communities

That we might share assumptions about listening reflects Suzanne Langer's (1953; 1979) notion of "discourse communities," that is, that culture, or collective life, depends upon a shared symbol system. Moreover, just as William Labov (1972) contributed to our understanding of "speech communities"—the shared set of norms regarding communication—we would hope to encounter established norms to indicate "listening communities."

"In an ideal world," according to Borisoff and Hahn (1992, p. 25), "where individuals share similar experiences, beliefs, ideas, goals, backgrounds, cultures and so on, the process of listening would be a simple act" Defining and negotiating discourse, speech, and listening communities, however, is not simple; rather, it is complex.

This complexity has been acknowledged in recent decades as studies on gender and communication have indicated that the "communities" into which women and men are socialized often result in distinct expectations for valuing and conveying listening (Bem, 1993; Borisoff and Merrill, 1991; Gumperz, 1962; Henley, 1977; Johnson, 1989; Kramarae, 1981; Lakoff, 1975; Nichols, 1980; Tannen, 1990; 1994; Wood and Inman, 1993).What is attended to, the context in which listening is facilitated, and the affective display of listening behavior have been the primary foci of studies on gender and listening. . This chapter examines the communication scripts for listening that have been written for men and women and considers how far we have come in establishing "listening communities."

Speech Versus Listening: Bi-Polar Spheres

> Everything is word, everything is only word ... we must grab culture by the word, as it seizes us in its word, in its language. . . . Indeed, as soon as we are, we are born into language and language speaks us . . . .
> (Cixous, 1976/1985, p. 7)

The "language" into which women and men are born reveals that the language we speak and that "speaks us" reflects division rather than unity, emphasizes differences instead of similarities. The language that speaks us is different for men and for women.

The dichotomous climate of men as speakers and women as listeners has its roots in Greek antiquity. Women's language was regarded as the voice of opinion and not truth. This voice, consequently, was devalued and relegated to the home. Men's voices, in contrast, were revered. They could be heard in public. More importantly, separating and valuing differently men's and women's communication made it increasingly difficult for the two sexes to converse. According to Elshtain, "women's communication in classical antiquity would have taken on the terms of their enforced isolation. That one sex almost exclusively inhabited a public sphere and the other sex the private may help to explain why so many men and women literally could not 'speak' to one another" (1982, p. 130). Silencing one group based on sex has had an enormous impact on society's attitudes towards listening. Women were the purveyors of emotions; men, the arbiters of fact. One group was expected to listen; the other, to speak. The interpretation by external society of how and where women and men should communicate resulted in internalized social constructs. Speaking up and out became associated with intelligence, activity, independence, strength, and competitiveness. These traits, in turn, became inexorably linked to men's sex-trait stereotypes. Listening and polite speech became linked to passivity, weakness, connection, emotion, and dependence. These traits, in turn, became associated with women's sex-trait stereotypes.

Sex-role behaviors acquired centuries ago are abundantly evident today. So pervasive, in fact, are the sex roles of men as speakers and women as listeners that they cross international boundaries. In a thirty-nation study by social psychologists John Williams and Deborah Best(1982) , these researchers and their colleagues found that the above-mentioned gender-linked communication stereotypes persist.

Self-concept influences how we interact with others. If men are expected to play the dominant role of speakers while women are encouraged to assume the ostensibly more passive role of listeners, then the desires and expectations each sex will have in a listening exchange with the member of the opposite sex will be affected.

Sadly, behind the conscious ego ideals of expected roles for each gender are what Keen calls the unconscious shadows (1991, pp. 44–45). Keen maintains that this discrepancy between the conscious ideal and the unconscious shadow "inevitably shapes the dance between the genders" (p. 44). Like Lerner (1989) and Rubin (1983) before him, Keen refers to the dichotomy within women's and men's own psyches as well as their interrelationships as "the choreography of the relationship between the sexes that has dominated the last era of human history" (p. 44). Thus, behind the male warrior image of the independent, extroverted, protector/provider who is supposed to be brave, bold, practical and angry is a fragile human being who has been socialized to eschew feelings, nature, and women. Similarly, behind the woman's image of the dependent, introverted nurturer who is supposed to heal, belong, be intuitive, passive, and emotional, is a strong human being who has been socialized to avoid power, anger, and men. By centering himself in the public, political sphere, man "has abandoned the familiar and domestic" (Keen, 1991, p. 44). By centering herself in the private, domestic sphere, woman "has abandoned the worldly and political" (Keen, 1991, p. 45).

As Keen suggests, the propensity for dichotomizing behavior according to sex has led to relegating men to the public domain of speakers and women to the private domain of listeners. Such dichotomizing, moreover, has allowed each sex to be the arbiters of communication within these respective spheres.

Implicit in dividing and privileging behavior according to gender lines is that this behavior, in turn, becomes the standard, or norm against which other, or different, behavior is then measured. Through such comparisons, the normative behavior for communication in a particular context acquires a kind of legitimate power or importance that seemingly may be impervious to challenge or change. The acknowledged traits for effective listening appear to privilege women's ways of communicating, although, as we will see in the next section, this privilege is qualified.

Listening Traits:
A Reflection of the Feminine Stereotype

The early Twentieth Century author, Brenda Ueland, articulates the powerful and creative force that listening can be:

> Listening is a magnetic and strange thing, a creative force. . . . When we are listened to, it creates us, makes us unfold and expand. Ideas actually begin to grow with us and come to life (1992, p. 104).

Ueland's essay is addressed to the adult who often forgets to "listen to our children, or those we love. . . . " (p. 104). If we take a moment to reflect on our own childhood and early professional experiences, we may find that what Ueland attributes to "forgetting" may be more a matter of never having learned how to truly listen in the first place.

For many of us, our early associations for listening are with obedience. These associations may follow us into adulthood. The parent tells the young child, "Now listen to me. You can't watch television until you've cleaned up your room." The teacher warns the students, "If you don't listen, you're all going to have to stay after school." The boss informs the young manager, "I'll listen to your proposals on how to have expenses; however, we've been experiencing serious losses in your unit." In each of these examples, listening is not a process of shared interaction. Rather, these examples are illustrative of explicit orders or veiled threats indicative of a power imbalance in the relationship. The parent, the teacher, and the boss clearly control the resources. In these instances, compliance—called listening—is demanded of the child, the students, and the worker. Thus, prior experiences with how the word "listening" has been used may inform how we come to construe this term. Such experiences, consequently, may diminish our ability to regard listening as an active process of mutual sharing. Overcoming prior experiences in order to value listening is our first challenge.

The second challenge to valuing listening may be related to the qualities that have been associated with effective and ineffective listening. In his seminal study on listening, Ralph Nichols (1948) asked 500 male and female college-age students to identify behavioral traits that may facilitate or impede listening. The following twenty-six positive and negative traits that emerged from Nichols' work have endured in the ensuing decades:

Positive Traits	*Negative Traits*
Alert	Apathetic
Attending	Defensive
Caring	Disinterested
Curious	Emotional
Effective Evaluator	Impatient
Empathic	Inattentive
Interested	Insensitive
Non-emotional	Interrupting
Non-interrupting	Quick to Judge
Other-centered	Self-centered
Patient	Uncaring
Responsive	
Understanding	

In their chapter on listening, Borisoff and Merrill (1991) observed a strong connection between the positive traits for effective listening and the sex-role and sex-trait stereotypes associated with women's behavior in U.S. culture—especially the terms attending, caring, empathic, non-interrupting, other-centered, patient, responsive, and understanding. Borisoff and Merrill noted as well the association of many of the terms linked to ineffective listening—especially the terms defensive, inattentive, impatient, insensitive, interrupting, quick to judge, self-centered, and uncaring—with the masculine stereotype for sex-role and sex-trait behaviors in U.S. culture. These connections led them to conclude that "It appears that in this culture, women acquire behavioral traits that conform to our expectation of the interested and empathic listener" (Borisoff and Merrill, 1991, pp. 60-61).

While we are by no means asserting that all women are other-centered, empathic, and understanding, and that all men are inattentive, insensitive and impatient, we are suggesting that the way gendered behavior for listening is acquired and valued in our culture may create a powerful barrier for men, in particular, to adopt the affective displays for effective listening that have been attributed to women's styles of communicating.

This leads to the third, and perhaps most complex challenge regarding listening behavior: the extent to which the perceptions of and expectations for listening behavior may be informed by the distinct communication scripts to which women and men feel compelled to conform. Much has been written in recent years connecting the failure, or *perceived* failure of listening—especially men's listening behavior—to marital conflicts (Beck, 1988; Rubin, 1983), relationship dissatisfaction (Duck, 1991; Hite, 1987; Tannen, 1990; 1994; Winokur, 1991; Wood and Inman, 1993), and to the dissolution of relationships (Duck, 1991; Fitzpatrick, 1988; Markman, 1992; Noller, 1987). Yet allegations that partners do not listen to each other may mask the real issues. We suggest two fundamental differences in the communication scripts for women and men that may give rise to the allegations that men and women do not listen to one another, especially in their personal relationships.

Listening for Feelings

Certainly men and women are capable of expressing their feelings. However in close personal relationships between couples, research suggests a qualitative difference in the kinds of feelings expressed, as well as in the cues attended to.

If we recall Elshtain's (1982) and Keen's (1991) assertions that women and men have inherited divergent legacies as listeners and speakers, we are not surprised that they would have access to different kinds of expression. Rubin (1983) in her work with male and female clients, Aries (1987) in her studies conducted with college–age students, and Beck (1988) in his treatment of couples, found that women gain closeness by talking about feelings. Moreover, they desire reciprocity in this type of personal disclosure from their partners. These same researchers found that while men do self-disclose, they are more likely to disclose and listen for facts than to reveal the emotional tapestry of their inner lives.

There are two essential factors that may discourage men from becoming emotionally vulnerable in their interactions with others. The first factor may stem from gender polarization. By dividing behavior according to sex, the resultant sex–role and sex–trait communication behaviors for both sexes become powerful lures for prescribing and limiting behavior. Sandra Bem (1993) suggests that once the mutually exclusive communication scripts for men and women are written, those who deviate from these scripts are apt to be regarded as "problematic" (p. 81); deviation from these scripts often is not tolerated.

Insofar as self-disclosing personal feelings is concerned, men have borne the brunt of negative sanctions. In the mid-seventies, for example, Derlega and Chaikin (1976) found that when men revealed personal problems in male-male and male-female dyads, they were viewed more negatively than when they remained silent. Conversely, women were regarded positively under the same interaction settings. Borisoff and Hahn (1992) observe that the negative assessment of men when they self-disclose under the aforementioned conditions might discourage them from doing so, *regardless* of how strongly men want others to listen to their feelings and emotions. It may be hard, then, for men to divest themselves of the mantle of the masculine stereotype, that is, of "the strong silent type," when they enter intimate relationships, for culture has taught them that others do not want to hear their feelings.

A recent study by Wood and Inman (1993) expands our understanding of self-disclosure by positing that the extant research and texts on interpersonal communication stress listening and speaking in face-to-face interaction as appropriate and valuable for self disclosure—the type of setting in which women are socialized and are, therefore, more comfortable. By ignoring the types of interaction settings in which men are more at ease and, therefore, more apt to self-disclose (for example, when engaged in activities), we privilege women's modes of communicating, thereby diminishing men's styles of expression. "To persist in dismissing ways of interacting that men seem to prefer and to excel in," Wood and Inman conclude, "impoverishes understanding of human communication" (p. 291).

We would add to Wood and Inman's conclusion by noting that urging either sex to adopt the behavioral modes of expression of the other gender may be flawed advice. Just as scholars who advised women to adopt masculine modes of communication in the work place (the "deficit" hypothesis; Henley, 1977; Kramarae, 1981; Lakoff, 1975) later abandoned this line of thinking, replacing it by encouraging at re-evaluation and expansion of what we value as effective communication in the work environment to *include* feminine communication styles (the "code switching" hypothesis; Borisoff and Hahn, 1995; Haste, 1994; Jamieson, 1995; Johnson, 1983; 1989; Tannen, 1990; 1994), we ought seek a similar re-evaluation of masculine communication styles in personal relationships and encourage men to become adept at employing multiple modes of expression.

Encouraging men to adopt feminine modes of expression, however, may be more problematic than urging women to expand the communication scripts written for them into the masculine domain. This leads us to the second, and more fundamental factor that discourages men from valuing emotional vulnerability in dyadic interaction. Those who write about gender and communication acknowledge that despite women's progress during the past several decades, our culture remains powerfully embedded in androcentrism, or male-centeredness.

Charlotte Perkins Gilman (1911) is credited with first articulating this term within the context of women's and men's relationship. She wrote:

> All our human scheme of things rests on the same tacit assumption: man being held the human type; woman a sort of accompaniment and subordinate assistant, merely essential to the making of people. She held always the place of a preposition in relation to man. She has always been considered above him or below him, before him, behind him, beside him, a wholly relative experience . . . . (1911/1971, p. 20).

Implicit in this "human scheme" is the *valuation* of men's communication. Implicit, as well, is the simultaneous *devaluation* of women's communication. Regardless of how sensitive as listeners men may want to be, the androcentric lens of our culture serves as a formidable barrier to expanding their communication scripts to include a feminine style of listening and self-disclosure.Androcentrism, according to Bem (1993), "so thoroughly devalues whatever thoughts, feelings, and behaviors are culturally defined as feminine that crossing the gender boundaries has a more negative cultural meaning for men than it has for women. . . . " (pp. 149–150). Such constraints, we would add, sadly closes the door to the full range of human experience and emotions for men.

If androcentrism limits what men may reveal while speaking and listening to others, we also might ask to what extent the masculine stereotype governs the affective verbal and nonverbal display of listening behavior. Furthermore, we might speculate about whether a failure to adopt feminine modes of expression for listening *implies* that men are not listening, or not listening as well as women. This leads us to the second fundamental difference in the gendered communication scripts alleging that women and men are not equally effective listeners.

The Nonverbal and Verbal Affective Display of Listening

Just as society instructs men and women differently about what they should reveal, it also provides gender-specific training in how to listen. While the listening texts referred to at the beginning of this chapter do not specifically divide their advice for effective listening along gender lines (especially in dyadic interaction in personal relationships), the strategies suggested to assure effective self-expression as well as attending and responding to others decidedly privilege feminine modes of communication.

Texts that address listening in personal relationships emphasize the benefits of "good" listening. In a productive communication exchange, speakers are enriched by being understood; listeners are enriched by being able to understand. These texts, moreover, emphasize the qualitative dimension of listening. The advice these works offer regarding mutually satisfying listening exchanges in dyadic personal relationships can be synthesized and summarized into the following two general categories: the nonverbal affective display of listening; and, the verbal content of messages that demonstrate effective listening. Both of these categories contribute to the listening process.

The Nonverbal Affective Display of Listening

Three dimensions of nonverbal communication play especially critical roles in conveying listening according to listening texts. The first dimension, kinesics, or body language, may signal our interest, or lack of interest, in the speaker. When we lean toward, or away from, the speaker; when we fold or unfold our arms; when we smile, or frown, or scowl—each of these actions may communicate volumes to another. Relatedly, when we achieve synchronicity, that is, literally being "in synch" with another's movements, we are signaling that we are attending or listening.

Oculesics, or eye contact, is the second nonverbal code that may demonstrate listening. When we gaze at a speaker, or look repeatedly at our watch, or glance down at a paper, we may be demonstrating respectively that we are listening, or are in a hurry, or are not fully interested in what the speaker has to say.

Paralinguistic cues, or the fillers we employ during interaction with another (for example, "I see," "uh–huh," "go on," etc.), compose the third nonverbal communication code that may indicate interest in and/or an understanding of the speaker's message.

While literally hundreds of books and journal articles have been written on nonverbal communication, we have two concerns regarding the aforementioned nonverbal cues and listening behavior.

The first concern relates to the process of an interpersonal encounter. A communication exchange is an active process: both the speaker and the listener are participants in this process. Nonverbal expression may signal to the speaker that the listener is attending to, is interested in, and/or understands the speaker's message. In other words, these cues provide signals to the speaker. The affective display affects the speaker. Does the absence of nonverbal markers necessarily imply a lack of attention, or understanding, or empathy? Nonverbal behavior, the literature tells us, is influenced by culture (Birdwhistell, 1970; Hall, 1959; 1966) and by socialization (Aries, 1987; Hall, 1984; Henley, 1977; LaFrance and Henley, 1994) . Therefore, if individuals have not been raised to employ the nonverbal cues which the texts on listening suggest are indicative of active and effective listening, are we to assume that such individuals are ineffective or "poor" listeners? The answer, of course, is that we cannot make this assumption. The obviousness of this discrepancy is often revealed in intercultural encounters, especially in a communication exchange between members of low and high context cultures. The advice advocated in the literature on intercultural communication is that we ought not judge others based solely on the lens of our own culture (a sign of ethnocentrism). Rather, we are encouraged to use the lens of understanding by suspending our judgments and endeavoring to enter the other's frame of reference (Barnlund, 1989; Borisoff and Victor, 1989; Hall, 1959; 1966, etc.).

The second concern deals with the subtler distinctions in the affect of nonverbal communication when communicating with members of the same culture. In their article on nonverbal sensitivity, Marianne LaFrance and Nancy Henley (1994) review the literature on gender and nonverbal communication which support that women, more than men, demonstrate more of the nonverbal cues (for example gazing, smiling, forward lean, head nodding, etc.), and are more adept at decoding nonverbal cues.

In light of these findings, we would again raise the question: are women, therefore, better listeners than men? This controversy has yet to be resolved. None of the studies on listening has demonstrated that either sex is a better listener in interpersonal communication, although the feminine stereotype for behavior, as indicated earlier, conforms more closely with Nichols' (1948) traits of the effective listener. Recent studies, in fact, suggest certain conditions that may *minimize* gender differences and nonverbal communication.

In the absence of status differences, for example, women and men were found to be equally adept at decoding nonverbal cues (Snodgrass, 1988; 1992, cited in LaFrance and Henley, 1994). Moreover, when status differences were introduced, Snodgrass (1992) found that neither women nor men were more nonverbally sensitive. It is important to indicate, however, that in these studies, individuals assigned to lower status positions demonstrated a heightened sensitivity to decoding the nonverbal cues of the individuals assigned to higher status positions. Further, we point out that these situations were contrived, that is, subjects were assigned roles, causing us to speculate about the extent to which the concept of the assigned role influenced subjects' performance at decoding nonverbal cues. In another study which considered self–esteem rather than status as the salient characteristic, John Daly (1990) found that individuals with a positive sense of self were able to listen more fully to others than were subjects with low self–esteem.High self–esteem subjects talked less about themselves, employed more conversational maintenance cues ("I see," "go on," etc.), and recalled more about their previous conversations with others.

While the above studies indicate that status and self–esteem may be critical factors affecting one's ability to decode and encode nonverbal cues, there are compelling reasons, according to LaFrance and

Henley (1994), *why* women are usually better at "performing" the nonverbal affective display of listening than men. They link this motivation to men's "greater social power relative to women in everyday social interactions" (p. 290). There is evidence suggesting that men *initially* are more attracted to high-expressive females than they are to low-expressive females (Sprecher, 1989), that in *dating* relationships males report greater satisfaction when their female partners self-disclose more than they themselves reveal (Millar and Millar, 1989), and, among *married* couples there is a positive correlation between the husbands' dissatisfaction with the relationship and the diminution of their wives' nonverbal expressiveness (Sabatelli et al, 1982).

To the extent that men are the arbiters of social power, women, it seems, are destined to be the arbiters of affective nonverbal display. LaFrance and Henley (1994) suggest that so long as power inequities persist, especially in the realm of social relations, it is unlikely that there will be significant changes in women's and men's nonverbal communication: "When power inequities are noted in interpreting research findings, socialization is often presented as the culprit that needs to be changed in order to bring about equality. But we, with others, see socialization as the means for perpetuating society's values, beliefs, behaviors, and power structures. Societal supports of inequality are what is basic and need to be changed. The phenomenon of gender will be more clearly understood in psychology only when power becomes a prominent item of the psychological agenda" (p. 308).

While the aforementioned studies indicate that decoding and encoding nonverbal cues may be simultaneously connected to power, status and self-esteem, *only* self-esteem has been directly linked to *listening*, and this factor, it seems, privileges neither males nor females.

The Verbal Content of Messages That Demonstrate Effective Listening

In 1961, Jack Gibb published an article on group communication processes in which he contended that communication is facilitated in *supportive* versus *defensive* communication climates. Fundamental to creating and maintaining a supportive communication climate is that communicators feel they have *equal* access to communication without being silenced or interrupted; that their expressed ideas, beliefs and concerns will be heard and valued in a *non-judgmental* and *non-evaluative* way.

Texts on diverse areas of communication, including those on listening, acknowledge Gibb's contribution to the communication process. The use of appropriate turn-taking, questions, and non-judgmental comments, for example, are ways to share ideas and feelings as well as to provide feedback to the speaker. These strategies often signal interest, empathy, and understanding.

As with their review of nonverbal communication and listening, the listening texts do not delineate the verbal components of effective listening along gender lines. However, a legacy of literature on gender and communication suggests that the socialization of women and men, stemming largely from cultural power differences, have contributed to women's greater proficiency in displaying the types of verbal expression (for example, the use of qualifiers, tag questions, hedges, etc.) reflective of the effective listener (Aries, 1987; Arliss, 1991; Belenky et al, 1986; Bem, 1993; Borisoff and Merrill, 1991; 1992; Haste, 1994; Jamieson, 1995; Kramarae, 1981; Lakoff, 1975; Maltz and Borker, 1982; Wood, 1994; Wood and Inman, 1993, etc.). We would caution, however, that the verbal *expression* of certain markers indicative of listening are not the sole indicators of listening. We would further suggest that effective listening, while perhaps in part a reflection of distinct gender socialization, may be demonstrated in multiple ways.

More than forty years ago, Theodore Reik (1954) observed that while men and women may assign the same *literal* meanings to words and expressions (as members of the same linguistic community), as members of distinct speech communities they hold divergent *interpretations* of these same words and expressions. Reik concludes, therefore, that misunderstandings between women and men may be "less a result of linguistic and semantic differences, but of emotional divergences when the two sexes use identical expressions" (p. 15). It is important to bring these differences to consciousness. While women and men may *hear* the same *message*, they may listen to the message differently. Two brief examples—the use of interruptions and providing feedback—may illustrate this difference.

We mentioned earlier that individuals feel they are being listened to when they have equal access to a communication exchange. Interrupting another has long been regarded as an indication of unequal access to such an exchange. Interestingly, however, how women and men *employ* interruptions when communicating with others has been linked to different motives. Interrupting another has been regarded as an indication of conversational maintenance when employed by women, and as a form of conversational control when employed by men (Aries, 1987; Mulac et al, 1988; Stewart et al, 1990). While the intentions of women's use of interruptions have not been challenged, the reasons why men interrupt have been disputed. Kathryn Dindia (1987), for example, suggests that opposite-sex conversations may be more awkward than same-sex interaction. Interruptions occurring in opposite-sex conversations, she concludes, may therefore be more a reflection of conversational overlaps than of direct attempts at dominance. Another explanation, recently posited by Deborah Tannen

(1990; 1994), suggests that men interrupt others and take up more speaking time because they are more uncomfortable with silence than women. We would suggest that much could be learned about interrupting patterns if, as was suggested regarding how nonverbal sensitivity is examined, perceived status, power, self–esteem, and the tone of the interruption are introduced as factors.

How gender differences in communication style may influence the *interpretation*, if not the actual intention of providing feedback in the listening process, is the second example. Women, as Gilligan (1982) and others have shown, attempt to reinforce connections and establish rapport through their communication with others (see also Belenky et al, 1986; Hall, 1984; Henley, 1977; Kramarae, 1981; Lakoff, 1975; Maltz and Borker, 1982; Rubin, 1983). They have been socialized to listen for feelings. Consequently, when women discuss problems and share experiences, the *process* of the discussion conveys empathic communication. Thus questions, for example, like the paralinguistic cues mentioned earlier, are often employed by women as a form of conversational maintenance.

Research suggests that men may convey empathy differently than women. In contrast to using questions as a form of conversational maintenance, men often employ questions to seek information, that is, to gather facts. In lieu of engaging in the *process* of communication as a means of showing empathy, men may offer solutions to show they are listening empathically.

The problem for many women and men when discussing personal concerns or problems, therefore, is that while women may offer what Tannen calls "the gift of understanding," and men call "the gift of advice" (1990, p. 50), the opposite–sex partner in the relationship may not regard "understanding" or "advice" as a "gift."

Psychiatrist Aaron Beck (1988, p. 75) suggests that, due to women's and men's differing listening styles, while one partner may intend respect and affection, the other partner may *interpret* the message as a sign of not caring, disrespect, or even as hostility. Borisoff and Hahn (1992) indicate that the lens of gender may erect a formidable barrier when women and men presumably are listening to one another. "Women often *accuse* their partner of not listening when they say: 'You're not listening!' Men often accuse their partner of not listening when they say: 'You're not focusing on the problem!' More than likely what both partners mean when they articulate these words is: 'I'm not getting the response I wanted!' Being listened to essentially becomes a metaphor for being accepted, valued, and understood" (p. 34).

Being accepted and valued are important components of listening. While acceptance and valuation are not explicitly included in the definitions for listening, they are undoubtedly implied. We suspect that when women, especially, claim that they are not being listened to, they are really alluding to these two implied components of listening. We suspect, moreover, that many women are justified in feeling this way. In the final section, we examine several conflicts submitted by our students that reflect that being listened *to* is experienced differently by women and by men.

Acceptance and Valuation as Reflections of Sex-Role and Sex-Trait Expectations

> I have noticed that in my dealings with all of my female friends, there is an open and carefree environment where I readily share my confidences, while with some of my male friends, there is always the need to prove myself. For example, if I talk about sports with my male friends, they'll quiz me about what I've read. *Though this is by all means a rather minor incident,* which hardly seems like a conflict, I believe that there is one because. . . . I have come to the conclusion that my male friends do not talk to me, but at me. (Mike, pre-law undergraduate student; Emphasis added)

Though Mike identifies his own insight as "a rather minor incident," he actually has hit upon a significant point, a distinction between women's and men's communication styles that often is noticed by women, rarely by men: the feeling of being talked at rather than with; the feeling of engaging in a verbal competition rather than a dialogue.

This observation, moreover, laces students' conflicts. One of the authors teaches a course on conflict management, where students are asked to present sample conflicts they experience. While initially in the course both the male and female students indicate that gender no longer is an area of concern, and that children today are being raised gender neutral (including their own experiences), Mike's observation was persistently, and often poignantly, reinforced in the sample conflicts presented by women. These cases indicate that when women complain about not being listened to, they are equating listening with being accepted and valued. The cases reflect the power of early childhood experiences in shaping the listening communities of women and men.

Overwhelmingly, in the cases presented, female students lament the fact that not only as children, but as adults, they are not listened to. They are getting a very clear message from their parents that not only are they different from their brothers, but as women (not as humans), they are less valued. For many of our female students, these discrepancies are troublesome, spanning age, geographic and ethnic background. Their concerns about their duties and privileges at home, as well as their career prospects, recur in their accounts. Consider these excerpts: "I think of my brothers as superior always," observes one senior from the Midwest. "My brother got more privileges. He had more independence and freedom," notes a 25-year-old

Mexican-American graduate student. And a 20-year-old African American from the Northeast expresses the perceived inequality of growing up female: "My brothers were allowed to pursue life with a zest that we were not allowed to possess. As a result, my brothers are spoiled. They feel that it is the woman's duty to care for the home and men shouldn't. As a result, they tend to look down on women and not listen to them."

These complaints were typical among women's voices, yet they are more than personal laments. These conflicts reveal a devaluation of the housewife role while simultaneously implying that that is the proper role of a woman. Clearly, the notion that men's lives and activities are more important is perpetuated, making highly problematic the ability of the female students to define themselves satisfactorily for both themselves and their parents. Karen, a 1-9-year-old psychology major, put it this way: "My mom feels that women should get the best education possible and work to establish themselves but that eventually the woman has to get married and give all this up to be a wife and a mother. I wish my parents would be more open-minded and not put limitations on what women can and can not do. I wish they would listen to *me*, and not to what society tells them is appropriate!" Typically, then, despite the assurance of the students that contemporary parents raise children in gender-neutral ways, the submitted cases suggest that many parents expect their daughters to work only until marriage, and that they then will make family their first priority; career and family are still seen as mutually exclusive.

We should hasten to point out that such thinking is not the exclusive province of mothers; fathers, too, are blamed for harboring the kinds of traditional values that create pressure to conform. Ann, a Michigan 22-year-old, recounts: "My dad wants me to focus my efforts after graduation on getting married and starting a family. Yet my brother went to work and then to law school and my father supported him. I wish there could be a simple way to persuade my father to alter his old ideas about what is proper for girls and what is designated for boys, but he refuses to listen. Another coed concluded, "I was beginning to see that no matter what, to my father I am just a little girl, and any suggestion I make at age 22 or 24 carries about the same weight as any suggestion I made at age 3."

The discrepant expectations parents instill in their children regarding appropriate gender behavior becomes incorporated into their value systems. The young women receive a very clear message: being *a mother* and taking care of the *home* are not regarded highly in a monetarily fueled economy, but that is the *proper* role of women. Such valuations can not help but affect the valuations the female students come to have of themselves, as a 21-year-old student from Chicago observed:

My mother would ask me to help with errands and ask my brother for assistance with repairs. Even though I was perfectly capable of setting up my own computer, for example, she suggested I call my brother for help. I'm supposed to listen to him solely because he's a man. *I am fully aware that this example is insignificant* . . . a mind set I have encountered since childhood. . . . The result it has on me is that I feel like she invalidates all of my endeavors. (Emphasis added)

Two points need to be made here. First, it is amazing how many times the students characterize their conflicts, or some element thereof, as "insignificant" or "inconsequential." Yet they clearly were of sufficient significance and consequence to be mentioned, and often to have been remembered for years. Second, we note that "invalidation" is a strong sub-text in many of the student reports, and almost always refers to ways in which women are devalued. Further, the two are mutually reinforcing, "if I am of little value then any complaint I have must be insignificant." Alternatively, "if I am bothered by these inconsequential matters I must be of little value."

The motivation for what Rubin (1983) calls "learned helplessness" does not stop in the home. If women and men continue to regard women's roles primarily as homemaker and caretaker, then, as another student indicates, "they will find it hard to picture women in any other role. They will find it hard to listen to women's voices."

The men who expressed family problems related to role expectations were relatively few in number. This is unsurprising —few men seek to deviate from the traditional role of provider The few who did were indeed sanctioned, as when Aaron, a 20-year-old communications major, recalls his father's response when Aaron told him he did not want to follow his father's footsteps and go into business: "He simply said that I would probably end up being just a housewife. To this day that comment still infuriates me, and makes me feel so inadequate. After that, I never felt he paid attention to me as seriously as he did to my brother." Again, note how a parent made a child feel inadequate, and that the denigrating role identified was "housewife."

From the sample conflicts presented by students, it is apparent that problems related to gender in our society have not been resolved. Their voices confirm that gender-based problems are more pervasive than they had initially thought. However, several tentative issues did emerge which may stimulate further research.

Progress or Status Quo?

We do not know how far we have come. Our sample conflicts are contemporary. Whether the situations facing these students are better or worse than those faced in the past we have no way of knowing. All we know, for sure is that the situation still is bad, although the fact that many of the issues were raised by male students is a hopeful sign. Additionally, since we asked for conflicts we did not gather any available evidence on positive gender interactions.

This We Believe; Voices of the Home

Relationship styles established early on have a powerful influence on the lives of young people, following them from childhood into adulthood. Perhaps most revealing are the students' analyses of the effects the conflicts have had on them. Especially compelling are the examples where the young men and women report feeling devalued. In the majority of examples this occurred when they believed that their parents would or could not fully listen to them.

We are not sure of what to make of the phenomenon of so many of our respondents downplaying their feelings, saying that the event being reported was "insignificant," or that they are probably making "too big a deal" of it. Perhaps they are feeling guilty about harboring grudges, about having *any* negative feelings, about not having solved the conflict. Or maybe they have accepted so thoroughly a negative valuation of "conflict" that they are incapable of facing painful ones without downplaying them. Perhaps there are other possibilities. At any rate, the language utilized is telling us *something*; we should attempt to discern what that something is.

We need some good solid research on the extent to which women and men repeat in their relationships with significant others the communication patterns they developed in their original families. Equally significant would be studies of those who have successfully shorn themselves of these original attitudes, especially if we could "get at" how those changes were effected.

Mathew McKay has argued that listening is both a commitment and a compliment:

> It is a commitment to understanding how other people feel, how they see their world. It means putting aside your own prejudices and beliefs, your anxieties and self-interest, so that you can step behind the other person's eyes. You try to look at things from his or her perspective. Listening is a compliment because it says to the other person: "I care about what is happening to you, your life and your experience are important." (1983, p. 14)

For the young women and men who strive to alter other's expectations of them, who try to carve out a new niche for themselves, it appears they risk losing both the commitment of understanding and the compliment of care from those they love.

Summary

The first three sections of this chapter examined the potential for establishing "listening communities." There are several barriers to such an establishment that are rooted in how sex roles and gendered behavior have developed and been valued. Our societal heritage has divided behavior along gender lines: men were relegated to the public domain as speakers; women were assigned to the private domain as listeners. This division resulted in both sexes being the presumed arbiters of these two skills. We explored how listening for feelings, self-disclosure, nonverbal and verbal communication may contribute to effective listening and suggested that what we call effective listening depends largely on the affective display of behavior—that is, effective listening relies on conveying to the speaker that he/she is being attended to, understood, and responded to. The literature indicates that women and men may convey this support differently. This difference, we acknowledged, is partly due to socialization; however, studies indicate that perceived power, status, and self-concept strongly influence listening behavior. These factors, we therefore contended, ought be considered when assessing men's and women's listening skills. In the final section, we presented student cases. We found that when individuals indicate they are not listened to, this is really a metaphor for not being accepted and valued. The female students' voices strongly reflected this concern. "Listening communities," we concluded, cannot be achieved until all individuals receive the commitment of being understood, accepted, and valued.

Exercises

1. This exercise considers perceptions of effective and ineffective listening, including such factors as context, gender, and status. The group is instructed to maintain a listening journal for minimally one week. In this journal they are asked to record instances when they feel they are being listened to as well as instances when they feel they are not being listened to. When describing each of these interactions, they should note the following: with whom they were communicating; the topic being discussed; the context in which the interaction occurred (at home, at work, in a restaurant, etc.); and, what specific behaviors (words used, nonverbal expressions, etc.) indicated that they were either being listened to or not. Following the assignment, the class may be divided into groups with each group asked to devise a summary sheet of markers for effective listening. Discussion would address whether or not group members found that gender differences in listening behavior and/or if other factors (such as role, power, context, etc.) influenced how they were listened to.

2. This exercise focuses on crosscultural listening. Group members are asked to interview members from another culture regarding what listening means to them: how they demonstrate listening; what kinds of behaviors (verbal and nonverbal) indicate that they

are being listened to. Individual and/or panel presentations would compare cultural differences and/or similarities. Such presentations might include whether or not there are gender differences in the expectations for listening behavior crossculturally.

3. This exercise addresses listening behavior at different stages of relationships. The group would be divided so that several individuals would interview dating couples, several would interview couples who are married for less than five years, and several would interview couples who have been married for more than ten years. All groups would develop and use the same questions that would address: how each partner in the relationship perceives his/her partner as a listener; what qualities influence this perception; whether or not the partner perceives that his/her partner's listening behavior has changed over time and what specific changes (if any) have occurred. Each group would present their findings. Discussion would address the extent to which relationship stages influence perceptions of listening.

4. This exercise considers enhancing listening behavior in specific relationships. Each group member is asked to think of one individual in their personal lives and one individual in their professional relationships who they feel does not fully listen to him/her. The assignment would be to write a statement indicating why they feel these individuals do not listen to them and what specific changes they feel these individuals could make in their behavior that could enhance their listening. Discussion would focus on the extent to which men or women were targeted and the types of strategies suggested (specifically, whether or not these strategies conform to the feminine stereotype for listening behavior).

References

Aries, E. (1987). Gender and communication. In P. Shaver and C. Hendrick, Eds. *Sex and Gender*. Newbury Park, CA: Sage, 149–176.

Arliss, L.(1991). *Gender Communication*. Englewood Cliffs, NJ: Prentice-Hall.

Barnlund, D. (1989). *Communicating with the Japanese*. Belmont, CA: Wadsworth Press.

Beck, A.T. (1988). *Love is Never Enough*. NY: Harper & Row.

Belenky, M.F., Clinchy, B.M., Goldberger, N.R., and Tarule, J.M. *Women's Ways of Knowing: The Development of Self, Voice, and Mind*. NY: Basic Books.

Bem, S.L. (1993). *The Lenses of Gender: Transforming the Debate on Sexual Inequality*. New Haven, CT: Yale University Press.

Birdwhistell, R. (1970). *Kinesics and Context*. Philadelphia, PA: University of Pennsylvania Press.
Borisoff, D. and Hahn, D.F.(Fall 1995). From research to pedagogy: Teaching gender and communication. *Communication Quarterly*, vol. 43, no. 2: 381-393.
Borisoff, D. and Hahn, D.F. (Fall 1992). Interrelationships between gender listening in intimate relationships. *Journal of the International Listening Association*, 6: 23-41.
Borisoff, D. and Merrill, L. (1992). *The Power to Communicate: Gender Differences as Barriers*. Second Edition. Prospect Heights, IL: Waveland Press.
Borisoff, D. and Merrill, L. (1991). Gender issues and listening. In Borisoff and Purdy, Eds. *Listening in Everyday Life: A Personal and Professional Approach*. Lanham, MD: University Press of America, 59-85.
Borisoff, D. and Victor, D. (1989). *Conflict Management: A Communication Skills Approach*. Englewood Cliffs, NJ: Prentice-Hall.
Brownell, J.(1986). *Building Active Listening Skills*. Englewood Cliffs, NJ: Prentice-Hall.
Cixous, H. (1976/1985). 'Le sexe où la tête?' , *Les cahiers du GRIF*, 13, Oct . 1976, p. 7. D.C. Stanton, Trans. 'Language and revolution: The Franco-American disconnection, In H. Eisenstein and A. Jardine, Eds. *The Future of Difference*. New Brunswick, NJ: Rutgers University Press, 1985, 73-87.
Daly, J. (Feb. 1990). Competent conversation. Paper delivered to the Iowa Ideas Forum, University of Iowa. Cited in S. Duck, 1991, *Understanding Relationships*, NY: Guilford Press, p. 43.
Derlega, V.J. and Chaikin, A.L. (1976). Norms affecting self-disclosure in men and women. *Journal of Consulting and Clinical Psychology*, 44: 376-80.
Dindia, K. (Spring 1987). The effects of sex of subject and sex of partner on interruptions. *Human Communication Research*, 13, 3: 345-71.
Duck, S. (1991). *Understanding Relationships*. NY: Guilford Press.
Elshtain, J.B. (1982). Feminist discourse and its discontents: Language, power, and meaning. In N.O. Keohane, M.Z. Rosaldo, and B.C. Gelpi, Eds. *Feminist Theory: A Critique of Ideology*. Chicago, IL: University of Chicago Press, 127-45.
Fitzpatrick, M. (1988). *Between Husbands and Wives: Communication in Marriage*. Newbury Park, California: Sage Publications.
Gibb, J.(1961). Defensive communication. *Journal of Communication*, 11: 141-48.
Gilligan, C. (1982). *In a Different Voice: Psychological Theory and Women's Development*. Cambridge, MA: Harvard University Press.

Gilman, C.P. (1911/1971). The *Man-Made World or our Androcentric Culture*. NY: Johnson Reprint.

Glenn, E.C. (1989) .A content analysis of fifty definitions of listening. *Journal of the International Listening Association*, 3: 21–31.

Gumperz, J.(1962). Types of linguistic communities. *Anthropological Linguistics*, 4, 1: 28–40.

Hall, E.T. (1966). *The Hidden Dimension*. NY: Anchor/Doubleday.

Hall, E.T. (1959). *The Silent Language*. Greenwich, CT: Fawcett Publications.

Hall, J. (1987). On explaining gender differences: The case of nonverbal Communication. In P. Shaver and C. Hendrick, Eds. *Sex and Gender*. Newbury Park, CA: Sage Publications, 177–200.

Hall, J. (1984). *Nonverbal Sex Differences: Communication Accuracy and Expressive Style*. Baltimore, MD: The Johns Hopkins University Press.

Haste, H. (1994). *The Sexual Metaphor: Men, Women and Thinking that Makes the Difference*. Cambridge, MA :Harvard University Press.

Henley, N.M (1977). *Body Politics*. Englewood Cliffs, NJ: Prentice-Hall.

Hite, S. (1987). *Women and Love*. NY: Alfred Knopf.

Jamieson, K.H. (1995). *Beyond the Double Bind: Women and Leadership*. NY: Oxford University Press.

Johnson, F.L. (1989). Women's culture and communication: An analytical perspective. In C.M. Lont and S.A. Friedley, *Beyond Boundaries: Sex and Gender Diversity in Communication*. Fairfax, VA: George Mason University Press, 301–16.

Johnson, F.L. (1983). Political and pedagogical implications of attitudes toward women's language. *Communication Quarterly*, 31: 133–38.

Keen, S. (1991). *Fire in the Belly: On Being a Man*. NY: Bantam Books.

Kramarae, C. (1981). *Women and Men Speaking*. Rowley, MA: Newbury House.

Labov, W. (1972). *Sociolinguistic Patterns*. Philadelphia, PA: University of Pennsylvania Press.

LaFrance, M. and Henley, N.M. (1994). On oppressing hypotheses: Or differences in nonverbal sensitivity revisited. In H. Lorraine Radke and H.J. Stam, Eds. *Power/Gender: Social Relations in Theory and Practice*. Thousand Oaks, CA: Sage Publications, 287–311.

Lakoff, R.T. (1975). *Language and Woman's Place*. NY: Harper & Row.

Langer, S.K. (1979). *Philosophy in a New Key: A Story of the Symbolism of Reason, Rite, and Art*. Third Edition. Cambridge, MA: Harvard University Press.

Langer, S.K. (1953). *Feeling and Form: A Theory of Art*. NY: Scribner's.

Lerner, H.G. (1989). *The Dance of Intimacy*. NY: Harper & Row.

Maltz, D.N. and Borker, R.A. (1982). A cultural approach to male-female miscommunication. In J.J. Gumperz, Ed. *Language and Social Identity*. Cambridge: Cambridge University Press.

Markman, H. (June 15, 1992). He said, she said: Couples therapy is the flavor of the month. Cited in P. Hoban, *New York*, 31-36.

McKay, D4. (1983). *Messages: The Communication Skills Book*. Oakland, CA: New Harbinger Publications.

Millar, K.U. and Millar, M.G. (1988). Sex difference in perceived self- and other- disclosure: a case where inequity increases satisfaction. *Social Behavior and Personality*, 16: 59-64.

Mulac, A., Wiemann, J.M., Widenmann, S., and Gibson, T.W. (1988). Male/Female language differences and effects in same-sex dyads: The gender-linked language effect. *Communication Quarterly*, 55: 315-35.

Nichols, P.C. (1980). Women in their speech communities. In S. McConnell-Ginet et al, Eds. *Women and Language in Literature and Society*. NY: Praeger.

Nichols, R. (1948). Unpublished dissertation from the State University of Iowa. Cited in L. Steil, L.L. Barker and K. Watson, *Effective Listening: Key to Your Success*. Reading, MA: Addison-Wesley Publishing Co., 1983.

Noller, P.(1987). Nonverbal communication in marriage. In D. Perlman and S. Duck, Eds. *Intimate Relationships: Development, Dynamics, and Deterioration*. Beverly Hills, CA: Sage Publications, 149-75.

Purdy, M. (1991). What is listening? In D. Borisoff and M. Purdy, Eds, *Listening In Everyday Life: A Personal and Professional Approach*. Lanham, MD: University Press of America, 3-19.

Reik, T. (1954). Men and women speak different languages. *Psychoanalysis*, 2: 3-15.

Rubin, L. B. (1983). *Intimate Strangers: Men and Women Together*. NY: Harper & Row.

Sabatelli, R., Buck, R., and Dreyer, A. (1992). Nonverbal communication accuracy in married couples: Relationship with marital complaints. *Journal of Personality and Social Psychology*, 43: 1088-97.

Snodgrass, S. E. (1992). Further effects of role versus gender on interpersonal sensitivity. *Journal of Personality and Social Psychology*, 62: 154-58.

Snodgrass, S. E. (1985).Women's intuition: The effect of subordinate role on interpersonal sensitivity. *Journal of Personality and Social Psychology*, 49: 146-55.

Sprecher, S. (1989). The importance to males and females of physical attractiveness, earning potential and expressiveness. *Sex Roles*, 21: 591-607.

Steil, L., Barker, L.L., and Watson, K. (1983). *Effective Listening: Key to Your Success*. Reading, MA: Addison-Wesley Publishing Co.

Stewart, L.P., Stewart, A.D., Friedley, S.A. and Cooper, P.J. (1990). *Communication Between the Sexes: Sex Differences and Sex-Role Stereotypes*. Second Edition. Scottsdale, AZ: Gorsuch Scarisbrick.

Tannen, D. (1994). *Gender and Discourse*. NY: Oxford University Press.

Tannen, D. (1990). *You Just Don't Understand: Women and Men in Communication*. NY: William Morrow & Co.

Ueland, B. (Nov.–Dec. 1992). Tell me more: On the true art of listening. *Utne Reader*, 104–09.

Williams, J.E. and Best, D.L. (1982). *Measuring Sex Stereotypes: A Thirty Nation Study*. Beverly Hills CA: Sage Publications.

Winokur, S. (June 1991). What happy couples do right. *Redbook*, 65–69.

Wolvin, A. and Coakley, C.G. (1988). *Listening*. Third Edition. Dubuque, IA: William C. Brown.

Wood, J.T. (1994). *Gendered Lives: Communication, Gender and Culture*. Belmont, CA: Wadsworth Publishing Co.

Wood, J.T. and Inman, C.C. (Aug. 1993). In a different mode: Masculine styles of communicating closeness. *Journal of Applied Communication Research*, 21, 3: 279–95.

CHAPTER 4

INTERCULTURAL LISTENING

T. Dean Thomlison

Points to be Addressed:

- The meaning of intercultural listening.

- Components of intercultural communication

- Crosscultural values and beliefs: how they influence crosscultural listening.

- Language as a factor in listening crossculturally.

- Nonverbal communication in the intercultural listening process.

- Cognitive processing: how thought patterns, high and low context, ethnicity, and stereotyping affect listening in intercultural contexts.

- Applications of effective intercultural listening.

Revolutions always begin in the mind. The way to save civilization and life itself does not lie in thinking up new technologies for ever more accurate and lethal weapon systems, but rather in liberating the mind from prejudices—political and social, national and racial—from arrogance, self-conceit and the cult of force and violence . . . our era is marked by sharp changes. So many events and transformations are taking place within a very short period of time in our country, in your country and in the world as a whole. We must make haste to remove the fears and threats looming over us, our children, and our descendants. Mikhail S. Gorbachev

We can hail the Russian people for their many achievements—in science and space, in economic and industrial growth, in culture and in acts of courage. Among the many traits the peoples of our two countries have in common, none is stronger than our mutual abhorrence of war. So let us not be blind to our differences—but let us also direct attention to our common interests and the means by which those differences can be resolved. And if we cannot end our differences, at least we can help make the world safe for diversity. For, in the final analysis, our most basic link is that we all inhabit this small planet. We all breathe the same air. We all cherish our children's future. We are all mortal. John F. Kennedy

We live in an era of human history that watched many ideological, political and physical barriers come tumbling down—from the Berlin wall that symbolized the forced division of a city, a country, and a people, to the cries for self-governance echoing around the world. Technology and transportation link the far corners of the earth thus greatly increasing exchange of information and ideas while diminishing the physical barriers of distance and time. The business world has literally become just that—now services and products are transferred between countries and continents in record numbers. Multinational businesses and organizations now send personnel in ever increasing numbers into a multitude of intercultural contexts.

Communication technology has progressed to the point we can now converse with people from other countries not only by telephone but also through teleconferencing. Mass communication advances have even provided us with the capacity to watch events unfolding anywhere in the world whether it be a revolution or an artistic presentation in a distant country. There is every indication the intercultural context for communication will continue to grow at an extraordinary rate.

As a result of these changes in political, transportation, technology, mass communication and organizational systems, we are in more contact with individuals from other subcultures, cultures and countries than at any time in human existence. In this sense, our planet is shrinking and intercultural contact is increasing proportionally.

This chapter explores major factors which influence listening when the participants are from two different cultures or subcultures. A better understanding of and sensitivity toward these elements of culture will enhance overall intercultural communication and listening effectiveness. Throughout the chapter, suggestions are provided for improving intercultural listening skills and for implementing both personal and professional applications.

It was suggested in Chapter 2 that you establish your own personal goals as you read each chapter. For this section you may want to begin with the general objective of increasing your overall listening awareness by learning more about cultural elements active in the intercultural communication process. You can add more specific goals as you proceed through the chapter.

Remember that to some degree all interaction with others involves crosscultural communication so the potential applications of intercultural listening skills are virtually unlimited. As Chapter 3 on listening and gender illustrated, even a person of the opposite sex who speaks the same language with the same regional accent and grew up in the same part of the country as you, is from a different culture in some sense. Keep in mind the many possible applications of intercultural listening as you read on.

Defining Intercultural Listening

Intercultural or crosscultural communication is described by Dodd (1987, p. 6) as a communication process in which the outcomes are influenced by cultural differences. Listening is defined in Chapter 1 as including the processes of receiving, attending, and assigning meaning. Thus, for purposes of our discussion, we will use the following definition:

Intercultural listening is communication in which the processes of receiving, attending, and assigning meaning are influenced by cultural differences.

A quick glance at these cognitive activities reminds us of the complexity of the listening process. This complexity and the barriers to effective listening are magnified when cultural differences are added.

Components of Intercultural Encounters

Whenever individuals engage in crosscultural contact there are several basic communication components usually present:

- Two different cultures, subcultures, and/or countries are represented.

- Two different sets of values and beliefs based on cultural heritage are operating.

- Two different primary language systems usually are represented by the participants resulting in one person having to operate in a secondary language or use a translator.

- Two different nonverbal systems are functioning in which the same behaviors may or may not be assigned the same meaning by the communicators.

- Two different sets of behavioral norms are operating at conscious and unconscious levels during the interaction.

- Two different world views are selectively screening information.

- Two different methods of thinking or cognitive processing may be in use by the participants.

An understanding of these intercultural communication components is essential to crosscultural communicators who want to
maximize their listening skills. *The primary goal of the effective intercultural listener is to reduce the level of uncertainty in the
communication process.*

CULTURE: THE FOUNDATION
OF ALL COMMUNICATION

The most significant influence on our communication is culture.
It is the foundation for all human interaction because we screen every
incoming message through the perceptual filter of our culture. There
is an inseparable link between communication and culture since according to Smith (1966), one cannot exist without the other. Wolvin
and Coakley contend that scholars in communication now recognize
that:

> culture is a primary determinant of all communication behavior
> (including listening) because an individual's culture essentially serves
> to define who he or she is and how he or she will communicate
> through his or her perceptual filter. . . The influence of culture is es-
> pecially prominent when one attempts to communicate across
> cultures (1988, 121).

As Chapter 1 points out, Western cultures as a whole place much
greater emphasis on speaking than on listening. Speaking is perceived
as the avenue to success. This tradition assumes listening comes naturally with no special effort. Even with the recent trend toward
predeparture courses for students who plan to study abroad and
crosscultural training for military, business and governmental personnel plus their families, the vast majority of these programs do not
focus directly on the listening component. Western cultures take listening for granted. Not surprisingly, there has been very little
intercultural listening research conducted.

In contrast, many non–Western cultures emphasize listening
rather than speaking. They give listening its rightful position in the
communication process—the center. Their traditions and cultural
heritage implicitly recognize that without the accurate receiving, attending to, and assigning of meaning, there can be no effective
communication. Furthermore, one's appreciation of life is significantly reduced without a keen listening awareness.

Several of these countries even have special ceremonies, rituals,
and art forms that incorporate the importance of the listening dimension while linking visual and auditory elements. The serenity of

walking through the beautiful public gardens of China and other Far Eastern countries can be a sensory experience not only from visual and olfactory perspective, but also from a listening perspective. These special environments were designed to encourage communion with nature and self.

Likewise, the Japanese tea ceremony, *cha no yu*, is a ritual which has been taught in minute detail since the Fifteenth Century. The ceremony is much more than boiling water, making tea and drinking it; rather, it is a highly symbolic, ritualized experience that encompasses all the senses. Even the simple act of pouring the tea has an aesthetic element to it as one listens to the gentle sounds of the hot liquid cascading into the cup. Learning to perform this ceremony correctly cannot be learned from reading books on the topic, of which there are many. Like Zen Buddhism, which influenced the development of this ritual, the tea ceremony can only be transmitted from a master to the disciple (Dalby et al., 1984, p. 93). This special teacher–student relationship also reveres listening and emphasizes its value in both the learning process and the tea ritual itself.

As Americans we are taught to be passive listeners rather than active ones. We have been conditioned to rely on the speaker of the message for motivation to listen. Our culture tells us to be *externally* motivated listeners. The most consistent and effective listening requires us to become *internally* motivated listeners—and this is especially true in the intercultural context.

We should keep in mind that intercultural listening is not to be used only when we talk with people from other countries. There are numerous subcultures in our own nation, our own state, and even our own hometown which require cultural awareness on the part of the listener. Our country is composed of a patchwork quilt of various unique ethnic, religious, socioeconomic, regional, and racial subcultures. They blend together when there are common goals and overlap when understanding is established. Accurate intercultural listening is one of the keys to mutual goal setting and increased crosscultural understanding.

Just as communication and culture are inseparable, so are listening and culture. In professional as well as personal intercultural interactions, there are several major elements of culture that listeners must understand if they wish to maximize their communication effectiveness. These include: (1) cultural values and beliefs, (2) language systems, (3) nonverbal systems, and (4) cognitive processing. (See Figure 1.)

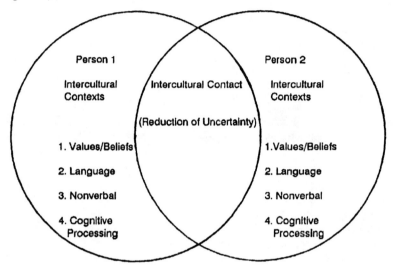

Figure 1. Elements of intercultural interaction

As we examine each of these elements of culture in the following sections, please keep in mind that they do not operate in isolation. They are an inter-connected web of finely tuned networks woven into a unique and highly complex system. All human communication is an ecological system in which there is an interdependence between all its elements. When a crosscultural context is added to the system, all the other components of the communication process are affected and must adapt accordingly.

We have a higher degree of predictability about those adaptations when both communicators basically share the same cultural background. This predictability is tremendously decreased when cultural variations are introduced to this complex system. However, these differences can also enrich our lives if we are open to new perspectives. An awareness of the following elements of cultural systems will increase our potential to move toward the goal of reducing uncertainty in our crosscultural listening.

Values and Beliefs

To be human is to have been enculturated. Basic values and beliefs about what is "right" and about how things "ought to be" done have constructed our cultural version of reality. They tell us what is "normal." As a result, these behaviors and ways of viewing objects, people, behaviors, and events feel "natural" to us. Values are the most subtle of our cultural patterns and yet the most influential for communication with someone from another culture. One way for us as intercultural listeners to develop more conscious awareness of values is to start by understanding and comparing our own values to those of other cultures. They are so subliminal that we often take them for granted. The ironic aspect of this subconscious indoctrination is that individuals from other cultures are quickly aware of many of the obvious indicators of our system of values and beliefs that we perceptually ignore.

Mark Twain once stated: "The only distinguishing characteristic of the American character I've been able to discover is a fondness for ice water "(Grove, 1984, p. 1). It is true that Americans are still notorious the world over for their preference for ice in their beverages whether it be water, beer, soda, or other libations. However, just as Twain noted that rumors of his own death were exaggerated, so was his claim that there is no unified set of general American values and beliefs. There are many excellent books describing American values that can be of aid to the intercultural listener in developing a greater awareness of their culture. For example, *Meet the USA* by Henry Steele Commanger and *Living in the USA* by Alison R. Lanier were both written for people visiting the United States from other countries. Most references to "American values" in such works allude to the generalized "mainstream" value orientations of a majority of its citizens. Of course, there will always be variations.

Robert Kohls has developed a helpful model contrasting American values with those of several other countries to illustrate how strongly divergent these perspectives can be (Kohls, 1984, p. 16). The following brief explanation of Kohls' thirteen categories provides an overview to facilitate intercultural self-awareness.

Kohl's Categories of US and Other Cultural Values

United States Values	Some Values in Other Countries
1. Personal Control Over Environment	Fate
2. Change	Tradition
3. Time and Its Control	Human Interaction

4. Equality/Egalitarianism	Hierarchy/Rank/Status
5. Individualism/Privacy	Group's Welfare
6. Self-Help	Birthright/Inheritance
7. Competition	Cooperation
8. Future Orientation	Past Orientation
9. Action/Work Orientation	"Being" Orientation
10. Informality	Formality
11. Directness/ Openness/Honesty	Indirectness/Ritual/"Face"
12. Practicality/Efficiency	Idealism/Theory
13. Materialism/Acquisitiveness	Spiritualism/Detachment

Personal Control Over the Environment

People living in the United States tend to believe that they can control nature. They eschew bad luck and view those who take a fatalistic approach to life as naive and lacking in personal initiative. It is not surprising, therefore, that Americans use an alarmingly high proportion of most of the world's natural resources! This same need to control affects our interpersonal communication styles. For example, Americans are often viewed by persons from other cultures as assertive, talkative and extroverted. Other cultures do not share the Americans' attitude toward control. In fact, the people of many other countries and even the first Americans (Native Americans) see many things as beyond human intervention. The destructive power of nature and the many diseases and blights that have historically touched these groups attest to the "fact" that some aspects of life are fated or in hands far stronger than those of human beings.

Father Halligan, a priest who directs The Center for Working Boys located in Quito, describes the fatalistic plight of many poor families in Ecuador:

> They are their own architects of misery. They have been led to believe that someone else, government, the church, will solve their problems. They don't realize the means are right at hand. . . . In this structure there are tools for change—food, education, people to trust. We try and teach them to take responsibility for themselves—they are not sick because God wants it, not a victim of circumstances. They are captain of their own life. We say "Don't look to what the Center will do for me, but what I can offer to the Center, to the movement of change" (Milton, 1987, p. 3).

Effective intercultural listeners know that such differences do not make these individuals lazy, naive, or lacking in personal drive.

To diminish misunderstandings between people from different cultures, it is important to acknowledge the differing belief and value systems that exist crossculturally. Individuals should refrain from stereotyping members of a particular culture because they hold beliefs, values, and attitudes that differ from their own. For successful intercultural communication to occur, we must listen for similarities and differences between cultures and avoid judging others based upon cultural variation. By being open to the ideas and views of others, we enrich ourselves.

Change

Americans see change as inevitable and positive. It is associated with development, progress, and growth. However, there are other cultures that can trace their heritage back thousands of years and that view change as disruptive, destructive, and evil. Because they value tradition so strongly, they regard change as potentially threatening.

As listeners we must keep in mind people can have different views of change from ours and still be informed and open to new ideas while cherishing their traditions. Sensitive listeners hear and respect these differences.

Time and Its Control

The average American values time. Interpersonal relations are often less important than getting "things" accomplished on time. We don't like to "waste" or "kill" time. American proverbs are full of references to the wise use of time, goal setting, and "spending" time today to enjoy results later. As we will see in a later section of this chapter, many other cultures are much less time-bound.

From a listening point of view it is important to be aware of the assumptions often made about those who do not follow our time perspective. Are they inconsiderate? Lazy? Uninterested? Unfriendly? Irresponsible?

Equality and Egalitarianism

Americans cherish equality and believe all human beings should have the same opportunities to succeed in life. In much of the remainder of the world status, class, rank, and authority are seen as facts of life which determine one's permanent place in society. Americans often display a lack of deference for societal position and rank, which members of other cultures may interpret as a lack of respect.

The effective intercultural communicator takes status differences into account in both listening and responding. Furthermore, the astute listener learns to decipher the spectrum of status levels through subtle cues and to show appropriate respect by not appearing to be overly familiar—especially to persons of higher status.

Individualism and Privacy

Since the Renaissance, the Western world has upheld individualism. Rugged individualism is especially coveted by Americans. Our "individual rights" and "personal freedoms" are protected by law. Each person is viewed as special and unique from all others. Although we join groups, each member is regarded individually. Many cultures believe that the individual is secondary to society and that the group, the family, the village, the tribe, the State, all come first. Thus, singling out an individual for recognition, for example, may appear to be an act of respect and graciousness to an American but it could prove embarrassing for many people from the Middle East, Asia, or Africa.

Individualism leads to the desire for and a belief in *privacy*. Kohls points out that many languages do not even have a word for this concept. While some cultures may regard privacy negatively—as separation from the group—for Americans it is a desirable state.

Intercultural listeners should keep these distinctions in mind and listen for information about family and social units. It is important to remember that introductory conversation about family and friends are just as important as any business or professional discussions that may follow, so do not treat them as "small talk" to be quickly dispensed with and forgotten. Also remember that part of this group orientation involves "saving face."

Self-Help

From the discussion of the last two values it becomes obvious that in the United States personal initiative is deeply admired. Americans revel in the stories of individuals who pulled themselves up from humble beginnings to succeed through their own efforts. Those born into wealth or power rather than "earning it" by personal accomplishment are not given the same admiration. However, much of the rest of the world operates on the opposite belief—you are born into a certain place in life rather than building your own status.

Thus, the intercultural listener must be aware that focusing on the *self* is particular to our culture. We have dozens of words beginning with the word "self" (i.e., self-reliant, self-interest, self-control, etc.). Kohls (p. 9) indicates that most other languages do not have equivalent words to the "self" words in English. Listeners should note the selflessness of their crosscultural partner and be sensitive to vocabulary usage. It is easy to see how this self-perspective could be easily misinterpreted as boastful, prideful, pompous, vain, or pretentious responses.

Competition

In the United States competition is encouraged in all walks of life—in the economy (free enterprise), the classroom ("Who knows the answer?"), business (which personnel were most productive), arts (who won the top award), medicine (which program has the latest technology), sports ("We're Number One"), and in a hundred other areas. Cooperation is an alternative in many other cultures—working *together* for the greater good of the cultural unit.

To be successful listeners in such contexts we must learn to listen to our self as we speak. This *intrapersonal listening* awareness will alert us to reduce responses which could appear antagonistic, combative, or overly aggressive. Furthermore, this competitive spirit can lead to one of the greatest barriers to effective listening—the tendency to use our listening time to develop counterarguments and refutations. In so doing we often miss key points or cues given by our partner. How can we "listen between the lines" if we are thinking about what we are going to say next to counter-attack? Instead, use thought time during listening to double check understanding and to concentrate on crossculturally appropriate responses that will reduce uncertainty.

Future Orientation

As we have already seen from earlier discussions of environmental control, individualism, and self-help, Americans are planners looking to the future. We are goal setters. A member of the Peace Corps teaching villagers about nutrition in the mountains of Guatemala recently wrote about a meeting with other volunteers:

> We discussed the reality of the frustration of not being able to see measurable results in our work. . . and while it helps to have discussed this phenomenon on an intellectual level so you can recognize and understand it, the reality of dealing with it can still be very difficult. Being good, goal-oriented Americans, many of us ask ourselves if this is the most productive use of our time (Benson, 1989, p. 2).

The intercultural listener will tend to process information based on the assumptions of his or her culture. If we assume moving toward a specified goal and accomplishing it is the highest priority then interpersonal sensitivity may be dulled. Realize that some traditional cultures, including much of the Moslem world, view future planning as a futile and potentially sinful act. While it is natural to regard and evaluate others from our own perspective, the sensitive crosscultural communicator will *actively listen* for differing conceptualizations of what is valued in order to make adaptations.

Action/Work Orientation

How can one accomplish all these future objectives? By taking action and by hard work, of course! This makes for an active lifestyle both personally and professionally. Our competitive values encourage us to "beat the competition" through hard work. Quiet introspection is not valued nearly as much as action. We like to "get down to work" and we often define ourselves in terms of our profession or "what we do for a living." This can create potential friction when, for example, a sales person from the United States discovers most of those on the client list are "on holiday." To many American business personnel Western Europe appears to be perpetually on vacation. "How can the Italians take those long lunch breaks and still run a business right?", they ask. "How do the French ever get anything accomplished when they are always on holiday?" "No wonder the British lost their empire!"

Pace is vitally important in all interpersonal communication but it takes on even greater significance in crosscultural situations. The goal-setting, action-oriented American who wants to "get down to business," "just get to the point," "stop beating around the bush," and "get to the bottom line" will be continually frustrated when communicating with persons of many, if not most, other cultures. As brash Americans our listening can be short-circuited by impatience when the person with whom we are communicating places equal value on deliberate, paced interaction and places more emphasis on the process than on the potential destination.

Instead of tuning out during what appears to be rather circuitous conversations, the aware intercultural communicator actively listens and participates in the transaction knowing that this process is as much a part of "business" as negotiating a price and agreeing on a contract. Effective intercultural listeners recognize that relationship is at least as important as content in ultimately reaching one's communication goals.

The Governor of Indiana, Robert D. Orr, became frustrated during a 1987 trade mission to the People's Republic of China after being given tours of many of China's sites. Orr called the tours "time-wasting" and declared at one point: "If I wanted to visit libraries, temples, churches, and museums and go shopping I could do that on a Sunday when the people here don't want to have meetings." He was quoted in newspaper accounts as having said: "I decided in that situation I was fed up and it was time to lay it on the line. I simply decided it was time to put my foot down and take the risk of stepping on some toes" (Clark, 1987). This demonstrates both the action-oriented American value system in operation as well as intercultural insensitivity. Ironically, Governor Orr was appointed Ambassador of Singapore, another Asian country, by President Bush in 1989!

Informality

In contrast to most other cultures, Americans are extremely informal and casual in their communication. Pomp and circumstance is not generally appealing to us. A supervisor will often encourage a subordinate to use the supervisor's first name. Teachers and professors tend to use first names with their students. Health care professionals and business people often do likewise with their patients and clients. Newly introduced people usually will resort to first names within a few minutes of conversation. Casual conversation and greetings are the rule rather than the exception even in business and professional settings. American dress also reflects this informality.

This informality could be interpreted by those from other cultures as inappropriate at the very least and at worst as a blatant display of disrespect. Intercultural listeners must pay special attention to the way introductory greetings are made to them so they can respond appropriately. Greeting rituals are very complex in some cultures so it is prudent to learn some culture-specific information beforehand.

For example, the business greeting for the Japanese consists of bowing, exchanging business cards, followed by a review of names and their pronunciation. The Japanese counterpart will usually emphasize how to pronounce their family name since they expect to be addressed formally. If a time comes in the relationship when first names are appropriate this will probably be explicitly discussed. A simple guideline is to maintain formality until and unless information to be more informal is received. This can be especially confusing in the case of the Japanese since they often extend their business from the office to the local night spots. To avoid offending others, it is important to listen to cues from the host rather than from the setting.

Directness, Openness and Honesty

Many societies conceive of indirect, subtle, and ritualistic methods of presenting unpleasant information as the most appropriate and humane approach to communication. Whether it be negative performance evaluations or "bad news" about something else, the majority of Americans utilize and prefer a direct approach. Furthermore, according to Kohls (p. 14) intermediaries are generally not appreciated by Americans. From the American perspective such indirectness only results in confusion and a loss of that valuable commodity that is so cherished—time. However, this frank openness may result in the loss of face for someone from another culture if we are not sensitive communicators and listeners.

Listening to these subtle hints and signals may result in turning a problem or impasse into a successful outcome. Intercultural training and business literature is filled with examples of personnel pushing for an affirmative response and finally politely receiving one, only to arrive home to the news that the "yes" has been rescinded equally politely. For example, one writer was told that her writing could not be used in a Chinese publication because it was so superior to the other articles that they would pale in comparison with her skillful use of words! In the long run much will be saved in time, money, "face" and/or results if we listen between the words.

Practicality and Efficiency

Americans value being rational, practical, and efficient. This is especially true in decision making. Rationality usually wins out over emotionality and subjectivity. We are more likely to ask "What will it cost?" or "How much will it take?" than to inquire "Is it aesthetically pleasing?" or "What does this say philosophically?" Of course, this pragmatic approach has led to Americans making more inventions than any other country in history. It also has led to more emphasis upon "practical" fields of study such as economics, business, management, and medicine rather than on fine arts, philosophy, or anthropology.

This "bottom line" approach can be used to plan and accomplish many physical goals but in some intercultural situations we learn more by listening than by switching into our rational problem-solving mode. The accurate assigning of meaning takes concentration and awareness.

Materialism/Acquisitiveness

There are many hard-working people in the world who will never accumulate one hundredth of the "things" Americans amass and call "necessities." A visit to any Third World country will make this abundantly clear. Americans see acquisitions as rewards for their labor and personal initiative. Social unrest has resulted from the disparity between the "haves" and "have nots" within the United States. The subculture of the poor and the homeless magnify the trend toward object accumulation. Problems with overflowing landfills for our garbage and calls for recycling highlight the fact that the United States is a throw-away society—we buy, use, and discard more material items than any other country in the history of the planet. A quick look around the room in which you are reading this book will reveal the extent of this value in your life.

In some Middle Eastern countries the value of spiritualism and friendship is so strong that just saying you like a piece of jewelry or a garment worn by another will immediately result in that object being offered to you as a gift. Many cultures view material things as the antithesis of spirituality and harmony, while others place special value on goods and wealth. For example, the cattle herdsmen of East

Africa revere their animals because of the wealth and status they provide (Dodd, p. 103).

Effective intercultural communicators listen carefully for cues to what members of other cultures value and adapt their behavior accordingly. Relationships will usually be much more important than any material factors during intercultural communication.

The thirteen values categories summarized above illustrate cultural diversity. Confucius astutely observed that "By nature men are nearly alike; by practice they get to be wide apart" (Seelye, 1985, p. 29). Although this was said five-hundred years before the birth of Christ, it is just as true today. We each have the same basic needs, yet we go about meeting those needs in very different ways. Seelye states: "An Eskimo might convey love and thoughtfulness to an elderly person by helping his friends and relatives hang him when he wishes to die; an American might manifest the same sentiment by attempting to prolong the life of an incurably sick elder in constant pain from cancer" (pp. 28-29). It is the way we go about meeting our needs which confuse and alienate individuals from each other.

Listening for our partner's basic needs can aid us in improving our crosscultural communication and transcending the divergent values that determine how we meet those needs. Cultural self-awareness is an essential tool in increasing our intercultural listening and overcoming the barrier of our own cultural bias.

While values, beliefs, and attitudes can separate cultures and be a source of misunderstanding, other elements of culture can be equally potent sources of miscommunication. The next section addresses language as a cultural dimension.

Language

I've decided that perhaps what I miss most about being outside the States is not hot showers or good steaks, but communication. Not only the means of communication (telephones, newspapers, reliable mail service) but the joy of interpersonal communication made "easy" by virtue of common language and culture. Many intercultural listening difficulties, obviously, are related to the process of trying to operate in a new language. In the beginning everything sounds like gibberish. It takes time and hard work to not only learn the sounds and how they combine to create meaning but then to be able to distinguish them in speech, recognize them, and remember what they mean. Attending conferences or agency meetings can be physically and mentally tiring because of the effort required to listen in another language; even social situations can be wearisome.

The point of all this is that it's difficult enough to process a foreign language in the comfort of a language lab at your friendly neighborhood university but when you add the competition of the sensory stimulation of a different culture it can become a monumental task. Bonnie Benson, Peace, Corps

Language is any system of signs, symbols, and/or gestures used to stimulate meaning and direct perception. Usually at least one of the two communicators in an intercultural situation is not using his or her primary language. All listening takes tremendous amounts of energy and mental concentration but when listening to or speaking in a non-primary language the energy output and communication anxiety increases. Hoijer observed: "to the extent that languages differ markedly from each other, so should we expect to find significant and formidable barriers to crosscultural communication and understanding" (1976, p. 116).

A basic principle of language is that meaning ultimately rests with the individual listener and not in the language itself. As a result, seldom will the exact same meanings be used even by a speaker and listener of the same culture. Adding the intercultural dimension to the communication process complicates the assigning of meaning further. An effective listener will consistently check with one's partner by paraphrasing what has been "heard" so any discrepancies can be corrected. Remember, the primary goal of the crosscultural listener is the reduction of uncertainty in the communication process.

Distinguishing Vocal Cues

In intercultural communication the ability to receive and attend to the particular sounds of the language will determine the success of the transaction. This is called discriminative listening by Wolvin and Coakley. This type of listening includes ability to recognize environmental sounds, detecting the structure of language, noting vocal cues, understanding dialects, and recognizing nonverbal cues (pp. 141-149). These skills are helpful in any listening situation, but in an intercultural environment they are essential.

Not all languages include the same kinds of sounds. For example, in the Kalahari Desert in Africa, there is a tribe whose language includes many clicks and whistles. The Yala people in Nigeria vary the pitch of certain words to change their meaning. A listener who is unfamiliar with languages such as these may not distinguish these sounds or recognize them as being meaningful. Of course, this could result in serious consequences. For example, a missionary in Nigeria in the 1960's preached an entire sermon about a spider because the word for Jesus Christ used the same sounds pronounced with a different pitch! A slight variation in pronunciation can make a world of difference in meaning.

The intercultural listener must actively discriminate sounds which may not appear to be significant yet are very different from one's native tongue. At first, the listener may be unable to interpret the sounds, but recognizing that they are present is an important initial step toward understanding. For example, The Listening Centre in

Toronto offers training to expand a person's listening awareness and range prior to beginning the study of a foreign language. Another aid to distinguishing vocal cues is the study of other languages. A combination of exposure to sounds that are distinct from the listener's primary language and practice in generating these sounds can increase discriminative listening skill. Within our own culture, we can distinguish many vocal cues fairly easily. However, we should not assume that the vocal cues of one culture or subculture are the same in a second culture or subculture.

Understanding Connotative Dimensions of Language

Successful intercultural communication requires more than understanding the denotative meaning of words. An ethnocentric, but common, response of many individuals engaged in crosscultural communication is to assume that if a word or idea has a certain meaning for *them*, it will have the *equivalent* meaning for the person with whom they are communicating. As Hall and Whyte indicate, however, such erroneous assumptions can lead to miscommunication as well as to unintentional insults: "Vocabulary, grammar, even verbal facility are not enough. Unless a man understands the subtle cues that are implicit in language, tone, gestures, and expression, he will not only consistently misinterpret what is said to him, but he may offend irretrievably without knowing how or why" (1976, p. 209).

The intercultural listener should be aware that speech includes two codes: restricted and elaborated (Bernstein, 1966). Restricted codes include verbal, nonverbal, and paralinguistic (vocal intonations, inflections, pitch, volume, etc.) messages that are very predictable and often in a "shorthand" understood by the two people. This may be technical language, "street language," idioms, and so on. Cultural or subcultural common ground provides the link so these shortened and specialized language components are understood without much explicit explanation. Elaborated codes, on the other hand, include verbal elaboration to explain what is specifically meant—meaning is verbally discussed instead of assumed. In many crosscultural contexts the listener will not be familiar enough with the restricted codes to assign meaning accurately, although listening for these codes with your eyes and ears can often help decode them.

Languages categorize meaning in a variety of ways. One language may not have words equivalent to the words of another language. Furthermore, different cultures use different idioms, have different types of life experiences, and use different concepts. Even the grammar differs. For example, the structure of Russian grammar makes it difficult to take personal responsibility for some acts. In English, there is no word that captures the meaning of the French *chez* which means at an individual's home or place. In Tagalog, there is no subjunctive mood (Sechrest, Fay, and Zaidi, 1982).

Even if the intercultural listener fully understands the speaker's message code, the message being sent may include concepts so new that they are incomprehensible. Tropical cultures have difficulty with the concept of snow since they have never experienced it. Another example is the Yala. If a Yala told an American that his child was as precious as salt, the American would not understand the significance. The American would probably not be familiar with the scarcity of salt experienced by the Yala. The intercultural listener can often use contextual and structural cues to decipher connotative meaning.

A brief example illustrates the care with which crosscultural communicators must listen not only to their *own* communication (intrapersonally) but to the *intended* response of the other (interpersonally). In the Japanese business culture, teamwork and consensus are highly valued instead of the individual "star system" which is encouraged in many U.S. companies (e. g., the employee of the week, the bonus system, salesperson of the year, etc.). Asking an individual a direct question may elicit the intended response but *not* the expected meaning. An embarrassing question may receive a polite but inaccurate reply.

Consider Borisoff and Victor's (1989) case of the engineering consultant from the U.S. who was sent to Japan to work on a mechanical problem for specialized equipment. Despite his desire to work alone, he was forced to work with a group of engineers and he resented the unwelcome imposition. After finally uncovering the source of the problem, he *insisted* on meeting with the president of the Japanese company. He asked the president if he knew what the problem was and how to correct it. The president answered "yes" and the consultant returned to the United States thinking the problem would be corrected, only to learn later that no corrective measures had been implemented. As Borisoff and Victor observe, only by understanding another culture's authority conception and social organization are we able to listen *effectively* and *accurately* to the communication of members of other cultures.

This tendency to accommodate at the denotative level while saying something very different at the connotative level is not limited to Asian cultures. In many cultures embarrassing questions may receive a polite but inaccurate reply. Likewise, leading questions may result in the desired response even though the answer has little relationship to the facts. For example, in Guatemala questions must be phrased carefully to avoid simply receiving an echo of the question. To get an accurate estimate of when a task can be completed one would not ask "Can you finish it by tomorrow?" Instead, ask "By when can you have it finished?" Intercultural listeners must be alert to the connotative dimension of language.

Recognizing How Language Affects Our View of Reality

It is vitally important that the intercultural listener be aware of the influence of language on thought and the social construction of reality. Edward Sapir and Benjamin Whorf developed the theory that language is not only a channel through which to report experience—it is also a shaper of thoughts, ideas, and ultimately our view of reality. Sapir wrote in 1929:

> Language is a guide to "social reality." . . . Human beings do not live in the objective world alone, nor alone in the world of social activity as ordinarily understood, but are very much at the mercy of the particular language which has become the medium of expression for their society. It is quite an illusion to imagine that one adjusts to reality essentially without the use of language and that language is merely an incidental means of solving specific problems of communication or reflection. The fact of the matter is that the "real world" is to a large extent unconsciously built up on the language habits of the group. . . . The worlds in which different societies live are distinct worlds, not merely the same world with different labels attached (Mandelbaum, 1949, p. 162).

Whorf also observed that language shapes our thoughts at a very fundamental level. He explained:

> We dissect nature along lines laid down by our native languages. . . . (T)he world is presented in a kaleidoscopic flux of impressions which has to be organized by our minds—and this means largely by the linguistic systems in our minds (1952, p. 5).

Whorf believed that our language influences all aspects of our lives as human beings. For example, the Hopi had great difficulty comprehending Christianity because they associate concepts with their physical, sensory world. As Hall (1969, p. 31) notes, the abstract concept of a "heaven" did not fit their thought structure.

Another example of the way we learn from our culture is how we perceive a misbehaving child. Anthropologists point out that English-speaking, Italian-speaking, and Greek-speaking cultures usually consider such behavior "bad" or "naughty" and admonish the child by saying "Be good!". However, the French say "Sois sage!" for "Be wise!" because their culture views such behavior as foolish, stupid, and imprudent. Swedish people say "Var snell!" and Norwegians say "Ble snill!"—both of which translate "Be friendly, be kind." In German the term used is "Sei artig!" meaning get back in step. Its literal translation is "be of your own kind," meaning "conform to your role as a child!" (Sinclair, 1954, pp. 28–29).

The Sapir-Whorf hypothesis claims that language plays a major part in what and how we experience our world at unconscious levels. If we accept this hypothesis, then intercultural listeners must be alert to the potential barriers generated by our *own* language system and its artificial organization of the world at large. Of course, the degree of perceptual variation will depend upon the level of dissimilarity between the languages used. Certainly languages with common roots such as Latin would have closer approximations of reality and thought structure than, for example, English and Arabic.

There are common elements in the languages of most cultures. For example, every language in the world uses some form of honorifics which are rules for the acknowledgment of position in the social hierarchy by demonstrating appropriate expression of deference and respect. Typically, we use different words when interacting with friends, family, and coworkers. Although more formalized in many cultures, there is some form of honorific operating whenever two people meet and greet each other. For instance, Japanese keigo or honorifics are explicit and expected. The appropriate form is determined by the nature of the relationship between the two communicators and the context of the interaction. Words and phrases are different even when using an honorific with the same person in different physical locations such as at work or at a bar (Dalby et al., p. 202). These fine distinctions require attentive listening and experience to master.

Listening to Non-Native Language

Most texts on intercultural communication concentrate on the perspective of the United States traveler or business person going abroad. Equally important to our social and economic relations with members of other cultures, however, is how we communicate with individuals who come to the United States.

When listening to a person from another culture, the American communicator should be patient, be quiet, and listen! It is interesting to note that while most United States travelers insist on speaking English when they go abroad, they also expect visitors to the United States to speak English. English remains the most widely used language for international business. Perhaps as a consequence, comparatively few Americans feel compelled to master a second language. It is important, therefore, for the sensitive intercultural listener to be alert to some common response tendencies when interacting with non-native speakers of English.

One very natural response is the tendency to become frustrated when a speaker cannot communicate his or her thoughts quickly. When United States communicators continually interrupt or complete the sentences of their communication partners, they are conveying impatience. Such responses, in turn, often serve to make the non-native speakers even more nervous and tentative in their assertions. It is important to recognize that non-native speakers will generally request assistance when they need help with a word or

phrase. Aware intercultural communicators listen to the entire message before responding and avoid dramatically changing their own
speaking style.

We have, on several occasions, heard non-native speakers of English say: "Please, don't shout. I can hear you." Many communicators
believe if they speak loudly, they will be understood better. Speaking
slowly and distinctly in a normal tone of voice is not only more appropriate but is also the least offensive speaking style when
communicating with non-native speakers.

Another response tendency is to stereotype the speaker's accent.
The inability to communicate in accentless English is not necessarily
a reflection of the speaker's intelligence. Yet, as Borisoff and Victor
(1989) report, many studies reveal that individuals tend to evaluate
the intelligence of foreigners based upon the strength of their accents.
The causes and debilitating effects of intercultural stereotyping are
addressed later in this chapter. However, if a communicator wants to
be a truly empathic listener and understand fully the speaker's message, he or she will refrain from judging others based on how and
how well they pronounce words.

This section on language has demonstrated that there is a wide
variation in language codes from culture to culture. Moreover, the
way individuals think, their concepts, ideas, values, and the very
words they use to express these ideas are subject to cultural variation.
By being aware of these cultural differences in language, intercultural
listeners can strengthen their ability to experience, acknowledge, understand, and interpret communication with members of other
cultures or subcultures.

These are just a few of the areas in which language awareness will
grow as the intercultural listener's skills develop. There is no substitute for experience! Listening with an open mind and a willingness
to acknowledge that what is different is not wrong, is vital to crosscultural understanding.

NONVERBAL

Nonverbal stimuli also require careful discriminative listening.
Numerous studies have shown that nonverbal messages are not the
same the world over (Hall, 1969; McAndrew, 1987; Mehrabian, 1971;
Morris, Collett, Marsh, and O'Shaughnessy, 1980; Schneller, 1985).
According to Birdwhistell's research, in an interpersonal conversation about 35 percent of the meaning is carried verbally and about 65
percent is conveyed nonverbally (Knapp, 1972, p. 12). Mehrabian (p.
44) claims that up to 38 percent of message meaning comes from the
vocal, 55 percent from facial and only 7 percent from verbal. These
figures have strong implications for all communication but take on
special importance when cultural variations are involved because they
are predominantly used unconsciously. An awareness of nonverbal

factors will significantly increase listening effectiveness since they play such a dominant role in the communication process.

Nonverbal behaviors are used to (1) complement verbal messages, (2) contradict verbal messages, or (3) replace verbal messages (Wolvin and Coakley, p. 150). When a communicator can anticipate intercultural contact it is advisable to review some of the "culture specific" information for that subculture, culture, or country as a means of preparing for some of the nonverbal interaction that will occur.

Crosscultural nonverbal communication has been the subject of literally hundreds of studies and texts. The authors of these works agree that understanding the nonverbal dimension is essential to communicate effectively with members of other cultures. Basic to this understanding is an awareness of the components of nonverbal communication and how, in turn, different cultures employ and interpret nonverbal cues. From a crosscultural listening perspective, the basic categories of nonverbal communication are kinesics, oculesics, proxemics, chronemics, vocalics and haptics.

Kinesics

Body movement, gestures, posture, and facial expressions are generally included in the study of kinesics. For listening purposes, behaviors which demonstrate attending and interest are particularly significant. In the United States these may include leaning forward slightly, appropriate facial display such as smiling or showing concern, head nodding to convey understanding, open body position, and eye contact (Hamilton and Glasgow, 1983). Attending indicators vary by culture so the American listener may not be communicating attentiveness in an intercultural situation by using these "natural" behaviors. Adaptation is a key to crosscultural communication and the observant listener can decipher many of the basic nonverbal codes of other cultures by paying close attention.

A listener's gestures and movements have the potential to discount all that is accomplished verbally. The Department of State is only too aware of this. Their files are filled with examples of government representatives with good intentions insulting their gracious hosts without even knowing it. For example, the American hand gesture meaning "OK" or good has a variety of meanings in other countries including being a very obscene gesture in certain Latin American countries, as well as in Turkey, Greece, and Malta (Morris et. al., pp. 108-114). The act of waving goodbye by moving the fingers up and down works well for North Americans but it would be interpreted as a summons to "come here" by people in Central America, West Africa, and India (Dodd, p. 173). Understanding and respectfully following another culture's denotative gestures or *em-*

blems is an essential ingredient of successful intercultural communication because they serve as substitutes for verbal statements.

In addition to variations in emblems, each culture varies in its use of illustrators, affect displays and regulators (Ekman and Friesen, 1969). *Illustrators* are nonverbal behaviors which accompany and complement the spoken word by accentuating, emphasizing, punctuating, elaborating, or framing what is said. Findings suggest illustrators serve two functions: (1) they aid the speaker in encoding difficult messages, and (2) they aid the listener in decoding messages (Cohen, 1977; Graham and Heywood, 1975). Illustrators do differ from culture to culture but not nearly as frequently as emblems.

Any gesture or facial expression which conveys information regarding the speaker's emotional state is an *affect display*. Ekman and Friesen have conducted numerous research studies on affect displays and believe they have isolated at least six facial expressions that are universally expressed by human beings. These include surprise, anger, fear, disgust, sadness, and happiness (Hickson and Stacks, 1989, p. 128). However, even if there are universal affect displays there are cultural variations regarding when, how, and in what context they are utilized. The listener must be aware of these differences to avoid being lulled into a false sense of security. For example, facial expressions can manage emotions in at least four ways. They can intensify, deintensify, neutralize, or mask a felt emotion (Ekman and Friesen, 1975).

Regulators control or regulate the flow of spoken messages. Borisoff and Victor (p. 69) indicate that although regulators have more similarities between cultures than emblems do, there will still be subtle variations. For example, head nodding in many cultures is used by the listener to indicate attending. However, in one culture or microculture it may mean "I agree" and in another it may mean "I understand." Regulators are especially important in intercultural listening because they provide subtle signals regarding when it is the listener's "turn" to speak.

Greeting rituals vary widely by country and culture. The North American handshake may have to be substituted by a bow with hands in front of the chest in many Asian countries. In some cultures a hug and kisses on both cheeks is appropriate. Greetings often differ according to the age, status, or sex of the person. In Japan one is expected to bow from the waist to a greater degree if the person is of higher status. Again, observation is the key. Most of us have heard or read about the more unusual or exotic examples of greetings used in a few cultures such as Matavai where a formal greeting following an extended separation includes scratching the head and temples of the other person with a shark's tooth until it bleeds! (Dodd, p. 181). However, these are rare exceptions. Most professional and even tourist contact between cultures will not have such unusual variations.

It may be comforting to know that even well informed intercultural "veterans" can misinterpret nonverbal behaviors. For example, in the United States the visual system carries the majority of emotional information very accurately. However, this varies in other countries where a show of emotion is sometimes more verbal and at other times more hidden. Problems can arise even for experienced intercultural communicators when they assume that emotional expression works the same in another culture or country. Incongruent or seemingly contradictory behavior may be complementary in another system of communication (McCluskey and Albas, 1978). Still, aware observers can "listen with their eyes" and learn a great deal about basic patterns of communication behavior in other cultures and microcultures.

Oculesics

Another aspect of nonverbal behavior of special interest to the intercultural listener is eye behavior. In particular, *eye contact* becomes important because of our tendency to associate it with listener display of interest and involvement in what the speaker is saying. Research indicates Americans associate eye contact with caring, concern, understanding, empathy, warmth, intimacy, and positive attitudes (Coakley, 1984, p. 3). McAndrew notes that norms governing nonverbal behaviors such as eye gaze vary widely from culture to culture. He points out low status persons typically have eye contact a great deal less while speaking than while listening and that even within American society there are different norms for looking behavior while speaking and listening for Blacks than for Whites (p. 318).

For example, Whites engage in nearly twice as much eye contact while listening as they do while speaking (Argyle, 1972, p. 229). When two Blacks communicate the speaker engages in more eye contact while speaking than while listening (LaFrance and Mayo, 1976). McAndrew's studies found significant variations in the way Pakistani and U.S. students perceived differences in the amount of looking during a conversation (pp. 317–320). Other studies have noted marked differences in eye contact when speaking and listening between American men and women (Coakley, p. 4).

In northern Nigeria it is a sign of extreme disrespect to listen while looking directly into the eyes of a superior (Singer, 1987, p. 86). Even cultures which use the same primary language can vary in their use of eye gaze. For example, although both English and North American listeners are socialized to look in the direction of the speaker's eyes, English listeners use a continuous gaze while the North Americans tend to look away from time to time (Hall, 1969). Therefore, eye–contact has significant implications for interracial, interethnic, intergender, and intercultural communication.

Crosscultural listening includes being aware of variations in *eye regulators* that control the flow of messages between speaker and listener. The listener must stay alert to the fact that status and dominance patterns can be misleading in intercultural environments as well. Even cultural patterns we think of as similar to our own will have some variations. For example, Hall observed that a proper Englishman pays strict attention during listening to be polite: "He doesn't bob his head or grunt to let you know he understands. He blinks his eyes to let you know that he has heard you" (1969, p. 143). An American taken off guard may interpret this eye behavior as rude or even belligerent because we have been taught not to stare.

As the above discussion illustrates, eye behavior can serve several different functions in a culture. Argyle, Alkema, and McCallin (1973) note that eye behavior can indicate the listener's level of cognitive or thinking activity, the emotional response of the listener, the extent of monitoring or attending by the listener, the listener's willingness to respond, and when the listener will respond. The effective intercultural communicator must be alert to the storehouse of information available in these oculesic cues both as a sender and receiver of messages.

Proxemics

Fixed feature space, semi–fixed feature space, territoriality, and distances between communicators are all parts of the study of proxemics. Proximity has a major influence on intercultural listening. In *The Hidden Dimension* Hall examines the many proxemic differences between England, Germany, France, Japan, and the Arab world. For example, Arabs consistently stand so close that one can feel their breath blowing on one's face. Hall explains: "However this habit is more than a matter of different manners. To the Arab good smells are pleasing and a way of being involved with each other" (pp. 159–160). When polite Americans avoid this closeness they communicate shame to their Arab counterpart. Likewise, many cultures in Central and South America have similar proxemic codes. Americans can unintentionally communicate a cool, "standoffish," untrusting, unfriendly message in such crosscultural situations.

In other cultures *appropriate distances* are greater than in the United States. These distances which seem so "natural" are in reality unconsciously learned. They will affect the communication process and can generate defensiveness unintentionally when violated. Even the degree to which people will *directly face* each other during a conversation varies by culture. To an Arab, viewing one's partner only peripherally from the side instead of facing the person is considered very impolite (Hall, 1969, p. 161). Appropriate interaction distances have been found to vary with sex, race, age, and ethnic groups (Baxter, 1970). Amount of appropriate eye contact can also be affected by interpersonal distance (Argyle and Ingham, 1972).

Seating arrangements at formal meetings and dinners are often structured much more precisely than in the United States. There are sometimes special locations or seats of honor for esteemed visitors or persons of higher status. Members of the host party usually will gesture or point with their eyes in the direction of the seat the visitor is expected to take in these situations.

Intercultural communicators can learn a great deal through observation of the distances and angles used by others during the conversation. Informed intercultural listeners focus on understanding and adjusting rather than on judging and jumping to quick conclusions.

Chronemics

Chronemics is the study of how time is perceived and structured in human communication. For the intercultural listener such aspects as arrival–waiting–departure time, when to move from introductory formalities into substantive information, and mono-chronic/polychronic time are important. Concepts of time differ greatly from culture to culture. Westerners tend to picture time in terms of three states: past, present, and future. As stated earlier, we "spend" it, "use it up," "waste" it and "save" it. However, in Japanese Zen time is viewed as a limitless pool. The present is most important. Navajo Indians see only the reality of the present (Klopf, 1987, p. 194).

Culture also affects our perception of "lateness" and "on time"— *punctuality*. In Latin America it would not be unusual to have to "wait" up to an hour for a business appointment. This is not meant to offend; it is simply the way these cultures define time. Similarly, the seemingly prolonged "chit chat" at the start of a business meeting or professional conversation emerges from that culture's sense of what is important and how time is to be utilized properly. Listeners in such settings must redefine their level of patience and redefine the meaning of this "use" of time. For example, in the People's Republic of China formal business discussions are preceded by the traditional sharing of tea. The aware communicator will avoid the cultural urge to "get down to business" during this preliminary ritual. Intercultural listening includes listening for the indicators of when it is appropriate to shift the topic of discussion.

North Americans prefer to "do things" one at a time in a systematic order. Time is a progressive linear path with a beginning and a end. This is known as a *monochronic* view of time. Although time perspectives are also related to influences such as personality, training, and hemispheric orientation, culture does affect our time perspective. For example, many cultures hold a *polychronic* perspective in which time is viewed more flexibly and in more of a cyclical fashion. African, Southeast Asian, Latin American, Middle Eastern, and Southern European cultures tend to operate on polychronic time

(Dodd, pp. 88, 190). Monochronic cultures tend to concentrate on doing one thing at a time, while polychronic cultures may combine a variety of activities simultaneously.

Patience must often be exercised by the intercultural listener when he or she is exposed to a different chronemic system. This is especially true when a monochronic listener is in a polychronic environment where it is easy to become frustrated by a seeming lack of organization or discipline with regard to how time is structured.

Vocalics

Vocalics encompasses any vocal–auditory behavior except the spoken word (Burgoon, Buller, and Woodall, p. 64). Such variables as pauses, silence, voice quality, pitch, intonation, inflection, accent, dialect, tempo, resonance, and vocalizations are some of the nonverbal behaviors included in vocalics. All cultures appear to have a vocalic pattern which is preferred and given higher prestige. Of course, there are also variations and deviations from these vocalic patterns in every culture. Most of these vocal behaviors are learned at an early age.

Much information can be communicated through *pauses* and *timing* during a conversation. For example, Americans tend to allow very little time between verbal statements in interpersonal transactions. Pauses are often longer in other cultures. In Japan people tend to feel more comfortable with less talk and longer pauses (Knopf, p. 195). Many international students who attend universities in the United States have difficulty participating in classroom discussions because of their different standards for silence and respect.

Silence is related to culture and it communicates as loudly as any words. The Velbellans of Italy are a very emotional people who are taught to be quiet from childhood. The Igbo culture of Nigeria is composed of very outgoing people except for certain culturally determined situations where deep respect is shown through silence. Some of these silences are even controlled by their law. The tolerance for silence among Finnish people is also strong and is often misinterpreted by unaware listeners as "slow" or "unintelligent" (Saunders, 1985). Bruneau (1973) notes that there are numerous communicative functions and meanings to silence. However, it takes a sensitive listener to decode its meaning especially in crosscultural situations.

Nonstandard speech patterns or *dialects* often result in stereotyping the speaker. For example, if a person speaks "Chicano" English the listener may rate the person as lower in intelligence, ability, success, and social awareness than someone who speaks in "standard" English (Bradford, Ferror, and Bradford, 1974). A person speaking in a foreign accent may also be stereotyped as of lower status or intelligence by the unaware listener.

Haptics

Tactile communication or haptics is also an important nonverbal behavior for the intercultural listener. Touch behavior varies greatly from culture to culture especially in greetings and leave-taking. For example, *greetings* vary from handshaking, to kissing, to embracing, to rubbing noses, to slapping backs—to name but a few. Cultural variations also exist regarding *who* touches whom, *where* one is touched, and *when* one is touched.

Some cultures are high-touch oriented while others are just the opposite. Sidney Jourard (1968) counted the amount of touching between couples in cafes in different countries. He counted 180 touches per hour in San Juan, Puerto Rico; 110 touches per hour in Paris, France; 2 touches per hour in Gainesville, Florida; and 0 touches per hour in London, England. Montagu states:

> Natural and cultural differences in tactility run the full gamut from absolute non-touchability, as among upper-class Englishmen, to what amounts to almost full expression among peoples speaking Latin-derived languages, Russians, and many nonliterate peoples. Those who speak Anglo-Saxon derived languages stand at the opposite pole in the continuum of tactility to the Latin Peoples. In this continuum Scandinavians appear to occupy an intermediate position (cited in Malandro and Barker, 1983, pp. 366–67).

Such variations in *touch orientation* will affect the communication process and the nature of appropriate listener response. For example, the Chinese culture is low-touch oriented to an extreme. A visiting communicator's attempt at being outgoing and friendly by slapping a Chinese dignitary on the back would be inappropriate and possibly insulting. English, Anglo-Canadian, Japanese, and German cultures tend to be non-touch oriented, as is the American culture, although there will be gradations in each case. In contrast, Israeli, French, Arab, Russian, Italian, and Latin cultures tend toward high-touch orientation.

Keep in mind that listening can be inhibited just by being in a different physical environment with many new and, to you, unusual visual stimuli. Your partner may look, dress, smell, and behave differently from what seems "normal". The crosscultural communicator must learn the culture-specific nonverbal behavior patterns of his or her partner to maximize communication effectiveness. However, even a general sensitivity and awareness of the categories of nonverbal communication will add to the listener's intercultural skills.

Cognitive Processing

Since intercultural listening includes the receiving, attending to, and assigning of meaning, the methods we use for information input and processing will have a direct impact on listening. All the cultural values, verbal codes, and nonverbal codes we have discussed so far must ultimately be cognitively processed into meaningful data by the listener. This section briefly reviews a few of the internal categorization processes that influence intercultural listening. These include thought patterns, contextual levels, ethnocentrism, and stereotypes. Although this is only a partial list of the many processes constantly operating during listening it will serve to demonstrate the complexity of cognitive processing for each communicator.

Thought Patterns

Cultural thought patterns refer to reasoning, decision making, pathways for thought processing, and the system of logic used by a selected cultural group. Information processing and thinking patterns do vary by culture. Western cultures tend to use an *Aristotelian pattern* which is linear in nature. Just as we view time in a monochronic way in which we divide it into pieces like a piece of rope with a beginning, middle and ending, we also think in a linear, sequential, time-oriented fashion. For example, Westerners use cause and effect reasoning. We believe each effect, symptom, or problem must have a cause. Find the cause and you control or solve the effect! Obviously, this view grows out of our values structure—we can control our environment, we can change situations, we can control time, and so forth.

By contrast, many non-Western cultures are more accepting of the world as it is. Furthermore, cultures with *configurational patterns* think in terms of mental pictures which are often not sequential and linear at all (Dodd, p. 49). Attempting to persuade developing countries to stop destroying their rainforests because they are affecting the entire world's climate through the greenhouse effect involves more than economic and social differences.

As we have already seen, variations in thinking patterns can affect the way people conceive of time. The listener who understands these variations in thought patterns will not be as surprised by the Latin American, polychronic business owner who conducts business interviews by inviting several people into the office who have unrelated business and then proceeds to conduct business simultaneously.

Crosscultural listening requires an awareness that there are cultural variations in the ways people think. In an international business setting, a salesperson's perfectly logical reasoning about why business should be conducted in a certain way or why their product is the logical choice to be purchased may not appear nearly so logical to their potential customer.

The linear, Aristotelian approach to categorizing the world can lead to intercultural misunderstanding and stereotypes of Americans. This way of thinking often results in an *either-or* approach to life. Either we do this or we do that! Either you are "good" or you are "bad." Either you are right or you are wrong. If you win, we lose. Either you are with us or against us. This form of cognitive pattern is reflected in our language with its abundance of bipolar adjectives (good/bad, right/wrong, responsible/irresponsible). As listeners it can limit the exploration of a vast area between the two extremes. In negotiations or business dealings listening for the "between" can often result in positive outcomes.

Contrasting with the either-or perspective is the *both-and* pattern prominent in many Eastern cultures and philosophies. They see reality as "more or less" or "both-and" on a continuum instead of one way or the other to the exclusion of all other possibilities. For example, the both-and view of medicine would say Western medicine can be useful and so can the ancient Chinese technique known as acupuncture. However, until recently the American Medical Association would not even acknowledge acupuncture as a therapeutic approach because it is impossible to explain how it works using Western medicine's view of how the body functions. This is either-or thinking; either our view of medicine is right or your view is correct, but certainly not both. The Chinese have no difficulty combining the two approaches to the healing process. Likewise, many shaman in South America take a both-and view in their healing approach. The both-and perspective says a person can be *both* good and bad, right and wrong, masculine and feminine.

It is important to become more aware of this polarization tendency as one listens to members of other political, religious, social, ethnic, or occupational groups, as well as people from other countries. It aids in avoiding categorical thinking in the assigning of meaning and allows for more open-minded listening. The listening process is short circuited if we categorize people, food, events, behavior, or options primarily into extremes (Thomlison, 1982, p. 217).

High and Low Context Cultures

As the amount of information available to the intercultural listener is increased there will be a proportionate reduction in the level of uncertainty. Some cultures aid the listener in their cognitive processing by providing explicit information about expectations and appropriate behavior, while other cultures provide only minimal information about what is expected behaviorally. *High–context* cultures expect one to know how, when, and where to act certain ways without ever telling the individual overtly (Hall, 1977). The context serves as the cue regarding what behavior is most appropriate (see Figure 3). For example, Japanese youngsters learn the very intricate system of how far to bow down when greeting people of different ages, relationships and status levels. They are seldom told overtly about this traditional approach to greeting behavior, yet they learn it from observation and modeling. They are simply expected to sense when it is proper to bow, be silent, or follow appropriate implicit rules of conversation. By contrast, information is explicitly provided

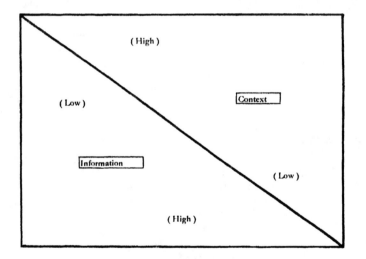

Figure 2. High context and low context cultures

in *low–context* cultures through detailed discussions of expectations and procedures.

On a contextual continuum, many Northern and Western European cultures would be on the low–context end along with North Americans. Many Middle Eastern, African, and Latin American cultures would be in the middle portion of the continuum. Many Far Eastern cultures such as Indians would be near the high–context end of the continuum (Dodd, p. 90). There will be exceptions and variations to these general patterns, but they may provide the intercultural listener with a beginning point from which to develop a deeper awareness and appreciation of their influence on information processing.

The contextual level of one's communication partner can have tremendous ramifications for an intercultural encounter. The degree of potential barriers is proportionate to the distance between the two cultures on the contextual continuum. Even an individual who has always worked in business organizations that have low-context cultures, for example, will have difficulties adapting to a high-context corporate culture in which expectations are not explicitly communicated. When the communicators are from different countries with marked differences in contextual levels, the intercultural listener must be especially sensitive to these variations. Hall makes the following observations about how context can influence the communication process:

> When talking about something that they have on their minds, a high-context individual will expect his interlocutor to know what's bothering him, so that he doesn't have to be specific. The result is that he will talk around and around the point, in effect putting all the pieces in place except the crucial one. Placing it properly—this keystone—is the role of his interlocutor. To do this for him is an insult and a violation of his individuality (1977, p. 113).

Contextual awareness can aid the intercultural listener in decoding potentially confusing and frustrating situations. It may also help the listener to avoid inappropriate responses which could result in negative outcomes in business discussions or personal conversations.

Ethnocentrism

Former United States Senator William Fulbright once said that Americans have "cultural myopia." Myopia is a visual defect in which distant objects appear to be blurred. Fulbright was correct but he left out one important detail—so does every other human being on the planet!

The belief that one's own culture or ethnic group is correct or superior to others is termed ethnocentrism. Since our world view has been shaped by our culture there is a natural tendency to evaluate that which is similar to our world as positive and that which is dissimilar as negative. The intercultural listener will be listening with a *natural bias* toward his or her own culture. This can generate quick judgments about anyone who behaves or looks different than we do. The result can be evaluative listening that can serve as a major barrier in the crosscultural communication process. This caution goes both ways. Your partner will likewise be listening to you through his or her own set of cultural screens and categories.

Neither can we assume that just because someone looks, acts, or speaks in a manner similar to us that the person necessarily has the same meanings for their words and actions as we have for them. Saying "no" may be a courtesy or politeness meaning "please ask again". As Chapter 3 indicated, gender differences in communication also contribute to a great deal of misunderstanding when men and women listen to one another.

Ethnocentrism results in the belief that we and our culture are the center of the universe. All incoming data is evaluated accordingly. Tourists the world over are notorious for comments such as "but why do they drive on the WRONG side of the road?" or "why don't they do it the RIGHT way?". The implicit and explicit messages about how to behave are often so subtle that it emerges in almost unconscious ways in our behavior and perception. These evaluative structures apply to everything from table manners to mourning a death. As Kim and Gudykunst observe: "Those who believe that their own culture is the only one—or the only 'real' one—treat communication patterns appropriate in other cultures, but not their own, as `mistakes' rather than `differences'" (1988, p. 22).

One of the basic barriers to effective listening is *judgmental thinking* during the listening process. Ethnocentrism serves to proliferate this barrier in intercultural communication situations. Moreover, as Dodd (p. 232) posits, individuals who are highly ethnocentric experience greater difficulty adjusting to and accepting intercultural experiences than do those individuals who are able to acknowledge—and, hopefully accept—different ways of viewing the world. Prejudice and ethnocentrism lead to decreased effectiveness in intercultural encounters (Kim and Gudykunst).

As Ralph Nichols noted more than 40 years ago, the truly empathic listener is able to listen more effectively than the individual who is unable to "feel with" another (1948). Listening empathically to members of other cultures, as well as to members of our own culture as Chapters 1, 2, and 9 propose, we can reduce ethnocentrism significantly and increase effectiveness in intercultural encounters.

Stereotypes

Ethnocentrism often leads to stereotyping other groups, subcultures, and cultures. For the listener this can mean responding to our collective label for a person instead of to the individual with whom we are communicating. Be careful of *labeling* an entire group as "unfriendly," "formal," "shy," or "reserved" based on one or two encounters. Clinard cautions:

> Beware of responding to a label rather than to an individual. Do not run the risk of making inaccurate or biased judgments and limiting your relationships and interactions. Be aware that people in other countries do have different tendencies, habits and expectations, but

each individual is also different. There is no way to anticipate all these differences. We must be sensitive and flexible" (1985, p. 39).

These stereotypes can influence our first impressions of others and, therefore, the entire intercultural transaction. Research indicates that human beings have a greater need to make *inferences* when dealing with people who are unfamiliar than when dealing with those who are familiar. Making these inferences or assumptions allows individuals to rationalize, explain, or make sense of actions or behavior that *differ* from their own. Frequently, however, those inferences that are based on the individual's own cultural background are interpreted differently in other cultures. The Middle Easterners' tendency to speak at close proximity (several inches) to the person with whom they are communicating, for example, may be the appropriate proxemic distance in their own culture; however, for the Westerner such a small spatial distance is considered aggressive. Quite logically, the American's judgment of Middle-Easterners as "pushy" originates from how Americans use spatial distance; not from the Middle-Easterner's use of space. Wrong impressions, incorrect interpretations, and inappropriate judgments abound as we increase the degree of unfamiliarity with our communication partner. Crosscultural communication is, therefore, fertile ground for stereotyping.

In summarizing some of the primary characteristics of stereotypes, Kim and Gudykunst state:
1. stereotyping is the result of cognitive biases stemming from illusory correlations between group membership and psychological attributes;
2. stereotypes influence the way information is processed, in other words, more favorable information is remembered about in-groups and more unfavorable information is remembered about out-groups;
3. stereotypes create expectancies (hypotheses) about others and individuals try to confirm these expectancies; and
4. stereotypes constrain others' patterns of communication and engender stereotype-confirming communication—they create self-fulfilling prophecies (pp. 117 – 118).

While it is nearly impossible for crosscultural listeners to step outside their own perceptual walls, it *is* possible to consciously examine our labels and expectations in order to defuse their impact on the information we are cognitively processing.

Listening is in one sense the imputing of meaning to experience. There is always more information than can possibly be processed so selection is an inevitable part of cognitive processing. As listeners we must keep in mind that no two people have the same personal *environment* of pressures, complexities, and experiences; no two people extract the exact same *stimuli* from their mutual communication environment since selection is inevitable; no two people experience stimuli the same because of differing sensory receptors; no two people possess the same *internal states* because of variations in our learning; no two people have the same *frame of reference* (Haney, 1967). Whatever confusions and barriers you are experiencing as an intercultural listener are also being experienced by your communication counterpart!

As our listening skills improve so will our intercultural adaptation. Nishida studied predictors of crosscultural adjustment and found that speaking and listening skills were closely related with interactional effectiveness. She also found people experienced less culture shock if they had a higher tolerance for ambiguity (1985, pp. 247-69). As we sharpen our intercultural listening skills, adaptation to other cultures and subcultures will be less stressful and difficult—both personally and professionally.

Applications

Examples of communication situations where intercultural listening will be important have been presented throughout the preceding discussion. These principles can be applied to any multicultural environment whether it be with a member of another race, ethnic group, religion, political group, or other subculture in your community or whether it be with a person from a different country and culture. The personal and professional applications are unlimited. Chapters 6–10 explore selected professional communication situations such as educational settings, organizational environments, service industries, doctor–patient interactions, helping professions, and lawyer–client transactions. All of these interactions have the potential to be intercultural encounters. We do not have to travel abroad to engage in transcultural communication or to practice becoming a more aware multicultural listener.

Listening training, cultural awareness, education, and practice can go a long way toward reducing the natural anxiety experienced by communicators confronted with intercultural contexts. Wolvin and Coakley point out that listening is influenced by several key factors "including time, age, sex, culture, self-concept, hemispheric specialization, physical/psychological state, and receiver apprehension . . . It should be clear, however, that a listener can overcome any negative, deterring influence by systematically employing the listening strategies in the communication" (p. 128). Among others, they recommend the listening strategies of active listening and appropriate feedback, as well as considerable practice.

Clinard, an intercultural trainer and consultant to corporations involved in international business, agrees that there is no substitute for preparation and practice:

Increasing your listening skills will require practice and self discipline. It is not easy, but the rewards are tremendous and come in many forms.

If you are involved in international work, listening will be your best tool for understanding the people with whom you work. Knowing labels and generalities frequently associated with a group may help alert you to possible differences, and help you avoid culturally biased assumptions. However, through careful listening you will come to understand individuals from cultures and countries different from your own (39).

Coming to appreciate the uniqueness of each communication partner is an important part of developing effective listening; but it is absolutely essential in an intercultural context.

Different business organizations have different corporate cultures which can be almost as distinctive and complex as those of other countries. Many of the listening suggestions offered in this chapter have direct applications for listening in corporate crosscultural situations. Furthermore, different countries have different corporate cultures. Flexibility in our communication will be very helpful in decoding corporate culture. As Dodd explains:

> Some Mediterranean cultures, for instance, expect greater authoritarian communication and control—the idea of requesting worker input may be difficult to accept at first. . . . the need for corporate flexibility is a significant element of intercultural consideration in these matters.

> Japanese corporate systems reveal some clear-cut methodologies and high levels of discipline and expectation. When Nissan came to Tennessee, it brought its corporate culture along. However, the company's success, as evidenced by low absenteeism and high performance, can be attributed to its cultural adaptation. Nissan melded its traditional corporate style of management into local culture in its attitudes toward friendliness, discipline, and listening (p. 124).

Ironically, one of the biggest barriers to improving our listening skills may be the assumption that we already know how to listen (Clinard, p. 39). Americans doing business overseas cannot rely solely on their American values and patterns of behavior. To compete in the international business arena they must recognize that there are different ways of thinking, relating, and behaving toward business associates. In a very real sense, there are different ways of doing business (McCaffrey, 1985).

Another area of international contact which requires intercultural listening at its best is in negotiations. These may be governmental, non-profit organizations, or corporate in nature. The more we know about other cultures the better will be the outcomes. Barnum and Wolniansky warn: "Nowhere do Americans pay so dearly for our crosscultural ignorance as in our international negotiations" (1989, p.

55). They note that crosscultural listening is vitally important in such discussions and that negotiations begin with the first telephone call or contact rather than with the first meeting or negotiation session. Negotiations are sometimes over before the first actual meeting and if our listening skills are poor we may not even realize it.

It is impossible to explore all the potential applications of listening skills in crosscultural contexts because of the multitude of possibilities. The advice of "think globally but act locally" may be an appropriate place to start. Individuals can begin applying these fundamental listening principles and skills in a hundred ways in their local communities. In both personal and professional applications, it is important to keep in mind that the major goal of an intercultural listener is to reduce the level of uncertainty in the communication and thereby increase the level of understanding.

Summary

The intercultural context for listening is complex because of the mostly unconscious nature of our acculturation and the many influences it has on the ways we process information. Throughout this chapter we have explored some of the primary barriers to listening when members of two different cultures interact. By understanding the major components of culture—such as values and beliefs, language, nonverbal codes, and cognitive processing—we can begin to practice more effective intercultural listening. Culture is the primary influence on our communication whether it be personal or professional.

We can never leave or set aside our own cultural heritage during crosscultural encounters, nor should we. However, listening will be enhanced if we can anticipate some of the potential difficulties which will inevitably be present during intercultural communication. Learning how to be an effective intercultural listener will help reduce the anxiety and stress which naturally accompanies new communication experiences. It can open doors to understanding and new perceptions that are boundless. The ultimate goal of the crosscultural listener is to reduce uncertainty in the communication process.

Crosscultural communication can be one of the most exhilarating and rewarding interpersonal experiences of our lives. It provides us with an opportunity to literally explore new worlds. Once we begin to become an active intercultural listener by opening ourselves to other cultures, perspectives, thoughts, beliefs, values and ideas, our world will be enriched and changed forever!

Exercises

1. This chapter indicates language can influence what we see and how we see it. Write down a list of words which especially affect

how you see events, people, and/or situations. (For example, a traditional English food is "steak & kidney pie." A large number of Americans refuse to eat this meal because of the word "kidney." It short-circuits their perception based on their culture—we don't eat kidneys! However, if not told what the dish is called before eating it, often the response is positive.) Hold a discussion in which these semantic reactions are shared.

2. Write down the following words on a piece of paper. Next to each write the words which come to your mind first. Don't think about it, just write them down quickly! (American, British, French, South African, Mexican, Black, Latino, Hispanic, Japanese, Iranian.) Discuss these stereotypes. What patterns emerged? How have the mass media contributed to these stereotypes?

3. Arrange to have an extended intercultural experience. You may want to volunteer to work in a soup kitchen for the homeless, help with the local meals-on-wheels program for the elderly, tutor an international student, or other experience in which you can practice your intercultural listening. During the experience keep a listening journal of (1) difficulties encountered based on your stereotypes, language, nonverbal differences, etc., (2) areas in which your listening improved such as deciphering accents, overcoming cultural biases, increase in level of open-mindedness, etc., and (3) what you learned about both your own and your partner's culture.

4. Invite a group of international students or community members who are from different countries to a discussion on intercultural difficulties. Ask each of the guests to describe how they honestly see Americans. During the discussion work on practicing your listening skills by paraphrasing the views of others to check for understanding, maintaining an unbiased perspective, and avoiding ethnocentric thinking.

5. Study the values of another culture or country and then compare the values with those you personally hold. How are they the same? How are they different?

6. Interview a business or professional person who has worked in another country. Ask for examples of communication successes and difficulties. Ask how important intercultural listening was to their experience abroad.

7. Interview an ethnic leader in your community about special traditions, activities, and celebrations of their group. What areas of misunderstanding exist between the group and other cultural

groups in the community? Summarize your findings in a written
or oral report.

8. As a group, list as many American proverbs as you can think of
on the left half of a flipchart or large sheets of newsprint. On the
right note the basic value being advocated by the saying or prov-
erb. Discuss what these values are and how they are reinforced in
our culture. A few examples are as follows:

Proverb:	Value:
A bird in the hand is worth two in the bush.	Practicality
There's more than one way to skin a cat.	Determination
God helps those who help themselves.	Initiative
If at first you don't succeed, try try again.	Persistence; work ethic

You may also want to consult Selwyn Gurney Champion's
book entitled *Racial Proverbs: A Selection of the World's Proverbs Arranged Linguistically* for examples of proverbs in other
cultures. If so, as one person reads these proverbs aloud the
group should closely listen and then call out the value being
advocated in each. How do these differ from those in your
own country? (Note: this exercise was modified from one
suggested by Robert Kohls in *Survival Kit for Overseas Living*.
Chicago: Intercultural Press, 1979, p. 30)

References

Argyle, M. (1975). *Bodily Communication*. New York, NY: International Universities Press.

Argyle, M., and R. Ingham. (1972). Gaze, Mutual Gaze and Proximity. *Semiotica*, 6, 32–49.

Argyle, M., R. A. Inghan and M. McCallin. (1973). The Different
functions of Gaze. *Semiotica*, 7, 19–32.

Baxter, J. C. (1970). Interpersonal Spacing in Natural Settings. *So-
ciometry*, 33, 444–456.

Barnum, C. and N. Wolniansky. (1989). Why Americans Fail at
Overseas Negotiations. *Management Review*, October, 55–60.

Benson, B. (1989). Letter dated July 15, 1–5.

Bernstein, B. (1966). Elaborated and Restricted Codes: Their Social
Origins and Some Consequences. In Alfred G. Smith (Ed.), *Communication and Culture*. New York: Holt, Rinehart and Winston.

Borisoff, D. and D. A. Victor. (1989). *Conflict Management: A Communication Skills Approach.* Englewood Cliffs, N. J.: Prentice Hall.

Bradford, A., D. Ferror and G. Bradford. (1974). Evaluation Reactions of College Students to Dialect Differences in the English of Mexican–Americans. *Language and Speech, 17,* 255-270.

Bruneau, T. (1973). Communicative Silences: Forms and Functions. *Journal of Communication, 23,* 17-46.

Burgoon, J. K., D. B. Buller and W. G. Woodall. (1989). *Nonverbal Communication: The Unspoken Dialogue.* New York, N.Y.: Harper & Row Publishers.

Clark, C. (1987). Orr Just Wanted to Get Down to Business—China Says Not So Fast. *Evansville Courier,* November 13, 1 & 3.

Clinard, H. (1985). Listen for the Difference. *Training and Development Journal,* July, 39.

Coakley, C. G. (1984). Attending Behaviors: A Research Perspective. Paper presented at the annual conference of the International Listening Association, Scottsdale, Arizona.

Cohen, A. A. (1977). The Communicative Functions of Hand Illustrators. *Journal of Communication, 27* (4), 54-63.

Commager, H. S. (1970). *Meet the U.S.A.* (Rev. ed.). New York, NY: Institute of International Education.

Dalby, L., P. Grilli, D. Hughes, C. G. Kanda, S. Longstreet, J. Spayde, O. Statler, and T. Trucco. (1984). *All-Japan: The Catalogue of Everything Japanese.* New York, NY: Quill.

Dodd, C. H (1987). *Dynamics of Intercultural Communication* (2nd ed.). Dubuque, Iowa: Wm. C. Brown Publishers.

Ekman, P. and W. V. Friesen. (1969). The Repertoire of Nonverbal Behavior: Categories, Origins, Usage and Coding. *Semiotica, 1,* 49-98.

Ekman, P. and W. V. Friesen. (1975). *Unmasking the Face.* Englewood Cliffs, N.J.: Prentice-Hall.

Graham, J. A. and S. Heywood. (1975). The Effects of Elimination of Hand Gestures and of Verbal Codability on Speech Performance. *European Journal of Social Psychology, 5* (2), 188-195..

Grove, C. L. (1984). *A Fondness for Ice Water: A Brief Introduction to the U.S.A. and Its People.* New York, NY: AFS International/Intercultural Programs.

Hall, E. T. (1977). *Beyond Culture.* Garden City, New York: Doubleday and Company (Anchor Books).

Hall, E. T. (1969). *The Hidden Dimension.* Garden City, New York: Doubleday and Company (Anchor Books).

Hall, E. T. and W. F. Whyte. (1976). Intercultural Communication: A Guide to Men of Action. In Joseph A. DeVito (Ed.), *Communication Concepts and Processes.* Englewood Cliffs, New Jersey: Prentice-Hall.

Hamilton, P. K. and W. A. Glasgow. (1983). An Experimental Study of the Effect of Listening Behavior on Self-Disclosure and Interpersonal Trust. Paper presented at the Central States Speech Communication Association Conference, Lincoln, Nebraska.

Haney, W. V. (1967). *Communication and Organizational Behavior* (Rev. ed.). Homewood, IL: Richard D. Irwin, Inc.

Hickson, M. I. and D. W. Stacks. (1989). *Nonverbal Communication Studies and Applications.* (2nd. Ed.). Dubuque, Iowa: Wm. C. Brown Publishing.

Hoijer, H. (1976). The Sapir-Whorf Hypothesis. In L. A. Samovar and R. E. Porter (Eds.), *Intercultural Communication: A Reader.* (2nd Ed.). Belmont, California: Wadsworth.

Jourard, S. M. (1968). *Disclosing Man to Himself.* Princeton, N.J.: Van Nostrand.

Kim, Y. Y. and W. B. Gudykunst. (1988). *Crosscultural Adaptation: Current Approaches.* Beverly Hills, California: Sage Publications.

Klopf, D. W. (1987). *Intercultural Encounters.* Englewood, Colorado: Morton Publishing Company.

Knapp, M. L. (1972). *Nonverbal Communication in Human Interaction.* New York, NY: Holt, Rinehart and Winston.

Kochman, T. (1986). Black Verbal Dueling Strategies in Interethnic Communication. In Y. Y. Kim (Ed.), *Interethnic Communication: Current Research.* Newbury Park, California: Sage Publications.

Kohls, L. R. (1984). *The Values Americans Live By.* Unpublished paper. Washington, D.C.: Meridian House International.

LaFrance, M. and C. Mayo (1976). Racial Differences in Gaze Behavior During Conversations: Two Systematic Observational Studies. *Journal of Personality and Social Psychology*, 33, 547-552.

Lanier, A. R. (1981). *Living in the U.S.A.* Yarmouth, Maine: Intercultural Press.

Malandro, L. A. and L. Barker. (1983). *Nonverbal Communication.* Reading, Massachusetts: Addison-Wesley.

Mandelbaum, D. G. (Ed.) (1949). *Selected Writings of Edward Sapir.* Berkeley: University of California Press.

McAndrew, F. T. (1987). Decoding Visual Dominance Among Pakistani College Students. *Journal of Social Psychology.* 127 (3), 317-320.

McCaffrey, J. A. and C. R. Hafner. (1985). When Two Cultures Collide: Doing Business Overseas. *Training and Development Journal*, October, 39-43.

McCluskey, K. W. and D. C. Albas. (1978). Differential Sensitivity to Contradictory Communication as a function of Age and Culture. *Journal of Cross-Cultural Psychology*, 9 (2), 167-178.

McCroskey, J. C. (1972). *Introduction in Rhetorical Communication.* Englewood Cliffs, New Jersey: Prentice-Hall.

Mehrabian, A. (1971). *Silent Messages.* Belmont, California: Wadsworth Publishing Company.

Milton, C. (1987) Letter dated August.

Morris, D., P. Collett, P. Marsh, M. O'Shaughnessy. (1980). *Gestures: Their Origins and Distribution*. New York, NY: Stein and Day.
Nichols, R. Unpublished dissertation. State University of Iowa. In L. Steil, L. L. Barker, and K. Watson. (1983) *Effective Listening: Key to Your Success*. Reading, MA: Addison-Wesley.
Nishida, H. (1985). Japanese Intercultural Communication Competence and Cross-Cultural Adjustment. *International Journal of Intercultural Relations*, 9 (3), 247-269.
Saunders, G. R. (1985). Silence and Noise as Emotion Management Styles: An Italian Case. In Deborah Tannen and Muriel Saville-Troike (Eds.), *Perspectives on Silence*. Norwood, New Jersey: ABLEX Publishing Corp.
Schneller, R. (1985). Heritage and Changes in the Nonverbal Language of Ethiopian Newcomers. *Israel Social Science Research*, 3 (1-2), 33-54.
Sechrest, L., T. L. Fay and S. M. Zaidi. (1982). Problems of Translation in Cross-Cultural Communication. In L. A. Samovar and R. E. Porter (Eds.), *Intercultural Communication: A Reader*. Belmont, California: Wadsworth Publishing Company.
Seelye, H. N. (1985). *Teaching Culture: Strategies for Intercultural Communication*. Lincolnwood, Illinois: National Textbook Company.
Sinclair, L. (1954). A Word in Your Ear. In L. Sinclair (Ed.), *Ways of Mankind*. Boston: Beacon Press.
Singer, M. R. (1987). *Intercultural Communication: A Perceptual Approach*. Englewood Cliffs, New Jersey: Prentice-Hall.
Smith, A. G. (1966). *Communication and Culture*. New York, NY: Holt, Rinehart and Winston.
Stewart, E. C. (1972). *American Cultural Patterns: A Cross-Cultural Perspective*. Yarmouth, Maine: Intercultural Press.
Thomlison, T. D. (1982). *Toward Interpersonal Dialogue*. New York: Longman.
Victor, D. A. and D. Borisoff (1989). Listening in CrossCultural Communication: Pseudoconflicts Exposed. Paper presented at the International Listening Association Conference, Atlanta, GA.
Whorf, B. L. (1952). *Collected Papers on Metalinguistics*. Washington, D.C.: Department of State, Foreign Service Institute.
Wolvin, A. and C. G. Coakley. (1988). *Listening*. 3rd ed. Dubuque, Iowa: Wm. C. Brown Publishers.

Chapter 5

MANAGING INTERPERSONAL AND TEAM CONFLICT: Listening Strategies

Patrice M. Johnson, and Kittie W. Watson

Points to be Addressed:

- Current definitions of conflict.
- The relation of communication to conflict management.
- Options for listening in conflict management.
- Listening interpersonally vs. listening in teams.
- Balancing advocacy and inquiry.
- Identification of listening behaviors related to inquiry and most appropriate to conflict management.
- Considerations for listening to manage team conflict.

Meredith Lopez leads a process improvement team at a Fortune 500 company chemical plant. The team monitors a plant maintenance process. Meredith believes the plant maintenance process would be improved if maintenance for each piece of equipment were reexamined and possibly performed less frequently. Increasing the intervals between maintenance events even by a few weeks would save money, reduce downtime, and use the maintenance staff more effectively.

A fellow team member, recognized by all as an expert mechanic with a great deal of knowledge about plant equipment, is strongly opposed to Meredith's position. He believes maintenance should be scheduled more rather than less often. He argues that even though maintenance costs would increase in the short run, in the long run the company would save money because the operating life of the equipment would be lengthened.

Each position has advantages and disadvantages. Meredith and her teammate debate the issue. Neither is willing to give in. Neither listens very effectively to the other's position. They know, however, that the team must decide on a single maintenance schedule. Obviously, they are involved in conflict.

No matter how accommodating we are, we must all deal with conflict and reconcile differing reactions to events. We must tackle our feelings of not being listened to and understood.

When most of us think about conflict, we think of friction, either between individuals or among team members. Whether it occurs between two people or within a team, the source of conflict is the same: the interaction of interdependent people who perceive incompatible goals and interference from each other in achieving those goals (Frost and Wilmot). According to Steinfatt and Miller, who examine conflict from a games perspective, a "major ingredient in conflict situations is the desire to gain something one does not possess and to hold onto that which one does possess . . . ." (p. 14). Conflict ends only when all individuals are satisfied that they have won or lost or that the advantages of ending the conflict outweigh the advantages of continuing it (Watkins, pp. 1–5).

As long as there are differing points of view, conflict is inevitable. In today's society, individuals who are reluctant to face conflict situations often find themselves unprepared for dealing with others personally and/or professionally. In fact, the ability to successfully manage conflict situations is a valued competency in today's changing organizations.

In many personal and professional instances, the oft-heard claim "Conflict is good for you . . . " is justified. Conflict does benefit relationships and team interactions when it results in greater understanding or in choosing the best response to an event. Productive conflict interactions occur when individuals move through disagreements by stating conflict issues, clarifying points of disagreement, confronting differences, and identifying consequences of not finding alternatives.

Although most people agree that conflict situations may have positive outcomes, in the midst of conflict our experience is negative. We feel threatened, tense, angry or attacked. We fear that conflict will destroy relationships and demoralize groups because it will lead to competitiveness, hurt feelings, bitterness, and ineffective action. We tend to place blame during conflict situations, without realizing that all those involved share responsibility for conflict. Conflict, like communication, is truly interactive in nature, and the outcome depends on how it is handled. How we respond or how we anticipate another person will respond influences the conflict situation.

Conflict confronts people with the need for change and readjustment. Since conflict interactions occur within changing environments, conflict communication is a dynamic process. To cope with conflict constructively, we must learn to adapt to the changing demands and constraints of the process.

When conflict develops, we try to resolve it. We attempt resolution because we believe all conflict can be resolved by choosing one of the offered responses to the event. However, it is important to note that some conflict is not intended to be resolved. Differences in taste and values can often be tolerated or even enjoyed as the spice of life. Think of all the products which cater to individual preference. You may love Italian food. Your best friend may live on burgers and fries. When you go out to eat together, you may sometimes choose a pizza place and other times go for hamburgers. Conflict over where and what to eat does not often emerge because both of you understand that you do not have to have the same eating preferences.

Another way of handling conflict is to manage it. Managing conflict means ensuring that people continue to talk. It does not necessarily mean resolving disagreements, even though successful conflict management must often precede resolution.

A number of theorists have presented models and formulas for conflict management and intervention (Borisoff and Victor, 1989; Fisher and Ury, 1992; Hocker and Wilmot 1985; Folger and Poole, 1984; Sillars, 1980; Stuart, 1980). Based on our personal and professional experiences, we believe successful conflict management strategies are based on the following three premises:

1. *Some apparent conflicts are due to misunderstanding rather than to fundamental differences.* By continuing to communicate, we may discover that we have much in common and disagree more about language than about substance.

2. *Some conflicts do not need to be resolved.* Often we can agree to disagree about world views and lifestyles, especially when we do not need to present a united front. You do not need to agree with your neighbor that wearing school uniforms simplifies dressing children and shows respect for education. You can each send your children to schools which reflect your values. Neither do you have to agree with your best friend that pizza is far superior to burgers and fries. Uniformity of opinion and conduct would make this a dull world indeed.

3. *Some conflicts cannot be speedily resolved* (Barker et al. 1995). Conflicts concerning value systems, educational backgrounds,

religious mores, personal interests, and ingrained political views may take decades or even centuries to resolve. Debates about such issues as environmental quality, abortion, and civil rights are likely to continue. Ethnic, religious, and political conflicts among nations may go on for generations. Think of the situations in Northern Ireland, the Middle East, and the Balkans.

The above premises suggest that continuing to communicate about the issues may be more important than identifying immediate solutions. Theorists propose that continuing to communicate improves the likelihood of successful conflict conclusion. If the lines of communication between speakers and listeners are maintained from the beginning of the conflict interaction, there is more potential for cooperation in ending the conflict (Littlejohn 194).

A key to maintaining this communication and, therefore, to conflict management is effective listening. The remainder of this chapter will focus on listening strategies which maintain communication during conflict situations.

Listening Options

Effective listening occurs when both speakers and listeners accept mutual responsibility for the success of communication and listeners practice listening behavior appropriate to the listening setting. Because most of us listen in habitual ways, becoming aware of our listening behavior and practicing appropriate listening under the stress of conflict may be especially difficult, but it is central to conflict management. We must know our listening options and be prepared to alter our behavior as circumstances change.

Knowing our listening options helps us to realize, for example, that making the appropriate listening choice for the setting increases our understanding of the speaker's message. When we understand and accurately interpret the message, we may find that areas of conflict are fewer than we supposed. We may also discover new areas of agreement to build on.

When Meredith makes the appropriate listening choice in listening to her teammate who disagrees with her about maintenance scheduling, she discovers that both she and her teammate are striving to save the company money while at the same time ensuring efficient equipment operation and that her teammate's opposition to her recommended maintenance schedule involves only one piece of equipment. The area of conflict is clearly limited. Resolution may be fairly easy to achieve.

Sometimes the appropriate listening choice for the setting requires us to just—listen. Listening, rather than speaking, becomes the objective. Obviously when we are listening and not speaking, potential occasions for conflict are reduced.

In most situations, appropriate listening increases our understanding of the speaker's motivation and values. When we understand another person, we may feel comfortable reducing conflict by agreeing to disagree. We may begin to accept the other's opinions and decisions, while at the same time holding to our own, without frustration, hostility, or the urge to make a convert.

Finally, listening is critical when conflict must be resolved. When we know what the issues are, we can make better decisions. By listening effectively, we can consider differing points of view and then apply suitable problem-solving and decision-making strategies.

Listening Interpersonally Versus Listening in Small Groups

Although listening is a major agent for managing conflict in both interpersonal and team situations, we may find the experience of interpersonal listening (in the dyad) very different from listening in a team. Since in the dyad we usually anticipate alternating roles—switching from speaker to listener and back to speaker again—the social pressure to listen is strong. When we know we will have to respond, we usually listen more carefully. In most dyadic interactions, we alternate between listening and speaking. Our time is often equally divided between the two.

In teams, however, we usually spend far more time listening than speaking. In a three-person group in which members participate equally, for example, each person will listen approximately 65 percent of the time. In a ten-person group, each person will listen 90 percent of time.

Consequently, the social pressure to listen is not as strong as in the dyad because the responsibility to respond is distributed among team members. When one person fails to respond, others usually will. Thus, team members may become passive in their listening behavior, relying on others to take responsibility for active listening.

However, to remain effective and efficient, teams need active listening from all members just as dyads do. Active listening is essential to understanding and interpreting message content accurately. Without an accurate assessment of message content, we cannot identify the issues at stake in a conflict.

Even so, we do not always listen effectively in teams, and we often fail to recognize those interpersonal situations which require that we listen more than we speak. Our failures lead to unsuccessful conflict management.

Balancing Advocacy and Inquiry

One factor which inhibits effective listening, whether in dyads or teams, is our tendency, as Senge et al. point out, to rely too heavily on *advocacy* in our communication. *Advocacy* is the practice of presenting and arguing strongly for our views, making our thought processes known. Advocacy shares: "This is what I think . . . This is how I see myself . . . This is how I see you." Most of us have had a lifetime of encouragement and practice in becoming capable advocates. Our culture tends to reward advocacy, whether in the education, business, or government arena.

The complement to advocacy is *inquiry*. *Inquiry* is the practice of discovering other people's views and assumptions, making other people's thought processes known. Inquiry explores: "What do you think? . . . How do you see yourself? . . . How do you see me?"

For many of us, inquiry skills are problematic. Further, when members of a dyad or team all are practicing advocacy, conflict is likely to occur and not likely to be well managed or effectively resolved. Each individual concentrates energy on presenting in the best possible light his/her views. No one expends sufficient time and energy on understanding and clarifying the views of others. Limiting the area of conflict and finding common ground in an advocate/advocate communication situation is not easy. Those involved become frustrated; feelings are hurt; positions hardened. We have all walked away from such situations bemoaning the fact that the others "just don't listen."

Three Listening Strategies

The listening behaviors which support inquiry skill development and therefore effective conflict management, both interpersonally and in teams, fall into three categories: *dampening, redirecting,* and *digging.* Dampening consists of those listening behaviors which rely on hearing out the speaker: listening with minimal response and maximum acceptance. Dampening contributes to conflict management by reducing the number of competing responses to events and allows the listener to develop an understanding of the speaker's assumptions. When we practice dampening behaviors, we temporarily refrain from advocacy—from articulating our opinions and feelings—and concentrate instead on listening to and accepting (i.e., dampening) the viewpoint of the speaker. Dampening is appropriate in listening settings requiring that we listen more than we speak out of either politeness or genuine love and concern.

Redirecting includes those listening behaviors which help manage conflicts by increasing understanding about message content. When we use redirecting behaviors, we respond to the speaker by asking questions, restating the message, and getting the speaker back on track. Redirecting is helpful in both interpersonal and team situations requiring message clarification and refocusing the speaker on key issues.

Digging is characterized by listening behaviors which rely on empathy and attention to nonverbal messages. Digging clarifies both content and feeling. When we use digging behaviors, we maintain communication by reflecting emotion. Digging is listening for feelings and is useful interpersonally and in teams when the real issues are obscured by emotion. Understanding emotion helps us to interpret the content in the proper context.

Now that we have defined the three categories for conflict management listening behaviors, let's examine each category and its specific behaviors.

Dampening

In some listening settings, the needs of one person to speak are so great that the appropriate response from others is to listen quietly. These settings usually occur in interpersonal relationships, i.e., in the dyad, though we can think of team situations which require dampening as well. Two listening behaviors in the dampening category are courteous listening and caring listening.

Courteous Listening

Courteous listening occurs when we listen out of politeness. In courteous listening situations, the listener remains relatively silent and uninvolved. The speaker and the listener do not alternate roles as we might expect in the dyad. We show concern for and interest in others or avoid giving offense by listening politely to our seat mate's problems during a transcontinental flight, to our great aunt's lengthy tale about her operation, or to a waiter's excuses about the slow service. We can listen attentively to team members as they introduce themselves, even to the garrulous administrative supervisor, who gives a blow–by–blow account of his twenty–five years with the company.

Courteous listening behavior is a useful conflict management tool. When your seat mate wants to talk about his/her problems, you can listen politely without feeling obliged to share your problems or give advice, i.e., advocate a particular solution. You can respond minimally with a friendly nod and disengage yourself at the first opportunity by looking away or opening a magazine. In situations calling for courteous listening, insisting on advocating your opinion may be interpreted as rudeness and evoke hostility. You can assume an attitude of acceptance without having to agree.

Caring Listening

Like courteous listening, caring listening requires us to listen more than we speak. However, we usually practice caring listening out of genuine concern for the speaker, and it therefore occurs most often in close personal relationships. When you listen sympathetically to your friend's fears about the success of an important job interview, even though it sounds to you as if the friend is being very pessimistic and exaggerating the possible problems (she already has three good job offers so how important could this last interview be?), you are engaged in caring listening. You are allowing someone close to you to express her feelings and emotions.

Unfortunately, it is sometimes the most difficult to listen patiently and attentively to people we care for. We become bored and turn away or we feel we know what the speaker will say next and we finish his/her sentence. Sometimes we give advice or advocate our position at the first opportunity. Such responses often lead not only to immediate conflict but also to long-term damage to the relationship. When your friend is recounting in detail the horrors of the previous day's interview, the appropriate response is caring listening rather than advocating the belief that the speaker is exaggerating and that the interview wasn't crucial anyway since she already has three good job offers.

A kind of caring listening is also helpful in less intimate encounters, especially when the other is angry or under stress. You are speaking to a client on the phone. A coworker rushes into your office with a report in his hand, a report you just completed. He begins to exclaim about an error in the report. You ask the client if you can call back in a few minutes. The coworker continues his tirade. He had a flat tire on the way to work; his son has the measles and the baby-sitter was late; the report is due on the boss's desk this morning and now an error must be corrected, and the secretary is on vacation. You know that he made the error, not you, and that it is minor and easily corrected. Now is not the best time to advocate your case, however. Caring listening is the appropriate response. If you must take an advocacy role at all, you should wait until your coworker is calm and objective.

We may use these dampening behaviors similarly in team situations, especially when the team first comes together and members have a need to become acquainted and feel accepted. Listening to other team members and indicating acceptance can keep communication open and build team spirit. At the beginning of the team meeting, we can listen to those lengthy introductions, and during the break, we can remain with the team and listen to small talk, when we might be tempted to check our messages and handle personal business.

As dampening behaviors, both courteous and caring listening depend on accepting the other's message. Remember—we use dampening when the other has a strong need to speak and when advocating would be rude or uncaring. If we disagree with the speaker, we refrain from advocating our point of view because we realize that the speaker's comfort is more important than the issues.

Redirecting

You may wonder how to keep meetings on track, especially during times of conflict. Redirecting is the key. Without redirecting, we make assumptions that may or may not be true. Redirecting involves asking questions to allow others to clarify and refocus their positions particularly after tangential comments, i.e., taking the inquiry role. Since clarifying message content contributes to successful conflict management in both the dyad and the team, we need to practice redirecting effectively. One type of listening behavior in this category is discriminative listening.

Discriminative Listening

Discriminative listening applies when we need to understand and to remember. It requires the ability to identify main ideas, follow the logic of the message, identify when the speaker has gone off course, pinpoint important details, and recognize the purpose of the message.

When we use discriminative listening, we *do not* imply that we will make a critical judgment. During your performance review, you may use discriminative listening to follow your boss's ideas about how better to close sales. You strive to understand and to remember her message. In the process, you ask questions to check your understanding and to refocus your boss when she or you lose track of key issues.

As a redirecting behavior, discriminative listening depends on fully understanding and remembering message content. In this type of listening, we refrain from criticizing message content, focusing instead on understanding. Redirecting requires that we maintain the inquiry posture, exploring what others think. We are then in a position to avoid those conflicts which grow out of misunderstanding and semantic arguments and to continue to communicate about substantive issues.

Digging

Digging is the third strategy for using listening to manage conflict. Digging is critical when the real agenda is obscured by feeling, self-interest, or lack of insight. Behaviors in the digging category occur when we attend and respond to the speaker's verbal and nonverbal messages/emotions. One type of listening behavior in the digging category is critical listening.

Critical Listening

We use critical listening when we listen to analyze and evaluate the speaker's message. Effective critical listening requires the ability to discern fact from fiction, separate fact from opinion, determine whether an argument is based on logic or emotion, maintain an objective attitude toward the speaker and the message, and clarify ambiguities (Steil et al. p. 31).

Used skillfully, critical listening is especially beneficial as a digging strategy in managing interpersonal conflict because it helps us to clearly identify the real areas of conflict. When you listen critically to a friend whose opinions on abortion differ from yours, you may discover that you agree about the importance of human life but disagree on when life begins. You may believe life begins at the moment of conception while your friend thinks life begins at a later point in fetal development. Or perhaps you both disapprove of abortion, but one of you thinks it should be allowed by law under some circumstances and the other does not.

When we use critical listening, however, we must control our tendencies to prejudge and to evaluate before we give the speaker a chance to complete the message. For example, during your performance review when your boss begins to talk about sales quotas, you may immediately conclude that you will not be appraised fairly because sales quotas are too high and you failed to meet them. You have evaluated the message before the speaker has finished speaking. Obviously, you now run the risk of a communication breakdown due to a significant listening error that results in faulty understanding of the speaker's message.

Response

The digging process is completed by the response, i.e., the listener reacts to the speaker's message; the listener gives feedback. Response possibilities range from nonverbal cues showing that we've received the message (smiling, frowning) to asking questions and requesting clarification. In contrast to redirecting questions, digging questions are intended to probe underlying feeling rather than message content. Whereas redirecting questions relate to the "What-do-you-think?" aspect of inquiry, digging questions relate to the "How-do-you-see-yourself?" and "How-do-you-see-me?" aspect.

A specific type of digging response is *reflecting*. Reflecting is restating the speaker's message and the feeling that goes with it, i. e., attending to the speaker's nonverbal messages/emotions. Because of our tendency as listeners to rivet attention on content, we often miss the emotional dimensions of both interpersonal and team interactions. Then we scratch our heads because we find ourselves embroiled in a conflict we didn't anticipate. When we reflect, we express the message and feeling in our own words; we paraphrase and check our paraphrase with the speaker to make sure we understand. *Empathy* is also a specific type of digging response. We have already established that one of the biggest obstacles to conflict resolution stems from our inability to listen to another person's point of view. When we do listen, we must communicate our empathy for the other. Empathic responses enable us to do just that—to communicate to the speaker that we understand. Genuine expressions of empathy serve to build supportive environments and reduce defensiveness. Usually when we listen to others, we judge what has been expressed. As we judge, our values, motivations, and experiences can influence what we have heard. When we are sincerely trying to empathize, we must suspend judgment and personal involvement until we have heard the entire message.

Empathic responses include *following.* Following encourages the speaker to continue talking. We have all had the experience of beginning to understand and to deal with our own feelings once we have talked about them adequately. Indeed, psychotherapy achieves emotional healing by encouraging the patient to talk out problems and internal conflicts.

Following responses consist of door openers, minimal encouragers, infrequent questions, and attentive silence. *Door openers* are noncoercive invitations that encourage speakers to begin talking. When you say to a coworker who comes from a meeting looking exhausted and depressed, "Looks like you've had a bad morning . . . want to talk about it?" you are using a door opener and allowing the other to surface feelings.

Minimal encouragers help speakers to continue talking. Nodding your head or saying "go on . . . really?" signals the speaker that you are interested in what he/she is saying. *Infrequent questions* help the listener to better understand the speaker without directing the conversation. Though we often need to ask questions/request clarification, we should not ask so many questions that we control the conversation and compel the speaker to respond to our agenda.

Attentive silence is probably the most important and most difficult digging response. Many of us feel so uncomfortable with silence that we fill pauses in conversation with questions, advice, and compulsive chatter. We don't allow speakers time to express themselves completely. During periods of silence, we should attend to and observe the other and think about what the other is communicating. The effective listener learns to both speak and listen as appropriate and feels comfortable with either (Bolton, pp. 40–48).

As we practice these digging strategies, we will be rewarded with greater success in conflict management because we will have acknowledged the importance of emotion in both interpersonal and team conflict.

Additional Suggestions for Listening to Manage Team Conflict

Since poor listening may be easier to hide as a member of a team than of a dyad, we must be especially alert to our team listening behavior.

Failing to listen by itself can trigger team conflict. Conflict can begin with the tension team members feel when others fail to listen. Think of your frustration at a meeting when team members failed to pay attention, interrupted others, responded inappropriately, or arrived unprepared because they did not listen to instructions. Perhaps the leader then scheduled another time-consuming meeting and asked you to issue a follow-up memo to members to reinforce what they "heard" at the meeting.

What about the time spent repeating instructions, policies, or problems because team members failed to understand the first time (or second or third)? The ensuing bickering and disagreement over details can distract team members from their objective. Significant conflict may never be examined and resolved satisfactorily and solutions to problems may not be optimum because of the failure to listen to and understand simple procedural and task information (Barker et al., pp. 81-82).

The Importance of Discriminative and Critical Listening in Teams.

We need to make skillful use of both discriminative and critical listening in groups. Discriminative listening contributes to our understanding and remembering what team speakers say. Without understanding and remembering, we are hardly in a position to continue communication or to choose among competing responses to events.

Critical listening allows us to judge and evaluate the speaker's message. Since teams are frequently charged with solving problems, making recommendations, or taking action, we must often move from managing conflicts to resolving them. At some point, we must choose among several competing options put forth by team members. Skill in critical listening helps us to make logical choices.

Some Final Suggestions

Remember—conflict within a team, if managed successfully, can improve the quality of decisions, stimulate involvement, and build cohesion. When you want to be sure to promote continued communication about the issues and perhaps even work out differences and reach agreements acceptable to all team members, use the suggestions below to guide your listening behavior (Barker et al., pp. 87–89).

Before the Meeting.

- *Think about the topic and the situation in advance.* In other words, prepare for the meeting. Be sure to go over the agenda and advance materials before the meeting begins.

- *Prepare yourself to listen actively.* Psyche yourself up before the meeting begins. Make a personal commitment to active listening.

- *Establish an environment conducive to listening.* Environmental distractions can allow us to rationalize poor listening. Before the meeting begins, minimize environmental distractions. Establish a comfortable, quiet, relaxed atmosphere for listening.

During the Meeting.

- *Avoid interrupting the speaker.* To the extent possible, give the speaker a chance to finish before you comment or ask questions. Some of your concerns may be laid to rest as the speaker continues. Withhold evaluation of the message until the speaker is finished and you are sure you understand it. In many cases the speaker's message is not so central to the team's purpose that it needs evaluation.

- *Seek areas of agreement with the speaker.* Instead of objecting, take a positive approach. Look for common ground to build on.

- *Search for meanings and avoid arguing about specific words.* Semantic arguments can be demoralizing and time-consuming.

- *Ask questions/request clarification when you don't under·
  stand the message.* Don't ask so many questions that you
  begin to control the speaker, but when you don't understand, ask whatever questions are necessary. Don't
  avoid questions because you think you will appear stupid in front of your colleagues. They probably have
  concerns similar to yours and will be grateful for the
  clarification.

- *Be patient.* You can listen faster than the speaker can
  speak. Use the extra time to think about and consider
  the speaker's message.

- *Compensate for attitudinal biases.* Acknowledge the perfectly human tendency toward personal listening
  barriers. If you have difficulty listening to someone
  older or younger than you, of the opposite sex, from a
  different ethnic group, competitive with you, less competent than you or whose mannerisms or personal
  appearance displease you, resolve to put aside your biases and listen for the message.

- *Listen for the speaker's principles, concepts, and feelings as
  well as the facts.* Isolated facts by themselves may be
  meaningless. You may misinterpret the facts when you
  miss the speaker's overall concept and the feelings expressed through nonverbals.

- *Compensate for emotion–arousing words and ideas.* Try
  to eliminate conditioned reactions by identifying your
  emotional triggers and counteracting their effects. Be
  objective.

- *Be flexible in your views.* Try not to be close–minded.
  Acknowledge that other views contradictory to your
  own may be possible and may even have some merit,
  although you cannot support them without reservation.

- *Listen even when the message is boring or difficult to follow.* Avoid the temptation to daydream when the
  speaker fails to excite and entertain. There may be a
  message of importance to you in what immediately
  seems boring or obscure.

After the meeting.

- *Review your listening behavior.* Resolve to continue effective behaviors and change poor ones. Remember—effective listening takes practice.

- *Review meeting outcomes.* Consider the contribution of effective listening to conflict management.

- *Prepare for the next meeting.* Go over your notes and take action as required before the next meeting.

As you reflect on your own listening behavior, keep in mind that both interpersonal and team conflict is inevitable. By listening effectively, however, we can frequently avoid the unnecessary conflict that stems from misunderstanding. We can sometimes simply agree to disagree. We can even resolve conflict by coming to decisions acceptable to all parties. Most importantly, we can manage conflict by keeping communication channels open, by balancing advocacy and inquiry.

Summary

In this chapter we discussed the importance of listening to conflict management, both interpersonally and in teams. We began by defining conflict, pointing out its positive aspects, and distinguishing between conflict resolution and conflict management. We discussed the difference between advocacy and inquiry, emphasizing the importance of developing inquiry skills. We then described three categories of listening behavior falling into the inquiry category and most appropriate to conflict management: dampening, redirecting, and digging. Our descriptions included analyses of the listening behaviors in each category. Finally, since poor listening may be easier to hide as a member of team than of a dyad, we offered additional suggestions for listening to manage team conflict.

Exercises

1. In your listening journal, record the interpersonal and team conflicts you become involved in. Each entry should include the following information:

   a. the parties to the conflict;

   b. the issues being argued;

   c. an assessment of the listening behavior of those involved, which describes the behavior and evaluates its effectiveness;

d. suggestions for listening behavior which would have improved the conflict process or outcomes.

2. Choose an issue—like drug use, environmental protection, abortion, or affirmative action—which is not likely to be resolved soon. Make a list of listening behaviors you can employ to keep the lines of communication open. Monitor your listening to see if you practice the behaviors.

3. In a small group, discuss the obstacles to managing conflict by agreeing to disagree. List listening behaviors you can practice to overcome the obstacles.

4. Observe the conflict management habits of close friends and family. Keep a log of interactions, noting especially the use of advocacy and inquiry. Consider whether these behaviors were used appropriately and how increased use of inquiry may have led to more successful conflict management.

5. Observe the listening habits of close friends and family. Keep a log of interactions which you believe called for dampening behaviors. Consider whether dampening behaviors were used appropriately and how improving dampening may have led to more successful conflict management.

6. After the next small group meeting you participate in, describe your efforts to practice discriminative or critical listening. Record the results of your efforts.

References

Barker, L. L., K. J. Wahlers, and K. W. Watson. *Groups in Process: An Introduction to Small Group Communication*. 5th edition. Englewood Cliffs: Prentice-Hall, 1995.

Bolton, R. *People Skills*. Englewood Cliffs: Prentice-Hall, 1979.

Borisoff, D., and D. A. Victor. *Conflict Management: A Communication Skills Approach*. Englewood Cliffs: Prentice-Hall, 1989.

Fisher, R., and W. Ury. *Getting to Yes: Negotiating Agreement Without Giving In*. 2nd ed. Boston: Houghton Mifflin, 1992.

Folger, J. P., and M. S. Poole. *Working Through Conflict*. Glenview, IL: Scott, Foresman & Company, 1984.

Frost, J., and W. W. Wilmot. *Interpersonal Conflict*. Dubuque, IA: William C. Brown, 1978.

Hocker, J. L., and W. W. Wilmot. *Interpersonal Conflict*. 2nd ed. Dubuque, IA: William C. Brown, 1989.

Littlejohn, S. W. *Theories of Human Communication*. Belmont, CA: Wadsworth, 1989.

Senge, P.M., C. Roberts, R. B. Ross, B. J. Smith, and A. Kleiner. *The Fifth Discipline Fieldbook, Strategies and Tools for Building a Learning Organization.* New York: Doubleday, 1994.

Sillars, A. L. "Attributions and Communication in Roommate Conflicts." *Communication Monographs* 47 (1980): 180–200.

Steil, L. K., L. L. Barker, and K. W. Watson. *Effective Listening: Key to Your Success.* Reading, MA: Addison Wesley, 1983.

Steinfatt, T., and G. R. Miller. "Communication in Game Theoretic Models of Conflict." *Perspectives on Communication in Conflict.* Eds. G. R. Miller and H. Simons. Englewood Cliffs: Prentice-Hall, 1974. 14–75.

Stuart, R. B. *Helping Couples Change: A Social Learning Approach to Marital Therapy.* New York: Guilford Press, 1980.

Watkins, C. "An Analytic Model of Conflict." *Speech Monographs* 41 (1974): 1–5.

Chapter 6

THE NEW DIGITAL PRESENCE: Listening, Access, and Computer-Mediated Life

Rob Anderson

Points to be Addressed:

- Listening skills and computer–mediated communication (CMC)
- Limitations of a source–based explanation of CMC
- Characteristics of an access theory approach to CMC
- Potential problems of on–line listening

A 10–year–old computer guru considers the Internet:

"In the short run, it may squish social relationships a little." (Kearney, 1995, p. 65)

I have friends who are dedicated computer techno–gurus, but I never expect to be one of them.

Like many people, I came late to the on–line party, and sat intimidated in the corner for a while. For several years I admired my computer more than I really used it, assuming that this box was destined to be simply my deluxe typewriter. Only recently have I worked up the courage to ask it to talk with me. Many of my friends could write a great chapter on computers from the perspective of electronic expertise. Others of us have a different credibility. I, for example, write from the perspective of naive, awestruck, semi-ignorant curiosity. Fortunately for me, this chapter need not describe how computer technology works, but concerns something more important to most of us: The revitalized importance of listening—interpretive responses to the varied forms of human speech—within the new media of electronic communicating. In addition to playing a central role in defining the quality of any human relationship (Berendt, 1985; Fiumara, 1990; Levin, 1985), listening seems critical (though not always in obvious ways) in establishing the revolutionary significance of computer-mediated communication (hereafter, CMC)[1] This essay suggests that we will understand CMC more thoroughly by comparing its essence with what we already understand about listening.[2]

CMC took many teachers and researchers by surprise. They thought they previously understood the ground rules of speaking and listening, writing and reading—but, it turns out, they were only kidding themselves.

Educators assumed for many years that these four basic skills of communication were already well defined and distinctive. Two of them involved oral messages; two involved written messages. Two were "sending" activities; two were "receiving" activities. While reading this book, you'll also discover that two of them—those involving written texts—are emphasized at all levels of Western education, while the other two—involving oral communication—are often taken for granted.

The ground rules for teaching students to communicate effectively were usually well laid-out. For example, educators assumed that the skills of talk were commonly understood and didn't take much effort, probably because most people talk every day, spontaneously and usually effortlessly, with a wide variety of friends and coworkers.

1 Some analysts (Santoro, 1994) reserve the term CMC for directly mediated forms of communication between identified persons, such as in e-mail or bulletin board systems, and use another term—like "informatics"—for database and information services phenomena. While this distinction is clear, it seems a bit artificial because the computer is clearly a mediating agency in both functions (and thus CMC is an appropriate umbrella term).
2 It would be unwise to tackle more in a brief chapter. Other sources (all of which are valuable) might be more theoretical (See Walther, 1993, 1996; and the many relevant articles in the journal *Computers in Human Behavior*, for examples), more technical (Gray, 1993), more skills based (Bruhn, 1995), or more oriented toward placing CMC in a wider context of social change (Chesebro & Bonsall, 1989; Jones, 1994).

Speaking and listening seemed to be immediate experiences, most common when people were interacting face-to-face. "Immediate," of course, suggests that something occurs without an intermediary, or without intervening or mediating circumstances. When 20th century electronic media of radio, television, and recording tape adjusted this assumption, the changes at least still seemed to resemble ordinary presence. In other words, many messages became more accessible over distance or over time, but they retained certain cues of the voice, the human image, or both, that are normally associated with immediacy. Another way of saying this is that as media become more and more "im-mediate" and sophisticated, they are *experienced* less and less like media. They seem almost to waft, to fade in and away, in a floating environment not experienced as machinelike, but as naturally involving. Therefore, while I might know intellectually that Oprah Winfrey isn't talking just to me (many of us have tuned in), or even talking to me right now (the show is taped) . . . and though I'm rationally aware that she doesn't even know who I am, it feels as if I'm addressed personally nevertheless.

At the same time, most analysts implicitly assumed writing and reading were more or less *non*-immediate experiences, involving distant encoding and deferred decoding. Reading and writing allow students to learn and even emulate literary or historical works on which the culture presumably depends. Therefore, these tasks were subject to more careful planning, seemed to depend on "higher" mental functions, and seemed more important to teach and learn. There were obvious differences of presence, too. The book I'm reading in Illinois may have been written in Mexico or Japan twenty five years ago, and my choice to read it may be only peripherally connected to the author's choice to write it. Writing therefore is considered a solitary act of creation and, except in an imaginative sense, as asocial as reading. In fact, a central myth of literature has always been the inspired, tortured, or bemused author who sat alone creating new worlds on pages that, after they were transported, became potent enough to move isolated readers to joy, to tears, or to action.

Once we reached the technological watersheds of the telegraph (which made writing and reading more interactive and spontaneous in an extended way) and the radio (which made speaking and listening spontaneous even when communicators were distant) in media history, our communication distinctions became more blurred. The speaking/listening arena, however, continued to be more immediate, spontaneous, multisensory, and, above all, social. The arena of writers/readers was still largely a "deferred" one in which reading is often radically divorced from writing in time and space. Writing and reading, therefore, encouraged styles that were often self-consciously strategic, unisensory, oriented toward persuasion, and, above all, individualized and often idiosyncratic. Writers spin out webs of thought and reasoning for their readers that listeners would never put up with from speakers, especially in an electronic age. Twentieth cen-

tury educators and researchers have assumed that the major characteristic of speaking/listening was its capacity for fixing presence (but
it was often so ephemeral); the defining characteristic of writ-
ing/reading, on the other hand, was its potential for transcending or
tolerating distance and absence (but it was often so durable that it became locked to particular historical moments and thus potentially
dated).

Written and spoken modes offered their own advantages, of
course. Speech, especially in face-to-face situations, provides more
holistic clues to meaning, including a speaker's appearance, vocal
tone, and gestures. Written texts invite, presume, and, in fact, shape a
more linear rationality. Newspapers have placed themselves at the
nexus of vast networks of context, and have been able to spin out
complicated stories and nuances that broadcasters can only hint at.
Still, in the midst of all this change, *what never seemed to change* was
that the point of origin, in effect, of news and entertainment—of information—was always *out there*. Someone elsewhere had to decide
that I needed to know what they wanted to say or write. Audiences,
in a sense, were at the beck and call of message producers. In the
process, they became consumers in the functional sense, in the service
of communication entrepreneurs.

However, "what never seemed to change" has changed.

Whereas message receivers have been waiting on senders throughout the century, the basic vocabulary of communication's
conventional wisdom is called into question by the new deferred
digital presence of on-line networks. Who are the senders now, and
who are the receivers? What is writing, and how does it differ conceptually from speaking, when writing is also immediate, and is not
only an instrument of presence, but often of real-time presence in
computer bulletin boards, "chat rooms," and on-line forums? How is
listening conceptually different from reading, when they are both
immediate experiences, and potentially equally ephemeral? And how
is our experience of communication affected by this emerging-
merging environment that emphasizes messages that do not necessarily seem directed or aimed at receivers at all, messages that seem
somehow to "float" between people? Floating messages function in
ways similar to how human speech is accessible to any listener within
earshot. Whereas directed messages presuppose the sender's
(predecided) purposes, floating messages presuppose the listener's
(potential) purposes. Reading in such an environment, it seems, takes
on central characteristics of listening, with interesting consequences
for presence and immediacy.

I've tried to address such questions by organizing this chapter
around two open and unresolved issues. First, what interpersonal
concepts are most appropriate to this radically blended communication system? Access and listening, for example, are two especially

important concepts for understanding on-line environments. Second, do serious social relationship problems emerge from our perhaps too-rapid and too-trendy embrace of on-line technologies?

Theoretical Questions: Communication as *Directedness* or *Access*?

Communication and Directedness Theory

> "We're on the on-ramp of the Information Superhighway—the engine's running—but we don't really know where we are going yet." (NBC vice-president, quoted in Newhagen, Cordes, & Levy, 1995, p. 174)

Although theorists generally agree that communication should not be seen as analogous to a pipeline or conduit, or, for that matter, a highway, most everyday conceptions of successful interpersonal or media communication essentially depend upon "aim, point, and shoot" or transportation assumptions. We assume that listeners listen *because* speakers decide to talk (although an equally strong case can be made for the converse), and that someone's talking because they have decided and intended to try to influence someone else by loading certain meanings into certain words and then transporting those words—almost as if they were containers—to an intended audience. Michael Reddy (1979) has called this common assumption the *conduit metaphor.*

This assumption is often prevalent in the mass media. Consider how you come to listen to a radio program, watch a television show, or read a newspaper. Your "reception" of, let's say, an infomercial about an exercise contraption, is near the end of a complex sequence of production decisions made by professionals. Although your own contribution is the consumer's choice whether to call the 1–800 number to order your Thigh-Twister or Ab-Flatter, many other people had to cooperate to send those words and images to you.

The *direction* or sequence of these decisions is clear enough. Someone was expected to do research on what kinds of pitch would be most effective with intended audiences who might be tuning in. (Sometimes this "research" is merely the previous experience of the communicators, creating routines and habitual assumptions about what audiences like.) Someone else brainstormed scenarios and alternative strategies that could fit both the goals of senders and the anticipated needs or desires of receivers. Others are paid to compare alternative messages, refine possibilities, and fit them to strategies by writing and producing the video. Finally, some celebrity with great thighs and a flat abdomen rehearses for days in order to sound appropriately spontaneous and inspiring as you pause briefly in your channel-surfing at the sight of the body you'd desperately like to have.

Even though researchers and teachers understand that interaction is far more complicated than implied by conduit assumptions, the fact that these usually *are* our assumptions affects how we define communication itself in everyday life: Producers do have audiences in mind, direct messages toward those audiences, and try to get their points "across." Aim, point, and shoot. To Berger, Berger, and Kellner (1974), "modernized" culture overvalues packaging and commercialization, and has to create consumers for all its packages. "If it is to be grasped in its full impact, modernization must be regarded as a process by which specific clusters of institutions and contents of consciousness are transmitted," they write (p. 119). Messages are designed to span the gap from sender to receiver. The metaphor of this "acrossness," this *directedness*, is revealing, and could be illustrated simply:

A ———> [message/package] ———> B

None of this should be surprising to anyone who has taken an introductory interpersonal or public speaking course lately. Yet the point is not merely that communication is more complicated than this simplistic model would suggest. Rather, until recently, these communication assumptions of directedness—while simplistic—were remarkably functional. Although they are misleading in serious ways, not the least of which was that they underestimated the listening and receptive aspects of interaction, social communication based on those assumptions was often successful and served valid functions. But even while we try to cling to transportation metaphors like "the information superhighway," computers have changed us irretrievably.

Communication and Access Theory

Access . . . signifies the ability to do what everybody else can do and to make use of what everybody else can use; access means the liberty to take advantage of resources. (Wurman, 1990, p. 45)

The abundance lies not only in the manipulation of text on one's own computer and data storage but also in the magical word which will replace libraries: *access*. As we have seen in previous chapters, the nature of digital text is characterized by linkage in an *essential* way. (Heim, 1987, p. 217)

Appreciating listening as essential linkage is not easy in a culture that appears to value message production more highly. We take many classes in how to write, and few in how to read. (Although we're expected to develop reading skills naturally, no one expects us to develop writing skills naturally.) Schools teach classes in public speaking, which are often required; almost no one is required to take public listening courses, and listening courses of any kind are unfortunately rare. People admire celebrities or charismatic friends who are loquacious, but we often label especially good listeners as too shy, wishy-washy, laid back, or timid.

Yet it is through listening that communicators ultimately create access to their culture's resources. Media moguls may imagine they're putting messages and meanings into our heads, but they're really only offering them to (toward?) us. Listeners can turn off, and often do. The gap between sender and receiver must always be sparked, at least in part, from the second pole, the listener's pole. And this means the distance must be bridged, at least in part, from the listener's experience. Despite society's directedness assumptions, listeners are not receptacles but active meaning-makers. This is their advantage, and this is their burden.

We now confront a new watershed of technology. Some have called this the time when we can look simultaneously backward and forward in order to recognize the varying influences of both "old media" and "new media" (See Rice & Associates, 1984; Taylor & Saarinen, 1994). Looking backward, we see the modernizing influence of transmitted packages, as Berger, Berger, and Kellner describe. Earlier, I suggested we could call this *directedness theory*. But looking forward, we see newer media that operate by the very different assumptions of what appears to be an *access theory*.

The new media stress certain characteristics more than older forms like print, radio, film, or television. Several interdependent characteristics are especially important:

1. They involve computers at basic levels of person(s)-with-person(s) connection. Consider:

- the shift from isolated single-author writing to "word processing," which often involves multiauthor manipulation of texts (Heim, 1987);

- shopping via the World Wide Web or researching via on-line databases like Lexis/Nexis or Dialog;

- highly interactive, talk-like writing via e-mail and electronic bulletin board services.

2. They involve merged media, merged human senses, and thus more immersive experiences. Consider:

- the extent to which satellite digital technology, computers, and phone lines have merged to facilitate viewer participation with, and control over, a myriad of specialized television channels;

- how "virtual reality" simulations immerse individuals' experience immediately in sensations that both are, and aren't, "present"—how virtual travelers can at the same time "be there" without leaving "here" (Rheingold, 1991).

3. They shift message responsibilities, thus involving audiences more as coauthors than as receivers. Consider:

- the branching choices invited by hypertext software, the versatile vastness of CD-ROM technology, and the multitude of "user"-determined choices in videodisks and CDs, all of which make messages available differently to different persons (in some new fiction, the question for the "reader/listener" isn't, "how does the story end?," but "how do *my* choices shape the ending?");

- messages that once were intended to serve a single purpose are now literally multifaceted and suggest multiple meanings (the programmers' work is infinitely reprogrammable by others); in terms of discourse, we are moving, in other words, from a modern era of statements and certainty into a "postmodern" era of questions, ambivalences, and linkages.

4. They rearrange time and place sensibilities. Consider:

- the linear cause-to-effect and here-to-there assumptions of directedness theory have given way to more multicausal views and message ambiguities;

- previous assurances of what is and isn't real no longer seem to apply. Where, for example, is the "original" message in an e-mail system to be found? When I send one e-mail to one person and what's called on my system a "cc" ('carbon—or complimentary—copy') of it to another person, neither literally is an original, and neither a copy, because both are composed at the same time, available to addressees at the same time, and their texts are indistinguishable apart from the headings. As each is sent, what's on my screen vanishes (unless I explicitly save a "copy"—of what?— for myself!). For the first time in the history of human communication, texts can be both originals and copies simultaneously.

In other words, our former habits of talking about communication are outmoded.

5. They blur the traditional modern concepts of power and responsibility. Consider:

- it used to be clear that to "respond" to a message, someone else needed to "author" it first. When revolutionary movements took over countries, they seized centers of message production (newspapers, broadcast facilities) first, because power meant the ability to control message production. Now, increasingly, the respondents—to the presence of databases, for example—reauthor, reconfigure or edit messages at will. Although persons seeking power have always sought to control access to information, anyone now interested in power must consider access first, not just as a consequence of message production. Corporate employees who are fired unexpectedly sometimes get their first clue when their e-mail account can't be accessed;

- it's harder with all this in mind to conceptualize brainwashing or propaganda as the imposition of outside or centralized authority on the will of helpless citizens; more worrisome is an information poverty in some social groups based upon differential access to common resources (See Barlow, 1995).

Notice how much all these overlapping characteristics depend less upon skills of encoding messages, and more upon either: (a) skills of "decoding" we have traditionally associated with listening, responding, and interpreting, or (b) skills that simply do not fit into the old categories.

The new media now fueled by an on-line culture are moving inevitably in the direction of a listening model. Immersion, coauthorship, interdependence, and interpretive responsibility are the keys to this new model. Effective listeners always have known they had to immerse themselves in a kind of ecology of experience; they've always known they were to some extent coauthors in communication; they've known that listening and speaking are not really separable, but are interdependent processes that co-create "presence"; they've known that social and political power has never resided solely with dictators, presidents, or charismatic speakers and writers, but also with the responsiveness and responsibilities of listeners. Listening is a phenomenologically different experience than observing or reading, in that sound surrounds us (Ihde, 1976; Ong, 1982). We listen, experientially speaking, *within* sound, not *outside* it, *to* it, or *toward* it. A listener turns—changes perspective—yet still can hear, for the sound refuses to be bound entirely by perspective or direction. With computers, we are similarly surrounded by the medium as it expects particular actions and responses from us. The medium is simultaneously an *extension of us* and *an environment for us* (McLuhan, 1964).

Computers are not just tools or even conduits, but create their own experiential listening environment that is becoming increasingly naturalistic and pervasive in human life. Even when distant computer users have different machines, monitors, and operating systems, they have no difficulty believing they are bringing up the "same" screen. Something informationally involving therefore surrounds communicators as if they were together, in a given physical place. They are, in fact together, but they've accepted as "given" a new type of nonphysical place. They are together in it, though they remain paradoxically apart from each other. Thus, even if we are "reading" texts within its boundaries, that reading is experientially closer to listening than it is to reading a book, for example. This point is very similar to Lanham's observations about the value of electronic texts, such as his own "hypertext" book, *The Electronic Word* (1993), "published" on computer disk.

The computer culture forces us to redefine what mediated communication means. The new media seldom appear to be "mass communication" (traditionally, the broadcasting of a single message structure to large audiences simultaneously), even when large groups gain access to messages. They are much closer in spirit to interpersonal communication, taken in its person–with–person sense rather than its face–to–face sense (although computer–mediated communication may be visual as well). Older directedness assumptions of mass communication and persuasive communication will no longer serve us well; what we recognize as human *presence* has been altered beyond recognition. Whereas directedness theory aims and points messages at audiences for predetermined purposes, access theory creates forums for messages within which persons develop access to information and to each other, in "real time" or "deferred time" experiences. Presence, which used to be idealized as immediate fleshly presence, can now be experienced in a mediated way. Presence can now be, in other words, deferred and distant—and this is not experienced in any way as contradictory (Anderson, 1994).

An access model of our new distant presence operates on different assumptions, and therefore must be understood differently. (The catchy phrase "distant presence" was evidently first used in the communication literature by Gozzi & Haynes [1992], but their application appears to refer to all electric media that span distances; therefore there are real differences from how I develop "presence" here.) In the old culture, messages and meanings were transmitted or transported; in the new, messages are offered, deposited and—in some sense—invested. Although it is an oversimplification, we might consider a database as the prototypical example of access theory:

A—>[Forum: Shared Access Messages]<—B

The basic assumption here is that certain communicators provide (contribute, upload, offer) messages to a commonly accessible forum that both *reflect* their own realities and that may *affect* the experience of others. By providing an array of messages, they construct and inhabit a new common site or space for talk, to which they themselves have access (they not only contribute, but also can respond), as well as creating something a wide variety of other agents can access. A good example of this is the "Experts" project on the on-line service called the WELL. Its premise is simple:

> If you have a problem or a question concerning any topic, from plumbing to astrophysics, you pose it. Then you wait seven minutes or a week. Sometimes nothing happens, and sometimes you get exactly what you want. In many instances, the answer already exists elsewhere in the WELL, and the topic serves as a kind of community librarian service that points the query toward the right part of the WELL's collection of information. And in some instances, the information requested exists in someone's head and that person takes the time to type it. (Rheingold, 1994, p. 60)

Availability is the key, *but transportation is in no sense the guiding metaphor*, as it was in the old media. Habitation—a living within—feels like a more apt metaphor. Rheingold, in fact, describes the communication system of on-line life in architectural and spatial terms—when you access different services or databases, it is very much like moving from room to room in a building (pp. 62-63). To interact in CMC is to inhabit a kind of space that is built by the communication itself.

Access theory also changes other aspects of where and how we live. Not long ago, a friend bought a new computer that had software for Prodigy, the commercial on-line information service, preloaded. An intelligent, educated, and sophisticated person, she nevertheless had trouble initially (as I did) in grasping the concept of e-mail. Her questions: "Why don't I have to have my computer turned on for people to 'send' me e-mail?" "How does the e-mail know where I live, or where my computer is located?" Her questions were motivated by the natural assumption that on-line communication is similar to what computer folks now derisively call "snail mail" (in which packages are first carefully addressed by senders so that a third party can take them directly by to their destinations) or similar to face-to-face expectations (people ideally ought to be in each other's immediate presence).

To understand on-line culture, though, we release our transportation and conduit assumptions because they are no longer functional. We move, again, to a listening model. As effective listeners have known all along, to "receive" a message, you cannot be just a receptacle; instead, you reach out to meet the message—the idea, the meaning, the feeling—at least halfway. The listening self is in motion, taking action, traveling, connecting, accessing.

My friend's e-mail address is not equivalent to her home address because it is a *different sense of place*, and therefore represents for human communication a *fundamentally different sense of presence*. A postal address is her home; an e-mail address indicates her electronic homelessness. If I post an e-mail message for her, it doesn't go to her, and it thus is not really "sent to her" at all. It resides in a computer neither mine nor hers that neither of us knows (in all likelihood) how to get to, and there it waits for her choice to access it.

This new CMC environment is analogous to Martin Buber's concept of "the between," which he claimed was the elemental reality of our human living (Buber, 1965a; 1965b). The analogy is ironic, because of Buber's notion that electronic technologies hindered dialogue; in another sense, though, it is quite helpful. Buber has shown that humans' fundamental presence for each other cannot be *psychological* but is *relational*. The "between" where we meet is where we really live and are present for each other, not in our minds. Similarly, on-line communication is conducted in a digitized "between" region.

While our culture has become more computer-saturated, we've noticed important clues that these newer forms of communication are experientially very similar to what we've previously understood as listening. Although many metaphors in these early stages of a new technology build upon the old directedness assumptions that are most easily recognized by written messages ("mail," "bulletin boards," etc.), increasingly the medium is morphing into re-oralized forms ("chat" rooms, "discussion groups," etc.). Ong (1982) would recognize this as an implication of "secondary orality," the developmental stage of human life that extends our former emphasis on literacy.

Indeed, in e-mail and real-time on-line discussion groups, people typically refer to their experience in speaking/listening terms rather than as writing/reading ("I tell them it's like using the phone only cheaper . . . I tell them they can talk to people all over the world if they want," "I say it's a way to talk to people all over the country from your computer"—bulletin board veterans quoted by Metz, 1995, p. 5), and most e-mail participants habitually emulate speech more than prose, producing short, relatively spontaneous, colloquial, and often unedited messages primarily designed to evoke replies. In addition, on-line enthusiasts supplement written messages with an array of symbols (often called "emoticons" or "smileys") designed to augment electronic messages with some of the nonverbal context on which listeners rely in face-to-face conversation. For example, read sideways to get this clue about a "speaker's" good will: :-) or this clue that the on-line speaker is really surprised or amazed: :-O.

Perhaps most important in the long run, we should note the unbureaucratic and conversational nature of the Internet, that vast system of interconnected computers that allows individual users to contact other users globally (so that theoretically no place and no person is "distant" in the older sense). The regulation of the Internet may be unbureaucratic (at least to this point), but it is regulated nevertheless. Its informal regulation mimics how everyday talk is coordinated; that is, the Internet's viability depends upon a humane, community-based or ensemble sense of how speakers and listeners can work together to guarantee the optimum quality and kind of use for the optimum number of persons. Internet protocol depends upon the assumption that large groups of people will not take unfair advantage of their opportunities to do just that, primarily because of implicit sanctions and emerging tradition. This, of course, is true more in the ideal than in how the ideal translates into practice, but most communication theorists are probably struck by how well, not how sloppily, the Internet works.

To summarize, new access theory assumptions of on-line communication recognize the listening needs of humans, not just their speaking and writing needs. As we interact with computers, we are immersed in many of the same ways as we are when surrounded by sound. We treat "electric writing" (Heim, 1987) as if it were speech—spontaneously with immediacy and the assumption of presence—and its reading therefore as if it were a new kind of listening. Recently, I read the announcement of a new chat room with a graphics dimension that allows participants to choose icons (pictures) to represent themselves; all who've logged on can watch (and presumably eventually "hear") as various characters (personae) "talk" within the virtual room. Such is our current preoccupation with computer simulation of the dynamics of face-to-face talk.

Access theory, arising out of new media technology, reminds us that receivers are not receptacles, and must "move toward" persons and messages rather than just waiting for them passively. This movement is to a new space, *a new distant and deferred presence*, that is strangely both unfamiliar and familiar. This sense of presence is unfamiliar because the old metaphors seem oddly dissonant; it is also familiar, however, as it legitimizes what philosophers like Martin Buber have shown to be the essence of communication.

Seductions of Trendiness:
Problems for Listeners in On-Line Life

Innovative trends can lead to trendiness. Many critics are worried that an uncritical acceptance of computer-mediated communication may reduce our ability to deal with communication problems in ongoing, open and humanistic ways. What skills are necessary for listeners in this new digital presence? A brief survey of the dangers of on-line culture will let us consider those skills more carefully.

1. CMC, while extending presence in some ways, still offers essentially *thin* versions of human presence.

While listeners in face-to-face contexts have multiple channels available to them, digital listeners may *feel* immersed in the process without really having access to the range of visual, auditory, vocal, and other nonverbal interpersonal cues that usually put messages in appropriate context. "For some reason," says Internet expert Tracy LaQuey (1993), "people become much more sensitive when they're on line, and they tend to blow things entirely out of proportion—for example, taking a couple of sentences originally meant to be humorous or sarcastic entirely the wrong way. If that happens, everything can go downhill quickly" (p. 71). Therefore, what listening researchers call "active listening" becomes especially crucial. Check out the assumptions you develop about others and their intentions. When appropriate, paraphrase the other's message and make explicit your developing interpretations. E-mail, to cite an obvious example, has developed an etiquette of brevity, but messages can become so abrupt and informal that writers (who are imagining—not facing—their readers) risk presuming too much. Always remind yourself to take full advantage of the essential interactivity of the medium.

2. CMC, at least in its current forms, offers new temptations of inauthenticity.

The popular press is full of stories about computer bulletin board participants or "chat room" users who try on new roles experimentally, and spin out elaborate lies about their everyday identities. Some stories are lurid (on-line romances between two people both of whom are misrepresenting their sexual preferences), but some are sad in other ways (people thinking they have to talk about cars they don't have, or people won't like them). Of course, people misrepresent themselves in non-CMC, too, but on-line listeners might want to remind themselves that it isn't necessarily cynical to be cautious about forming rapid first impressions on the basis of the content of another's disclosures. "Joan," a Compuserve chat regular in the 1980s, inspired many people with her experience of overcoming multiple physical injuries caused by a horrible disfiguring car accident that also left her mute and depressed. This was fine, except that "Joan" turned out to be a New York psychiatrist named Alex, who "in real life, IRL, was neither disabled, disfigured, mute, nor female." He had just "become obsessed with his own experiments in being treated as a female and participating in female friendships" (Rheingold, 1994, p. 165).

3. CMC could deflect face-to-face presence, and forego its benefits.

There is always the danger of this new digital listening becoming more important than going out to meet people face-to-face. The stereotype of the computer "nerd" is unfair and often vicious, but within it is this kernel of truth: Instead of profiting by increased social contact, some people cloister themselves with electronic technologies behind closed doors. A recent popular film, "The Net," dramatized the identity dilemmas of computer junkies and fashioned an intriguing adventure out of them. A young woman working out of her own home invested so much of her life as a technical on-line consultant that when the bad guys discovered how dangerous she could be to their plan (you get the picture; their actual motives aren't germane), they were able to "vanish" her identity, making her essentially a nonperson. By breaking into various computers ("hacking"), they made changes that shifted her identity to another person entirely. Her neighbors didn't know what she looked like, and even her coworkers knew virtually nothing about her non-on-line personality. Not able to access her financial accounts, government records, or other proof of who she was, she could barely think of anyone with whom she'd maintained a recent face-to-face relationship. Although hardly a profound movie, "The Net" does serve as a cautionary tale about how many of the bright and exciting opportunities afforded by CMC also carry a potentially dark side. To what extent do our identities increasingly reside in the traces of digital records rather than in the experiences of people who interact with us as embodied communicators? We would be wise to take such questions seriously, and not assume that they only come from slow learners and technological foot-draggers.

We have other problems of interpersonal communication to confront also. Even assuming that CMC can have interpersonal quality, could an uncritical immersion in on-line culture increase your access only to very narrow corridors of culture? While Sandra Bullock played the central role in "The Net," many attracted to the new CMC form of semi-isolation from face-to-face interaction evidently are men (Cobb, 1995), and we might assume too that inexperienced or ineffective interpersonal listeners are especially tempted to make this substitution. We already know that many other social groups (such as African-Americans) are seriously under-represented in on-line life, and that the cost of computer equipment makes certain kinds of access an economic privilege, too (See Barlow, 1995). Instead of expanding our awareness of otherness, on-line culture may provide new narrow-listening enclaves of sexism, racism, and classism.

4. CMC's access assumptions paradoxically may encourage people to become lazy listeners and ill-informed knowers.

"An axiom of the hypertextual environment," write media philosophers Mark Taylor and Esa Saarinen, is that "the speed of information processing is inversely proportional to the rate of retention of the information processed" (1994, p. "speed 9"); with more rapid dissemination of information, we get more rapid forgetting. If this seems odd, consider how the information environment has changed lately. If vast amounts of information are instantaneously available, why should we have to remember or know anything independent of what the database can provide immediately on call? In a total access environment, what is the value of *human* recall, indeed of traditional information-retention education itself, apart from remembering how to ask the computer your question? "I can always look it up" could be the emerging mantra for digital communicators, and in this attitude lies a danger if it suggests that you don't need to listen carefully in order to learn. The new challenge for everyday citizens is to quit thinking of face-to-face listening in terms of raw information processing, and redefine it largely in terms of "discriminative listening"—interpreting the links between unsolved problems meaningfully. Accuracy will fade somewhat as a criterion for listening effectiveness; discernment and evaluation will become increasingly important. Accuracy implies a content orientation, and we now live in a process-oriented era.

As an example of the difference between retention listening and discriminative listening in an on-line culture, imagine yourself as a student in tomorrow's lecture hall at the local college. Do you bring paper and pen to scribble furiously the content of Professor Smart's lecture? Although you might want to jot some notes about the good professor's insights, your own hand-held or laptop computer give you virtually instant access to the same range of information available to Dr. Smart. You need not try to record many facts in your notes. Still, that doesn't mean you don't listen. It's literally not the amount of information that is the problem, nor the possibility of retaining it accurately from the lecture to the final exam. No, the major problem you face is listening carefully enough—and in a discriminating, thoughtful mode—to the lecture to hear new ways to synthesize the information or new ways to apply it creatively. In the new computer-mediated environment, teachers are freed to de-emphasize information retention and emphasize how information and decisions may be linked creatively. However, if teachers and students continue to define education as directed information transfer through oral communication, then many learners will decide unfortunately that this brand of education just isn't worth their time.

5. CMC often diminishes responsibility for message content, which can diminish quality control in disseminating knowledge.

This issue is related to the previous concern. Access theory, as it becomes institutionalized, will proliferate information. We'll have more and more information, but paradoxically, we'll be less and less sure about its validity. Even now, many critics are worried about the tendency of some on-line communicators to get their medical advice from forums, libraries, and bulletin board systems. Although thousands of reputable journals, magazines, and newspapers are available through the Internet and commercial services, a quack, a prankster, or an ignoramus can upload authoritative-sounding advice just as easily. Academic and scientific journals, for instance, employ blind review procedures to ensure quality control of what is published. Yet the nature of "publishing" is changing, and it's far from clear whether electronic sites can ever maintain the same kinds of oversight of quality that paper information systems did. It's wonderful to have millions more bits of information to retrieve, but what about a system with millions of additional opportunities for that information to be just plain wrong, maliciously misleading, or unintentionally misinterpreted out of context? CMC listeners will need to be careful in developing their own contextual criteria for determining what they need.

6. CMC's access-driven theory presently concentrates on information, which isn't necessarily a guarantee of access to a more dialogic system of response.
One point I stress in classes is that an audience's listening style in many ways regulates a speaker's speaking style. By "regulates," I do not mean that listening style fully determines what will be said, but that when speakers note certain reactions in their audiences, they are likely to try to adjust to meet newly perceived challenges. In other words, the fact that someone is listening, along with the shape of their listening, becomes a valuable feedback system in and of itself. An access model of CMC, carried to its logical conclusion, runs the danger of creating—from a speaker's perspective—the challenge of overcoming a sense of audiencelessness even though the *actual* audience might be huge. At the very least, feedback will take new forms, and more of the overt responsibility for reporting it will fall upon listeners. Electronic listeners must respond not just by using information but by contributing relevant messages to the broader cultural conversation. Although speech scholar Stephen Smith (1994) foregrounds the potential for a "polyphonic national public dialogue" (p. 91), historian and media critic Mark Poster (1995) is not encouraged about the potential for a new "public sphere" emerging from Internet culture: "True, the Net allows people to talk as equals. But rational argument rarely prevails, and achieving consensus is widely seen as impossible. These are symptoms of the fundamentally different ways identity is defined in the public sphere and on the Net" (p. 135).

Another fear that concerns communication theorists is that a new access model invites new forms of control, even including new censorship dangers. Almost paradoxically, although the new technologies offer vastly increased interactivity, there is also a corresponding shift from what legal theorist Monroe Price (1995) calls "open terrains of speech" (where whoever chooses to listen is invited to do so) to "closed terrains" (where listeners' access is controlled by their wealth, prestige, or in-group membership). As access becomes paramount, *who gets to listen in* and *when they can listen* become issues that invite regulation. He perceives our communication system as moving from an open theater-like metaphor to something quite different:

> One example . . . is the conception of the public library and public information sources. Formerly a reservoir of books and materials available to all at no charge, the "library" is reemerging as a variety of databases, information to be metered, charged by the minute or the megabyte. Far more is available, more conveniently, but not in the conventional form of the common building with wooden chairs and tables and books available, without a fee, to all alike (Price, 1995, p. 68).

The move to closed speech and information terrains raises many vexing questions for democratic decision-making, and for the definition of public citizenship itself. Communication planners should recognize that even though CMC technology is itself potentially highly interactive, access to that technology (literally, *access to the access* to information) is not itself automatically easy or interactive.

7. CMC opens up new dangers for invasion of privacy; citizens are more vulnerable to unwanted "listening in" from others.

Paradoxically again, our newfound opportunities for access to information solve one problem while raising the potential for another. One advantage of CMC for consumers is the opportunity to shop at home. We can now follow stocks from home, do research on companies we may want to work for, download test results for new cars or stereos, make elaborate travel plans, or even sample musical and literary works. Communicators should be aware, however, that listening in on the world of commerce this way is equivalent to being listened to. Listening in this tightly webbed environment literally becomes another form of message-sending. Poster (1990) warns:

> Today's "circuits of communication" and the databases they generate constitute a Superpanopticon, a system of surveillance without walls, windows, towers or guards. The quantitative advances in the technologies of surveillance result in a qualitative change in the microphysics of power. Technological change, however, is only part of the process. The populace has been disciplined to surveillance and to participating in the process. Social security cards, drivers' licenses, credit cards, library cards and the like—the individual must apply for them, have them ready at all times, use them continuously. Each transaction is recorded, encoded and added to the databases. Individuals themselves in many cases fill out the forms; they are at once the source of information and the recorder of the information. Home networking constitutes the streamlined culmination of this phenomenon: the consumer, by ordering products through a modem connected to the producer's database, enters data about himself or herself directly into the producer's database in the very act of purchase. (p. 93)

A clear implication of this problem: As citizens and consumers are able to gain more thorough access to information and to other people, we also expand *their* access to areas of our lives that were previously private. The line between public and private blurs. Some listening from others we crave; other listening from others we consider eavesdropping. Is that line blurring, too?

8. CMC paradoxically could invite listeners to overspecialize their listening, tuning out many possibilities of otherness.

In *Being Digital*, Nicholas Negroponte, the Director of the Media Lab at MIT, presents quite a persuasive case for a personalized electronic newspaper (1995, pp. 152-154). No longer would you need to read all that news that doesn't concern you, those things you might skip over and try to ignore anyway, those things that annoy or anger you about the news selections of reporters and editors. Instead, the digital revolution now can provide software that lets you preconfigure the news you want to know about. You can enter your preferences, and while you're sleeping the electronic newspaper will be assembling itself according to your personal dictates. Negroponte describes all this in a chapter appropriately titled "Personal Filters," and the resulting news could be called, he jokes, *The Daily Me* (p. 153). Ideally, says Negroponte, such a newspaper could be equipped with a kind of "knob" for dialing up (or down) personalization, so that on some occasions you'll want to scan only those things you know will be personally relevant to you, while other times you may want to explore some wider issues.

Some days, this innovation sounds incredibly helpful. Mostly, it sounds scary. How, for example, do you already know what will be relevant for you tomorrow, unless you paid careful attention to yesterday's, last week's, or last month's, news? One essential element of listening is the capacity for being surprised. Effective listeners haven't already made up their minds.

The electronic paper provides the technological enabler for filtering out all the news about conservatives from the papers of liberals, and vice-versa. David Duke supporters can eliminate all the news about Jesse Jackson from their newspapers . . . except, if they so stipulate, any negative stories. One of your neighbors might opt for an all good-news format, without murder stories, while your own paper could be all sports or entirely national financial news without all those annoying reports of racial unrest downtown. Granted, listening is always selective at some level anyway, and large newspapers are always going to be read somewhat selectively. Yet, when citizens go to the polls, or serve on juries, they vote on the same issues. We should be wary of technological advances that invite people to fragment listening further. The militia-based right and the radical progressive left may not like each other, but at least they're "on the same page" in today's *Post, Times, USA Today* or *Monitor-Index*. A virtual paper that artificially slivers our access to certain kinds of news is not necessarily an advance for anything other than selfishness, even though it may multiply the number of possible slivers.

Summary

As computers become more central in our lives, opportunities for communication change in both radical and subtle ways. With CMC, our assumptions even about what constitutes communication change at the same time. Communication is no longer the process put in motion by a sender envisioning what messages will do to receivers; it is no longer essentially a speaker's or writer's game with messages *directed* toward audiences. Instead, active listening now becomes the communication skill that must be mastered if persons are to be competent in the new deferred presence mandated by digital culture. That culture encourages *access* assumptions now.

It's not as if all bets are off, but people are understandably somewhat puzzled about how to negotiate these new demands on communicating. No longer is it clear who is a sender and who a receiver. Who is responsible for a message in an environment like hypertext when "receivers" don't just receive, but actually coauthor or re-form the text itself? Nor are originals and copies of CMC messages always distinguishable any more. *Now* and *here* don't seem to define the only time or the only place for us to be present for each other. Forms of mediated presence are possible as well. Persons seem to be here and there at the same time, or present somewhere together at different times, mixing time and space. Computers sometimes seem like tools for our communication, sometimes like media for containing and sending our messages, sometimes like extensions of ourselves, sometimes like artificially intelligent others with whom we can communicate, and most often like environments in which we live, immersed as if in the midst of sound.

To understand listening as a "between" process is to take the first step toward understanding the new on-line culture. Yet there are dangers, too, and new demands placed upon listeners, in computer-mediated communication. Achieving a "virtual community" (Rheingold, 1994) is possible, but involves different practical skills than public communication has ever demanded before. Many of us delayed careful consideration of CMC until absolutely necessary. Waiting too long, I paid a price for delaying while I simply used these Macs as glitzy editorial assistants. Now I'm listening better, but with so much to hear catching up seems impossible. . . .

Exercises:

1. (If you consider yourself a computer rookie):

    a. Ask a computer-savvy friend if you can join him or her at the keyboard during a conversation on-line in a forum or chat room. Listen both for how the conversation flows and for how your friend decides when to reply.

    b. Investigate several different methods of obtaining an e-mail address for yourself.

2. (If you consider yourself a more experienced computer user):

3. Locate an "electronic book" on floppy disk or CD-ROM. (Richard Lanham's *The Electronic Word*, published in a hypercard version of the University of Chicago Press in 1993, is especially appropriate for students interested in communication). Read through several chapters, using all the interactive features of an electronic text environment. How is this kind of reading different from turning pages in a normal book? Do you think there are advantages to ink-and-paper books that electronic publishing will never achieve?

4. Interview an experienced reference librarian at a large library to discover how many—and which—databases are available to you free of charge, and which topics they cover. Plan a schedule for yourself in which you'll access and research several databases most closely related to your personal interests (history? Art? Education? Politics? Religion?).

5. Discuss with several friends what it feels like to be known and accepted in a community (a sports team, a particularly cooperative neighborhood, a club, a sorority or fraternity). In your opinion, is such a sense of interpersonal support possible on-line in what Howard Rheingold calls "virtual communities?" Why or why not? Compare your opinion with those of other people who have read this chapter. What kind of evidence would support - or refute - your stance on this issue.

References

Anderson, R. (1994). Anonymity, presence, and the dialogic self in a technological culture. In R. Anderson, K. N. Cissna, & R. C. Arnett (Eds.), *The reach of dialogue: Confirmation, voice, & community* (pp. 91-110). Cresskill, NJ: Hampton.

Barlow, J. P. (1995, March-April). Is there a there in cyberspace? *Utne Reader, 68,* 52-56.

Berendt, J. E. (1992). *The third ear: On listening to the world* (T. Nevill, Trans.). New York: Henry Holt.

Berger, P., Berger, B., & Kellner, H. (1974). *The homeless mind: Modernization and consciousness.* New York: Vintage Books.

Bruhn, M. J. (1995). E-mail's conversational value. *Business Communication Quarterly, 58,* 43-44.

Buber, M. (1965a). *Between man and man* (R. G. Smith, Trans.). New York: Macmillan.

Buber, M. (1965b). *The knowledge of man: A philosophy of the interhuman* (M. Friedman, Trans.). New York: Harper & Row.

Chesebro, J. W., & Bonsall, D. G. (1989). *Computer-mediated communication: Human relationships in a computerized world.* Tuscaloosa, AL: University of Alabama Press.

Cobb, N. (1995, June 7). Gender styles clash on the internet. *St. Louis Post-Dispatch*, pp. E1, E5.

Fiumara, G. C. (1990). *The other side of language: A philosophy of listening* (C. Lambert, Trans.). London: Routledge.

Gozzi, R., Jr., & Haynes, W. L. (1992). Electric media and electric epistemology: Empathy at a distance. *Critical Studies in Mass Communication, 9*, 217-228.

Gray, S. H. (1993). *Hypertext and the technology of conversation: Orderly situational choice.* Westport, CN: Greenwood.

Heim, M. (1987). *Electric language: A philosophical study of word processing.* New Haven, CN: Yale University Press.

Ihde, D. (1976). *Listening and voice: A phenomenology of sound.* Athens: Ohio University Press.

Jones, S. (Ed.). (1994). *Cybersociety: Computer-mediated communication and community.* Thousand Oaks, CA: Sage.

Kearney, M. (1995, March-April). Whiz kid anonymous. *Utne Reader, 68*, 65.

Lanham, R. A. (1993). *The electronic word: Democracy, technology, and the arts.* Chicago: University of Chicago Press Expanded Book (Hypercard Version).

LaQuey, T., with Ryer, J. C. (1993). *The internet companion.* Reading, MA: Addison-Wesley.

Levin, D. M. (1989). *The listening self: Personal growth, social change and the closure of metaphysics.* London: Routledge.

McLuhan, M. (1964). *Understanding media: The extensions of man.* New York: Signet.

Metz, J. M. (1995). Computer-mediated communication and the question of culture. *The New Jersey Journal of Communication, 3*, 1-25.

Negroponte, N. (1995). *Being digital.* New York: Random House.

Newhagen, J. E., Cordes, J. W., & Levy, M. R. (1995). Nightly@nbc.com: Audience scope and the perception of interactivity in viewer mail on the internet. *Journal of Communication, 45(3)*, 164-175.

Ong, W. J. (1982). *Orality and literacy: The technologizing of the word.* London: Methuen.

Poster, M. (1990). *The mode of information: Poststructuralism and social context.* Chicago: University of Chicago Press.

Poster, M. (1995, November). The net as a public sphere? *Wired*, *3*, 135-136.

Price, M. E. (1995). Free expression and digital dreams: The open and closed terrain of speech. *Critical Inquiry*, *22*, 64-89.

Reddy, M. (1979). The conduit metaphor. In A. Ortony (Ed.), *Metaphor and thought*. Cambridge: Cambridge University Press.

Rheingold, H. (1991). *Virtual reality*. New York: Summit.

Rheingold, H. (1994). *The virtual community: Homesteading on the electronic frontier*. New York: HarperPerrenial.

Rice, R. E., & Associates. (1984). *The new media: Communication, research, and technology*. Beverly Hills, CA: Sage.

Santoro, G. M. (1994). The internet: An overview. *Communication Education*, *43*, 73-86.

Smith, S. A. (1994). Communication and the constitution in cyberspace. *Communication Education*, *43*, 87-101.

Taylor, M. C., & Saarinen, E. (1994). *Imagologies: Media philosophy*. London: Routledge.

Walther, J. B. (1993). Impression development in computer-mediated interaction. *Western Journal of Communication*, *57*, 381-398.

Walther, J. B. (1996). Computer-mediated communication: Impersonal, interpersonal, and hyperpersonal interaction. *Communication Research*, *23*, 3-43.

Wurman, R. S. (1990). *Information anxiety*. New York: Bantam.

Chapter 7

LISTENING AS AN INDISCREET PUBLIC ACT: Or Eavesdropping Can Be Fun

Gary Gumpert and Susan J. Drucker

Points to be Addressed:

- Listening as a public act: intended and unintended receivers

- The detached observer and listening: Life as a *flâneur*

- Conversational participant listening, indirect performance, observational listening

- Eavesdropping and the Communication Medium

Consider a recent theater piece done at, or near, Lincoln Center in New York City this past Summer. "C'est la Vie" was billed as an audience-as-voyeur theater piece. The audience was seated outside of the theater, equipped with binoculars and radio headphones, and treated to 11 different interwoven dramas played out in the windows of a nearby hotel with a soundtrack broadcast through the head-

phones tuned to an FM frequency providing dialogue (Holden, 1995).[1]
     Much has been written about listening as an important variable of interpersonal communication, but little has been said about the importance of listening as a public act. This chapter deals with the joy of listening to the conversations of others in public places such as parks, shops, streets, cafes, restaurants, on public transportation, in beauty parlors, barber shops, and churches; it links such activity to more orchestrated and mediated contexts including theater, television, radio, film, telephonic, computer communication.

Listening as a Public Act: Intended and Unintended Receivers

     Presentation of an image of oneself, or persona, occurs in interpersonal interaction which in turn is effected by the context in which such interaction takes place. Private and public relationships differ in many ways, one of which is the degree to which communicators have an expectation of privacy. When private relationships take place in public places communicators are placed in an environment in which unplanned, uncontrolled and sometimes undesired listeners join the audience. Intended and unintended receivers may influence the interpersonal communication taking place in such places. The very possibility that strangers may become unintended receivers may well shape interpersonal performances yet public places have historically served as significant sites of interaction, providing social orientation, information, entertainment and human associations.
     According to the *Oxford Universal Dictionary* the etymology of the word "eavesdrop" can be traced to 1606 and refers to standing "within the 'eaves-drop' [the projecting edge of the roof] of a house in order to overhear secrets; hence, to listen secretly to private conversation." But what brings us to thinking about "eavesdropping" as a serious communication issue? For the last decade we have been focusing in on the changing character of public space – those places where people interact on a face-to-face basis. Plazas, parks, cafes, pubs, streets, shops, banks, coffeehouses, community centers, churches, beauty parlors, barber shops, and malls are among those sites offering the possibility to talk, listen and observe. We were, and continue to be, concerned with the disintegrating conditions of ur-

---

[1] French Director Veronique Guillaud created the show which includes characters such as a newlywed couple, an Eastern European immigrant and a local visitor and a New York Jewish family all being watched over by an angel. Reviewers noted that the premise might have been fun if it provided a greater illusion of voyeuristic transgression and the fun of uncovering someone else's secrets (Holden, 1995).

ban life and are equally provoked by the dominating values of suburbia. Social opportunities are endangered amid the dwindling absence of street activity, the rising fear of outdoor encounters, and the demise of a public vibrancy. We believe that these changes are connected to altered patterns of transportation, industry, and communication technology. We have described and discussed these developments elsewhere noting the importance of public social interaction as a quality of life issue (Drucker & Gumpert, 1991).

In this chapter our focus is somewhat narrower although nevertheless far-ranging in breadth. We are specifically pre-occupied with the notion that men and women need the opportunity to gather outside home and office, that on occasions they need the opportunity to be outside the boundaries of either home or work among others. Sociologist Ray Oldenburg (1989) has characterized such places as the "third places."

> The third place is a generic designation for a great variety of public places that host the regular, voluntary, informal, and happily anticipated gatherings of individuals beyond the realms of home and work (Oldenburg, 1989, p.16).

Public spaces are unique environments in which such options can be explored, because their venue allows for diversity with elements of the serendipitous. Stimulation, information, correlation (how one fits in to the outside world) and the overcoming of loneliness are all communicative options offered by the medium of the public space.

The unique blend of interactional opportunities offered by the medium of the public space are embodied within sociologist Erving Goffman's social approach to human behavior. Goffman (1974) distinguishes face engagements or encounters from unfocused encounters. Face engagements take place when there is perceived mutual activity and a relationship is developed and sustained via both verbal and nonverbal means. Individuals have the opportunity to present the self in conversation (Goffman, 1974). In marked contrast to face engagement, the unfocused encounter described by Goffman is interaction in public places in which others are acknowledged without paying direct attention to those sharing spaces, that is to say, other individuals are accessible for conversation or encounter but not engaged (Littlejohn, 1989).

The Detached Observer and Listening: on Being Social Alone

Sometimes there is a need to be among others, but alone (by alone we mean unaccompanied by cellular phone, walkman, discman, beeper or other designated human companion). The idea is not a new one. There is a remarkable short poem by the French writer Charles

Baudelaire (1970) in which he describes another poet wandering among the Parisian *Crowds*.

> Multitude, solitude: identical terms, and interchangeable by the active and fertile poet. The man who is unable to people his solitude is equally unable to be alone in a bustling crowd.

> The poet enjoys the incomparable privilege of being able to be himself or some one else as he chooses. Like those wandering souls who go looking for a body, he enters as he likes into each man's personality. For him alone, everything is vacant; and if certain places seem closed to him, it is only because in his eyes they are not worth visiting.[2] [3]

In literary theory the Flâneur (the word comes from the French" to stroll") came to refer to a nineteenth century "lounger or saunterer, an idle man about town" (The Oxford Universal Dictionary on Historical Principles, 710). According to a contemporary critic, John Lechte, the flâneur "turns into the walker in search of novelty, governed by fashion, and more or less powerless to resist the inexorable tide of consumerist culture" (Lechte, p. 103). There is a clear connection between Baudelaire's collection of poems and contemporary post–modernist criticism. The transitionary medium is Walter Benjamin and his famous The Work of Art in the Age of Mechanical Reproduction (pp. 384–408). According to Elizabeth Wilson, Professor of Media Studies at the University of North London Benjamin saw the "metropolis as a labyrinth".

> It is Baudelaire's obsession with 'spleen' that Benjamin takes as a pointing towards the deeper meanings of the urban spectacle and the *flâneur*'s apparently inconsequential existence. At the heart of Benjamin's mediation on the *flâneur* is the ambivalence toward urban life. . . a sorrowful engagement with the melancholy of cities. This melancholy seems to arise partly from the enormous, unfulfilled promise of the urban spectacle, the consumption, the lure of pleasure and joy, which somehow seem destined to be disappointed, or else are undermined by the obvious poverty and exploitation of so many who toil to bring pleasure to the few (Wilson, p. 73).

The flâneur is the detached critic, the emancipated dilettante without connection, the outsider who strolls, examines, notes, and judges. And because of his detachment, he (and later she), would not be without his (or her) critics. The flâneur is a citizen without re-

---

2 See also *Flowers of Evil*.
3 The sexist nature of Baudelaire's view of the poet and the flâneur is significant. The rise of the female flâneur is linked to the arrival of the large department store, Bon Marche, in Paris which signals a shift in the shopping habits and activities of women. Clare Oliva Parsons is currently completing her dissertation, "Women and the Walk: Female Flanerie and the Aesthetics of Public space in 19th Century Europe," at Harvard University in the Department of Comparative Literature.

sponsibility, disconnected from community, able to be mobile and free without the restraints and obligations of community. The flâneur spent time in picking up gossip (Wilson, 1995, p. 62) taking pleasure in eavesdropping. The joys of gossip have long been recognized as "one ingredient that defines human life" (Wernick, 1993, p. 76). According to Patricia Meyer Spacks, gossip recaptures the experience of intimacy, trust, human association; it is a form of closeness (Spacks, 1985, p. 60) even for the detached observer.

But the reality of capitalist consumption embraces a cornucopia of attracting goods and compelled men and women. The growth of leisure time, of the possibility of activity not spent in the hardship of survival, emphasizes the social outside. The vitality of American cities in the last two centuries, until recently, was very much characterized by the spectacular activity and variety which could be found by simply walking down the street. It was a canvas of interest that was freely available (and remains that way in most European cities) for a public which required visual and auditory stimulation and has the luxury to indulge.

If we now look at the American social values at the turn of the 20th century, we see the rise of privacy as the dominating value (strangely similar to the motivation of the detached flâneur who defined privacy as the right to be let alone) and the shifting of life from the uncontrollable exterior to the controllable interior. But urban delights are limited by a commuter constituency, the very rich, and the impoverished. Rural life is dwindling at an alarming rate, and suburbia is characterized by an automobile philosophy, shopping, strip malls, superstores, and residences of quiet, safety, and no visible social life. Yet, we believe there remains a need for social variation and stimulation. How many of you would respond affirmatively that you have a need to be with others in a third place? How many of you would respond affirmatively that you have a need to be with others alone? How many of you have the opportunity to be alone with others? How many of you would admit to being card-carrying eavesdroppers when you are alone with others?

Current developments and our quest for privacy (probably more aptly described as safe isolation) could not have occurred without the swift evolution of media technology. The shifts and changes in communication that have occurred in the last 150 years are awesome—photography, motion pictures (from black and white to color), telegraphy, the typewriter (from the manual introduced by Remington in 1874 to electric typewriters to wordprocessors), telephony (from the party line to the cellular phone), sound recording (from acoustical to digital, from disc to tape to CD), radio (from wired to wireless, from AM to FM and short wave), typography and high-speed printing, television (from live to film to tape to disc), xerography (and copies galore) facsimile, high band and broad band satellite transmission, the computer and its countless variations of digitizing information.

But all of this begins with the strange human need to reach out and be heard by others. Without the absolute necessity to feel and touch others, all of that magical technology is meaningless - - except perhaps to preserve what once was and has passed. There is, however, something seductive about the technology of communication and we have begun to rely upon technologically assisted or mediated communication and even to prefer that mode to the old, particularly because it is safe, because it is convenient, because it is efficient and requires less physical energy, *forgetting that there are qualitative differences between the two.* The mediated functional alternatives that we choose emanate from inside controlled private space.

What can be clearly demonstrated is that most of us opt for alternatives for social stimulation. Instead of coping in an environment based primarily on physical interaction, more and more of our time is spent with relationships which exist in mediated, primarily electronic, space. Specifically, much of our flánerish activity, our formerly strolling view of others, has shifted into a mediated form. An early classic example of such a shift was the party–line telephone – intrinsically constructed to listen in on, but also structured with an ethic that condemned the practice . It is short trip from listening to others on the telephone to surfing the Internet and exploring computer bulletin boards.

Venturing into public space alone in physical or electronic space (Gumpert & Drucker, 1992) offers the opportunity to engage in three distinct types of listening activities defined by the degree of active involvement of the receiver: 1) First there is *conversational participant* listening in which the intended or recognized receiver is engaged in interaction with a sender (i.e. conversations among friends while walking down a street, talking with a merchant, etc.); 2) *indirect performance* in which the sender is aware of the receiver's interest although that receiver may be unintended (i.e. a performance is given for the listener); 3) *observational listening* in which the fact that one is listening is unknown to the sender, perhaps unwanted (i.e. eavesdropping). Much work has been done with regard to the first type of listening so it is our intention in this chapter to provide a communication frame, a typology of active observer and observational listening (eavesdropping) from which we can establish a contemporary theory of isolated disconnected interaction by focusing upon the following variables:

Typology of Eavesdropping

Unmediated (face to face)	Mediated (micro or mass media)
Intentional	Unintentional

Public (known)	Clandestine (unknown)

Eavesdropping and the Medium

The intimate process of eavesdropping has always been linked to specific media. What characterizes the connection is the distance that is maintained between voyeur and subject. One does not intrude. One does not become involved and alter the course of action. Listening to someone else's conversation requires an ideal distance which does not violate the nature of the conversation or reveal the presence of the third party participant. We generally conceive of eavesdropping as an unmediated, unplanned event—one that occurs at a specific site.

But all of us have fantasized about the possibility of being the fly on the wall, to be invisible and watch and listen to the unfolding events. We can point to all sorts of mediated events, more formalized and stylized constructions, which permit the auditor to get closer and remain invisibly intimate. From a literary perspective consider the appeal of the genres of the diary (never only intended for the self) and the autobiography. Their attraction is their intimately revealing, yet distant relationship, between writer and reader.

There was and is a form of theater which has been experientially described as having the fourth wall removed thus revealing a slice of life enfolding before the audience. This unique relationship between audience and performer was recently articulated in a review of a solo performance of the Romanian pianist Radu Lupu at Carnegie Hall. The following caption introduced the review: " A pianist Whose Intense Subjectivity Turns Listeners Into Eavesdroppers." Critic Edward Rothstein said:

> He doesn't really seem to care if anybody is listening; he is playing as if for himself, giving the music an unusual immediacy. Mr. Lupu's stage persona reinforces the impression of solitude. He strides deliberately on stage sits down at a straight-backed chair and gets down to work as if there were nobody else in the room. There is no showmanship, no courtship of the audience, no display (Rothstein, 1994, p. C15).

Similarly film and television can convey this sense of revelation without intrusion when it is treated as an unobtrusive medium. So one of the primary characteristics of mediated eavesdropping is the transparency of the medium; its convention of pretending not to be present as a channel of communication. In short it is an inconspicuous medium - - which it is not, of course. Thus, the camera cannot break the agreed to distance, cannot penetrate the acceptable boundaries established by participants and the conventions of the medium and genre. Any violation of the tacit conventions renders the fragile aesthetic agreement null and void.

Computer-mediated communication, particularly on-line chat rooms, offer new opportunities for interaction and voyeurism with the awareness that others are on-line in the room but not keyboarding their way into the conversation. If one really wished privacy, private rooms are only a keystroke away. "Public" rooms are occupied with voyeurs listed on screen replete with names—real and otherwise.

A matter of Intentionality

The participants of eavesdropping may or may not be aware that they are part of an ongoing event. From the perspective of a communication model we have at least a minimum of a dyad existing along with a monad (one person listening) and sharing some part of a visual or/and acoustical space. Two scenarios are possible. First, it is the intent of the eavesdropper to listen and/or watch interacting individuals who are unaware of the intentions of the third party (an incidental relationship results). Second, is the intent of at least one member of the dyad to perform for the outsider. Both members of the dyad need not be aware of the performance yet a relationship is established. At times all of us have performed for others outside our immediate arena of conversation.[4] In *The Fall of Public Man* (1977), sociologist Richard Sennett suggests that for most of our history, people have reveled in the opportunity to "play act" in public, to try on different roles and enjoy the company of strangers (p. 338)."[P]layacting requires an audience of strangers to succeed, but is meaningless or even destructive among intimates" (Sennett, p. 29). So physical and electronic spaces are required to support public activities in which some degree of distance and detachment are essential.

In a sense we create a relationship with a third party who benefits from our performance through eavesdropping.[5] When at least one of the parties intends or is consciously aware of the third party listener, this is an intended eavesdropper.

---

[4] One vivid example of a parent publicly talking to a child comes to mind. We talk to display our children and our parenting techniques to others. One way we do this is to involve the child in a dialogue in order to demonstrate the verbal abilities or very precociousness or idiosyncrasies of the child. Adults also exhibit their talents at relationship building or the to exhibit patience or wisdom.

[5] This concept is akin to the legal doctrine of third party beneficiaries found in the law of contracts. Most rights under contracts are limited to those in a recognized relationship known as privity yet there are situations in which a non-contracting party (i.e. a stranger to a contract) may have an enforceable right under the contract.If a third party is an intended beneficiary, that is to say, one whose benefit was intended by at least one of the contracting parties, the third party has an enforceable right.If the benefit is unintended, no right exists (Calamari & Perillo, 1977).

This explains, in part, the extraordinary phenomenon known as talk radio.[6] Think of the complexity of that act. Two people have a conversation overheard by several hundred thousand or several million other persons. Both are aware that they are not alone, but on a vast acoustical stage where intimacy is public. Each has the intention to let others eavesdrop on a simple although complexly facilitated event.

Interpersonal Eavesdropping v. Institutional Surveillance

Eavesdropping is an interpersonal communication activity which may be fun and harmless but has ethical implications. The ethical dimensions of informal interpersonal eavesdropping relate to rightness or wrongness of communicative activity. It is significant to note that a review of the literature of communication ethics reveals that the issue of eavesdropping is not considered directly in works dealing with interpersonal communication ethics (Johannesen, 1990; Jaksa & Pritchard, 1988). It has been suggested that interpersonal communication in general is unethical when there is interference with freedom of choice (DeVito, 1995) so that subversion of the sender's choice in who receives a message (i.e. the act of unintended eavesdropping) would be viewed as unethical.

Eavesdropping has been industrialized and its spirit of fun been subverted. A telephone call to the help desk of a computer software company is accompanied by a warning that "this telephone conversation may be recorded for reasons of quality control." Governmental and police agencies wiretap phones in their quest to gather evidence. Banks, without permission, photograph and/or video tape their customers in order to protect themselves against robbery and fraud. Some companies place small television cameras behind the counter in order to supervise their cashiers. With the rise of theft in megastores, hidden security microphones are being introduced in addition to the usual (and accepted?) technology of visual surveillance. Dime–sized microphones are being placed somewhere among clothing racks so that stores can determine whether customers are working together in acts of theft (Kilbourn, 1995, p. 6). According to the owner of one such supplying security company:

> A system for a small store, with eight microphones and an endless–loop machine, would cost about $7000.00...They're starting to put

---

[6]"Broadcast-teleparticipatory communication" describes media simulated interpersonal communication which is quasi public and quasi private in nature. A caller calls in a radio or television program and conducts a conversation with an on-air personality as if it were a private telephone conversation although aware of the public performance dynamic. The host is aware of need to control the caller for commercial purposes within proscribed restricted language codes (Cathcart & Gumpert, 1986, p.34).

them in supermarkets...restaurants have them in the kitchen because a lot of stuff goes out the back door (Kilbourn, 1995, p. 6).

A number of legal and ethical issues regarding the rights of employees and customers come to the foreground. While it is a major concern of ours, it is not our intent to focus on these ethical and legal issues at this time. However, one particularly interesting legal observation must be made. According to the *The New York Times* article, some companies are shying away from introducing audio surveillance technology into their stores, because of potential legal repercussions. What is important is that Federal law recognized the concept of eavesdropping and "prohibits eavesdropping unless one of the two participants in a conversation knows about it. A minority of states require that both people know."[7] Yet, there are institutionalized forms of eavesdropping conducted with assumed consent by virtue of entering a particular location such as an elevator or store.

Stores using audio systems can inform people by posting a warning that typically says, "Audio monitoring on premises," The manufacturers of the gear enclose the warning stickers in their shipments... [According to Jeffrey Meuse, the president of one of the security companies] "The question is whether the stickers are noticed" (Kilbourn, 1995, p. 6).

In Line and On-Line

Waiting in line (in the queue), while perhaps an annoyance or necessary evil because of the distribution of scarce resources or crowding, provides the opportunity to see and talk to others as well as to listen in on the conversation of others. Each culture trains its own in the art or conventions of standing in line. The line at the ATM machine, the supermarket checkout or the deli counter provide possible chance meetings (face engagements) or eavesdropping opportunities (unfocused interaction). It is to be noted that the queue is shifting from the physical sites of public interaction to electronic sites. The bank branch, once an important arena of social interaction

---

[7] There are little known, seldom enforced laws which ban and criminalize some recording. Participant monitoring, when at least one party to a conversation is aware of a secret recorder or transmitter, is permitted by federal law and the law in 40 states. Therefore, it is legal to secretly record your own telephone conversation and then transmit it to a third party (Safe Streets Act, 1987). A participant tape recording is equated with recounting your own conversation to a third party. The Federal Communications Commission does require telephone companies to prohibit telephone subscribers from recording conversations unless all parties to the conversation are told of the recording in advance either with an announcement or a beep tone (Use of Recording Devices in Connection with Telephone Service, Docket No. 20840; 86 F.C.C. 2d 313 (1981); 48 Fed. Reg. 51,773 (1983).

is being phased out by bank policy. The shift is linear from lines waiting for a bank teller to waiting for an ATM machine to 24 hour a day contact on the telephone line with a non-branch operator to 24 hour computer connection "on-line" without any connection with a local branch. The psychological shift from the physical "in-line" to the metaphorical "on-line" is significant[8] as we move from occupying shared physical space to a wire.

The shift from the unpredictable collision with strangers in public space to a more emancipated, controlled and safer connection with others in a mediated universe, is a complex one. You might ask what is the connection of the concept of the flâneur with the world of cyberspace? How many people have a computer? How many people subscribe to on-line services such as America Online or Prodigy in order to participate in or observe Bulletin Board" discussions? How many people subscribe to CRTNET—Communication Research And Theory Network? How many people surf the World Wide Web? How many are citizens of virtual communities?

Howard Rheingold described the on-line experience as follows:

> People in virtual communities use words on screens to exchange pleasantries and argue, engage in intellectual discourse, conduct commerce, exchange knowledge, share emotional support, make plans, brainstorm, gossip, feud, fall in love, find friends and lose them, play games, flirt, create a little high art and a lot of idle talk. People in virtual communities do just about everything people do in real life, but we leave our bodies behind. You can't kiss anybody and nobody can punch you in the nose, but a lot can happen within those boundaries. To the millions who have been drawn into it, the richness and vitality of computer-linked cultures is attractive, even addictive (Rheingold, 1993, p 3).

Imagine a world in which you are connected to everyone, without having to reveal yourself to anyone. Think of the opportunity to participate in or watch the on-line discussion of sexual fantasy without having to reveal your identity. Reflect over the amazing ability to link up with organizations, individuals, libraries, causes, data bases, governments, museums, etc. all over the world without leaving your keyboard and screen. Universal access and convergence suddenly become commonplace. In a review of the 10th Annual International Conference and exposition on Multimedia and CD-ROM, Wendy Anson comments: "To be a latter day Walter Benjamin who could stroll cyberspace at will, with no bounds, a flanuer in Paris. To be able to move about 'at random' in a 'hypertext' universe where one could invent connections and spark new synthesis" (Anson, 1995).

---

[8] One might question whether "on-line" derives from the use of the telephone line (wired communication) for computer-mediated communication or whether it is a metaphor for the turn taking sequencing associated with waiting for the distribution of a scare resource

Life on-line provides each of us with the opportunity to become "media flaneurs," adventurers who never leave the room, but interact with those with whom we do not share community. We may stroll the channels, telephone lines, stations, chat rooms and web sites selecting moments in other people's lives in which they can perform and exit. We "channel surf" or "netsurf" from program to program, site to site, from situation to situation, from momentary connections, strangely encapsulated in a protected warm safe place while taking excursions into electronic space. It is the serendipitous gambol without commitment that excites, titillates and brings satisfaction along with anonymity and protection. Face-to-face or body-to-body requires different energy and obligations without the guarantee of experiencing the pleasure of eavesdropping.

Summary

The act of public interpersonal performance and public listening (eavesdropping) are important socializing agents which require public spaces. Traditional opportunities for this communicative activity are threatened by the decay of cities and public spaces. Public life is shifting into the more controllable, safe confines of electronic public spaces in which eavesdropping opportunities abound. But do not confuse quality and function. Listening and watching others on the Internet is a substitute for a former experience. If we choose a personae without a face or a face without a body, life will be a virtual hell....but you will be safe!

Since eavesdropping on conversations raises ethical problems, it is not recommended that one rush out and engage in such activity. Yet, in a regulated, highly organized world, there is a need for the unplanned, the surprise, the unorganized, the incidental encounter. There is a degree of exhilaration and discovery inherent in the possibility of happening upon observation or the thoughts of others making public listening opportunities particularly appealing. The *flâneur* represents a figure in history who relished this act of public listening.

People have long ventured from home for outings for pragmatic and pleasurable experiences. Public spaces are vital to the personal and political life of a society, offering sites of significant communication and contexts for important forms of listening but the literature in the field of listening has yet to focus upon the unique situational demands generated by communication opportunities and activities of listening in public places. This chapter suggests three such types of listening in public places: (1) conversational participant listening by a receiver intended or recognized by the sender; (2) indirect performance in which the receiver's interest is known to the sender although that receiver may be unintended resulting in a performance for the listener; (3) observational listening, typically considered eavesdropping, when the receiver is unknown to the sender. As an ever increasing amount of time is spent in mediated activities removed from traditional public places, the art of public listening is shifting into a mediated realm. As aliases and anonymous persona are available to media consumers, the life of the *flâneur* is becoming available to all.

Exercises:

1. This exercise focuses upon the traditional sites of public social interaction where conversational listening, observational listening and indirect listening take place. In every major city around the world, establishments with the description café have come into being, which despite their immense variety, national characteristics and functional particularities, ultimately continue to offer what the coffee–house trade has offered since its inception, namely a blend of refreshment, games, entertainment and *education. Observe:* Dwell time—how long do people stay. What do they do? (read, converse, sit and watch others?) What is the percentage of patrons who come alone? Are there regulars who seem to know one another or know the staff? Do conversations start up between patrons at different tables?

2. This exercise illustrates the movement of public listening from the physical realm to that of electronic public space. Get on–line and access a public chat room. Identify yourself (using your password and alias), greet other members in the chat room and then remain "silent." Observe reactions of others in the chat room. Are others aware of your presence? Are they performing with an awareness of your presence? Do others seek to engage you in conversation? Are you permitted to remain silent? What are the ways you may violate the rituals of chat rooms?

3. This exercise illustrates the movement of public listening from the physical realm to that of the mass media realm. Tune in to a talk radio program. Observe the nature of the broadcast teleparticipatory relationship. Does the caller indicate an awareness of the large audience listening? Does the caller act as if this is a private interpersonal interaction? What is your relationship with the on–air host. Is the host a friend? An acquaintance? Someone who angers you? If you are a regular listener, do you recognize some of the people who call in? Can you describe two such regulars?

4. This activity underscores some of the opportunities to listen in public places. Many of the activities which draw us to public places are crowded and necessitate waiting in line. Waiting in line

may be necessary due to over crowding or limited clerks or waiters. The use of lines, the rituals and norms and the role of queues for interpersonal interaction vary from culture to culture. Choose one: Bank line (waiting for a teller);One ATM (automatic teller line); One Supermarket line; One Movie line/or Store line.

Observe: (1) Who talks to whom? How are conversations started? How are conversations ended? (2) Do people on line appear to be eavesdropping on the conversations of others around them? (3) What are the rituals of the line? Who breaks the line? How are rules enforced? Are security guards or other "officials" present to enforce rules?

References

Anson, W. (1995, May). Intermedia '95. *Postmodern Culture* v. 5, n. 3.
Baudelaire, C. (1970). *Paris Spleen, 1869.* Trans. Varese, L. New York: New Directions Books.
Benjamin, W. (1977). The Work of Art in the Age of Mechanical Reproduction. In J. Curan et. Al., (eds.). *Mass communication & Society.* London: Edward Arnold, pp. 384- 408.
Calamari, J.D. & Perillo, J.M. (1977). *Contracts.* St. Paul, MN: West Publishing Co.
Cathcart, R. & Gumpert, G. (1986). Mediated interpersonal communication: Toward a new typology. In G. Gumpert & R. Cathcart (eds.). *Inter/Media: Interpersonal Communication in a Media Age.*(Third Edition). New York: Oxford, pp. University Press. Pp.26-40.
DeVito, J. (1995). *The Interpersonal communication book* 7th edition. New York: Harper Collins.
Drucker, S. & Gumpert, G. (1991). Public Space and Communication: The Zoning of Public Interaction, *Communication Theory,* Vol.1 No. 4, pp.296-310
Goffman, E. (1974). *Frame Analysis: An essay on the organization of experience.* Cambridge: Harvard University Press.
Gumpert, G. & Drucker, S.(1992). From the Agora to the Electronic Shopping Mall," *Critical Studies in Mass Communication,* 9, June, pp.186-200
Holden, S. (1995, August 5). Some Hi-tech voyeurism for a Summer evening. *The New York Times.,*
Jaksa, J.A. & Pritchard, M.S. (1988). *Communication ethics: Methods of analysis.* Belmont, Calif.: Wadsworth.
Johannesen, R.L. (1990). *Ethics in human communication.* 4th ed. Prospect Heights, Ill.: Waveland Press.

Lechte, J. (1995). (Not) belonging in postmodern space. In S. Watson & K. Gibson (eds.). *Postmodern cities & spaces.* Cambridge, MA: Blackwell Publishers. pp. 99–111.

Kilborn, P.T. (1995, May 25). In a growing number of stores, hidden security microphones are listening. *New York Times*, p. 6.

Littlejohn, S.W. (1989). *Theories of human communication.* (Third Edition). Belmont, CA: Wadsworth Publishing Co.

Oldenburg, R. (1989). *The great good place: Cafes, Coffee Shops, Community Centers, Beauty Parlors, General Stores, Bars, Hangouts, and How They Get You Through the Day.* New York: Pergamon Press.

Rheingold, H. (1993). *The Virtual Community,* Addison–Wesley.

Rothstein, E. (1994, Jan, 20). A pianist whose intense subjectivity turns listeners into eavesdroppers. . *New York Times*, p. C 15.

Sennett, R. (1977). *The Fall of Public Man.* New York: Alfred P. Knopf & Co.

Spacks, P.M. (1985). *Gossip.* New York: Alfred P. Knopf & Co.

The Oxford Universal Dictionary on Historical Principles, Oxford: At The Clarendon Press: 1955 580.

Wernick, R. (1993). When it comes to gossip, we're all-ears listeners. *Smithsonian.* Pp. 76,78.

Wilson, E. (1995). The invisible flaneur. In S. Watson & K. Gibson (eds.). *Postmodern cities & spaces.* Cambridge, MA: Blackwell Publishers. pp. 59–79.

Chapter 8

LISTENING IN THE EDUCATIONAL ENVIRONMENT

Carolyn Coakley and Andrew Wolvin

Points to be Addressed:

- Listening is the most frequently-used communication form at all levels of education and the most central to the student's learning success.

- Teachers, students, and parents listen the way they have learned to listen.

- The effective listening teacher is an effective listening model to students.

- Students have the responsibility to acquire listening skills and positive listening attitudes in order to listen to classroom instruction, other students, and parents.

- Parents should be effective listening models and listen appropriately in parent–teacher conferences.

- Teachers, students, and parents constitute the learning "team" which can function most effectively through skillful listening behaviors.

Into the educational environment come the three major participants: the teacher, the student, and the parent. They arrive as individuals, but partners they should become; for, as Friedman (1980) notes, "the deeply interdependent, critically significant parent-teacher–student collaboration should be carried out by people who have an open, honest, mutually respectful partnership" (p. ix). Each of the three participants comes with a primary purpose: the teacher comes primarily to teach; the student comes primarily to learn; and the parent comes primarily to determine the learning success of the student. All participants share the common goals of having a genuine concern for the student's well-being—of helping the student get the best education possible.

The participants attempt to accomplish their purpose by means of communication—through speaking, listening, reading, writing, and engaging in nonverbal cues. But, of all the forms of verbal and nonverbal communication, the communication form that is most basic, most utilized, and most central to the student's learning success at all levels of education is *listening*. Steil (1982) stresses the essential role that listening has for each participant's purpose:

> Students at all levels must be able and willing to listen or little learning will occur. In addition, the effective listening of teachers is critical for students' inquiries to be heard and answered. Finally, the effective listening of . . . parents is central to any school's successful coordinated effort (p. 2).

Yes, listening is the most basic of the language arts. Listening is the first language skill to appear in children; they "listen before they speak, speak before they read, and read before they write" (Lundsteen, 1979, p. xi). Thus, an individual's ability to speak, read, and write—as well as to master complex intellectual skills, such as reasoning—is directly or indirectly dependent upon his or her ability to listen. This dependency is apparent when we consider that speech development is derived from one's imitation of others' sounds, reading development is heavily contingent upon auditory discrimination ability as well as ability to recode letters as sounds, writing development is greatly affected by listening vocabulary, and critical thinking is influenced by the way one processes messages.

Listening is the most frequently used communication form at all levels of education. Over the past fifty years, studies investigating the amount of time elementary, secondary, and college students are expected to engage in the four major forms of communication have consistently revealed that listening is the primary form used in the classroom. Wilt (1950) found that elementary school students are expected to spend 57.5 percent of their classroom time listening; of their total listening time, 54 percent is spent listening to the teacher, 31 percent is spent listening to each other, and 15 percent is spent listening to other auditory activities (such as sound films, singing, radio, and choral activities).

Investigating the time secondary students are expected to listen in the classroom, Markgraf (1957) discovered that they were supposed to listen 46 percent of their classroom time (or, 53 percent of the classroom time if study hall periods were omitted from consideration); 66 percent of their listening time was spent listening to the teacher (with English teachers talking 97 percent of the time), and 24 percent was spent listening to their peers. Also examining secondary students' supposed-to-listen time, Corey (1940) found that high school students were expected to listen to their teachers (who talked two-thirds of the classroom time) 66 percent of their classroom time.

Studying the expected classroom listening time of both secondary and college students, Taylor (1964) found that "close to 90 percent of the class time in high schools and colleges is spent in listening to discussions and lectures" (p. 3). Bird (1953), exploring the amount of time college women are expected to listen in the classroom, reported that listening consumed 42 percent of their verbal communication time. A more recent study, conducted by Barker et al. (1980), revealed that college students spend 52.5 percent of their total verbal communication time engaged in listening.

Significantly, these studies show that students are expected to listen for more than half of their classroom time. Moreover, listening is the communication form most central to the student's learning success. Devine (1982b) supports this premise by noting that "listening is primary in all learning, in that it comes before speaking, reading and writing in the development of all communication skills" and "listening seems to be the primary means by which all incoming ideas and information are taken in" (p. 25).

Indeed, listening is so integral to the learning process that Conaway (1982) determined that listening comprehension is the critical factor in the attrition and the retention of college students: "Among the students who fail, deficient listening skills were a stronger factor than reading skills or academic aptitude" (p. 57). Likewise, Legg (1971) found that students who listen effectively are more successful in their schoolwork and can achieve beyond their mental capabilities as measured by intelligence tests, while students lacking in listening skills may be "slower in developing mental abilities than those who are higher in listening ability" (p. 129).

Furthermore, in three surveys cited by Brown (1987), college students ranked listening as being a more important factor than reading in achieving academic success. Lacking proficiency in listening, then, can handicap the student in both the processes of communicating and learning, two activities critical to the student's success at all educational levels.

Moreover, the need for listening proficiency is recognized in federal initiatives to strengthen educational outcomes for secondary school and for post-secondary students alike. For example, the U.S. Department of Labor (1991) established a SCANS commission to identify what critical skills were essential for high school graduates to function effectively in the workplace. The basic skills of mathematics, reading, writing, speaking, and *listening* were determined to be at the core of preparation for graduates to enter the workplace (p. xviii). Likewise, the U.S. Department of Education has identified in its national education goals, Goals 2000, a significant communication objective for all college graduates: "The proportion of college graduates who demonstrate advanced ability to think critically, communicate effectively, and solve problems will increase substantially" (National Education Goals Panel, 1992, p. 5). The "communicate effectively" outcome includes *listening* along with speaking, writing, and reading.

Recognizing the importance of developing listening competency, educational institutions are beginning to provide direct instruction in listening. With increasing frequency, entire courses devoted to the study of listening behavior are offered in may colleges and universities (Wolvin, Coakley, and Disburg, 1991, 1992). Additionally, some attention to the study of listening is offered in basic speech communication courses in colleges and universities (Perkins, 1994). Unfortunately, no recent surveys of listening instruction on either the elementary or secondary educational levels have been conducted, so it is difficult to ascertain just how much instruction in listening proficiency is provided to students bfore they enter college. It is interesting to note, however, that a considerable amount of corporate classroom time is devoted to training employees in listening behavior ("1994 Industry Report," 1994, p. 49.)

It is evident, then, that we must recognize that each of the participants—the teacher, student, and parent—comes to the educational environment with a different level of listening proficiency. Simply stated, *each listens the way he/she does because he/she has learned to listen that way.* How does one learn to listen?

One of the most pervasive premises found in listening literature is that an individual learns to listen by observing the way parents and significant others listen. Initially, these "others" may be guardians, grandparents, older siblings, day care workers, etc.—anyone with whom he or she interacts regularly over a long period of time. In other words, adults' listening behaviors serve as models for children's listening behaviors. If children observe parents who "constantly talk *at* each other and do not respond to each other's feelings, . . . communicate their judgmental attitudes through their posture or facial expression, . . . give each other and their children little acknowledgment —the children will mimic their behavior" (Burley–Allen, 1982, pp. 22– 23). If children observe that these "others" are interruptive, look stern, ignore feelings, or turn away, these children will mimic these behaviors when they are listening to others.

Similarly, if children observe parents who communicate *with* each other and respond appropriately to each other's feelings, communicate their openness through their nonverbal cues, and acknowledge that they are listening and striving to understand and, when listening to the children themselves, observe turn-taking signals, maintain a non-judmental expression, acknowledge children's feelings, and engage in attending behaviors, children will mimic these behaviors when listening to others.

When these children leave home and enter day-care facilities or schools, new adults become their listening models. Again, if these new "significant others" are ineffective listeners, children will incorporate their negative listening behaviors. Similarly, if the new adult models are effective listeners, children will incorporate their positive listening behaviors.

In addition to learning to listen from adult models, individuals learn to listen through both informal and formal listening training or through no listening training. In the home, for example, parents or guardians may informally teach elementary listening skills such as "the skill of listening-without-needless-interruption at the dinner table" (Arnold, 1973, p. 36). In the classroom, teachers may informally teach listening skills such as physically preparing for listening or engaging in attending behaviors, or they may formally teach listening skills such as how to improve one's concentration, how to determine the purpose(s) for listening, how to ask questions to insure understanding, etc. Or, in the home or classroom, children may not receive any listening training and, thus, continue to learn to listen by observing adult models who may be ineffective or effective listeners.

Each of the participants, then, comes to the educational environment with a different background in listening. This background consists of having had ineffective or effective listening models as well as having had informal and/or formal listening training or the lack of either or both. To reiterate, *each listens the way he/she does because he/she has learned to listen that way.*

Listening During Transactions in the Educational Environment

In the educational environment, the transactions involving the three main participants are those between teacher and student, student and student, student and parent, and parent and teacher. While all transactions involve these participants, the setting is not always the classroom.

Listening in Teacher/Student Transactions

The Teacher

Effective listening teachers provide effective listening models to their students. By demonstrating effective listening behavior, teachers show that they regard listening as a critical communication skill. In his four-step MAPP listening plan, Stammer (1981) places Modeling before the other three steps—Assessing, Preparing, and Practicing. Another educator who has stressed the importance of teacher modeling is Radford University President Donald Dedmon (1983):

> The heart of the teaching transaction is skilled oral communications. Teachers must consistently practice them and encourage the practice of them by their students. The good teacher is both a good speaker and listener. The latter may, indeed, be more important than the former (p. 19).

Still another educator, Friedman (1983), describes how a teacher—as a model listener from the first day of class till the last day of class—can create a classroom climate conducive to effective listening.

> When students enter the classroom for the first time, they look to the teacher and wait for the messages that will tell them what to expect. Simultaneously, the teacher is sizing them up. Each is alert, attentive, listening. From that moment on, they will spend most of their time together trying to gain and hold each others attention, striving to understand and be understood, determining where they stand with each other, silently judging and evaluating—in short, they will be concerned with listening (p. 4).

Together, Stammer, Dedmon, and Friedman emphasize that teachers must *model effective listening consistently* during every communication transaction in the educational environment. Teachers who consistently exhibit effective listening behavior, in turn, elicit effective listening behavior from others, demonstrate that they do what they teach, and convey to others that listening is a valued skill.

Numerous listening educators have described the listening knowledge, attitudes, and skills that the effective listening teacher should possess. While it is beyond the scope of this chapter to include all that has been recommended, many of the recommendations made by Lyle (1987 and 1989), Stewig (1974), Lundsteen (1979), Cooper (1984), Devine (1982a), Rence (1985), and Coakley (1993a/b) can be noted.

As a *planner* the model listening teacher:

1. values listening as a skill that needs to be modeled and taught;

2. realizes that students have difficulty sustaining attention for long periods of time;

3. considers the length of students' attention spans as he/she plans daily lessons;

4. plans carefully his/her instructions so students can clearly understand them;

5. plans explanations that are clear, precise, and concise;

6. organizes each daily lesson in a logical sequence so that it can be easily understood;

7. plans ways to restate ideas if students do not understand them at first.

One aspect of an individual's frame of reference is sensory acuity. The sharpness or keenness of our senses can affect our listening effectiveness.

In other words, our sensory acuity refers to how well we can hear . . . how well we can see . . . how well we can smell, taste, and feel. If we can hear well, we can engage in the first step of listening. But, listening is more than hearing.

8. plans for times during the class period when students can orally share their thoughts, questions, and concerns with him/her;

9. anticipates questions students might ask about daily lessons and prepares answers;

10. creates instructional lessons from a comprehensive listening framework (taxonomy/scope and sequence) of well-defined listening skills that build upon each other and are repeated and reinforced;

11. prepares advance organizers (pre-lecture discussion) to assist students in understanding daily lessons that are to be presented orally.

Today, we are going to examine three ego states that operate within each of us. What does ego mean to you? How have you heard the term used? What does 'She has a big ego' mean to you? In the sentence, 'He is in a grumpy state,' what does state mean to you? What other states might one be in?

12. includes in daily lessons a variety of listening experiences for students;

13. plans instructional activities that reinforce cognitive development in listening;

14. plans instructional activities that focus on a full range and a variety of listening situations and functions;

15. sets up classroom listening expectations and—with students — consistently practices them; and

16. provides a physical atmosphere conducive to effective listening (by adjusting seating to the best acoustical advantage; attending to temperature and ventilation; and minimizing external distractions).

As a *presenter*, the model listening teacher:

1. speaks with directness, clarity, and adequate volume;

2. practices the "once–only" rule for giving instructions and making important announcements.

   (First day of class) I follow the once–only rule for giving instructions. We will have a trial period of two weeks after which time I will put this rule into effect. From that time on, I will no longer repeat instructions because you have not been listening. I will clarify the instructions if they are not clear to you, but I will not repeat them. When you ask for clarification, I expect you to accompany your request with a statement of what you do understand about the instructions.

3. teaches listening in connection with all subject areas;

4. assists students in determining how listening skills and strategies learned in class are applicable to other areas of students' lives;

5. establishes with students the purpose(s) for which they should listen in class.

   While I am reading the story, I'd like for you to think about why Marlon acted as he did to his brother. Be ready to share your thoughts with the class when I have completed the reading of the story.

6. strives to create a social, psychological, and physical classroom climate that encourages students to take risks and share information orally and to listen openly;

7. gets the attention of a student/students before he/she speaks;

8. avoids needlessly repeating his/her messages;

9. encourages listening by limiting the amount of talking that he/she does;

10. is consciously aware of his/her nonverbal behaviors that may distract others and tries to keep those behaviors under control;

11. does not routinely repeat students' responses; rather, encourages students to listen to each other;

What is your opinion of Sung's statement regarding allowances? Maria?

12. times messages well; for example, avoids delivering messages as students are leaving the class room; and

13. provides positive reinforcement for students' effective listening.

As a *listener*, the model listening teacher:

1. understands the communication process and is able to explain it clearly to his/her students;

2. understands the listening process and is able to explain it clearly to his/her students;

3. varies (according to the type of thinking—reflective thinking, immediate recall, etc.—required) the time given to students to think and respond after he/she asks a question;
   Why did Johnny want the money so badly? (Pause)
   Sherwyn? (Pause)

4. is comfortable with silence as he/she waits for students to respond;

5. encourages students to continue speaking when they hesitate;

6. does not supply student speakers with words when they are "grasping" for words, phrases, thoughts, etc.;

7. engages in attending behaviors (direct eye contact, comfortable interactional distance, responsive facial expression that matches the speaker's concern, receptive bodily posture, sincere head nodding and verbal expressives such as "uh huh" to indicate understanding, a warm and pleasant voice tone, and silence) as he/she listens to his/her students speak and expresses his/her interest in/appreciation for what they say;

8. sets aside his/her personal concerns while he/she is in the educational environment;

9. gives his/her complete attention to student speakers;

10. concentrates actively on what a student is saying;

11. is consciously aware of the nonverbal messages he/she sends as a listener;

12. shows that what his/her students say to him/her is important to him/her and may be important to others;

13. asks students what their words mean to them;
    What is your meaning of "redneck"?

14. establishes quality listening time to listen to students before and after school as well as during class;

15. demonstrates verbally and nonverbally that he/she is approachable and encourages his/her students to speak with him/her;

16. provides a supportive climate that says, "I'm here"/"I care"/when students discuss personal problems with him/her;

17. is a patient listener;

18. listens to one student at a time;

My, I'm popular this morning! Now, who was here first? I believe it was Steve. Let me listen to Steve, and then I'll listen to Mary, Francisco, and Nakia—in that order.

19. listens to a student's complete answer after he/she has asked a student a question;

20. does not communicate to students that he/she is just waiting for him/her to finish speaking;

21. does not interrupt speakers;

22. withholds judgment about a student's idea(s) until the student has completed the message;

23. keeps his/her emotions under control while he/she is listening;

24. is aware of his/her biases and controls them while he/she is listening;

25. recognizes and "reads" his/her students' nonverbal messages;

26. listens "between the lines" for what students are not verbally saying;

27. "reads" students' feedback messages;

28. listens for and reflects his/her students' thoughts and feelings (See Long, 1978, for a complete discussion of the teacher as a reflective responder.);

Elonda: I don't think I can finish this story. I'm so discouraged. I don't understand half of he words.

Teacher: It's frustrating to be asked to understand an essay that's beyond your reading level, isn't it?

29. does not verbally or nonverbally respond to students until they have completed their messages;

30. listens empathetically without advising or judging;

31. checks for accuracy of understanding (by paraphrasing, asking questions, etc.) when he/she is not sure he/she understands students' messages;

Are you saying that you are more concerned with your grades than you are with learning?

32. gives prompt and thoughtful responses to students' questions;

33. listens to all students equally well;

34. listens equally well during the morning and during the afternoon;

35. cares genuinely about students;

36. cares genuinely about how his/her listening behavior affects his/her students;

37. is aware of his/her own listening behaviors and how he/she is listening; and

38. consistently demonstrates effective listening attitudes and skills.

While the preceding list is not exhaustive, it can serve as a valuable checklist for teachers to assess their own listening effectiveness as they both prepare for interactions with students and actually interact with students. Believing in the positive effect that model listening teachers have on their students, Lundsteen (1976) suggests that the ideal results would be as follows:

> As the teacher acquires these . . . desirable behaviors, he or she seeks to pass them on to the students who begin to employ them also. Thus, almost every modeled teaching behavior influences and is then copied by the pupil (p. 348).

Teachers can further assess their listening effectiveness as they consider the listening knowledge, attitudes, and skills that the students with whom they interact should possess.

The Student

Many listening educators (for example, Devine, 1982a, p. 56; Weaver, 1972, pp. 10–11; Lundsteen, 1979, pp. 59–61) as well as many states (35 states as of 1990, when Van Rheenen and Casmir separated data pertaining to listening and speaking practices) have identified listening skills, attitudes, and/or knowledge that students should possess. According to Lundsteen, who has examined goals and objectives of numerous states, the state of Maryland's K–12 listening framework is a "model" for other states (Lundsteen, 1989, personal conversation). Agreeing with Lundsteen, the authors present Maryland's goals and subgoals as an example of the many "lists" of listening behaviors that exist:

GOAL *1*: Use the stages of the listening process to understand aural messages
Subgoals:

1. Determine purposes for specific listening situations

2. Focus on the listening task

3. Discriminate among received aural and accompanying visual messages

4. Assign meanings to the messages received

5. Use self-monitoring techniques to assess listening effectiveness

GOAL 2: Listen for a variety of purposes
Subgoals:

1. Listen to comprehend the content of messages and the intent of speakers

2. Listen empathetically to help speakers clarify their thoughts and feelings

3. Listen critically to evaluate the validity of a message and the credibility of the sender

4. Listen for recreation and aesthetic pleasure

GOAL 3: Develop a positive attitude toward listening
Subgoals:

1. Develop a willingness to listen actively, openly, and responsibly

2. Develop a curiosity about and interest in listening to a variety of topics and people

3.   Value the significant role of listening in human experiences (Maryland State Board of Education, 1988)

While all of Maryland's goals and subgoals may be applicable to students during some communication transactions with teachers, the most commonly-used knowledge, attitudes, and skills are those listed in Goal 1 and its subgoals (covering knowledge about the listening process, purposes of listening, and self as a listener), Goal 3 and its subgoals (covering attitudes toward listening), and Goal 2-Subgoal 1 (covering comprehensive listening skills). Unlike Maryland's broad-based framework that includes essential listening knowledge, skills, and attitudes, a majority of listening educators' and states' "lists" of what competent listening students should possess focuses on comprehensive listening skills such as the following:

- prepare physically and mentally to listen
- determine the main idea(s) of a message
- recognize the general structure of a speaker's message
- determine a speaker's pattern of organization
- identify transitions
- note significant supporting details
- determine the interrelationship between main ideas and supporting details
- detect and assign meaning to nonverbal behaviors
- distinguish between relevant and irrelevant materials
- develop a variety of note taking styles
- adapt note taking style to the presentation style of the speaker
- use structural analysis and contextual clues to assign meanings
- anticipate the speaker's direction
- summarize the speaker's main ideas
- link new information with prior learnings
- follow oral directions
- follow a sequence of ideas
- determine the speaker's purpose
- formulate questions
- check for accuracy of understanding by asking questions, paraphrasing, etc. (Coakley and Wolvin, 1985)

Although a focus on comprehensive listening skills is understandable, especially considering that the major purpose for which students listen to teachers in the educational environment is to comprehend (that is, to understand the information that teachers impart), the possession of these skills—though absolutely essential—is of little significance if the student does not have a knowledge base about listening and positive attitudes toward listening.

Knowledge about listening includes knowledge about many relevant aspects such as knowledge about the communication process, listening process, role of listening in the communication process, importance of listening, purposes of listening, and self as a listener. (See Wolvin and Coakley, 1996, for a complete discussion of each of these aspects.) Particularly important in student-teacher transactions is the student's understanding of the role of feedback or overt responding. While feedback is not intrinsically a part of the listening process, it is an essential component in the communication process, and it is the means by which a teacher knows if a student does or does not understand the teacher's message. A common complaint among teachers is that students today are passive—are not responsive; in fact, one professor recently created a dummy, seated the dummy in the front row of his classroom, and then lectured to the dummy—just to show his students that the dummy was as responsive as they were.

For successful communication to occur during teacher-student transactions, students must understand the essential role of—and then apply—useful, supportive feedback. Also of major importance is that the student understand himself/herself as a listener, "for listeners must know what they are doing before they can improve their listening skills" (Coakley and Wolvin, 1989, p. 1).

Along with possessing comprehensive listening skills and listening knowledge, students must also possess positive listening attitudes if they are to be competent listeners when interacting with teachers. Goal 3 and its accompanying subgoals of Maryland's listening framework lists many of these essential attitudes—attitudes that are displayed both verbally and nonverbally.

Effective student listeners are basically interested people; they are interested in many topics and in many people. Likewise, they are curious—curious about what they do not know. They willingly seek to learn by listening. They approach each classroom listening situation with this question: What does this teacher (and my classmates) have for me? Then, they listen for what will be useful to them—useful now or in the future.

If a subject is not particularly interesting to them or if the speaker is not a particularly interesting presenter, they still listen, for they are looking for that which is valuable rather than that which is interesting. Also, they are open-minded; they are open to others' ideas (even when these ideas are expressed in emotionally-charged language), willing to share in problem-solving rather than debating, and amenable to reconsider their own behavior, views, values, and attitudes rather than view them as being absolute, definite, unquestionable. They welcome new information and new points of view, for they know that the more information they have and the more points of view they have listened to and then soundly evaluated, the more informed decisions they will make. Too, they realize that even people they do not particularly like may have useful ideas; thus, they do not let their feelings toward a teacher (or classmate) interfere with their listening to that teacher's (or classmate's) ideas.

Furthermore, effective student listeners are responsible; they know that they share in the responsibility for successful communication, and they willingly accept—with the teacher (or classmate)—at least 50 percent of this responsibility. An integral part of this responsibility is to motivate themselves to listen—rather than to rely on the teacher (or classmate) to motivate them. In addition to being motivated by listening for what is in the message for them, they are motivated by other personal rewards such as enjoyment, friendship, respect, praise, fulfillment of basic needs, educational or financial gains, etc. They know that listening is not a passive act; rather, it is hard work—especially to focus, resist or eliminate internal and external distractions, and refocus attention on the teacher (or classmate). Thus, they come to a listening situation ready to "sit up, work hard, and listen" as well as to be responsive nonverbally and verbally.

Among the many other attitudes that competent listening students should demonstrate in student-teacher transactions are two very important attitudes— patience and caring. Effective student listeners are patient because they care about how their listening behavior affects each teacher's (and classmate's) self-esteem. Rather than engaging in distracting signals that show impatience and insensitivity, they engage in attending behaviors (which have been described in the discussion of the model listening teacher); rather than interrupting, they observe turn-taking signals; and rather than beginning to speak before getting another's attention, they wait until they have that person's attention before they begin to speak.

Perhaps the most important attitude—underlying all others—is that effective student listeners care. They care about themselves as listeners, care about teachers (and classmates) as human beings, and care about how their listening behavior affects those other human beings. (See Coakley, 1993a, for a complete discussion of all attitudes discussed here as well as other attitudes the competent listening student should possess.)

Listening in Student/Student Transactions

While many student/student transactions occur within the immediate educational environment (classroom, halls, cafeteria, counselors' offices, etc.), many others extend beyond the school to public libraries, dorms, homes, etc. Also, while many of these transactions relate to classwork, many others relate to personal concerns that affect students' learning in classrooms. Regardless of the settings or the topics of the transactions, effective listening plays a major role, and competent student listeners are skilled in that role.

For effective listening to occur in student/student transactions, students must possess the same listening knowledge, skills, and attitudes as they need when interacting with teachers. (These are described in the previous section.) However, they also need to possess some additional listening skills and one other essential listening attitude.

Among the additional skills that students need to cultivate are withholding judgment, maintaining emotional control, creating a supportive communication climate, and applying sound criteria for student speakers and message evaluation (Goal 2—Subgoal 3 of the Maryland listening framework). Maintaining emotional control and withholding judgment until the message is fully understood are critical when class discussions are being held and, according to Arnold (1973), difficult for student listeners to do: . . . they [students] find it hard to listen to classmates. . . .

> The problem extends all the way to graduate school: recently a professor told me he was seriously considering giving up graduate seminars because of the inability of students to hear each other out (p. 36).

Competent student listeners make final judgments about a classmate's message only after they have completely understood (comprehended) the message. As they listen to the message, they ask themselves questions such as "Am I judging before I have gained a complete understanding of the total message? Does my premature judgment show on my face? Have I stopped listening in order to plan how I will respond or to plan a rebuttal?

These "catch" questions assist student listeners in "catching" themselves in the act of judging prematurely. The skill of withholding judgment requires much self-control and emotional control, but with awareness of what arouses them and persistent practice in changing their reaction tendencies, students can remain open to other students' points of view. Additionally, competent student listeners should create a supportive communication climate during class discussions. Through their verbal and nonverbal responses to others, they create a climate in which classmates feel free, safe, and comfortable in expressing themselves.

The last classroom skill (though there are certainly others) is applying sound criteria for student speakers and message evaluation. Among the critical listening sub-skills in which student listeners are competent are the following:

- recognize the influence of source credibility

- evaluate the credibility of the source

- recognize possible speaker bias, prejudice, attitudes, and point of view

- recognize argument structures

- judge validity of arguments detect and evaluate reasoning

- identify fallacies in reasoning

- detect propaganda

- evaluate evidence

- distinguish among facts, opinions, and inferences

- identify emotional appeals

- resist the influence of emotion-laden words

- draw conclusions from the talk (See Wolvin and Coakley, 1996, for a complete discussion of critical listening.)

In student/student transactions, one additional attitude that the student listener needs to cultivate is being other-oriented; that is, the student suppresses the desire to talk. Rather than having his or her ideas be the focus of the discussion, the other-oriented student listens to classmates' ideas. When other students present their ideas, the listener acknowledges their messages by asking for more background information, more supporting evidence, more personal points of view, etc. Though Bostrom (1988) describes the speech classroom, his comments are applicable to any classroom where there are student-student transactions:

When you enrolled in this course, you probably thought that your major job would be preparing and delivering speeches. While that is surely important, you can now see the importance of active, attentive listening. No speaker can do well without listeners. No one can have a significant public speaking experience without an audience, and your job as a member of the audience is vital to your classmates.

Clearly your classmates need a friendly, supportive group that shows interest in the topic and the situation. Boredom, disinterest, and hostility are terrible "turnoffs," even if exhibited by only one audience member . . . (pp. 48–49).

Another purpose for which students listen to students—mostly out of the classroom—is to empathize (Goal 2–Subgoal 2 of Maryland's listening framework). Also known as empathic and therapeutic listening, empathetic listening "is listening to provide a troubled sender with the opportunity to talk through a problem" (Wolvin and Coakley, 1996, p. 265). The need for empathetic listeners is apparent wherever there are students who have problems, problems ranging from failing a class or not being asked to the homecoming dance to dealing with a drug-abusing parent or dealing with the death of a friend.

While many students daily serve as empathetic listeners, only a few have been given intensive training through such programs as the hot line, crisis intervention, and peer-counseling programs. In addition to training students in focusing attention, demonstrating attending behaviors, and developing a supportive communication climate (three skills discussed previously in this chapter), such programs also sharpen students' skills in developing empathy and responding appropriately, two additional skills that the competent listening student possesses.

The skilled listening student knows the importance of demonstrating empathy, that is "thinking and feeling with another person" (Wolvin and Coakley, 1996, p. 279). This importance is emphasized by Carkhuff (1969): "Without an empathic understanding of the helpee's world and his difficulties as he sees them there is no basis for helping" (p. 173). Having empathy, then, is essential for the student listener to make appropriate responses.

Rather than focusing on self, discounting the speaker's feelings, philosophizing, blaming, evaluating, or advising (as the untrained student tends to do), the trained listening student responds reflectively—that is, he or she reflects the troubled student's thoughts and feelings. By making reflective responses and listening and listening and listening, the skilled listener provides the troubled speaker with the opportunity
to "work through" the problem and come to his/her own solution. (For a complete discussion of therapeutic listening, see Wolvin and Coakley, 1996.)

Listening in Teacher/Parent Transactions

When referring to the teacher/parent relationship, writers and speakers must frequently use the term "partnership." For example, the Rev. Jesse Jackson, spearheading a campaign in Prince George's County, Maryland, in September, 1989, urged parents to get involved—and to stay involved—in the schools by forming a partnership with their children's teachers. Likewise, the National Education Association (NEA) encourages parents to meet with their children's teachers to "help build strong parent-teacher partnerships" (NEA, n.d.).

While there are numerous opportunities for parents to get involved and interact with teachers (including participating in volunteer programs such as serving as an aide in the classroom, cafeteria, or nurse's office or on the playground; a resource person in the career lab, writing lab, or computer lab; a tutor; a chaperone for a school event; a fund-raiser for school "extras"; an interpreter for non-English- speaking students or other parents; a sign language expert; a host for school-related social events; etc.), the majority of parent/teacher transactions occur during classroom observations, PTA meetings, school performances (such as sporting events, variety shows, and plays), school rituals (such as graduation), back-to-school nights, telephone conversations, and conferences. Regardless of the context or purpose of the teacher/ parent interaction, listening plays a major role.

Although telephone conversations may be considered "conferences" (and should be prepared for by whoever initiates the calls), the emphasis in this section will be on the role of listening in face-to- face conferences. These conferences may be general ones organized by schools or specially-requested ones arranged by teachers or parents. It should be noted that "parent," as used throughout this chapter, may also refer to a grandparent, foster parent, or other person acting as guardian.

The Teacher

Just as the teacher prepares to listen to students in the classroom, the teacher prepares to listen to parents in the conference. One means of preparation is physically preparing the meeting area so that it will be conducive to listening; the area should be quiet and free of external distractions. Also, the area should be free of physical barriers; that is, comfortable chairs should be arranged conference style so teacher and parent(s) will be of equal status (MSTA, 1989, p. 7). To maximize listening time, the teacher should also mentally prepare for the conference.

Mental preparation includes (1) scheduling time between conferences (for the purposes of making notes about the previous conference and preparing for the next one); (2) preparing a conference checklist of items to cover (such as the student's academic achievement, physical and general health, attendance and lateness, social and emotional relations, work and study habits, special talents or aptitudes, etc.) (Ornstein, 1988, p. 8)—or— planning a general but flexible agenda of what will be covered (including the previous mentioned items as well as a review of the student's specific strengths and achievements and one of the student's "high-priority, well-focused area needing improvement" along with a proposed plan of action) (MSTA, 1989, p. 6) ; and (3) preparing a work folder for each student (Friedman, 1980, pp. 7–8)

During the conference, the effective listening teacher serves as a mode listening teacher. Article after article and checklist after checklist reviewing what teachers must do to have successful conferences with parents stress the need to LISTEN. For instance, Ornstein (1988) suggests three principles that should be followed; the first one is "Be a good listener. . . . Teachers must be sensitive to the parents' need to communicate their concerns or feelings" (p. 8). Also, included in the Maryland State Teachers Association "Effective

Conference Checklist" is the advice to "Listen to all [that] parents are saying" (MSTA, 1989, p. 7).

The model listening teacher begins by creating a supportive communication climate in which all involved are truly partners. After expressing genuine appreciation for the opportunity to interact with the parent(s) and informing them of the conference time frame so that the parent(s) will not feel "resentment at being cut off at the end of the allotted time" (Friedman, 1980, p. 6), the teacher—recognizing that the parents have their own agenda—encourages parents to express the goals they have for their time with the teacher. Friedman (1980) recommends the following as an appropriate opening: "Is there anything you would like to say or ask about your child's experiences in school this year?" (p. 12). This opening allows parents to express the major concerns they would like addressed, demonstrates the "teacher's receptivity and interest in them" (p. 12), and assists the teacher in identifying agenda priorities. At this point, the teacher engages in two other listening skills—checking for accuracy of understanding (through questioning, paraphrasing, and reflecting thoughts and feelings) and making written notes of the parental concerns. Adding the understood parental concerns to his/her prepared agenda, the model listening teacher then previews "what is to come and establishes joint responsibility for the ensuing dialogue" (p. 13).

As the conference progresses, the model listening teacher continues to employ effective listening skills and attitudes. In addition to using those skills previously mentioned, he/she:

- engages in attending behaviors

- concentrates on the parents' messages

- is other-oriented (that is, does not monopolize the discussion but rather seeks parents' thoughts and feelings)

- asks brief questions for clarification

- withholds judgment (rather than reacting before completely understanding) as he/she listens   to parents answer his/her open-ended questions about the child or present some other message

- is patient (that is, gives parents ample time to answer questions, explain concerns, etc., and employs "wait time" when a parent pauses but appears to still have more to say)

- accepts and acknowledges parents' views without necessarily agreeing with them

- demonstrates empathy and encourages parents to express feelings (by saying "What makes you feel inadequate as a parent?" rather than denying their feelings by saying "Now, you know you really don't feel that you're an inadequate parent")

- "listens" to the nonverbal feedback of parents and encourages them to express their concerns by making comments such as "I'd like to hear what's on your mind" or "You seem to be uncomfortable with what I just said; could you share that with me?" (Friedman, 1980, p. 35).

The model listening teacher also engages in listening behaviors that ensure better understanding and encourage the retention of the main concerns covered. To these ends, the teacher does not use educational jargon, such as CRT's and CAT's (MSTA, 1989, p. 7), is receptive to questions parents might have or clarifications parents might request, and asks parents to paraphrase (such as "I would like to know what basic messages you are getting from what I've said" and draw conclusions from the data he or she has presented (Friedman, 1980, p. 22).

Two other listening skills that the model listening teacher engages in are maintaining emotional control and responding appropriately. The NEA stresses the need to "stay calm" (n.d.). The MSTA recommends that teachers "avoid becoming defensive" (MSTA, 1989, p. 7). Both educational associations give meaningful advice, but maintaining emotional control when parents send, for example, blaming messages (such as "My child did well in school until she came into this classroom") and evaluative messages (such as "Your method of grading is very unfair") is difficult. However, the effective listening teacher, by utilizing a method proposed by Friedman (1980), can remain rational and respond appropriately by doing the following:

. . . the response should be divided into two corresponding parts—agreement that the behavior did occur (if it did) and disregard of the judgment component. The parent's remarks should be viewed as an attempt to draw the teacher into a "who's right, who's wrong" debate that has no basis in reality. In other words, if the parent's comment is "You require too much homework," instead of reacting "I don't give too much at all," the teacher might respond, "Yes, I ask them to do about an hour of homework each night. Is that difficult for your son to complete?" Or, the teacher might agree to the judgment, but without guilt or remorse, "Yes, I have required more than many students can handle." When problems are framed without blame the discussion can proceed effectively into the problem–solving stage" (pp. 44–45).

Another way of rationally dealing with blaming and evaluative messages is also proposed by Friedman (1980):

. . . teachers need to be sensitive to the feelings developing within themselves and in the dialogue with parents. When a sense of exasperation seems to arise in one's self or in the other's voice, face, or words, a shift in conversation needs to take place. The pattern itself can be pointed out, but without judgment or blame. Then, they can work together to change it (for example, "We seem to be arguing over who is at fault, rather than considering what we can do about the problem"). . . . A return to clarifying and reaffirming the shared basic goals of the conference can help to reemphasize the initial purpose from which the participants are drifting ("We both want Tom to do better, let's not lose sight of that.") (pp. 55–56).

As Friedman (1980) notes, teachers need to be conscious of the conference "climate" and "vibrations" and adapt skillfully to them (p. 56). (If conferences do lose their cooperative spirit and those involved cannot control their emotions, teachers should end the conferences and resume them when all parties are in control of their emotions.)

After the conference has focused on the student's strengths and one high-priority, well-focused area needing improvement has been described—not evaluated—by the teacher (such as "Karen did not do her history project" rather than "Karen is lazy") and one high-priority, well-focused area needing improvement has been agreed upon by all parties, the teacher may indicate understanding of the problem area by summarizing or may ask the parents to summarize their understanding. Then, together, the teacher and parents work to develop an action plan.

In establishing the action plan, both the teacher and the parents seek and listen to each person's opinions and come to agreement. After a plan has been formulated and the means by which progress will be communicated has been established, one or more of the individuals involved summarize the action plan. The teacher/parent interaction then concludes with all parties again expressing their appreciation for having had the opportunity to confer together.

The Parent

The parent, too, prepares to listen to the teacher in the conference. Before attending the conference, he or she mentally prepares by talking with the child and determining what, if anything, the child would like to have discussed with the teacher.

Also, if there is a second parent who cannot attend the conference, the attending parent asks that parent for any concerns, questions, etc. Additionally, the parent makes notes of what he or she would like to discuss: for example, the parent might note aspects about the "child's life at home, personality, problems, habits and hobbies" (NEA, n.d.) that the parent feels is important for the teacher to know; concerns about the programs and policies of the school; ways he or she and the teacher might work together for the purpose of helping the child do well; and questions about the child's progress (such as "Is my child in different groups for different subjects? Why?", "How well does my child get along with others?", etc.) (NEA, n.d.). To maximize the use of speaking and listening time during the conference, the parent should prioritize his or her list so that the most important ones would most likely be discussed.

The parent (like the teacher) begins the conference by creating a supportive communication climate. After clearly introducing him or her self and stating the name of the child, the parent expresses honest appreciation for the opportunity to interact with the teacher. Wintrol (1989) emphasizes the importance of showing appreciation: "We are quick to criticize when things go wrong; we are quick to request help when needed. We also need to be quick to appreciate when things go well or when we know extra effort and time is being given on behalf of our child" (p. 14).

Perhaps what is most important in creating a supportive communication climate is that the parent enters the conference with a positive, cooperative attitude toward the teacher rather than with a negative, competitive attitude. Chapman (1988) stresses the importance of parents' being positive: "You want to work together if possible, since your main objective is to help your child" (p. 9). Friedman (1980) observes the importance of both parents and teachers being cooperative:

> They must work to develop a fundamental sense of c mpatibility or of being on the "same side." Each must feel points of contact, understanding, and common ground with the other. Each should sense that the other knows and accepts where the other is "coming from" (p. 23).

Thus, to attain the best conference results, the parent leaves subjectivity, unrestrained emotions, defenses, and biases at home when he or she attends a teacher/parent conference.

The effective listening parent does not lose sight of the objective of the conference. Many a parent, when entering a school, has flashbacks to his or her own school days. Having the teacher as a captive listener, the parent often has the urge to relate school day experiences to the teacher. There is also the parent who, finding the teacher an empathetic listener, begins to discuss his or her own problems rather than the child's. With the limited time allotted for a conference, the listening parent suppresses the desire to talk about self and focuses instead on the child.

Even when the parent is focused, the parent does not monopolize the conversation. Both parent and teacher seek—and listen to—the other's opinions regarding the child. While the listening parent demonstrates all of the listening skills and attitudes that the listening teacher demonstrates, some actions have been recommended specifically for parents. "Listen, ask questions, observe" are the three actions Chapman (1988) stresses for parents to engage in during teacher/parent conferences (p. 9). She suggests that if the parent does not clearly understand a point made by the teacher, the parent should ask for clarification. For example, the parent should ask for an explanation of educational terms initials, and concepts that are unclear to him/her. Or, if the teacher makes a generalization about the child (such as "Marco is rowdy") without citing specific instances that prompted the teacher to make the general statement, the parent should ask for specific, supporting instances.

Further, she suggests that the parent ask specific questions about the child's behavior and then listen to the teacher's answers; the parent should listen "between the lines" to sense how caring the teacher is about his/her students. Chapman (1988) notes that asking the following question is essential: "What can we do at home to foster our child's performance at school?" (p. 10) This question, according to the NEA (n.d.), "is the most important part of the meeting. It will become your action plan." Lastly, she suggests that the parent observe the classroom environment to detect the personality of the teacher. Following this suggestion could provide the listening parent with a better understanding of the frame of reference from which the teacher is speaking. The NEA (n.d.) recommends still another listening skill that the parent should practice at the end of the conference: summarize the decisions that the parent and teacher have reached regarding the student's action plan so that the parent understands what the teacher is to do at school and the parent is to do at home.

After the conference is over, the parent continues to listen. First, he or she listens to the child. Both Chapman and the NEA suggest that the parent discuss the conference with the child. The parent listens to the child's opinions and then compares them with the teacher's. Additionally, the parent discusses the action plan with the child and determines—through listening to the child's paraphrasing—that the child understands what needs to be done. Finally, the parent maintains regular contact with the teacher to discuss the progress that the child is making.

With both teachers and parents demonstrating the listening skills and attitudes discussed in this section, it is likely that more teachers and parents would develop a gratifying partnership.

Listening in Parent/Child Transactions

Although the parent/child transaction is removed from the educational setting, a common topic of discussion between parent and child is school. In fact, the results of a survey investigating the listening behaviors of high school students and their parents revealed that (1) according to parents, school is the topic that their children most frequently discuss with them, and (2) according to students, school is the topic that their parents most frequently discuss with them (Coakley, 1986).

Thus, it seems appropriate to include in this chapter a section on listening in parent/child transactions since both the parent and the child are expected to listen to discussions about school. Unlike previous sections, however, this section will not separate the two participants; rather, the two will be combined, and the accent will be on the parent as an effective listener to his or her child.

Effective listening parents know the importance of listening to their children. They know children do need what fifteen-year-old Marit Hedstrom expresses: "Some parents don't listen. That's what kids really, really need. The kids come to them and really want to talk to them and share their problems with their parents. Some parents don't listen, don't want to know . . . (Gardner, 1982b, p. 14). They also know what Norman and Harris (1982) posit: "The key to real communication with young people is the readiness to listen and care about what they say even when we don't agree" (p. D2). And, parents do what they know: they listen.

Effective listening parents, likewise, know the importance of serving model listeners. Thus, parents accept the model role in hopes that the child will sense the importance of effective listening in relationships, as described by Komaiko (1961):

> A child first learns to listen by imitating others. He watches his parents, and if they listen to one another with interest and respect, he comes to sense the rightness of having a give-and-take relationship with people. Even more important to the kind of listener he will become, is how his parents listen to him. If at home he finds only talkers, but no listeners, he may pack up his problems and lug them elsewhere—or worse, seal them inside of himself (p. 80).

Additionally, effective listening parents know that listening is not an act that can be commanded; rather, it involves skills that must be taught and attitudes that must be developed. Just as parents accept the model role, they accept the teacher role (unlike many parents that Komaiko (1961) describes below) in hopes that the child will learn to be a skillful and willing listener:

> Most parents . . . act as if just commanding attention is the best way to get it—"Listen," we say. "Pay attention," we plead. Whatever phrase we adopt for demanding a listening ear and a comprehending mind, one thing is certain—no child ever learned to listen properly and well, simply because he was ordered to do so. Listening actually has far more to do with emotions than it does with just hearing (p. 80).

One of the most important listening attitudes that listening parents possess is a willingness to listen. They invite the child to talk about his or her daily activities, school affairs, schoolwork, feelings, concerns, etc. And, when they sense that the child is troubled, they invite the child to share his or her feelings: "You seem depressed. Did something happen at school? May I help in some way?" Parents recognize, though, that "some . . . youngsters . . . prefer no talk at all when they're upset. For them, Mom or Dad's presence is comfort enough" (Faber and Mazlish, 1980, p. 34). When a child is silent or says that he or she does not want to talk about what is on his or her mind, it is often enough for a parent just to say, "Okay, I'll be here if you want to talk later."

Parents also recognize that the time to invite communication is often not as soon as a child returns home from school (or as soon as the parent returns home). Rather than firing questions at the child ("How did you do on your math test? Was it hard? Were you prepared for it?") as soon as the parent and child see each other, the parent pleasantly acknowledges the child's presence and then gives the child a chance to tell or not to tell about his or her events of the day.

Additionally, parents recognize—and strive to teach the child—that there are inappropriate times for the parent to engage in effective listening; such times are as soon as the parent returns home, while a parent is preparing dinner, when a parent is talking with someone else, or when a parent is too tired. Parents know that there are times when they must agree with Procaccini, author of Parent Burnout: "Parents haven't the energy to listen; they're emotionally drained from making money and taking care of their own parents. And listening well is more exhausting than chopping wood" (Klingaman, 1989, p. D1). While there are times when parents do not have time to listen or are too tired to listen, listening parents recognize that they must make time to listen. This time may be scheduled time, such as uninterrupted "sharing time" scheduled each day (Sayre, 1984, p. 7) or family meeting time scheduled each week. Or, the time may be when "spontaneous moments—on the couch, in the car, over a cup of tea—can happen" (Goodman, 1988, p. 92).

Indeed, making time to listen is a critical problem recognized by communication experts who recommend that parents and teens make appointments if necessary or change schedules ("Let's talk at 10 o'clock" or "How about if I get up a half hour earlier tomorrow") (Klingaman, 1989, p. D-7). The listening parent, when necessary, commits to a specific time—and then keeps his or her commitment.

Among the other listening attitudes that listening parents possess are being honest, patient, open minded, and caring. For instance, when parents do not have time to listen to their child at a particular moment, they say they do not. Parents know that their impatience and distraction will be apparent and, thus, prevent them from being an effective listener. Later, when the two do interact, the parent does not rush the child, for the parent realizes that listening —true listening—often requires much time and patience and that patience is not demonstrated by interrupting.

Listening parents also remain open minded and allow for differences of opinion; "permitting youngsters to disagree with us shows them that we're strong enough to be challenged (and big enough to back down if necessary)" (NEA, 1971).

Winship, author of the syndicated teen-age column, "Ask Beth," likewise, stresses the importance of being an open minded listening parent: "Parents need to treat them as important individuals, which means listening. And it means allowing them to have opinions. You don't have to agree with it, but you've got to listen to it" (Gardner, 1982a, p. 14). A parental response of "I disagree with you" shows an open mind, whereas a response of "How dare you think that way" shows a closed mind. Lastly, listening parents have a caring attitude— a caring attitude about the child, their relationship with the child, and about the effects that their listening behavior has on the child's self-esteem. One of the most meaningful ways that parents show their caring attitude is to listen to their child; by listening, the parent is saying he following:

> You are . . . saying that your child is important enough to be heard; you are teaching her that it pays to explore and share inner feelings. You're telling your son that his thoughts are worth your putting your busy schedule on hold. Perhaps most important, you are saying to your child, "I care about you" (Goodman, 1988, p. 94)

Serving as teachers by example, listening parents demonstrate effective listening skills, too. In addition to being competent in many of the other skills that have been previously mentioned in other sections of this chapter, competent listening parents are especially skilled in engaging in attending behaviors, withholding judgment, and responding appropriately.

Attentive parents put down the newspaper, turn off the television, shut the door, and do all that they need to do to free the setting from external distractions. Then, they use their entire bodies to focus fully on the child and show that they are available: eye contact is maintained, facial expression shows involvement, body is open, etc. As parents listen, they withhold judgment. One commonly-made judgment that listening parents do *not_* make is that the topic of the child's concern is not significant.

Parents know what the NEA (1971) states:

> What is "important" is a relative matter, and if children learn at an early age that what they consider to be major concerns are treated as minor concerns by their parents, we should not be surprised if they become increasingly less communicative and more secretive as they get older (no page).

And, parents know what Goodman (1988) vividly describes:

> Children's concerns are different from ours. You may no longer fear eating the black part of the banana or crumple when someone calls you names, but the emotions behind these situations are universal. Never laugh, suggests Dr. Formica, unless your child is laughing too.

Give her the freedom to express her feelings and views without fear of ridicule or judgment (p. 94).

The other most commonly-made mistake that effective listening parents do **not** make is quick judgment about the child's message. Rather than listening to the child's verbal and nonverbal messages to learn the child's feelings and thoughts, ineffective listening parents quickly judge the rightness or wrongness of the child's comments. The judgmental face and judgmental response appear almost instantaneously. One fifteen-year-old boy warns parents about the possible effects of their being judging before fully comprehending:

> Whatever they have to say, let them talk; then give your views. Don't jump to conclusions. I feel that half the kids aren't ever listened to. They don't have any say in matters after a while; they don't even talk any more . . . . Norman and Harris, 1982b, p. D2).

Being attentive and non-judgmental, listening parents also respond appropriately as they engage in "active listening." Active listening, popularized by Parent Effectiveness Training author and workshop director Thomas Gordon, is listening intently to the verbally—and nonverbally—expressed thoughts and feelings of the speaker and reflecting—without making a value judgment—those thoughts and feelings back to the speaker.

Ginott (1969), author of Between Parent and Teenager, cites many examples of individuals engaging in active listening. The following is an example as described by a parent:

> Oliver, age thirteen, came home from school in an ornery mood. He had a lot of homework plus an assignment he hadn't finished in school. He said he hated his teacher because she kept piling on work.
>
> I resisted the impulse to preach: 'Well, it's not your teacher's fault. You have only yourself to blame. If you had finished the work in class, you wouldn't have to do it at home.' Instead, I said, You do have a lot of work: Spelling, arithmetic, and social studies, all in one day.' To my surprise Oliver answered, _I'd better start right away. I have lots of work to do' (pp. 70–71).

Like Oliver's parent, effective listening parents resist giving responses that are blaming and judgmental; they also resist giving other inappropriate responses such as those that focus on themselves ("You think your day was bad. In the office, there was...."), discount the child's feelings ("Oh, don't worry about it; tomorrow will be brighter."), philosophize ("Life is full of disappointments. The sooner you realize that 'hard knocks' abound, the sooner you will leave your dream world."), or advise ("Well, let me tell you what you should do. Tomorrow, in each of your classes...."). Instead, listening parents, engaging in active listening, empathetically respond by reflecting the child's thoughts and feelings ("It must really hurt when your classmate makes fun of you.").

Listening in the educational environment, then, involves the transactions of the student, teacher, and parent as the key communicators in the process. Since students learn to listen effectively through instruction and role models, it is important that both teachers and parents provide effective training in and modeling of listening behavior for their children. Likewise, all three participants must be willing, active listeners who assume their share of the responsibility for the successful outcome of the communication transactions.

To build a true learning "team," it is necessary for teachers to listen to students, students to listen to teachers, students to listen to their peers, parents to listen to teachers, teachers to listen to parents, parents to listen to their children/students, and children/students to listen to their parents. The success of any and all of these transactions is dependent upon all participants adopting appropriate, effective listening attitudes and behaviors and applying them with responsibility and care.

Exercises

Teacher/Student

1. The teacher will have audiotapes and videotapes of his/her teaching—leading class discussions, lecturing, interacting with individual students, facilitating activities, giving directions, and engaging in many other teaching behaviors. The teacher then plays back the tapes, and carefully analyzes his/her presentation and listening behaviors—verbal, vocal, and nonverbal behaviors. Note spatial distance; eye contact; touching behavior; vocal variety and possible interpretations of volume, rate, pitch, and tone; bodily movement; gestures; facial expressions; verbal clarity and conciseness; word choice; complexity of sentence patterns; verbal and nonverbal formality and informality; attending behaviors; wait time; teacher–talk time versus student– talk time; responses to students; amount of teacher repetition; timing of messages; patience; amount of teacher interruptions; emotional control; etc. He/She notes behaviors with which he/she is dissatisfied and works toward minimizing or eliminating them. He/She continue experimenting with and practicing various behaviors, taping, and analyzing the tapes until he/she becomes a model presenter and listener (Coakley, 1993b, pp. 13-14).

2. After a teacher has given students instructions, he/she typically asks, "Do you understand what you are to do?" Frequently, students —whether they understand or not— will nod that they do understand (or will give no response).

Instead of asking "Do you understand ...?", the teacher asks, "What do you understand that you are to do?" and calls upon students to paraphrase his/her instructions. After a student has given his/her paraphrase, the teacher asks all other students to signal—nonverbally—whether or not they agree with the paraphraser's message.

Student/Student

3. To encourage students to listen to other students' answers, the teacher regularly and randomly calls upon a student to paraphrase another student's answer to a question, comment during a discussion, question, etc. Additionally, the teacher encourages students to ask each other questions related to their comments (Coakley, 1993b, p. 21).

4. The class establishes a "listening corner" in some fairly secluded area of the classroom. This designated area serves as a place where a troubled student may go when he/she feels the need to have someone to listen to him/her. Another student serves as an empathetic listener for the troubled student (Coakley, 1993b, p. 22).

Parent/Child

5. Schedule a time each week for family sharing time, when all family members are equal. Each member airs what is on his/her mind, but before one member can speak, he/she first summarizes (to the previous member's satisfaction) what the previous member has expressed.

6. The parent practices responding reflectively to the following messages expressed by teenagers:

"I've had a miserable day. Nothing has gone right. I did poorly on my math test, I forgot my speech, and I couldn't get the pom routine straight."

"I don't know what to do. I don't know if I want to go on to school or work. I'm having a tough time deciding."

"John told me today that he thought we should break up for a while. He said he thought that we were getting too serious and that we should see other people."

Teacher/Parent

7. Prior to a teacher/parent conference, the parent mentally prepares by listing and prioritizing questions/concerns that he/she would like to have addressed during the conference.

8. Following a teacher/parent conference, the teacher sends to the parent a note stating his/her understanding of the action-plan decisions made at the conference and asks the parent to confirm the accuracy of the teacher's understanding.

9. Following a teacher/parent conference, the parent draws up a one-page "executive summary" of the points the teacher has made.

References

Arnold, J. (1971). Who listens? The Independent School Bulletin, 33, 36–38.

Barker, L. L., Edwards, R., Gaines, C., Gladney, K., & Holley, F. (1980). An investigation of proportional time spent in various communication activities by college students. Journal of Applied Communications Research, 8, 101–109.

Bird, D. E. (1953). Teaching listening comprehension. Journal of Communication, 3, 127–128.

Bostrom, R. N. (1988). Communicating in public: Speaking and listening. Edina, MN: Burgess Publishing.

Brown, J. I. (1987). Listening—ubiquitous yet obscure. Journal of the International Listening Association. 1, 3–14.

Burley–Allen, M. (1982). Listening: The forgotten skill. NY: John Wiley & Sons.

Carkhuff, R. G. (1969). Helping and human relations, Vol. I. NY: Holt, Rinehart and Winston.

Chapman, J. K. (1988). Advice for parents. PTA Today. 14, 9–10.

Coakley, C. G. (1986). Parents' and teenagers' listening behavior. Unpublished study, High Point High School, Beltsville, Maryland.

Coakley, C. G. (1988). Teaching effective listening. Unpublished work.

Coakley, C. G. (1993a). Teaching effective listening. New Orleans: Spectra Publishers.

Coakley, C. G. (1993b). Teaching effective listening—Teacher's companion book. New Orleans: Spectra Publishers.

Coakley, C. G., & Wolvin, A. D. (Eds) (1989). Experiential listening: Tools for teachers and trainers. New Orleans, LA: Spectra Publishers.

210   *Listening in Everyday Life*

Coakley, C. G., & Wolvin, A. D. (1985, July). State of the art of lis-
    tening: For Education. Paper presented at the International
    Listening Association Summer Conference, St. Paul, MN.
Conaway, M. S. (1982). Listening: Learning tool and retention agent.
    In A. S. Algier & K. W. Algier (Eds.), Improving reading and
    study skills (pp. 51-63). San Francisco: Jossey-Bass.
Cooper, P. J. (1984). Speech communication for the classroom
    teacher (3rd ed.). Dubuque, IO: Gorsuch Scarisbrick.
Corey, S. M. (1940). The teachers out-talk the pupils. School Re-
    view, 48, 745-752.
Dedmon, D. N. (1983). Education: Confirming what we know. Vi-
    tal Speeches, 50, 19. Devine, T. G. (1982a). Listening skills
    schoolwide: Activities and programs. Urbana, IL: NCTE/ERIC.
Devine, T. G. (1982b). Teaching study skills. Boston, MA: Allyn
    and Bacon.
Faber, A., & Mazlish, E. (1980). How to talk so kids will listen and
    listen so kids will talk. NY: Avon Books.
Friedman, P. G. (1980). Communicating in conferences. Urbana, IL:
    ERIC Clearinghouse on Reading and Communication Skills.
Friedman, P. G. (1983). Listening processes: Attention, understand-
    ing, evaluation. Washington, D. C.:   National Education
    Association.
Gardner, M. (1982a). Building bridges of mutual respect. Christian
    Science Monitor, Nov, 3, 12-14.
Gardner, M. (1982b). You have to listen. Christian Science Monitor,
    Nov, 1, 12-14.
Ginott, H. G. (1969). Between parent and teenager. NY: Avon
    Books.
Goodman, S. (1988). Are you listening? Parents, 63, 89-94.
Gordon, T. (1970). Parent effectiveness training. NY: Peter H. Wy-
    den.
Klingaman, M. (1989). Parents must learn to tune in to teen signals
    for help. The Evening Sun, Jan. 19, D1, D7.
Komaiko, J. R. (1961). The fine art of listening. Parents, 36, 41, 78,
    80.
Legge, W. B. (1971). Listening, intelligence, and school achievement.
    In S. Duker (Ed.), Listening: Readings II (pp. 121-133). NJ:
    Scarecrow Press.
Long, L. (1978). Listening/Responding: Human-relations training
    for teachers. Monterey, CA: Brooks/Cole Publishing Cmpany.
Lundsteen, S. W. (1979). Listening: Its impact on reading and the
    other language arts (2nd ed.). Urbana, IL: NCTE/ERIC.
Lundsteen, S. W. (1976). Research review and suggested directions:
    Teaching listening skills to children in the elementary school,
    1966-1971. Language Arts, 53, 348-351.

Lyle, M. R. (1987, March). Teaching listening, K–12. Paper presented at the International Listening Association Convention, New Orleans, LA.

Lyle, M. R. (1989, March). Training trainers to teach teachers. Paper presented at the International Listening Association Convention, Atlanta, GA.

Markgraf, B. (1957). An observational study determining the amount of time that students in the tenth and twelfth grades are expected to listen in the classroom. Unpublished master's thesis, University of Wisconsin.

Maryland State Department of Education. (1988). English language arts—A Maryland curricular framework. Baltimore, MD: Maryland Department of Education.

Maryland State Teachers Association. (1989). How to build parent support. MSTA Action Line, Aug. 23, 6–7.

National Education Association. (n.d.). Making parent–teacher conferences work for your child, pamphlet NEA 202-1087–F.

National Education Association. (1971). How to get your child to listen to you. Washington, D. C.: NEA.

National Education Goals Panel (1992). The national education goals report. Washington, D. C.: National Education Goals Panel, p. 5.

Nichols, R. G. (1966). Listening instruction in the secondary school. In S. Duker (Ed.), Listening readings (pp. 242–243). NY: Scarecrow Press.

"1994 Industry Report." (1994, October). Training, p. 49.

Norman, J., & Harris, M. (1982). Teen–agers just want their parents to listen. Denver Post, Feb. 18, D2–D4.

Ornstein, A. C. (1988). The parent–teacher conference. PTA Today, 14, 8–9.

Perkins, T. M. (1994). A survey of listening instruction in the basic speech course. Journal of the International Listening Association, 8, 80–97.

Rence, M. (1985). Project listen: Good listeners are winners. Unpublished paper of Project LISTEN, San Juan Capistrano, CA, June, 7–9.

Sayre, J. M. (1984). Helping the child to listen and talk. Danville, IL: The Interstate Printers and Publishers.

Stammer, J. D. (1981). MAPPing out a plan for better listening. Teacher, 98, 37–38.

Steil, L. K. (1982). The secondary teacher's listening resource unit. St. Paul, MN: Communication Development, Inc.

Stewig, J. W. (1974). Exploring language with children. Columbus, OH: Charles E. Merrill Publishing Company.

Taylor, S. E. (1984). What research says to the teacher: Listening. Washington, D. C.: National Education Association.

United States Department of Labor. (1991). What work requires of schools. Washington, D. C.: U.S. Department of Labor, p. xviii.

Van Rheenen, D., & Casmir, M. H. (1990). The status of state practices in speaking and listening skill assessment: 1981–1009. Paper presented at the Speech Communication Association Convention, Chicago, IL.

Weaver, C. H. (1972). Human listening: Processes and behavior. Indianapolis, IN: Bobbs-Merrill.

Wilt, M. E. (1950). A study of teacher awareness of listening as a factor in elementary education. Journal of Educational Research, 43, 631.

Wintrol, J. (1989). When kids and schools are out of step. Washington Parent, Sept./Oct., 14.

Wolvin, A. D. (1984). Teaching teachers to listen. Curriculum Review, 23, 17–19.

Wolvin, A. D., & Coakley, C. G. (1988). Listening (5th ed.). Dubuque, IO: Brown & Benchmark Publishers.

Wolvin, A. D., Coakley, C. G., & Disburg, J. (1991). An exploratory study of listening instruction in selected colleges and universities. Journal of the International Listening Association, 5, 68–85.

Wolvin, A. D., Coakley, C. G., & Disburg, J. (1992). Listening instruction in selected colleges and universities. Journal of the International Listening Association, 6, 59–65.

Chapter 9

LISTENING TRAINING: The Key to Success in Today's Organizations

Lyman K. (Manny) Steil

Points to be Addressed:

- Listening in the 1990's: a key to success in organizations
- The SIER model for effective listening
- General principles for understanding and developing listening
- Guidelines and approaches to listening skills training in organizations.

Listening has been, is, and will continue to be the primary communication activity used by most people throughout the world. Listening has always been central to the personal, professional, social, educational, and family success of every person. Thus, listening training is doubly important to all professionals who are interested in, and responsible for, the full development of employees within an organization.

In the 1990's and beyond, a simple yet significant fact for human development and training remains: Job success and development of all employees, regardless of title, position, or task, will continue to be directly related to the employees' attitudes toward, skills in, and knowledge about listening. Moreover, all professionals directly responsible for training and development, in all organizations, are in an excellent position to have a positive impact on employees' listening and learning experiences. Most important, management, leaders, and human resource professionals are in a position to insure that effective listening training is available throughout the organization, from the top down and across all functions. The basic key to effective listening development within today's organizations is two-fold. First, effective listening training and development requires a balanced focus on enhancing appropriate listening Attitudes, Skills, and Knowledge (ASK). Our ASK Model (Figure 1) clarifies that there is no quick-fix to listening training and any training that only focuses on skill development (i.e., 6 tips and 17 techniques) is doomed to minimal long-

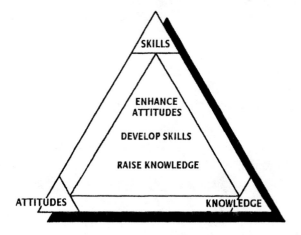

term impact.

Figure 1 – Listening ASK Model

The second key to maximizing effective listening training resides in specific and individualized profiling and assessment. Effective development requires tailored training based on such identified individual characteristics as personality traits, listening strengths and weaknesses, habitual patterns, and operational attitudes, skills, and knowledge. Without specific and individualized profiling and assessment, any training will be generalized and less than effective[1].

Operational Definition

Listening is the complex, learned, human process of Sensing, Interpreting, Evaluating, Storing, and Responding to oral messages. (See Figure 2.)

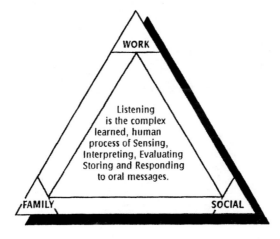

Figure 2 – Listening definition

Effective listening consists of the interconnected activities of Sensing, Interpreting, Evaluating, Storing and Responding. (See Figure 3)

---

[1] An example of such profiling and assessment tools utilized with our clients is: Personal Listening Profile (Form A & B), copyright 1980, Communication Development, Inc., and Personalysis, copyright 1975, James Noland.

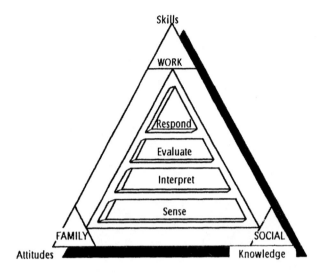

Figure 3 – S. I. E. R. Model

Sensing is the first stage, where the sender's message enters, or does not enter, the listener's stream of consciousness (sensory mechanism). The second stage is the *interpretation* of what was sensed, which leads to mutual understanding (or misunderstanding). The third stage involves *evaluation*. Evidence is weighed, fact is separated from opinion, the reasoning process is analyzed, agreements and disagreements are registered, and judgments are made. *Storing* is the necessary mortar between each stage, and *responding* is crucial to complete the whole act of listening. Responding allows listening to come full circle and is crucial for judging the success of the listening act as a whole. *Sensing, interpreting,* and *evaluating* are internal acts; *responding* is an external act.

These four stages must occur in order, as the message must be fully sensed before it can be adequately interpreted. Correct interpretations must precede effective evaluations. And, of course, an intelligent response cannot be made until the listener has properly sensed, interpreted, and evaluated the sender's message.

Listening is an active skill, in spite of a long and strongly held misconception that it is a passive behavior that primarily requires interest, attention, and focus. Effective listening requires that the listener assume at least 51 percent of the responsibility for effective communication.

Finally, the "Steil Law of Listening" is helpful. Remember the word *law* and the formula L = (A x W)2. Simply put, L (Listening) = (A (Ability) x W (Willingness)) (Steil, 1983, p. 21–24). Without the necessary listening abilities, no amount of willingness to listen will result in effective listening. On the other hand, a person can possess the necessary skills and abilities, but not be willing. Without both components, a person cannot be a successful listener. Trainers can enhance the listening attitudinal/motivational base, skills/behavior base, and knowledge base of employees in organizations.

Purpose and Objectives

Any careful reflection on most training and development programs will establish that individual development through training in listening is the foundation on which all other training and development programs can (and should) be built. Such descriptors as *basic, vital, necessary, crucial,* and *central* are clearly appropriate when considering the importance and purpose of training in listening for most employees, in most jobs, at all levels. Since listening skills are central for the learning of most other skills, listening training should be an initial, major, and basic component of any core training program. Moreover, such listening development efforts should be reinforced in all subsequent training.

Recognizing that the overwhelming majority of all employees have never participated in any significant listening training and do not listen as effectively as they should, or could, and that the resulting costs are extraordinary, the general objective of listening training is simply to help employees develop listening attitudes, skills, and knowledge. The ultimate objective is to prepare each employee to be an efficient and effective listener in all situations. Specific objectives include:

- Increasing employees' insights into the importance of, role of, needs for, nature of, and problems, costs, and rewards of listening.

- Assessing individual listening habits, abilities, and skills.

- Developing listening skills and technique to improve individual and organizational listening effectiveness.

General Principles

The following nine principles are relevant to maximizing the understanding and development of listening:

1. We are all communicating beings.
2. Listening is central to success in all personal, professional, family, social, educational, and other endeavors.
3. Listening is the primary communication activity.
4. Although effective listening (knowledge, attitudes, and specific skills) can be taught and developed, it generally is not.
5. As a result of this lack of training, most people develop inadequate listening habits and behaviors.
6. Poor listening is costly.
7. The rewards of effective listening substantially exceed the costs of development.
8. Listening involves more than hearing: The complete act involves the four stages of sensing, interpreting, evaluating, and responding.
9. Individuals listen for a variety of purposes, including phatic (relationship binding), cathartic (emotional release), informational (shared data), and persuasive (change or reinforce belief and achieve action) purposes.

Each purpose requires similar but different skills.

As noted, the costs of poor listening are overwhelming. Specifically, poor listening can result in exorbitant wastes of time, money, productivity, profitability, sales, human relationships, self-esteem, reputations, health, and lives. Examples include rescheduled meetings, wasted materials, lost sales, management-labor disputes, divorce, missed opportunities, airplane disasters, and losses in wars.

Moreover, the higher a person moves within an organization, the more important effective listening is. Studies affirm that listening time increases with position advancements. On average, middle managers and above spend approximately 57 percent of their work time listening. Some top-level executives report that they spend nearly 80 percent of their communicating time listening. In a 1978 study by Harold T. Smith of Brigham Young University, certified administrative managers were asked to identify managerial competencies, reduce them to the top 20, and then rank them according to how critical the managers thought each was to their jobs and success. The No. 1 ranked competency, viewed to be supercritical to professional success, was listening. Since the relevance and importance of effective listening seems obvious, a discussion of listening in historical perspective is in order.

Historical Perspective

For more than half a century, numerous studies have examined the role and significance of listening as a human behavior. Among the early researchers, Paul T. Rankin had the most impact and stands out as most noteworthy. From 1926 to 1929, Rankin carefully identified and analyzed the communication—reading, writing, speaking, listening (1926). Over the years, Rankin's findings have been confirmed by the work of other researchers[2].

In sum, this collective research indicates that listening is clearly the predominant, most utilized communication behavior. And listening has continued to be our first learned, most used, and least taught communication activity (Figure 4).

	Listening Writing	Speaking	Reading	
Learned	First	Second	Third	Fourth
Used	Most	Next to most	Next to least	Least
Taught	Least	Next to least	Next to most	Most

Figure 4. Communication Activities and time spent learning, using, and teaching each (Steil, 1983).

More than 40 years of research, spotlighting the low level of effectiveness and efficiency of the average listener, reinforces the need to develop listening skills. The pioneering research of Ralph G. Nichols (1948) ("the Father of Listening) is still applicable today: the low level of retention (25 percent effectiveness within 48 hours) of the average listener, the characteristics of effective and ineffective listeners, and the specific factors that account for differences in listening comprehension (Steil, 1977). Most important, the long-term consistency of the data highlights the challenge and opportunity faced by training and development professionals.

Although listening development has been largely and generally neglected at all levels of education and training, there have been exceptions. Since 1948, listening has been a fully credited course of study at the University of Minnesota, and thousands of students have

---

[2] For example, Bird (1956); Wilt (1949), pp. 115–36; Markgraf (1947); Breiter (1957), pp. 745–52; Corey (1940); Steil (1977); Barker, Edwards, Gaines, Gladney, & Holley (1980), pp. 101–109; and Steil, deMare, & Summerfield (1983), pp. 9–36.

completed the ten-week course entitled "Effective Listening." Over the years, a limited but growing number of other educational institutions have offered listening instruction. And a very small number of consultants, consulting firms, and corporate training departments have also developed creative, well-founded, and effective listening development programs.

Since 1978, three major events have enhanced listening training efforts throughout the world. In 1978 the federal government amended the Primary–Secondary Education Act, mandating for the first time the inclusion of listening as a basic competency to be taught in our elementary and secondary schools. This focus on a "return to the basics," or "forward to the basics," or developing "minimal competencies" has had a strong impact on the interest in listening development at all levels.

A second event advancing listening also occurred in 1978 when the Sperry Corporation (now Unisys) undertook a major listening development and advertising program. Sperry's commitment to listening grew from a basic position that effective listening was central to its business and managerial philosophy and commitment. The corporation's motto—"We Understand How Important It Is To Listen"— was communicated throughout the Western World. In addition, Sperry is the corporate model in developing listening training programs for its employees. In five years of its program, Sperry trained more than 40,000 employees, at all levels (chairman of the board and down), in more than 20 countries around the world. Moreover, Sperry extended its listening training efforts to selected public audiences throughout the United States, Canada, and Europe.

The 1979 formation of the International Listening Association (ILA) was the third major event. The ILA currently consists of members representing education, industry, business, government, military, consulting, counseling, and publishing from 46 states and 10 countries. The purpose of the ILA is to promote the study and development of effective listening through:

- Establishment of a network of professionals.

- Exchange of information, including teaching methods, training experiences, and materials.

- Research on how listening affects humanity in economics, education, race, culture, and international relations.

Recognizing the fact that the overwhelming majority of our existing workforce (as well as those entering) are not well-developed, effective listeners, the personnel management, human resources development, training, employee relations (communications), and productivity improvement professionals face a great challenge and opportunity. In fulfilling both, there are essential conditions that should be met.

Essential Conditions

As listening is a sine qua non of today's workforce, some essential conditions are suggested. To maximize any internal listening training and development, such training should:

1. Be related to larger organizational philosophies, objectives, and policies.

2. Be supported by top-management commitment.

3. Be specifically and adequately budgeted.

4. Start with top management.

5. Be provided to all appropriate personnel with a top-down priority order.

6. Be enhanced with parallel training and group reinforcement.

7. Be reinforced over time with appropriate extended recognition and rewards.

8. Be offered as a core program and also be integrated into all other appropriate training and development programs. It should be seen as more than a simple, "quick fix" solution.

9. Be based on tested, proven materials and methodologies.

10.   Be professionally facilitated by trained, knowledgeable, and skilled listening specialists.

General Approaches

Beyond these essential conditions, at least four general approaches can be used to provide listening training and development opportunities. These include internal organizational training programs, external consultant training programs, external to the organization training programs, and individual self-development programs. Each approach has advantages and disadvantages.

Internal Organizational Listening Training Programs

Numerous organizations have developed their own corporate/organizational in-house listening training programs. Such in-house programs are (1) developed and presented by internal staff members, (2) developed by an external consultant and adapted and presented by internal staff people, or (3) built around commercially available programs and materials. Advantages and disadvantages of the internal approaches are worth reviewing.

Potential advantages of internally developed programs include:.

- Specific knowledge of the needs of potential participants and sponsoring department or units.

- The ability to tailor specific programs to the organization and its employees.

- The ability to coordinate and integrate listening development with other training efforts.

- The efficient use of internal resources, and potential cost–effectiveness.

Potential disadvantages of internally developed programs include:

- Limited knowledge of listening research, tests, methods, and materials.

- Fiscal inefficiency due to potential costly "reinvention of the wheel."

- Possible reduced program credibility and organizational acceptance.

- Possible inability (due to positional differences) to effectively train organization members of higher position, rank, and status (such as the chief executive officer, president, senior vice president).

- Reduced focus and attention due to multiple demands and ongoing responsibilities.

- Possible loss of program continuity due to internal mobility and turnover of staff members.

In sum, effective internal listening programs have been, and can be, developed and presented with special attention to the essential conditions previously discussed.

External Consultant Training Programs

Many organizations contract with specially trained listening development consultants for the development and presentation of listening programs. Such programs range from stock or canned prepackaged programs to tailor-made programs. Depending on the organization's intent and usage of such programs, a number of potential advantages and disadvantages exist.

If a knowledgeable, skilled, experienced, and professional consultant or consultant group is retained, the potential advantages include:

- A program based on current, broad, and relevant materials, methodologies, and resources.

- Use of a tested and proven program and facilitator/instructor.

- The consultant's objective, bias-free orientation.

- Heightened program credibility because of perceived outside specialist role.

- The ability of the consultant to draw on numerous other experiences.

- Fiscal efficiency and heightened cost-effectiveness because it is unnecessary to "reinvent the wheel."

- The ability of the consultant to work at all organizational levels.

- The ability of the consultant to focus full attention on the development project.

- The consultant's contribution of fresh, new, stimulating materials, concepts, stories, and approaches.

Potential disadvantages of using external consultant programs include:

- Challenge in selecting effective consultants.

- Consultant's limited view of client's big picture.

- Difficulty of coordinating internal and external staff efforts.

- Lack of acceptance if consultant is viewed as an unknowing outsider.

- Extra cost for qualified resources.

The critical questions in using external listening consultants center around the selection, the specific use, and the management of such resources. Overall, with proper and careful selection (discussed later), use, and management, external listening consultants may serve any organization in an expert, productive, cost-effective, efficient manner. If not properly selected, used, and managed, external listening consultants will be costly and ineffective.

External Organizational Listening Training Programs

A third approach available for listening development is the use of programs offered by numerous external agents. These include regularly scheduled, for-credit university or college courses of full quarter or semester length. In addition, a growing number of listening seminars and workshops (ranging from a few hours to two or three days) are offered throughout the world. Such programs obviously hold advantages and disadvantages, but the most important caveat centers on the necessary careful evaluation of the specific program (objectives, methodologies, materials) and the instructor/facilitator (background, knowledge, training, skills, recommendations).

Potential advantages of external programs include:

● Programs that are readily available and that require no internal creation.

● Credit for degree or certificate programs received by program participants.

● Programs that have credibility.

● Lengthy, in-depth programs that may allow extended participant development.

● Programs that may allow extended participant practice and application.

● Flexible programs that may be completed outside work hours.

● Programs that may provide a fresh perspective and allow freedom for self-disclosure and risk taking.

● Programs that allow for combined organization and individual support and initiative.

● Programs that may increase participant motivation.

● Programs that are available at a range of costs.

Potential disadvantages of external programs include:

- Programs created externally without specific consideration of corporate, organizational, or individual participant needs.

- Program and instructor quality that may be difficult to assess, monitor, and change.

- Involved participants isolated from other organization members.

- Lack of desired parallel training for all organization members.

- Likely extinction of newly developed attitudes and behaviors because of lack of reinforcement.

- Difficulty in integrating program gains into other internal programs.

- Wide range of program and instructor quality.

In sum, external listening development programs are available, and although variable in nature and quality they offer opportunity to both the organization and the employee. In creating a full portfolio of training opportunities, the external program can fill an important gap. When choosing any external program, careful evaluation of the program and instructor is the most critical challenge faced. If the evaluation is sound, the use of external programs can be effective in terms of both cost and skills acquired.

Individual Self-Development Programs

A substantially different method in the development of listening is the individual self-development approach. In this approach, individuals chart their own reading, studying, observing, and practicing program. A plethora of materials regarding the behavior of listening is available and, with guidance from training professionals, can be helpful. In reading about the importance and role of listening, related problems, and ways to improve listening, a person will become sensitive and directed to this issue. Of course, individual self-development programs have both advantages and disadvantages.

Potential advantages of individual self-development programs include:

- Complete flexibility of time.

- Complete range of treatment, with as much or as little coverage as desired.

- Low cost
- Extensive array of available reading materials.
- The opportunity to fit a reading program to individual learning styles.
- The opportunity to increase self-initiative and motivation.
- The opportunity to focus on special subtopics and issues.

Potential disadvantages of individual self-development programs include:

- Limited or no opportunity for listening development practice or coaching.
- Limited opportunity to receive group feedback and reinforcement.
- Lack of the organizational group orientation.
- Total dependence on individual motivation.
- Primary dependence on written materials.
- Limited knowledge, awareness, or availability of necessary materials.
- Limited opportunity for use of before-and-after listening tests.
- Limited opportunity for evaluation beyond written self-tests.

Obviously, the success of any individual self-development program depends largely on the self-motivation of the individual. In addition, reading about listening is not equivalent to the more complete approaches of the other programs. Yet such efforts can be productive for the employee. Most important, training, development, and personnel specialists should be prepared to direct and assist anyone interested in developing an individual self-development program.

Participants

Regardless of the development approach taken, any careful consideration of the importance of and the need for listening development will suggest that all members of any organization will profit from focused listening training. Any consideration of the benefits of parallel training and the rewards of group reinforcement through a broad organizational application will support this claim.

On the basis of many years of listening training and development experience with several hundred organizations and scores of individuals throughout the Western world, three observations stand out:

- The best, most effective listening development programs have included—in fact, have started with—the highest level people (regardless of function) within the organization.

- The most productive programs have involved organization members at all levels (regardless of job function).

- The most cost-effective programs are organized around an ordered, prioritized selection process with broad participation across the organization.

Any listening development program that starts at the top, moves down and out, and prioritizes participant selection and involvement in a planned fashion will avoid a "bandaid" approach to listening training. This prioritized selection of participants will result in parallel training and heightened reinforcement. Moreover, developing a strategy for selection will allow a greater tie to organizational philosophies, objectives, and policies.

In prioritizing participant selection, consideration of organizational and individual needs should dictate. On the basis of assessed needs, employees in primarily people-oriented positions should of course receive first priority. Individuals in positions of management, sales, customer service, research and development, training, engineering, and secretarial services are examples.

A final note of caution is in order. Many highly positioned and very successful people (with obvious listening development needs) often hold the mistaken opinion that they have little or no need to participate in a listening development program. Moreover, many people erroneously believe that they're okay; if they could "only fix those other people, everything would be fine!" At best, collective and parallel training, from the top down, where needed, will enhance both individual and organizational listening.

Leader Skills and Requirements

Whatever approach is taken to develop the listening knowledge, attitudes, behaviors, and skills of today's workforce, the role of the trainer, instructor, facilitator, or consultant is critical. Consequently, specific skills and requirements are mandated.

First, at minimum, listening trainers must be knowledgeable in the following areas:

- History of listening development.

- Role, value, and importance of listening.

- Broad array of listening research.

- Levels of listening effectiveness and efficiency.

- Real costs and rewards of listening.

- Characteristics of effective and ineffective listeners.

- Purposes, steps, and stages of listening.

- Various definitions of listening.

- Role of responsibility in listening.

- Variety and value of listening assessment tools.

- Variety of listening development materials.

Second, listening trainers must be skilled presenters and seminar/workshop leaders.

Third, they must be:

- Effective listeners in order to role model desirable listening attitudes and skills.

- Aware of their personal listening weaknesses and strengths.

- Involved in a self–development plan for their own listening enhancement.

Simply put, anyone involved in helping others become better listeners must be a knowledgeable, skilled presenter and an effective and growing role model.

The selection of qualified leaders and consultants deserves critical attention, especially in light of the growing interest in listening training. The point was recently reinforced by an evaluation of a major training directory, that listed more than 80 individuals and organizations as available "listening trainers, consultants, and developers."

Careful evaluation indicated that just two years earlier, this same directory had no heading dedicated to listening. More than half of those listed had no special training, knowledge, or experience in listening development. When directly queried, several admitted they had no specific program in listening but had modified, or were modifying, other related programs. Finally, several known, knowledgeable, skilled, and effective listening training professionals were not listed.

In selecting or developing a listening program, the "buyer beware" caveat would seem obvious. However, it may not be enough. The following questions should be asked of anyone (either external or internal) being considered as a listening trainer:

Trainers' Background and Training

What is the specific extent and nature of their listening training?
Who have they studied with or been mentored by?
What professional listening-related associations do they belong to?
What special experiences or qualifications do they have?

Trainers' Listening Development Experience

How long have they taught listening?
How many listening programs have they taught?
How many people have they trained specifically in listening?
What were the job levels of the participants in the program?
What were the job functions of the participants?
What organizations have been involved?
Who (including facilitators and participants) can be contacted for recommendations?

Program Questions

What are the general and specific objectives of a typical program?
What is an outline of a typical program?
What is the range of appropriate participants?
How can the program be modified for various (function and level) participants?
What assessment procedures are, or can be, used?
What training activities and exercises are, or can be, used?
What training materials are, or can be, used?
What training media (tapes, films, video) are, or can be, used?
What post-training tests, exercises, activities, and readings are, or can be, used?

Such questions, of course, must be raised within the specific context of the organization's listening development needs, interests, resources, and program plans. But one must not underestimate the critical importance of selecting a knowledgeable, skilled, and professional trainer to develop and conduct the listening training.

Materials

There is a plethora of materials available for developing listening attitudes, skills, and knowledge. For the experienced listening trainer, the availability of such materials poses little problem. However, for the uninitiated or newly developing trainer, the available material may well seem to be scattered and confusing. The challenge of finding useful material is complicated by the fact that only a limited amount of such materials is commercially available. In addition, some of the commercially packaged material will not serve all training participants, will need instructor modification, may be of marginal quality, or may not be easily available. In fact, regarding the last point, it is important to note that some old, but effective, materials are periodically taken out of print.

The most productive approach to identifying and locating usable listening training materials is through affiliation with professional associations, such as the International Listening Association, where one can share with other professionals involved in listening development. Of course, appropriate permission for use of copyrighted and proprietary materials is mandatory.

Content and Coverage

Obviously, the content and coverage of any listening development program must be based on the organization's and the individual participant's objectives and needs. In addition, the budget, the instructional resources, and the time allotted for training will affect the content and coverage. Such training can be as short as a few hours of introduction, or it can be a few days of extended focus or a number of weeks of in-depth training. In addition, such training can be offered during a continuous period or it can be spread out over time.

Although the content of such programs can be very varied and there is no one way to develop listening, let's consider as an example the objectives and content of a popular and effective one–day listening seminar.

Length. One day (six to eight hours with appropriate breaks).

Participants. Professionals, managers, supervisors, sales representatives, service representatives, support staff, and others who want to improve their listening knowledge, attitudes, and skills.

General objectives. This seminar is introductory and intended to help each participant become a more effective and efficient listener. It will allow participants to discover the role and value of listening, the characteristics of good and poor listeners, and ways to become a better listener. Participants will initiate a personal strategy that can be used in developing long–term listening improvements.

Additional general objectives include:

- To develop an appreciation of the listener's role.
- To develop respect for listening as a medium of learning.
- To become aware of poor listening habits and their causes.
- To identify and eliminate poor personal listening habits already acquired.
- To develop the basic understandings, attitudes, and skills essential to efficient and effective listening.

Specific Objectives. Each participant will begin to increase his or her individual insight and understanding of:

- The role of listening in the communication process.
- The importance of listening for complete communication.
- The importance of efficient listening abilities for the individual.
- The misconceptions that perpetuate poor listening.
- The causative factors of poor listening.
- The various purposes of communication.
- The methods for improving listening abilities.
- The complexity of the listening task.
- The different types of listening situations.
- The stages of the communication/listening process.

Each participant will also begin to develop the following *attitudes and appreciations*:

- A desire to become a better listener.
- An appreciation for necessary listening skills.
- An appreciation of the potential knowledge to be gained through improved listening.
- An appreciation of the role played by the listener in oral communication.
- An appreciation for the speaker in all cases.

- An attitude of shared responsibility in oral communication situations.

- An appreciation of the various types of listening situations.

- An appreciation that effective listening demands energy.

- An appreciation of the costs of poor listening.

- An appreciation of the rewards and benefits of effective listening.

Each participant will begin to develop *observable, measurable increased skill in*:

- Communicating with others.

- Preparing to listen.

- Eliminating exterior environmental distractions.

- Responding to both verbal and nonverbal messages.

- Listening for different purposes.

- Eliminating, or controlling, personal biases.

- Determining the speaker's pattern.

- Locating the central idea of the speaker.

- Evaluating supporting evidence.

- Withholding judgment.

- Using the difference between thought speed and speech speed.

- Considering ideas rather than isolated facts.

- Anticipating the speaker's direction.

- Taking notes.

- Planning to report.

- Sensing the full message.

- Accurately interpreting message meaning.

- Effectively evaluating the message.

- Responding in a manner appropriate to the situation.
- Improving listening proficiency.

Brief Outline

A 3,000-year oversight: Listening.

Listening assessment: How well do you listen? Willing yourself to listen well.

How you spend your communication/listening time.

The 25 percent efficiency level.

The costs of poor listening.

Listening elements and purposes.

The 51 percent responsibility challenge.

The SIER model—sensing, interpreting, evaluating, and responding.

Improving your listening skills: Identifying and controlling distractions. Identifying and controlling emotions. Identifying and using structures.

Developing a strategy for personal enhancement.

Strategies, Procedures, and Techniques

In any listening development program (with the exception of the individual self-development approach), a variety of strategies, procedures, and techniques should be used. Usually, these will include a combination of individual pre-seminar assessment, pre-seminar reading, lecture, large- and small-group discussion, and group and individual exercise and practice. In addition, participants will profit from the use of appropriate audio and video exercises, written inventories, films, slides, and overhead visuals. A logical oral-to-written mix would be a ratio of five to one, favoring the oral/aural approach. Of course, each program should include extended opportunity for individual practice and group discussion. In addition, each program should allow significant time to map a direction and plan a strategy for post-seminar individual self-development. If time allows, each seminar should provide individual post-seminar assessment.

In sum, although the strategies, procedures, and techniques for listening development will be affected by the available time and desired scope, the best guide is to build the program around strategies, procedures, and techniques that require and allow directed and practiced listening.

Evaluation

A number of wide-ranging tools for evaluating listening attitudes, skills, and knowledge exist, but only a few of these are standardized with established norms for comparing data[3]. In addition, many of the commercially available tests measure a very limited component of the total listening process. Moreover, many of these tests make claims of worth beyond their due.

At their best, listening test materials should evaluate individual knowledge about listening, individual attitudes toward listening, and specific listening skills or behaviors. Such evaluation should answer the following questions for each individual listener:

- How do I evaluate my listening skills?

- How do I perceive other people's analysis of my listening skills?

- How do others evaluate my listening skills?

In addition, these materials should include open-ended questions as well as criteria-based questions with specific factors to be measured. Of course, they should allow comparison to others materials. Finally, the time frame should allow for before-and-after evaluation.

Summary

As noted, listening has been, is, and will continue to be the primary communication activity used by people throughout the world. Effective listening is indeed central to the personal, professional, social, educational, and family success of every productive person. More than a third of a century ago, Nichols and Stevens wrote the very thought-provoking book Are You Listening? In their concluding remarks, they said:

---

[3] See: Brown-Carlsen Listening Comprehension Test, CDI, 25 Robb Farm Road, St. Paul, MN 55127; Watson-Barker Listening Test, Spectra, P. O. Box 1708, Auburn, AL 36830.

In the years ahead more and more of us will have the opportunity to sharpen our listening abilities while receiving guidance from experts in this field. . . . When this transpires, we shall have taken a long stride toward greater economy in learning, accelerated personal growth and significantly deepened human understanding (1957, pp. 221–222).

As we look ahead to the next 25 years, the significance of their conclusion is greater than ever. We must develop individual knowledge about, attitudes toward, and skills of listening. As all professionals positioned to meet this challenge act, extraordinary gains will be made.

Exercises

1. Talk with training managers, trainers, or those responsible for contracting with trainers in an organization in your area. These individuals might be in a human resource development department, personnel, or some other less obvious department. Ask them some of the questions listed in this chapter about training programs, trainers, and participants in their organization.

2. Talk with members of organizations in your area who have participated in one or more training programs. Ask them questions related to the quality of the trainer, the content of the training program, and the results.

3. Prepare an audiotape of between 5 and 7 speakers. Speakers should be males and females who represent diverse speaking styles and/or accents (i.e., New York (city) dialect, Southern or New England (regional) accents, foreign accents, etc.). Speakers should speak in succession for approximately one minute each on a topic they choose (i.e., my favorite vacation, what I like about my work, etc.).

   Play the audiotape to the class or seminar group. After each speaker's segment has been played, ask the group to write down a description of the speaker (physical appearance, age group, nationality, educational background).

   Once all of the speakers have been evaluated, the group should compare its responses. Were descriptions similar/dissimilar? Discussion should follow about the importance of communication in organizations—especially the image conveyed on the telephone where listening not only enables individuals to communicate clearly, but includes as well our propensity to stereotype or group individuals on the basis of how they sound. (Borisoff, 1990)

4. Class or seminar members should prepare an assessment of 3–5 professionals with whom they come in contact over a designated period (i.e., several days, weeks, a month). The local dry–cleaner,

the waitperson in the coffee shop, the dentist or physician, a colleague at work may be among the professionals selected. Each group member should answer the following question: What is your perception of this individual as a listener? Explain your response fully. (Borisoff, 1990)

5. We each play different roles in life: friend, son/daughter, lover, spouse, worker, student. Evaluate your listening strengths and weaknesses in the different roles you play. The group should compare their findings. Do any patterns emerge regarding when we are good or poor listeners? (Borisoff, 1990).

References

Barker, L. L., Edwards, R., Gaines, C., Gladney, K., & Holley, F. (August 1980). An investigation of proportional time spent in various communication activities by college students. *Journal of Applied Communications Research*, 8, 101-109.

Bird, D. E. (June 1956). This is Your Listening Life. *Journal of the America Dietetic Association*, 32, ,534-36.

Borisoff, D. (1990). Impression management: Developing effective listening and speaking strategies. Paper presented at the New York State Reading Association Conference, Kiamesha, New York.

Breiter, L. R. (1957). Research in Listening and Its Importance to Literature. Unpublished masters thesis, Brooklyn College.

Corey, S. M. (1940). The Teachers Out-Talk The Pupils. *School Review*, 48, 745-52.

Markgraf, B. R. (1947). An Observational Study Determining the Amount of Time That Students in the Tenth and Twelfth Grades Are Expected to Listen in the Classroom. Unpublished master's thesis, University of Wisconsin.

Nichols, R. G. (1948). Factors Accounting for Difference in Comprehension of Materials Presented Orally in the Classroom. (Unpublished doctoral dissertation, State University of Iowa.

Nichols, R., & Stevens, L. A. (1957). *Are You Listening?* New York: McGraw-Hill.

Rankin, P. T. (1926). The Measurement of the Ability to Understand Spoken Language. Unpublished doctoral dissertation, University of Michigan.

Steil, L. K. (1977). A Longitudinal Analysis of Listening Pedagogy in Minnesota Secondary Public Schools. Unpublished doctoral dissertation, Wayne State University.

Steil, L. K., Barker, L. L., & Watson, K. W. (1983). *Effective Listening: Key to Your Success.* New York: Random House.

Steil, L., deMare, G. & Summerfield, J. (1983). *Listening . . . It Can Change Your Life.* New York: McGraw-Hill.

Wilt, M. E. (1949). A Study of Teacher Awareness of Listening as a Factor in Elementary Education. Unpublished doctoral dissertation, Pennsylvania State College.

Chapter 10

LISTENING IN THE SERVICE INDUSTRIES: It Makes Good Cents

Judi Brownell

Points to be Addressed:

- The unique requirements of listening in service organizations.

- The customer's role as "partial employee" in the service encounter.

- The role and tasks of the service manager.

- The advantages of a behavioral approach to listening instruction in service industries.

- The specific listening needs of service managers, employees, and customers.

- The ethical concerns in listening training.

- The implications of a growing service economy.

"Your enjoyment guaranteed. Always" (Firnstahl, 1989, p. 29). Service organizations are the fastest growing segment of the US economy. In 1995, almost eighty percent of the labor force was engaged in some form of service activity (Statistical Abstracts, 1995). That number will continue to increase.

Service is a unique commodity; it can't be stored in inventory or wrapped in bright colors (Davidow & Uttal, 1989). Researchers have attempted to make the concept more manageable by identifying its nature and its attributes. Service has been explored from an organizational perspective and from the guest or client's viewpoint. As various characteristics emerge, we can more clearly distinguish the attributes of service relevant to human communication in general and listening in particular. Our interest is in the interpersonal communication process; therefore, our focus is on the service encounter itself. We examine those interactions that require face–to–face interaction between the provider and the consumer (Vandermerwe & Chadwick, 1989).

Nowhere else does the consumer play as important a role as in service organizations. From 1,500 room resorts to "bed and breakfasts," from the service departments of high–technology companies to the local repair shop, from health care professionals to plumbers and electricians, service providers are everywhere. By definition, "superior service" is service that meets or exceeds the customer's expectations; without the customer's participation in the process, the concept of service is meaningless. Effective service delivers what the customer wants or expects. The primary task of all employees in the service business, therefore, is to listen well.

Our discussion unfolds in the following manner. First, a theoretical perspective emphasizing the role listening plays in facilitating the linking of customers' and service providers' perceptions is explored. A discussion of the stages of the service encounter further highlights the critical need for effective listening skills. Next, the notion of service manager as culture leader is examined. Managers are responsible for shaping attitudes and values that employees must then communicate during service delivery. Moving from the manager–as–culture–leader perspective, the final sections of this chapter examine issues related to training service employees. A behavioral model of listening is presented and its usefulness discussed. Ethical issues related to listening training, as well as the problems unique to the service industry, are examined. Finally, the importance of listening to the future of the service industry is explained.

As a participant in the service encounter—whether delivering or receiving services—it is essential to understand the role of listening in this unique context. Effective service is only possible to the extent that all parties understand the rules that govern communication encounters, recognize their listening responsibilities, and strive to improve listening effectiveness.

The Service Employee-Customer Relationship

Reliance on high levels of customer/provider interaction for service delivery poses a unique challenge both for managers and their service staff. Since the customer participates in the service encounter, it is difficult to control service quality during high contact situations. In a sense, customers become "partial employees," since they actually participate in the production of the service they receive (Barrington & Olsen, 1987).

Consider this. A guest is dining in an upscale restaurant. The customer is undecided about what to order and discusses the merits of several dishes with the server. The server suggests ways that various dishes might be modified to meet his dietary demands. When the meal arrives, the dish has been prepared either: (l) correctly, because the customer communicated these ideas clearly and the service person listened well and accurately communicated her perceptions to the cook, or (2) incorrectly, because messages regarding the customer's order were unclear, discounted, or incomplete.

You can readily see how the customer affected the final product and how important effective listening was at each stage. In service organizations, especially those that require prolonged and direct interaction, the customer's perceptions and whims often shape the service encounter. The activities of all "regular" employees are affected directly and immediately by the participation of these "outsiders." The customers are the real bosses; failure to listen to their voices can directly affect an organization's bottom line.

Because the customer participates in the creation and delivery of the service he or she seeks, each encounter is unique and unpredictable. The nature of any transaction depends on several variables, including: the type of service, the specific tasks required, and the particular customer's skills, motivation level, and personality. The customer-service provider relationship can be viewed as contractual, for it implies a set of mutual expectations held by each party regarding his or her rights, privileges, and obligations. When a repairperson comes to your home, you don't expect him to sit down in your living room and watch television with your family. You assume he will enter your home, take care of his specific business with a minimum of personal conversation, and leave immediately when the job is complete.

While some interactions have well-developed rules governing the actions of both participants, others are more ambiguous. In such cases, the parties involved in the encounter must closely attend to the other's behavior in order to make appropriate communication choices. While a server asks for your decisions on a variety of clearly specified dimensions, a therapist must personalize the relationship to a much greater extent as she adapts to your unanticipated and unpredictable responses. The more complex and ambiguous the relationship, the more important it is that both parties demonstrate effective listening behavior.

Coyne (1989), in fact, has drawn attention to this aspect service by distinguishing three types of encounters: environmental, transactory, and assistance-based. He explains that customers hardly notice environmental encounters unless they are inadequate or unless something goes wrong. In this type of interaction, rules are clear and guidelines well-developed; both customers' and service employees' behavior tends to be predictable. Rules and guidelines define such aspects as: the rights of the customer, the time needed for the production of the service, and the approximate outcome of the effort.

Do you readily recall, for instance, what a bellman says as he carries your luggage and checks your room? It's likely that you would remember only if he goes to the wrong room, insults you, or otherwise draws attention to his behavior. Hostesses and others with formalized roles are seldom personal or unique in their approach; consequently, the need for careful listening is reduced.

Brief encounters, like checking in at a hotel, are routine for the provider yet allow for some degree of individualization. Although customers have expectations regarding the outcome of the encounter and the effort they will need to expend, their behavior may be unique and unexpected. Service employees in these positions are frequently called upon to answer questions, solve problems, and modify their usual performances based upon unique characteristics of the guest—culture, status, or personality. Consequently, the need for effective listening is considerably greater than in environmental encounters, where the employees' routine is seldom disrupted.

Assistance-based encounters are the most problematic since the degree of customer participation and, therefore, the degree of uncertainty, is highest. Customers are unsure of the expected outcomes, and providers need to establish themselves as competent and trustworthy during the course of the interaction (Coyne, 1989, pp. 71–72). Participants in these encounters must be skilled listeners as they negotiate their specific relationship and learn of the others' expectations.

When there is a high degree of customer involvement in the service process and, in addition, a correspondingly high degree of ambiguity in the tasks to be performed, the potential for disruption of the service process increases. This is particularly true when customer performance is unpredictable or substandard. A real estate agent, for instance, must gather a considerable amount of information from her clients as well as make her own assessment regarding their financial status, their meaning for words like a "modest" house or a "fair amount" of privacy.

When rules about how to behave are imprecise—as in the assistance-based encounters—the customer directly and significantly affects service quality. In a sense, this level of involvement causes the customer to view the service employee as part of the product he or she is buying. A doctor, for instance, affects the customer's perceptions of whether the service was satisfactory; the consultant or trainer is herself part of the service package. These providers' listening behaviors are critical to the success of the encounter. Service, without question, emerges from the coordinated efforts of both service employee and customer.

The interactions between service employee and customer have been studied in a number of ways. Mills and Morris (1986) advocate viewing the customer as a "partial employee" who participates in the creation of his or her own service. They describe the process through which both parties come to understand their respective roles and relationship.

Customers as Partial Employees

Since the constant coordination of activities between service provider and customer depends upon the each person's listening ability, it is helpful to examine the process in greater detail. Mills and Morris (1986) explain the stages of the service encounter from a customer's first contact with the provider to the time the organization is ready to terminate the relationship. Their process model defines the stages of customer involvement in the creation of complex services. We discuss examples of both transactory and assistance–based encounters. At each stage of the relationship, the importance of listening to effective service delivery becomes apparent.

Pre-encounter: Customer Expectations

Every customer comes to the service encounter with a set of expectations and personal skills. These are most likely developed through previous observation or participation in similar encounters. Thus, most customers have some idea of the service the organization provides and the role he or she is going to play in the production of the service. It is obvious, however, that individuals who don't share the same set of assumptions—whose background or culture is different from that of the providers'—will experience difficulties in the service process.

As organizations become multi-national and service is more and more frequently delivered across cultures, we will witness an increasing need for providers who listen well in order to understand unique assumptions and needs. Women, people of color, the disabled, and other minorities will likely play increasingly important roles in the service process. Although it would be helpful for the provider to assess each customer's pre–encounter expectations and characteristics, in most cases this is not feasible. It is not until they begin to interact, therefore, that customer and provider become aware of one another's expectations and personal skills.

Initial Encounter: Negotiation and Role Making

The service employee, as the primary contact between the organization and the customer, is likely to be the major source of influence during the early stages of the relationship. The employee must not only perform the appropriate organizational role behaviors, but he or she must also engage in activities that enable the customer to establish a corresponding set of appropriate behaviors. The service representative is a boundary spanner (Likert, 1961), translating the organization's set of expectations and rules to the customer while simultaneously interpreting and responding to the customer's needs and demands. When customer role readiness is low, the processes of role negotiation and boundary spanning becomes particularly difficult.

It is during the early stages of the relationship that respective roles are being negotiated, or "made." Role making (Graen & Cashman, 1975) is a process by which participants who are functionally interdependent work through how each will behave under a particular set of circumstances. Effective service employees must perceive, understand, and interpret relevant cues within this sensitive situation—and respond to them appropriately. Sales clerks must determine when to offer their help and when to leave the customer alone; doctors must know when to probe a patient for additional information and how insistent to be when making recommendations.

The stress created by highly ambiguous situations can lead to low levels of commitment and consequently higher turnover. The more qualified the employee—the better his or her listening skills—the more likely she is to feel in control of the situation and the less likely she will be to experience high levels of stress. In addition to ambiguity, several other factors influence the service encounter.

Variables in the Service Process.

Behaviors that meet the minimum quantitative and qualitative standards of performance have been called "dependable behaviors" (Katz & Kahn, 1966). Service employees who display dependable behaviors are able to "get by"; their performance is acceptable and does not draw attention to their role. Although the dependable behaviors that define a given role are taught to regular employees, such is not the case with regard to customers. While traditional service employees are deliberately selected, trained, and socialized (Simon, 1976), the organization's customers are seldom pre-selected or trained for the role they will play. An employee's extended relationship with a company allows the necessary time for socialization; the brief involvement of customers in the organization's operation, on the other hand, limits its ability to prepare these "partial" employees to respond effectively in the service situation.

Clearly, customers must possess the necessary skills and personality to perform their role well. It is often the service providers' responsibility, at each stage, to determine whether the customer has the appropriate knowledge and ability to function effectively and assume this responsibility. If a customer seeking a creative business logo has no sense of composition, color or design, he or she is in no position to advise or participate in the creation of the product. As the customer's role expands, the listening skills of both parties become an increasingly critical factor. This becomes particularly significant as the number of service organizations increases and more of everyone's time is spent in service encounters.

Another potential difficulty is the customer's inability to determine the degree of effort a provider has invested in the service and if, in fact, he has really been well-served. This lack of clarity in judging service quality tempts some service providers to undersupply or oversupply the service. Problems arise when the customer is naive and his expectations are unclear—when he is unable to determine exactly what "good service" means.

Perhaps some of the best and most powerful examples come from the health care field, where even experienced customers are often at a loss to determine the extent of the service rendered. Numerous other services, such as therapy and financial management, are also prone to these problems. In such instances, it is the service provider's responsibility to educate consumers and thoroughly answer all questions regarding the nature and extent of the service to be rendered. The balance of status and power between customer and service representative is also of interest, especially with regard to how it affects the interpersonal dynamics of the encounter. At times, the power of the customer over service employees sets up an imbalance in the interpersonal relationship and creates unique demands on the listening behavior of service staff. Customers who see themselves at a higher status are not likely to listen well.

In other cases, the reverse may be true; customers who enter service encounters with low status and little credibility are often extended less discretion than others and are subjected, as Mills and Morris (1986) point out, to the "burden of proof process" (p. 732). In such cases, the customer must work to establish himself as a legitimate recipient of the service. Teenagers who are ignored by the service staff in expensive department stores, patients on medicaid who cannot get health care, or women who dine alone in restaurants all are occasionally victims of this perceived status relationship.

As we have seen, among the many variables that arise in the process of service delivery are the customer's expertise, personality, status, and motivation. It is reasonable to expect that customers will not perform spontaneously as effectively as service employees. Although their self-interest is best served by defining and enacting the role behaviors that are required for efficient, effective service, such is not always possible. Customers may not have the ability or the motivation to perform effectively; as a result, costs to both the organization and the customer are heightened as a result of the customer's inappropriate or disruptive communication behaviors. In other cases, differences in perspective and prior experience may result in very different assumptions, attitudes, and behaviors.

Ending the Service Relationship

In some cases, the nature of the service may be such that the customer and the service provider disagree about when the customer's participation should end. Health care and consulting services are examples of relationships where closure is imprecise. On occasion, the organization must work to dissolve the association while maintaining good relations. Although the organization may want the customer to repeat her business in the future, a prolonged relationship may prove costly. Organizations must document service completion while at the same time encourage customers to return for future business. There is little research on how organizations manage this sensitive process. It is obvious, however, that accurate understanding of the individual customer, acquired through effective listening, is essential.

A Service Encounter:
The Front Desk at Starlite Hotel

The customer's perception of service quality comes as a direct result of the way he or she is treated in a specific encounter (Worsfold, 1989). If we look closely at a brief example of one service situation, we see why it is essential that employees who have customer contact be skilled listeners.

Heather is working the front desk and has had a difficult and stressful shift. A middle-aged woman rushes into the lobby. She steps up to the front desk, slightly out of breath, and asks if there have been any messages for her that morning. "I'm sure if there were messages for you, you would have gotten them," Heather says, sorting through credit card receipts.

Heather should have realized that the woman was upset; her off-handed response did not satisfy the woman's need for reassurance that she had not missed a message.

A more appropriate response would have been:

"I don't think there's anything for you. We get messages to our guests as soon as they arrive. If you'd like, though, I'll double check." Heather immediately goes to the computer and verifies that there is no message.

The woman continues, "Please, then, I'd like to leave a message for Mr. Raymond. Tell him to meet me as soon as possible at the Take-A-Break. If he gets in after 1:00 p.m., however, he'll have to check with my friend Jamie who is staying at the Crestwood. Her number is 902-4460. I really have to catch him before I leave this afternoon."

"Sure, no problem," Heather mumbles, snapping her gum.

Heather should have taken the message down as she listened and then read it back to the guest. Her response was abrupt and did not create an image of competence or good listening. She did not communicate concern or interest in the guest's problem.

A more appropriate response would have been:

"One moment," Heather replies as she positions herself at the keyboard. "Okay, please continue." Heather takes the message, then reads it back to the guest. "If there's anything more we can do," she offers, "just let me know."

"Well, there is one thing," the woman pauses. "I just realized that check-out is at 1:00 p.m. and my flight doesn't leave until 3:30 p.m. Could I keep my room for a few hours longer?"

"I'm sorry," Heather replies. "Our policy is to have guests check out at 1:00 p.m."

Again, Heather did not respond appropriately. She is dealing with a reasonably skilled guest who already knew the hotel's check out policy. She should have demonstrated her interest in serving the customer and meeting her specific needs by making some problem-solving efforts on her behalf.

A more appropriate response would have been:

"We're expecting a large number of convention guests in this afternoon, so your room will need to be cleaned as soon as possible. Would it help if we could find a quiet lounge with access to a telephone where you could wait? Your bags, of course, will be held for you as long as you like here in the reception area."

As a guest, you can feel the difference between an employee who is paid to perform emotional labor, and a caring, helpful service provider. Paying attention to the customer, focusing on his or her needs, listening carefully, all are prerequisite to establishing a positive customer- service employee relationship.

How service employees and customers can best acquire the knowledge, skills, and dispositions to perform effectively while in the service creation process is a growing management concern (Mills & Morris, 1986). Although the service organization has much to gain by shaping attitudes, expectations, and behaviors before the initial service contact, the job is complex and costly. A great deal of the burden has fallen on the shoulders of the service manager, whose responsibility it has become to establish a service environment that communicates important aspects of the organization's culture both to its regular and to its "partial" employees.

Service Managers as Culture Leaders

Organizational goals and accompanying service strategies must set all employees heading toward the customers' priorities (Albrecht & Zemke, 1985). Service initiatives often fail because the effort improves service in ways the customer doesn't really care about—the organization hasn't listened. In this section we emphasize the importance of listening to the customer in determining organizational goals, and in developing managers who are able to guide all employees toward service-centered values.

Successful Service Organizations Listen to Customers

Peters and Austin (1985) call customer listening a "watchword" (p. 15), describing a philosophy they learned from talking with the chairman of Allergan, a subsidiary of SmithKline Beckman. The philosophy, called naive listening, draws attention to the importance of staying in touch with the direct user—the one who knows what he or she wants from the service or product. Going directly to the home owner, the patient, the housewife, prevents SWAG (Scientific Wild Ass Guesses) and ultimately increases profitability. The authors note that a wide range of businesses, including Milliken and Company, 3M Corporation, General Electric, and Wang, have profited from a strong focus on listening. Milliken, in fact, has opened a customer listening college for its employees (Peters & Austin, 1985, p. 19). The power of listening, without question, is a largely untapped resource. The bottom line, Albrecht and Zemke (1985) believe, is this: "If you're not serving the customer, you had better be serving someone who is" (p. 106).

Large scale, holistic listening, Ulrich (1989) argues, results in positive outcomes for both the organization and the individuals it serves:

> In the turbulent and increasingly competitive 1990's, firms need to go beyond customer satisfaction to focus on customer commitment. The totally satisfied customer says, "My needs have been assessed and met, so I feel good about dealing with this firm." The totally committed customer says, "We have developed interdependent, shared values, and strategies to the extent that our separate needs can best be met through long-term devotion and loyalty to each other" (p. 19).

As we have seen, service management demands flexibility and responsiveness; it demands effective listeners. In high contact systems, the customer affects the time of demand, the exact nature of the service, the length of the encounter, and even the service quality itself. These factors, coupled with the high degree of uncertainty in day-to-day operations, makes high contact service systems the most difficult to manage efficiently (Chase, 1978, pp. 137-138). The "pure service" businesses—hotels, restaurants, health centers, schools—are among the most challenging operations to control from a management perspective.

The Manager's Role

The most vital link in our communication web is the middle manager who must gather and filter information in all directions to ensure that everyone, both within and outside of the organization, is marching together. In fact, when alumni of the School of Hotel Administration at Cornell University were surveyed in 1993, they were asked what academic preparation they felt was most essential to their career success. Ranked at the top of a list including all functional areas of management was communication.

Some (Barrington & Olsen, 1987) believe the lack of management skill in service organizations is responsible for most industry criticisms (*Business Week*, 30 October 1971; *US News and World Report*, 9 July 1979). Although service delivery often falls to line employees, service quality is heavily dependent upon management style and philosophy; few other industries are so affected by the specific individuals who create and control services.

One of management's toughest but most important tasks is the communication and development of a culture that promotes and rewards a strong "listening environment" (Brownell, 1994) among employees. This type of culture fosters quality service. An example of this attitude was expressed simply through a story the management of one hospitality industry told its new employees. The story has become part of the cultural myths of that property, setting up a model for appropriate behavior. The story goes:

> A guest was checking out of the Sunset Motel, chatting informally with a member of the front desk staff. He then went outside in front of the Hotel to catch a cab. As the cab pulled away, the doorman noticed that the man had left one of his bags on the sidewalk. The doorman immediately checked with the front desk, where the employee remembered that the man had said he was headed to a board meeting at a company several miles out of town. The two employees looked up the address, and the doorman hailed another cab and headed out to return the guest's bag.

The story's messages are quite obvious: (1) take the time to know your guests personally, (2) take initiative, (3) work together, and (4) the service concept extends beyond the employee's job description. When stories and myths are used to send important messages regarding organizational culture and philosophy, the employee as listener becomes an essential concept.

Since service is difficult to measure and to evaluate, these stories describe what effective service is within a particular context.

Hospitality managers, in particular, must deal with employees who have low levels of motivation, few clear lines for career advancement, and modest salaries. These factors often make it difficult to develop a caring and competent staff. Managers rely on informal networks to strengthen the service culture. They use the myths and stories that circulate among employees to communicate important messages regarding quality and professional behavior. Quality, as Peters and Austin (1985) repeat, is not a technique; it's a matter of passion and pride—values that are instilled through the daily activities of organizational members (p. 118).

Managers also communicate organizational values through their own daily activities. Leaders who believe listening is important demonstrate the behaviors they value on a day-to-day basis. When employees have a role model, they witness for themselves the difference a skilled listener can make. Managers who listen to their employees create an atmosphere that encourages increased participation on all levels. A high degree of face-to-face information-sharing heightens employee trust. Involving employees in decision-making and problem-solving activities is likely to increase their commitment to the organization and to their work group. Employees must see themselves as valuable resources and, whenever possible, be empowered to make decisions and act in the best interests of their customers and their organizations.

The MBWA (managing by walking around) approach not only enables managers to hear from their employees, but the more frequent contact also creates opportunities to coach and provide feedback. Regular reinforcement and feedback lets employees know their manager is "listening." Managers who closely observe their employees can take advantage of daily on-the-job situations to modify and improve performance. Observing employees as they interact with customers allows managers to witness what Albrecht and Zemke (1985) call "moments of truth," those all-important customer contacts that shape the customer's perceptions of the organization and its services.

Again, the voice of the customer also influences organizational policies and practices. Management must understand the role their customers play in shaping the company's mission as well as its daily behaviors. Any misunderstanding on the part of either party will have implications for how satisfied each is with the relationship. Since customers are a key element in the service industry, their contributions might be optimized by bringing them into the system as legitimate members. Mills and Morris (1986) explain:

> It may be beneficial for some services to foster an environment for innovative and spontaneous behaviors on the part of the client, since this can lead not only to new solutions and issues of future use . . . but also to greater satisfaction . . . (p. 733).

Ulrich (1989) takes one of the most extreme positions, advocating that the customer be involved directly in the organization's human resource practices. He takes the concept of "listening" to the customer and extends it to suggest that these people have an opportunity to interview managers, taste the dishes of prospective chefs, and provide input into the development of employee reward systems. The primary outcome of such customer–oriented practices, he argues, is not only a product in keeping with market demands, but a stronger customer commitment as well.

Listening: Training and Development Concerns

In addition to the manager's role as culture leader, he or she often acts as a change agent through direct involvement in training and development efforts. This section examines the listening needs of managers and customer contact employees, and presents a behavioral model of listening instruction that appears to have potential in the service industry. Beginning with a brief look at how communication behaviors in the service encounter are assessed, the discussion continues with a description of the HURIER listening model. A study using this framework to identify the perceived listening skills of hospitality managers is presented. Finally, the ethical issues that arise from a behavioral approach to listening training are reviewed.

Assessing Service Needs

A study by the Technical Assistance Research Program notes that the average customer tells nine to ten of his or her friends when service from a particular organization has been unsatisfactory (O'Connell, 1989, p. 66). In addition, one author reports that most businesses never hear from up to ninety-six percent of their unhappy customers. This should be frightening news for service managers, especially since assessing and controlling service quality is neither easy nor straightforward. Bromley (1987) observes:

> The perception of reality is the reality. . . . Whose perception should we focus upon to determine the reality? Should it be the perception of the hotel or of the company's management? Or should it be the guests' perception of the service . . . or should it be from the line employee's view of how management treats them and how they treat the guest? (p. 4)

What is good service? What behaviors are desirable in service personnel? What, exactly, will guarantee customer satisfaction? The answer is elusive; service is not only difficult to define, but difficult to measure and evaluate. As one author writes, "Good service has nothing to do with what the provider believes it is; it has only to do with what the customer believes is true" (Davidow & Uttal, 1989, p. 84). The intangibility of effective service has been a constant concern for those who seek to improve employee performance.

At the least, customer service requires "high touch." Effective service delivery depends upon flexible, warm human contact (Davidow & Uttal, 1989). A recent study, in fact, reports that people skills were more closely associated with effective service and successful management than any other attribute. Worsfold (1989) defines these people skills as "understanding people, caring for people, interest in people, and the ability to communicate" (p. 58). It is readily apparent that these attributes also describe the effective listener; an individual who is other-centered and who truly enjoys providing quality service. Teaching employees to "care for people" or to "be interested" poses significant challenges for the organization.

The presence of the customer, as we have seen, also makes assessment difficult. As Peters and Austin (1985) put it, "The customer perceives service in his or her own unique, idiosyncratic, human, emotional, end-of-the-day, irrational, erratic terms" (p. 83). The "service package," the combination of some physical aspects with face-to-face interaction, must somehow be precisely defined so that service organizations not only know exactly what they're looking for in their employees, but so they can control the nature and quality of the service they deliver.

Efforts to assess service have taken many different forms. Most instruments, like the Customer-Service Assessment Scale (CSAS) proposed by Martin (1986), distinguish the human, face-to-face encounters (the convivial dimension or warmth) from more procedural (mechanical) aspects (pp. 80-81). Martin's instrument for assessing the convivial dimension includes such aspects as: attentiveness, friendly tone of voice, use of customer's name, positive attitude, and customer feedback.

Using this tool, the two service dimensions (convivial and mechanical) are placed on a grid resulting in four service arenas. Businesses are then described as: (1) The Freezer: We don't care (low conviviality, low mechanical), (2) The Factory: You are a number. We are here to process you (High mechanical, low conviviality), (3) The Friendly Zoo: We are trying hard, but we don't really know what we're doing (Low mechanical, high conviviality), and finally (4) The Full Balance: We care and we deliver (high mechanical, high conviviality) (Martin, 1986, pp. 83-84).

Clearly, service employees can be taught to demonstrate "dependable" mechanical skills far more quickly than the convivial skills. It is obvious if a front desk clerk cannot use a computer; it's much more difficult to recognize exactly why the hostess didn't seem friendly or why the mechanic was perceived as untrustworthy. Increasing workforce diversity further complicates these issues.

Regardless of the inherent challenges, however, service organizations realize that communication skills are essential. Formal training efforts have increasingly focused on effective communication, and human resources managers have begun to acknowledge and emphasize active listening as a core competency for all employees.

Status of Listening Training

The status of listening training in service organizations is difficult to measure precisely, largely because—even in programs dealing extensively with listening skills—the word "listening" itself is often omitted from course titles. Training programs capture participants' interest by emphasizing the results of training or the contexts in which the training will be applied rather than the skill itself. Training time is valuable, turnover is often high and, in order to capture interest in highly competitive markets, topics must link directly to practical tasks. Seminars in which listening skills play a key role are often given such titles as: "Effective Customer Service," "Handling the Difficult Customer," or "Improving Employee Morale." The language of training in a highly practical, applied industry has often obscured the main goal of the session—to prepare employees to listen more effectively. Only recently have listening seminars been accurately labeled and offered under such titles as: "Effective Listening for Quality Service," "Listen to What Your Employees Are Telling You," or "Increase Productivity Through Effective Listening."

The next section focuses on the practical matter of identifying the listening behaviors essential to effective service, and the issues and challenges involved in listening training.

A Model of Listening Behavior

A behavioral model of listening makes sense for a number of reasons. As Bromley (1987) suggests, service organizations are concerned with perceptions; employees respond to their perceptions of their manager's interest and understanding, customers formulate their perceptions on the basis of how service employees behave in that all-important encounter. Managing impressions seems to be the name of the game; the industry cannot afford sincere, concerned managers who come across as silent and aloof or shy service employees who project an image of disinterest because they communicate the wrong signals to customers.

When a behavioral model is adopted, results–oriented training programs guarantee not only that participants do in fact listen more effectively after training, but that they will be judged to be more effective listeners by customers, employees, or colleagues. The important questions become: What do employees and customers in this organization *mean* when they say that employees are listening? On what specific indicators are judgments of listening effectiveness based?

One framework that has proven useful in both assessing listening behavior and in designing training programs is the HURIER model (Brownell, 1996). This system clusters listening behaviors into one of six different skill areas: hearing messages, understanding messages, remembering messages, interpreting messages, evaluating messages, and responding to messages.

The HURIER model was developed after careful examination of the existing literature with emphasis on those aspects identified by Nichols (1956), Barker (1971), Floyd (1985) and Steil and his colleagues (1983). The standardized tests most frequently used to assess listening competence (Barker and Watson, 1984; Brown-Carlson, 1955; Bostrom, 1983) were also reviewed. Focus groups consisting of both managers and their subordinates were audiotaped as they discussed their listening concerns. A wide variety of specific listening behaviors were identified, and a conceptual framework was then developed for clustering these behaviors around six skill areas. Each area represents a different focus in the listening process, and includes such concerns as the following:

- *Hearing*: behaviors related to concentrating, avoiding distractions, and preparing to listen

- *Understanding*: behaviors related to sharing vocabulary, note taking, and identifying the main points being presented

- *Remembering*: behaviors related to long term memory techniques

- *Interpreting*: behaviors related to understanding the affective component of messages and communicating empathy

- *Evaluating*: behaviors related to analyzing the validity of messages, their logic and reasoning

- *Responding*: behaviors related to verbal and nonverbal responses

The HURIER model suggests that each skill area, although inter-related, can be identified and developed as a separate component of the listening process. Rather than viewing listening as a unitary, covert process (Weaver, 1972; Sperritt, 1962), the HURIER model proposes that specific listening behaviors can be isolated and clustered around six discrete skill areas. Service providers can then describe "effective" or "ineffective" listening in terms of specific behaviors that can be observed, identified, learned, and practiced. This model provides trainers and human resource professionals with a practical way to assess needs and tailor training programs.

A Study of Managerial Listening in the Hospitality Industry

Since middle managers serve as key links in numerous formal and informal communication networks, their listening behavior has a direct impact on the culture and operations of the organization. We have seen that, in their role as culture leaders and in carrying out their responsibilities for developing employees, managers who are perceived as effective listeners have a decided advantage over their peers. Managers who listen well encourage supportive, positive communication climates which in turn affect employees' attitudes and work-related behaviors (Sypher & Zorn, 1986; Lewis & Reinsch, 1988). A workplace characterized by openness, trust, and employee participation is also characterized by the perception of effective managerial listening.

To discover how managers' listening is perceived by subordinates, a 26-item questionnaire was developed using behaviors representing each of the six areas of the HURIER model. Hospitality managers were asked to indicate the extent to which they believed they displayed each of the 26 listening-related behaviors on the job. A companion questionnaire, consisting of the identical listening behaviors, was distributed to each manager's subordinates. Subordinates were asked to rate their manager on the same 26 items. Background information was also requested from both the managers and their subordinates (Brownell, 1990).

The results of this study provided: (1) individual feedback to each manager, who was able to compare his or her self-rating for each question with the mean of his or her subordinates' ratings, (2) organization-specific information regarding the specific indicators employees use to make judgments about their manager's listening ability, and (3) organization-specific information regarding the management population's overall listening strengths and weaknesses, as measured by their self-reports and their employees' ratings. This information facilitates the development of tailored listening training.

Further, this study verified the presence of discrete listening factors almost identical to those proposed in the HURIER model. The first factor, sensitivity (interpreting), was the most significant in determining the employees' perceptions of their manager's listening effectiveness. Using the five factors (See Listening Components, below), comparisons were made between the managers' self-perceptions and their subordinates' perceptions of the manager's behavior.

Listening Components

1. Sensitivity (Interpreting)
2. Understanding/Recall(Understanding/Remembering)
3. Objectivity (Evaluating)
4. Attention/Concentration (Hearing)
5. Information sharing/Feedback (Responding)

As might be expected, managers gave themselves higher ratings on all factors except understanding/remembering. Manager and subordinate ratings were most discrepant in the area of sensitivity; while managers believed they recognized employee feelings and projected empathy, subordinates disagreed that their managers recognized and responded appropriately to their emotional needs.

When the self-perceptions of hospitality managers were compared with the self-perceptions of managers from high-technology organizations (Table 1), some striking differences became apparent. On a 7-point scale, the mean self-rating for hospitality managers on behaviors related to sensitivity was 5.8 compared to 5.0 for the high-technology group. The factor related to information-sharing also revealed a significant difference; while the mean of non-service managers was only 5.3, hospitality managers gave themselves a 6.2. Hospitality managers gave themselves lower ratings than their high-technology peers in understanding/recall and evaluating messages.

Table 1
A Comparison By Listening Components

Listening Component	Hospitality Managers	Industry Managers
1. Sensitivity	5.0	5.8
2. Understanding/Recall	5.9	5.4
3. Nonjudgmental	5.7	5.5
4. Attention/Concentration	5.4	5.4
5. Information sharing/Feedback	5.3	6.2

How did the "good listeners" (those whose subordinates' ratings placed them in the top twenty-five percent of the group) differ from the "poor listeners" (those whose subordinates' ratings placed them in the bottom twenty five percent)? In general, those given the highest ratings had held their current positions less than one year, compared with the "poor listeners" who had been in their positions for more than six years.

Perhaps most disturbing, however, was the discovery that managers who were assigned the lowest overall ratings by their subordinates still thought of themselves as good listeners. Accurate self-perceptions are important for all types of communication training. Unless managers are aware that their listening skills are inadequate, it is unlikely that development efforts will be effective.

Finally, what are the characteristics of the subordinates who assigned particularly high or low ratings to their managers? Three variables, all themselves correlated, appear particularly significant: (1) the degree of familiarity with the manager, (2) the frequency of communication with the manager, and (3) subordinates' satisfaction with their job and with their relationship with the manager.

Now that you know how one specific listening study was conducted, you may be more aware of what is required to obtain accurate and complete information about listening in organizations. As is evident, listening researchers have a long way to go before they understand the exact nature of listening or how it influences business relationships. It may be helpful at this point, however, to put the information we do have into perspective by looking at how it might guide our future training efforts.

Listening Training in Service Industries

Effective listening begins at the top and filters down through division heads, middle managers, shift leaders, frontline employees, and finally to the customers. In fact, listening has been identified as one of the key success factors for middle managers who aspire to senior management positions (Brownell, 1994). Service organizations cannot afford gaps in their training efforts, nor can they afford a bandaid approach. Top management must make a commitment to include listening training as an on-going part of the organization's activities. As Peters and Austin (1985) constantly remind us, the organization's management demonstrates its values by what it pays attention to. All organizational members must pay attention to their listening, day in and day out.

Values and common goals must be shared; frontline staff must know that their division managers not only verbally support, but understand and practice, the same principles they learn in their training sessions. It stands to reason that, due to their role as culture leaders, managers are among the first group to be trained. In light of the need for organization-wide training, a final task is to use our behavioral model to clarify the listening needs of all three groups: managers, service employees, and customers.

We have discussed the fundamental managerial tasks and have examined the results of a study that revealed hospitality managers' self-perceptions of their listening behavior. An organization-specific assessment or communication audit would provide specific, accurate information regarding a particular population's needs. If the hospitality managers studied are typical of those in other service organizations, however, we can conclude that managers tend to see themselves as better listeners than do their subordinates. Therefore, they must first recognize the need to improve their listening skills and be highly motivated to continue skill development. They must develop strong attitudes about the importance of listening, and be able to recognize examples of effective and ineffective listening in their daily activities.

Although different types of services and different job situations require emphasis on different competencies, two of management's most fundamental skill areas are: sensitivity (interpreting), and information sharing and feedback (response). Managers of the future, our successful culture leaders, must learn to use intuition and sensitivity in their decision–making to create true listening environments. They need to recognize and respond to the more subtle cues their workers send. The ability to link the perceptions of diverse groups, to communicate effectively with the minority employee, requires sensitivity and empathy. As the workforce becomes more diverse, the skills associated with this listening component will become increasingly valued.

Effective managers also create a listening environments that facilitate information sharing. Unless communication channels are open, managers will find it difficult to determine their employees' needs and concerns. In their role as coach, and in all employee development activities, the importance of timely and accurate feedback cannot be underestimated. Employee participation and involvement can only be facilitated if managers share information. High levels of employee participation, made possible through constant manager–employee interaction, often encourage a strong sense of organizational commitment as well.

Service Employees' Listening Needs

The listening needs of service staff differ only slightly from those of management. We have seen how these employees represent the organization to the customer and how important their listening skills are in establishing relationships with customers. All service employees must manage their impressions. As we have discussed, customers must perceive the service person as interested and concerned. This requirement, which has been described as emotional labor, distinguishes effective service employees. Attention and concentration are prerequisite to establishing positive customer relationships.

Although the specific skills required will again depend upon the individual's position, understanding and recall also become important to the service employee as he or she must use information from the customer—either acting on it or passing it along to another destination. Unless messages are accurately understood and correctly recalled, an endless chain of problems may result. Our earlier discussion of the service employee–customer encounter emphasized that individuals who interact directly with customers must develop sensitivity (interpreting); they must be able to interpret their partner's nonverbal cues and consider emotional as well as logical aspects of the situation. The degree to which this skill becomes important depends upon the type of interaction; environmental encounters would require a much lower degree of sensitivity than transactory or assistance–based.

Although it is clear that effective organization–wide training begins with commitment at the top, some feel that too few resources have been spent on developing frontline employees (Albrecht & Semke, 1985). Listening training may increase morale and demonstrate the organization's support of their service staff who, as Albrecht (1988) notes, provides not only physical but also emotional labor. Dealing constantly with unhappy or dissatisfied customers creates a stressful, isolated response that can be moderated by increasing the employee's communication competence.

Again, such training must be perceived as meaningful by the employees, and must become an on–going opportunity to receive instruction and feedback. The most effective training efforts are combined with individual coaching on the job and continuing reinforcement. As part of a team supervised by managers who themselves value and demonstrate effective listening, employees can be integrated into a service–based culture.

Customers' Listening Needs

Much has already been said about the customers' role in the service encounter and the importance of their communication behaviors in the delivery of service. The benefits of directly involving customers in the organization's human resource activities have also been presented. It is clear, however, that as "partial employees"—often temporary and uncommitted—the organization has much less control of its customers. Even if it did, what skills and attitudes would be most helpful to foster? And, importantly, how would customers acquire the attitudes and competencies that would enable them to perform more effectively?

Accurate understanding and recall are perhaps as important to the customer as to the service employee. Customers must become knowledgeable about the service and align their expectations with the type of service provided. Customer training, then, may come in the form of efforts to familiarize the customer with services and products prior to the actual service encounter. If customers understand the nature of the service and the role they are to play in advance, they are less likely to experience dissatisfaction with the provider, and service personnel will confront fewer conflicts.

The customer as decision-maker must establish criteria and judge the service choices available. During the service encounter, customers must listen critically to determine whether or not the information they receive is valid, reliable, and complete. Skills related to making sound judgments (evaluating) and thinking critically cannot help but better prepare consumers to make all kinds of decisions in a competitive, democratic society.

Organizations can assist in preparing customers to carry out their critical thinking tasks by encouraging access to information and by making the nature and extent of their services clear so that customer expectations more closely match the provider's objectives. Service personnel who view themselves as resources, who willingly provide information and discuss possibilities with their clients and guests, not only help their customers but also contribute to their own credibility and reputation as well.

Clearly, everyone engaged in the service process benefits from effective listening skills. The areas highlighted above suggest how training in specific listening components might contribute to more effective service. If organizations begin with a thorough needs analysis for employees at all levels, training can be targeted to meet specific organizational needs. The best possible environment is one in which on-going training is combined with on-the-job coaching and constant feedback. A behavioral approach to training enables human resource professionals to identify specific needs and target training efforts. This approach seems best suited, too, to organizations that depend on their employees to create an image of concern and competence.

A Question of Ethics

One engaging issue that emerges from a behavioral approach to listening concerns the fundamental philosophy of service mentioned many times earlier: What the customer perceives is the reality. If we train service employees to act like effective listeners without generating any accompanying sincere interest or personal commitment, are we corrupting the system? Are we concerned with gathering accurate and complete information from our market only so that it can be used to create the impressions we desire? One recent article on training service personnel (Barrington & Olsen, 1987) raises just these questions:

> Since interaction is the most important and yet the most vulnerable part of service delivery, management must make a special effort to pre-control as much of the interaction as possible. One way of doing this is to create a framework that we call "service repertoire," which service personnel can easily follow in a majority of the situations they will face. It is accomplished by preparing each of the service personnel to perform as actors in a play. . . . One caveat is that although the

service personnel's responses are rehearsed, they must appear to be automatic as well as genuine before the trainee leaves the classroom and faces the customer (p. 137).

Although behavioral models of listening do not imply lack of genuine caring or interest, their applications must be monitored to ensure that efforts are not misdirected. Only when listening is sincere and viewed as a part of the total service process does its significance become fully realized. Taken in isolation, the development of specific behaviors without accompanying positive attitudes and internal motivation may have no real meaning either for the employee or for the customer.

The connectedness of all aspects of our society is becoming increasingly apparent; decisions and actions in one department, one organization, one region often have profound, although not always immediate, consequences for many others. The implications of each choice, at any level, must be carefully considered. Service organizations must be prepared to address ethical issues related to training as well as the ethical concerns that will continue to emerge in the future.

Into the Future

Good service, in many respects, is good listening. Communication in service organizations is profitably viewed as a web of interrelationships among the management, the service staff, and the customers. Each thin connecting strand depends upon the integrity of the entire network for its strength (Frank & Brownell, 1989). The spider web image is a useful one, for it draws attention to the pervasiveness of communication in this industry and the limitations of formal, one-way communication channels to accommodate the information that flows not only within the organization, but across front desks and tables and counters and out to the public as well. As managers work to bridge perceptual differences among employees and create common assumptions and values, service employees reach outward, linking the customer to the service provider. Listening, in our model, serves as the glue that holds our web's fragile strands together, that enables individuals to span gulfs in understanding and viewpoint among these different groups. As more workers operate in service roles, the boundary between employees and customers will become less pronounced. Vandermerwe and Chadwick (1989) clearly indicate the growing need for effective service employees:

As we forge ahead towards the year 2000 . . . interest in services has mushroomed. The media, from daily newspapers to academic journals, point out the massive shift to service-dominated economies and the consequent managerial challenges. . . . the fact is that the whole world is the domain of business service activities today (p. 79).

In order to thrive in highly competitive, rapidly changing environments, service employees must learn to listen well. The costs of not listening are high. As America moves toward a service economy, we will find ourselves increasingly on both sides of the counter. Effective listening, wherever we stand, will bring organizations and their publics closer to a common vision of what it means to provide quality service.

Summary

This chapter presents a framework for viewing the customer-service employee relationship. Emphasis is on service encounters that are ambiguous and complex, those interactions that require both the service employee and the customer to modify their behavior in light of the others' performance. Listening is the process through which this alignment of perceptions and expectations takes place. It is through these interactions, too, that customers become "partial employees," as they influence the nature and quality of the service they receive.

The role of the service manager as culture leader is also explored. Effective listening is presented as an essential tool in carrying out managerial tasks. Managers convey the organization's mission through myths and stories as well as by example. Employees must understand the organization's purpose and share common values. Managers link employees' perceptions and align the perceptions of customers with the organization's goals. Effective managers instill commitment, facilitate active employee participation, and encourage customer involvement.

Listening training is an essential organizational development activity; it must be among the core competencies of every individual engaged in the service encounter. A behavioral model of listening is presented and its applications to the hospitality industry discussed. Behavioral models appear to have potential in an industry concerned with perceptions of listening effectiveness. The findings of one study of hospitality managers indicate that: (1) managers often perceive themselves as better listeners than do their subordinates, and (2) listening behaviors are perceived in terms of five independent factors (sensitivity, attention/concentration, understanding and recall, objectivity, and information sharing/feedback). Manager, service employee, and customer listening requirements are discussed using components from the behavioral model. Ethical issues regarding behavioral models are also explored. These issues, and others related to the delivery of quality service, will gain in significance as we become an increasingly service-based economy.

Exercises

1. Interview two service employees. Ask them the four questions below, plus at least two of your own:

   (a) What type of customer do you find most difficult to listen to? Please elaborate.

   (b) What would you like customers to know before you see them? Do you think this preparation would make your job easier?

   (c) Do you see yourself as an effective listener? Please tell me something about your strengths and what you do to keep listening in difficult situations.

   (d) Think about your manager's listening behavior. What skills or techniques do you find particularly helpful?

2. In a small group, generate two examples of each of the following types of service encounters. Be as specific as possible about the incident, including how the conversation/interaction progressed:

   (a) Environmental

   (b) Transactory

   (c) Assistance–based

3. Using the examples generated above, choose one from each category to role play. Make sure your situations illustrate the differences between the three types.

4. Observe customer service employees over the next week. Record as much as you can about each encounter, including:

   (a) The type of encounter

   (b) The overall setting and nonverbal environment

   (c) Specific characteristics of the service employee's listening skills

   (d) The degree to which the service employee demonstrated customer-centered behaviors

5. In a small group, select two well–known service organizations.

   (a) Discuss the extent to which each has "listened" to the customers (naive listening). What would you like each of these organizations to know? If appropriate, write a letter to their customer service representatives, describing ways in which they might respond to your perceived needs.

(b) As a customer, how might each of these organizations better prepare you for the service encounter?

6. You join an organization as a middle manager and realize that no one listens well. What would be your first steps in an effort to create a stronger listening environment?

7. What do you think about listening training for the purpose of preparing employees to simply create perceptions of effective listening? Do you feel that there is any ethical problem when a trainer's goal is for participants to look like they are listening with little concern for their actual listening competence? What other ethical concerns do you project will arise within the next few years in service industries?

8. Compare the HURIER model presented in this article with other models of listening that you know (for example those in other chapters of this book). What are the strengths and weaknesses of each? How are their uses different?

9. Using the HURIER model, assess your own listening strengths and weaknesses. In what areas are you skilled? Where might you focus your energy to improve still further?

10. How can service organizations prepare customers to be better listeners?

References

Albrecht, K. & Zemke, R. (1985). *Service America—doing business in the new economy.* Homewood, IL Dow-Jones Irwin.

Albrecht, K. (1988). *At America's service—How corporations can revolutionize the way they treat their customers.* Homewood, Il: Dow-Jones Irwin.

Armistead, C. G. (1989). Customer service and operations management in service businesses. *The Service Industry Journal,* 9 (2), 247–260.

Barker, L. (1971). *Listening behavior.* Englewood Cliffs, NJ: Prentice-Hall, Inc.

Barker, L. L. & Watson, K. (1984). Watson–Barker Listening Test. New Orleans: Spectra, Inc. Barrington, M. N. & Olsen, M. (1987). Concept of service in the hospitality industry. *International Journal of Hospitality Management,* 6 (3), 131–138.

Bonoma, T. V. & Lawler, J. C. (1989). Chutes and ladders: Growing the general manager. *Sloan Management Review,* 30 (3), 27–37.

Bostrom, R. (1983). The Kentucky Comprehensive Listening Test. Lexington: Listening Research Center.

Bromley, S. (1987). The specialist: Coming soon to your local hotel. *FIU Hospitality Review*, 5, 1-4.

Brown, J. I. & Carlsen, G. R. (1955). Brown-Carlson Listening Comprehension Test. New York: Harcourt, Brace, and World.

Brownell, J. (1996). *Listening: Attitudes, Principles, and Skills*. Boston: Allyn & Bacon.

Brownell, J. (1994). Creating strong listening environments: A key hospitality management task. *The International Journal of Contemporary Hospitality Management*, 6(3), 3-10.

Brownell, J. (1994). Managerial listening and career development in the hospitality industry. *Journal of the International Listening Association*, 8, 31-49.

Brownell, J. (1990). Perceptions of listening behavior: A management study. *Journal of Business Communication*, 27(4), 401-416

Chase, R. B. (1978). Where does the customer fit in a service operation? *Harvard Business Review*, 137-142.

Coyne, K. (1989). Beyond service fads—Meaningful strategies for the real world. Sloan Management Review, 30 (4), 69-76.

Davidow, W. H. & Uttal, B. (1989, July). Service companies: Focus or falter. *Harvard Business Review*, 4, 77-85.

Firnstahl, T. W. (1989). My employees are my service guarantee. *Harvard Business Review*, 4, 28-31, 34.

Floyd, J. (1985). *Listening: A practical approach*. Glenview, Illinois: Scott, Foresman, and Company.

Graen, G. & Cashman, J. (1975). A role-making model of leadership in formal organizations: A developmental approach. *Leadership Frontiers*. (Ed.) J. G. Hunt and L. L. Lawson. Kent, Ohio: Kent State University Press, 143-165.

Katz, D. & Kahn, R. (1966). *The social psychology of organizations*. New York: Wiley.

Lewis, M. H. & Reinsch, N. L., Jr. (1988). Listening in organizational environments, *The Journal of Business Communication*, 25, 49-67.

Lovelock, C. H. and Young, R. F. (1979). Look to customers to increase productivity. *Harvard Business Review*, 168-178.

Martin, W. B. (1986, May). Measuring and improving your service quality. *Cornell Hotel and Restaurant Administration Quarterly*, 80-87.

Mills, P. K. & Morris, J. H. (1986). Clients as "partial" employees of organizations: Role development in client participation. *Academy of Management Review*, 11, 726-735.

Nichols, R. G. (1956). Listening is a 10-part skill. Nations' Business, 45.

Noe, R. A. (1986). Trainees' attributes and attitudes: Neglected influences on training effectiveness. *Academy of Management Review*, 11 (4), 736-749.

Northcraft, G. & Chase, R. (1985). Managing service demand at the point of delivery. *Academy of Management Review*, 10, 66-75.

O'Connell, K. (1989). The service challenge: An essay review. *The Journal of Management in Practice,* 1 (1), 66–67.

Owens, E. L. (1987, February). Effective managerial communication skills increase productivity. *Data Management,* 22–25.

Pearson, A. E. (1989). Six basics for general managers. *Harvard Business Review,* 4, 94–101.

Peters, T. & Austin, N. (1985). MBWA (Managing By Walking Around). *California Management Review,* 28 (1), 9–34.

Peters, T. & Austin, N. (1985). *A passion for excellence.* New York: Warner Book.

Simon, H. A. (1976). *Administrative behavior.* (3rd ed.) New York: The Free Press.

Statistical Abstract of the United States. (1995). US Department of Commerce, Department of Census. Washington, D.C.

Steil, L. K., Barker, L. L. & Watson, K. (1983). *Effective listening: Key to your success.* New York: Addison–Wesley Publishing Company.

Sypher, B. D. & Zorn, T. E., Jr. (1986). Communication–related abilities and upward mobility: A longitudinal investigation. *Human Communication Research,* 12, 420–431.

Ulrich, Dave. (1989). Tie the corporate knot: Gaining complete customer commitment. *Sloan Management Review,* 30 (4), 19–27.

Umbreit, W. T. & Eder, R. W. (1987). Linking hotel manager behavior with outcome measures of effectiveness. *International Journal of Hospitality Management,* 6 (3), 139–147.

Vandermerwe, S. & Chadwick, M. (1989). The internationalization of services. *The Service Industry Journal,* 9 (1), 79–93.

Worsfold, P. (1989). A personality profile of the hotel manager. *International of Hospitality Management,* 8 (1), 51–62.

CHAPTER 11

LISTENING AND THE HELPING PROFESSIONS

William E. Arnold

Points to be Addressed:

- The role of listening in therapeutic communication.

- Listening with the five senses.

- The differences among informational listening, empathy, and relational listening.

- The implications of empathy in listening.

- The professional versus the amateur helper.

- Being a friendly helper.

- Crisis—a special need for listening.

- Listening—a key to crisis resolution.

Robert, age 43, had just completed 20 years with the corporation only to be "let go" because of the economic conditions. When his wife comes home, Bob is crying and keeps repeating, "what are we going to do?" After a few hours, they agree that Bob should see a counselor.

Peggy had been dating Mark for almost six months. When she got back to her apartment, she began to cry and scream that Mark had raped her. Jill, her roommate listened as Peggy described the situation.

April and Jim had wanted to have a family but confirmation of April's pregnancy by their physician left them in shock. Both were just twelve months from graduation from law school and they were not prepared financially or emotionally for this child. For help they turned to their minister.

In each of these circumstances, one person was being asked to serve as a helper. The counselor and the minister were trained for that role but the roommate, Jill, had to assume that role because she was there. In addition to being a helper, the three shared a second and critical role of listener. Peggy, Robert, April, and Jim all needed someone that they could talk to who would listen. As a result of this contact, all three of our listeners became "unofficial" members of the helping professions.

When this chapter was first conceptualized, it had a different title: Listening in a Therapeutic Setting. While the emphasis on therapy may be enlightening, most of us are not nor will we ever be therapists. However we can, like Jill, be called upon to listen in a helping relationship. It is important at this point to caution that we must be realistic in our appraisal of situations where professional therapy is needed. For example, my experience with crisis hotlines would suggest that Jill should encourage Peggy to see a professional therapist just as Robert's wife did for him. Some problems require professional therapeutic counseling. Our task is to both listen to the person about the situation and encourage the person to get professional help when necessary.

The remainder of this chapter will focus on three key components of listening in the helping relationship. First we explore briefly the types of relationships that we have with others. Second, we present a model of listening and then apply it to the helping relationship. Finally, we integrate the concepts of empathy, helping, and therapeutic listening.

Relationships with Others

We must begin with an understanding of the types of relationships in which we can find ourselves. (For a more detailed discussion of this topic, see Chapter Two.) To have a relationship, we must initially have communication contact with another person. If, after we make contact with a stranger, we find that we want to continue interaction with that individual, we enter into a personal relationship.

As we travel around the country or sit in a waiting room, classroom, or restaurant, we establish casual relationships. These relationships may not last more than a few minutes or a few hours. If that interaction develops we may find a need for a more involved or intimate relationship. We want to know more about the other person just as she or he wants to know more about us. That process of getting to know another person is called mutual self disclosure. Each person learns something about the other person. We may talk and listen to thousands of ideas with someone before she/he becomes our significant other or best friend. In fact, a person becomes your best friend because you can tell them anything and she/he is there to listen. In these personal relationships we may be a helper one day and a helpee the next.

We have professional relationships with physicians, dentists, nurses, barbers, beauticians, teachers, and others. We listen differently to them as they do to us. The counselor and therapist fall into this category. These are the relationships that are discussed throughout Part Two of this book. Clearly, our expectation as to the level of listening provided by each of these individuals would differ as well as what might be mutually self disclosed.

In the previous chapter, Brownell presented listening in the service environment. We would not expect the same level of listening from our physician or therapist as we might a bartender. We would expect our physician to be very attentive to all of the physical and emotional messages that we might be sending. Our therapist must listen to both what we say and what we fail to say. We would expect our therapist to know the content of our messages as well as our feelings. The bartender, on the other hand, wants to know if we need anything else (another drink), but knows the tips are better if she/he listens.

In concluding this section on relationships, it is important to underscore the role of listening. Regardless of who we are: friend, therapist, casual acquaintance, or spouse, we may find the relationship taking on the characteristics of a helping relationship. If we become the helper or the helpee, we need to understand the importance of listening in that relationship.

Listening Issues

To apply listening to the helping professions, four critical issues must be addressed. First, listening must be thought of as *more* than hearing. While all listening scholars know that hearing is a step in the listening process, there is disagreement as to the scope of listening. Glenn (1989) provides us with fifty different definitions of listening. These definitions however focus on the *aural* message. Only eight make mention of the various nonverbal cues which must be considered when we explain the listening process. We use *all* of our senses when we listen to another person. We *see* the other person as she or he is talking. We are *aware* of the olfactory sense as well as appearance. The combination of the messages received by our senses is what we listen to. Such messages can complement or contradict each other. When I listen to the words "I love you," for example, I expect the sender to give me eye contact, touch my hand, and speak in a sincere voice. Anything less suggests I may be listening to contradictory messages. If a child looks down, fidgets, and speaks in a soft voice when she or he says that someone else took the cookie, we are not likely to trust the verbal message.

The last example offers a second important issue for our listening model: We listen to *verbal* and *nonverbal* messages. Research tells us that approximately 60–70 percent of our communication is nonverbal so the same percentages could apply to our listening behavior (Birdwhistell, 1970). We also know from the study of nonverbal communication that we listen to the nonverbal message giving it greater credibility than the verbal when they are contradictory.

Third, for listening to be complete we need to respond to the speaker verbally and nonverbally. The response is necessary to complete the listening cycle. If we use the slinky model of communication I am arguing that feedback (listening) has to be included.

The final issue that should be addressed is what we mean by empathy. Do I have to feel your pain or walk a mile in your shoes to be empathic? In the newspaper advice columns, you find numerous examples of folks who are trying to be empathic by saying "I know how you feel about the loss of your mother because my cat died last week." Do you see the cat's death as the same as the loss of your mother? I doubt it. Would it not be more empathic for me to listen and say, "You are in a great deal of pain over your mother's death." I will never experience child birth but I could be an empathic listener as wife, daughter, or friend went through it. As a listener we cannot share the feeling but we can understand the feelings and let that person know we understand. An empathic listener does not diminish our feelings or offer advice before we are ready for it. We will come back to this last point later in the chapter.

Listening Model

By combining all of the issues just discussed, I would like to offer you a model of listening that will undergird your use of listening in helping relationships. Figure One visualizes the key components of the model. This model contains two dimensions of listening: information seeking/empathy and relationship orientation/task orientation. We are focusing on the verbal and nonverbal response to another person within these dimensions. On one dimension, a listener can be very task-oriented which focuses on information seeking or informational listening. This listener would respond with such statements as "Tell me more," "Would you elaborate on that," or "Give me the details."

Reporters and some physicians are good examples of high information-seeking listeners. The physician asks: How long have you had the pain? Where does it hurt? Describe the pain. What are you taking for it? At the other end of the continuum, a blank look or a person who does all the talking is doing little task-oriented listening. In fact if we encounter someone who does all the talking, we can only give an information-seeking response nonverbally by leaning forward, or nodding our head if we are trying to be positive in our response. A yawn or looking away should suggest little information seeking to this person. Goss (1983) presents a detailed discussion of the information approach to the study of listening.

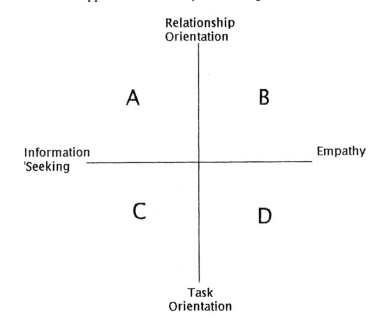

Figure 1. Listening Dimensions

The other end of the continuum reflects a focus on the relationship. The ends of the information seeking/empathy continuum, then, can focus on the other person or on one's self. If the focus is on the other person you are being what I would define as an empathic listener. This empathic listener would respond with "you sound upset, would you like to talk." Nonverbally, it might be like putting your arm around a person who is feeling badly. If you focus on yourself, you might respond by saying, "I know just how you feel, I lost my favorite pen." Clergy and therapists are trained to be other-oriented in their listening. We don't expect a counselor to listen by telling us how s/he feels.

As you can see in the figure, we can be a listener anywhere on the two dimensions. When we are a helper we can shift to the upper right quadrant. When we are over-stressed we may move to the lower left quadrant. Averaging our listening activities for a day we might be somewhere in the middle. There is no right place to be at all times. We have to be flexible in our listening. Since this chapter focuses on the helping relationship, we will expect the listener to be in that upper right quadrant.

To see if you can distinguish listening responses, identify the quadrant for each of the following. The correct answers are at the end of the exercises at the end of the chapter.

Sample One:

Samantha: The world seems to be in a state of turmoil.
Len: What do you mean?
Samantha: With the crisis in the Mideast, we appear headed for a calamity.
Len: Do you predict war in the Mideast?

Sample two:

Samantha: I am really quite upset by the whole thing.
Len: You do sound bothered by it.
Samantha: Yes, I just can't get Ron out of my mind since he
left.
Len: Would you like to talk about it?

Sample three:

Samantha: It sure is hard to get ahead financially.
Len: I can relate to that, my savings account is empty.

Sample four:

Samantha: I just made the final cut for that new position the company is offering.
Len: I like my job

Now that you understand the model, you are ready to differentiate the types of listening responses.

Listening Responses

We indicated early that a person can make a verbal, nonverbal, or both as listening responses. Taking the nonverbal responses first, O'Heren and Arnold (1991) described several key positive and negative nonverbal behaviors which we make in response to another person. These behaviors include eye contact, forward lean, head nod, and facial gestures on the positive side, and lack of eye contact, glance away, and backward lean on the negative side. We make these nonverbal responses whether we are listening for information or with empathy. If we are interested in the topic, we might lean forward and provide greater eye contact. If the topic does not interest us or annoys us, we might lean back or begin to look away.

How do we listen verbally? Consider the following verbal responses we can give a speaker. Essentially, there are five possible verbal responses that we make as a listener whether we are paying attention to the speaker or not.

- No response if you say and do nothing.

- Same subject response (*Same*)—if the speaker says something about a topic, we respond to the same topic.

- Minimal verbal response (*Min*)—if the speaker says something, we respond with a "huh," "UH," or "yeah."

- Tangential response (*Tan*)—if the speaker says something about a topic, we respond on a related issue.

- Different response (*Dif*)—we change the subject as if we were not even listening.

We will not spend much time on the first, since we are interested in responses.

Below are four responses to a statement by a speaker (Joan), which you could make that illustrates each of these responses:

JOAN: I would really like to go to a movie tonight.

Example 1: "A movie sounds good to me." [Same]

Example 2: "U–huh." [Min]

Example 3: "I would like to go to dinner tonight." [Tan]

Example 4: "I wonder what is on the Communication test?" [Dif]

At this point we have a model of listening that is based on information seeking and empathy and consists of both nonverbal and verbal responses as listening behavior. Even armed with this knowledge, we cannot be certain that a person has listened even if he/she gives us the appropriate positive nonverbal listening behavior and an apparent verbal response. How many times have you maintained eye contact and nodded your head yes, and then could not remember what was said? Perhaps we were faking listening to that person when we were preoccupied with something else. While we will not get into a debate as to how we know whether a person is really listening, it is helpful to integrate the types of verbal listening responses into the listening model presented earlier.

On one part of the continuum, we described the information seeking listening behaviors. We would predict that a listener seeking information might ask many questions on a variety of related and even unrelated subjects. We would expect the information seeking listener to provide a greater percentage of tangential and different listening responses to a speaker. A diagram all of the listening responses in an information seeking conversation, might look like the graph in Figure 2.

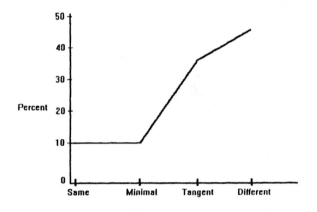

Figure 2. Listening responses in an information–seeking conversation

In the next graph representing relational listening, it should be noted that the total number of listening responses equals 100 percent and that about 70 percent of the responses were on the same topic.

The key is to note the difference between the diagram (Figure 2) reflecting informational listening and the one that follows (Figure 3) representing listening in a helping relationship. In the helping relationship, the listener wants to *provide* empathy and allow the speaker the opportunity to talk fully about what she or he wants to talk about.

In everyday normal conversation we might have some of each of the types of listening responses. Figure 4 might reflect a composite of normal conversations. We have not completed the research to qualify normal conversations.

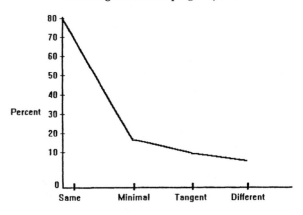

Figure 3. Listening responses in an empathic conversation

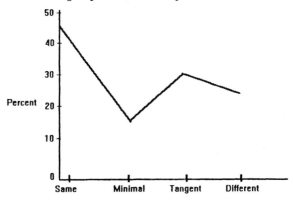

Figure 4. Listening responses in a relationship conversation

Now that we have looked at verbal and nonverbal listening responses, we need to focus on the relationship dimension which most authors call empathy. In a helping relationship we need to rely on empathic listening responses.

Levels of Empathy

To complete our general understanding of listening in a helping relationship, we need to look at Carkhuff's (1969) work on empathy. He has described the type of listening behavior that fits the right hand side of the continuum and identified the levels of listening that are appropriate for counselors working in a clinical setting. These same levels have been applied to all people in the helping professions including religious counselors, physicians, and crisis center volunteers.

Carkhuff offered five levels of empathy which go from no empathy (level 1) to telepathic empathy (level 5). To help you remember each level, we can describe them as colors.

At the first level (red) the verbal and behavioral expressions of the helper do not attend to or detract significantly from the expressions of the helpee. Red (level one) represents a listening response that fails to even recognize that someone is communicating with you. For example, someone tells you that he/she is feeling bad, and you ignore the person and start talking to someone else. Clearly you are not at all empathic. The person expected some kind of response and you chose to ignore him/her. The color red was selected because it signifies a "stop" in conversation with the speaker. This is not the response one should make unless you feel your life is in danger. You would not, for example, want to give an empathic listening response to an ominous-looking stranger on the street corner at midnight.

If this red response did not occur with some regularity in our listening repertoire, we could ignore it. but it does occur too often. Have you every felt like talking about some particular problem, and you got a red listening response in reply? How did you feel? Did you see that person as empathic or egocentric? In sum, a red response is a nonlistening response and therefore not empathic at all. As we have said throughout this book, to *listen,* you must be responding to a stimulus. In this case, you are ignoring the stimulus or helpee.

Carkhuff suggests that a level two (yellow) response from a helper distracts noticeably from the communication of the helpee. The helper focuses on his/her own ideas rather than on the helpee's. This yellow (level two) offers some, but not much, improvement. In this interaction, the listener recognizes the existence of the other person but little else. Suppose, you just got a nev' job which you want to share with your best friend. "Guess what Bob, I got a new job, just today!" Bob responds, "If you think *that's* great, I just got promoted." Remember the example of the physician earlier in the chapter.

This is the "I can top that" listener. This type of listener recognizes your existence only long enough to get to his or her point. Again, this is not one of the preferred empathic listening responses. As a listener, you need to do more than just acknowledge others' existence. If they need a friendly ear, they do not want to hear about your problems or about how *you* can top whatever they have said.

Yellow was selected because it symbolizes the transition from red to green. It is the beginning of recognition for the helpee leading to a truly empathic response. Like the red listening response, a yellow response is not really appropriate because such a response signals to the speaker that his or her concerns are not really important, and he/she is not worth your time. In our model the response quickly moves from other to self. It is at the next level, however, that we are beginning to achieve empathic listening.

We should comment that people use a yellow response because they believe they are being empathic. For example, I told everyone of my flood damage in my home from a broken hose. All but one out of about 60 people immediately told me about their flood. Thus all gave me the yellow yes but response. I suspect they thought that they were empathic. Trying to be a green listener, I pursued their flood rather than switching back to mine.

A green response (level 3) is the first *true* sign of empathy by a listener. Carkhuff states that the expressions of the helper in response to the helpee are essentially interchangeable with those of the helpee. Listening at this level indicates to a speaker that you have heard both the content *and* feeling of his/her statements. While you cannot always read feelings from the content of a verbal statement, the speaker's nonverbal messages can facilitate understanding. For example, I might say that I am angry with the way society treats the homeless. You, as a helper, would need my tone of voice and other paralinguistic cues to know both feeling and content.

If this is the first time that you have heard of levels of empathy, you might think the level three green response sounds like a parrot that mimics. I say that I am angry with the way society treats the homeless, and you respond (listen) by saying, " You sound upset by the way the homeless are treated." This green response should encourage me to continue expressing my views. If the response is conveyed with sincerity and conviction, I will want to continue the conversation and tell you why I am upset. We may not always use the exact same words but we want to convey to the helpee that we understand the feelings and content which she or he expressed to us.

When we move to a blue listening response (level four), we begin to offer the other person advice. Carkhuff says the helper is about to add to the expressions of the helpee in such a way as to express feelings on a level deeper than the helpee was able to express. As indicated above, you need to have a special relationship with the other person you can offer advice. Have you ever offered advice to a classmate or a colleague? If he/she tries it and it does not work, you get the blame. Other times, you get an immediate response like, "Yes but, if I do that I will…." Most people let us know when they want our advice. A close friend, a significant other, or a client seeing a counselor will be more open to advice. Each of these helpers can provide advice because it comes from intimate knowledge of the helpee as a result of the relationship.

The last empathic listening response, is labeled a violet response (level five). It could best be described as a telepathic response. Carkhuff suggests that a helper is capable of going significantly beyond the feelings and thoughts expressed by the helpee. An example happened not too long ago. A former student called, and I immediately asked her for the two pieces of news she had to report. She said, in fact, she did have two pieces of news and wanted to know how I knew. A lucky guess or a sixth sense, I am not sure why I felt that should expect two items, but I did. Professional counselors, skilled and experienced at reading into behavior, can provide violet listening responses. This level is of little practical value to us in everyday relationships, since it cannot be learned or consciously controlled.

It is important to have a good understanding of how listening functions in both a general interaction and in a helping relationship which calls for empathy. Let us explore the helping profession from the listening perspective. We will look; at the *range* of helping professions extending from the psychoanalytic or therapeutic approach to what a friend might do when serving as a helper. The *goals* of listening differ, as well as, *how* you might listen to the person.

We can classify helpers into at least three categories. Category one contains all of the degreed *professional counselors* and *therapists.* The therapist's goal is to be the empathic listener for the person with emotional and related problems. In category two, we have the *trained volunteer* who serves the local crisis center or hotline. You and I are in category three because we have the least training to prepare us for the role of *helper.* In fact, we are a helper solely because the helpee designated us for that role. Let's talk about each of these categories as they relate to listening and helping.

To understand the therapist's role we need to know the steps that he/she goes through to help the client. The goal of the professional therapist is to help the client restructure his or her personality in order to help the individual develop a more positive and rewarding personal existence. Therapists deal with such psychological issues as personal conflict, depression, and even suicide. They usually work with a long term commitment to help the patient adjust to society. Like the development of any relationship, the therapist must establish contact with the helpee. He or she must show the patient concern, genuineness, empathy, and support. We will talk about how these behaviors are manifested in verbal and nonverbal listening later in this chapter.

Once contact has been established, the therapist listens for information, feelings, and the unsaid in order to determine the problem and its scope. To collect this information, the therapist usually focuses on the past to determine it's impact on the present. Finally, the therapist develops a plan of action with the helpee including some goal setting. The helpee is involved in the development of this plan otherwise it is not likely to be implemented.

Throughout this lengthy process, the therapist serves as a mirror of the thoughts and feelings of the helpee. As suggested in the beginning of this chapter, the therapist is attempting oneness with the patient. He or she tries to feel with the patient. Carkhuff and others have determined that the more successful therapists are those who can demonstrate the greatest empathy for the patient.

The crisis intervener differs in a couple of ways from the therapist. First, the intervener seeks to help the helpee find resolution to the immediate crisis. If a person calls the hotline threatening suicide, the helper will not attempt to develop a long term relationship. The helper will listen to determine the immediate threat of suicide. If the threat is low, the helper will assist the helpee restore some level of functioning. The helper might also suggest that the potential victim seek professional counseling to deal with the deep issues facing the helpee. Once a level of functioning is restored, the relationship usually ends.

Finally, all of us may serve as helpers to those around us. Suppose your best friend calls you at 10:00 PM one evening and says that he is going to commit suicide. What do you do? When you commit yourself to help, you have decided to become a true helper and enter that helping listening relationship. We can choose to help or not to help but if we say yes, our listening and communication behaviors are similar to those of the therapist and hotline volunteer. Like the latter, we must deal with the immediate situation. We too must determine the severity of the situation. We listen for the cues that our best friend provides us.

As you can see, in a helping relationship the professional listener is trained and prepared to make a long term commitment to the patient/client/friend. As a helper we may have that same long term commitment to a friend but not as a long term helping listener. If a long term commitment is needed for therapeutic listening, a professional is required. Like the hotline worker' we will take a more active role with the helpee than the therapist. We want to help our best friends deal with the immediate situation at hand.

Therapeutic listening, helping listening, and our own everyday listening differ by degree. While the professional counselor and hotline volunteer have more professional training and practice at listening in a helping relationship, they apply the same basic principles that everyone applies when they enter a helping relationship.

In concluding this chapter, it is essential to describe the approaches that we can take in our verbal and nonverbal listening behaviors in the helping relationship. These are applicable to the therapist, the volunteer, and to the friendly helper.

Approaches to Verbal and Nonverbal Listening Behavior

Rather than prescribe specific verbal and nonverbal behaviors it is more productive to suggest verbal and nonverbal strategies for establishing a relationship with the helpee. The exact words, phrases, and nonverbal behaviors that individuals select are highly personal. In fact, it may be necessary to try many words and behaviors to get through to the helpee.

In a study of empathy and verbal responses, Arnold and Johnson (1992) found that best friends, counselors and even strangers were perceived as more empathic when their messages sounded competent and comforting. The person needed to be sincere and friendly. Through words and actions we must help the person reduce the anxiety and emotionality of the immediate situation. When we are asked to listen in a helping relationship, there is likely to be tension, stress, and even volatility present. An excited voice, nervous behaviors, rapid speech on your part would not be calm and comforting. When we have a heated argument, both parties tend to talk louder and faster. The gestures become more obvious. We are trying to reduce the immediate crisis nature of the relationship.

When we are in the helping relationship we may need to be more direct in our listening. Unlike the therapist who keeps saying, tell me more, we will have to assist the other person as to the options. I am not proposing that you tell him/her what to do. Rather, you explore options and leave that person with choices. For example, if your friend says she really has trouble with a particular coworker, you should explore what is meant by trouble. Once that has been discussed, and your friend still wants to talk about the problem it would than be useful to explore optional solutions. The good green listener knows when the other person just wants to let off steam and when they want to go further toward a solution. We have no magic tips to help you decide what to do. Remember, communication and listening are processes that can be modified as long as you keep talking.

Focusing on the present and the future will help the other person more than focusing on the past. There is always the tendency to ask why. Why did my spouse leave me? Why did she have to die" Why can't I pass an algebra exam? In the listening environment of the helping relationship, we are not trying to conduct a psychological examination. We are trying to reduce the pain; lower the stress; and have the other person focus on the future.

In addition to these three strategies and the use of empathy, we might include the basic Boy (Girl) Scout laws: That is, a helper must be trustworthy, loyal, helpful, friendly, courteous, kind, and sometimes cheerful. We have to listen in such a way that we have the confidence of the people we are trying to help. We began with their confidence when they turned to us, so we must listen effectively to maintain it.

Finally, as suggested throughout this chapter the helper must demonstrate empathy for the helpee. If the above approaches are applied with the green level of empathy, we are well on our way to being effective listeners in a helping relationship. We need to reflect back to the helpee the content and the feelings that she or he is expressing. The better we know the person, the more we may be able to listen between the lines for what is not said or expressed nonverbally.

We have come full circle from relationships and listening to empathy and the helping process. Listening is central to any helping relationship whether it is between a client and a therapist or between you and your best friend. We must develop the empathic side of our listening behavior when we are asked to serve as a helper. We must perfect both types of listening if we are to be effective in our day-to-day relationships.

Summary

This chapter has identified the unique role of listening in the communication process with special emphasis on the helping relationship. We have not developed a detailed discussion about the professional role as an empathic listener since there are complete texts on therapeutic relationships and empathy. Rather we have tried to identify how individuals fit the helping relationship and how we can serve others when they are the helpees in a problem or crisis. We can all be helpers listening to the verbal and nonverbal messages of friends with greater empathy.

Exercises

1. Read each of the following dialogues and determine the levels of listening (Carkhuff) response:

    A. JOHN: That boss of mine really does not understand me.

       JANE: I have always liked him myself.

    B. JAN: Would you like to have dinner now?

       FRANK: What time is it?

    C. GEORGE: I am very upset with that math instructor and the grade that I got on the test.

JEAN:　　　Perhaps you should talk to the instructor about the grade.

Now go back and provide a green (level three) response for each.

Find a friend and practice providing empathic type responses to each of the following situations:

A. FRIEND:　I feel that we are drifting apart. We seem to be going in different directions and no longer share the same things. I am disappointed.

YOU RESPOND:

B. FRIEND:　I am so happy. The weather is just great. I feel like doing something silly.

YOU RESPOND:

C. FRIEND:　I feel really miserable. I just lost that promotion to that *&@i¢$&.

YOU RESPOND:

Were you able to give a response that was empathic without agreeing with what your friend said? You do not have to agree with a person to be empathic.

What were the barriers to listening empathically?

What were the difficulties that you experienced?

3. Find two other people with whom to practice this exercise. Select a topic for discussion that is somewhat controversial. Ask one friend to talk about the topic for several minutes. You should then try to repeat back (a green, level three response) to that person both the content and the feelings that she or he communicated to you. The third person should listen to determine if you were able to capture the content and the feelings expressed. You can repeat this exercise sitting back-to-back so that the facial expressions cannot be seen.

What were the difficulties that you experienced?

What were the barriers to listening?

Were the feelings difficult or easy to identify?

Did the back to back session make it harder or easier? Why?

4. Watch a soap opera on daytime television. Describe using the three categories of informational, relationship, and empathic lis-

tening, the types of listening behavior typically used. Was the listening appropriate for the circumstance?

What nonverbal listening behaviors would you use if your best friend came to you upset over the loss of his/her parent?

Answers to model: 1-D, 2-B, 3-D, 4-C.

References and Additional Sources

Aguilera, D. C. & Messick, J. M. (1974). *Crisis Intervention: Theory and Methodology*. 2nd edition. New York, NY: Mosby.

Arnold, W. E. (1990). Listening: A conceptualization. Paper presented at the International Listening Association Convention, Indianapolis.

Arnold, W. E. (1989). Listening and information processing. Paper presented at the International Listening Association Convention, Atlanta.

Arnold, W. E. (1980). *Crisis Communication*. Scottsdale, AZ: Gorsuch Scarsbrick.

Arnold, W. E. and Johnson, J. (1992). Perception of empathic messages and message sources. *Journal of the International Listening Association, 6,* pp. 83–88.

Birdwhistell, R. L. (1970). *Kinesics and Context: Essays on Body Motion Communication*. Philadelphia: University of Pennsylvania Press.

Bohling, H. and Arnold, W. E. (1990). Alzheimer's patients and caregiver's listening cues. A paper presented at the International Listening Association Convention, Indianapolis.

Boy, A. V. and Pine, G. P. (1982). *Client-centered Counseling A Renewal*. Boston: Allyn and Bacon.

Brammer, L. M. (1973). *The Helping Relationship: Process and Skills*. Englewood Cliffs: Prentice Hall.

Bruneau, T. (1989). Empathy and listening: A conceptual review and theoretical directions. *Journal of the International Listening Association, 3,* pp. 1–20.

Carkhuff, R. (1969). *Helping and Human Relations*. New York, NY: Holt, Rinehart, Winston. 2 vols.

Glenn, E. (1989). A content analysis of fifty definitions of listening. *Journal of the International Listening Association, 3,* pp. 21–31.

Goss, B. (1983). *Processing in Intrapersonal Communication*. Belmont, CA: Wadsworth.

Lobdell, C. L. and Gluc, J. M. (1990). Measuring listening: An applied test. Paper presented at the International Listening Association, Indianapolis.

Lobdell, C. L., Sonoda, K. T. and Arnold, W. E. (1993). The influence of perceived supervisor listening behavior on employee commitment. *Journal of the International Listening Association, 7,* pp. 92–110.

O'Heren, L. W. and Arnold, W. E. (1991). Nonverbal attentive behaviors and listening comprehension. *Journal of the International Listening Association, 5*, pp. 20-24.

Stone, H. (1976). *Crisis Counseling*. Philadelphia, PA: Fortress Press.

Watson, K. W. and Barker, L. L. (1984). Listening behavior: Definition and measurement. *Communication yearbook, 8*, pp. 178-179.

Wolvin, A. D. and Coakley, C. G. (1988). *Listening*. 3rd edition. Dubuque, LA: Wm. C. Brown.

Zimmerman, R. and Arnold, W. E. (1990). Physicians and patients perceptions of actual versus ideal physicians communication and listening behaviors. *Journal of the International Listening Association, 4*, pp. 92-110.

Chapter 12

THE LAWYER-CLIENT ENCOUNTER: Listening for Facts and Relationship

David A. Victor and Cindy Rhodes Victor

Points to be Addressed:

- Listening in the context of the practice of law.

- The relative importance of listening as a basic communication skill for attorneys.

- The specific components of listening in the context of the lawyer's profession.

- Ways to strengthen legal listening skills.

An attorney is only as effective as his or her ability to communicate. While admittedly an attorney's occupation rests on the interpretation and application of the law, attorneys must impart that information to others. A mere knowledge of legal facts and even a keen interpretation of legal trends are in themselves only a small portion of the lawyer's day-to-day work. Instead, the vast majority of an attorney's time is spent on communication-related tasks.

The Importance of Listening in the Practice of Law

Many of these communication-related tasks revolve around the attorney's ability to listen actively. While some communication theorists such as James Weaver (1983) have paid particular attention to listening as a necessary skill for lawyers, the importance of listening has not, as a rule, been particularly recognized by the legal community.

Indeed, in a survey in which attorneys assessed the time they spent in various communication activities, listening was consistently ranked as being of lower importance than writing or speaking skills in such listening-intensive activities as oral argument (Cotton, 1986). Still, listening was ranked as the most important skill in such legal activities as counseling and interviewing witnesses and clients (Cotton). Moreover, Cotton (p. 39) found that in every category or rank with the exception of junior associates, all attorneys surveyed ranked listening as the basic communication skill (over reading, speaking and writing). Sole proprietors and junior partners spent the most hours per day listening, while for senior partners, speaking tied with listening for most hours spent during the day.

Listening, then, takes up a high proportion of the experienced lawyer's time. Its very frequency makes it a point of importance. Yet listening as a work-related skill should merit a lawyer's attention for more than simply the amount of the working day it consumes. Instead, listening is a skill which—in its various components—directly influences an attorney's effectiveness in a wide variety of job-related tasks. Effective listening skills are most crucial in the lawyer-client relationship. The lawyer must actively listen to the client not only to ascertain the facts of the client's legal problem, but also to determine whether the client has presented an incomplete or biased picture of the problem and to assess the emotional state of the client in relation to the legal problem.

Components of Active Legal Listening

In Chapter 2 of this book, Purdy cites seven components of the listening process: volition, focused attention, perception, interpretation, remembering, and response and receptivity to the human element. Each of these components is described below in its relation to the practice of law (although for our purposes, we have combined response and receptivity to the human element into a single category). Each component plays an important role in defining the listening skills an effective attorney needs and directly influences specific activities related to the lawyer's profession, including client counseling and representation.

Volition: Developing a Desire to Listen

Until fairly recently, the role of listening in the practice of the law had not received much emphasis. Law schools traditionally provided their students with little if any training in practical communication skills or even in those legal activities such as counseling clients or interviewing witnesses (Gee and Jackson, 1982; Stevens, 1983; Cotton, 1986).

Instead, law schools have promoted the study of the content—as opposed to the practice—of the law. Even the teaching method in many law schools tends to emphasize the knowledge of the law itself and the ability to build a foundation for legal interpretation based on precedents. Generally speaking, law students as a group are not particularly well-trained in interpersonal communication skills, including listening. Trained instead in a system which emphasizes research and document preparation, these law school students graduate to become attorneys who may believe that the law stands somehow apart from any interpersonal skills. These new attorneys may decide that what matters is the ability to construct a case based on the interpretation of the law, not the relationship of the lawyer with a client, or even a witness or judge.

Such training may result in new attorneys who view their main function as the interpreters of the legal code to the ignorant lay person. It is possible, therefore, for the inexperienced attorney to develop the attitude that the lawyer's job is to talk, while listening is primarily the client's task.

Few things could be farther from reality. Those lawyers who hold fast to such a view never develop good listening skills precisely because they have no desire to listen. It is significant that in her survey of the importance of listening among attorneys at various stages of their careers, Cotton found that only junior-level associates (that is, beginning attorneys) ranked listening as a comparatively unimportant skill. While many lawyers doubtless never develop a liking for listening, few survive the perils of an unwillingness to listen for very long. Those attorneys who lack the will to listen find themselves host to a bevy of professional difficulties. Unexpected revelations of damaging facts and testimony blindside them in trial. Unhappy former clients brand them as arrogant. Judges surprise them with unexpected rulings or unfavorable assignation of court dates. To the extent that the nonlistening attorney can label these occurrences as simply unfair or the fault of other parties, he or she can rationalize the source of the difficulties and put off the need to develop listening skills. Yet such excuses, as Cotton's study suggests, tend to fall flat with continued experience in legal practice.

As a result, volition is the first step lawyers must take to develop needed listening skills. Only when they overcome their law school training which deemphasized listening and other interpersonal skills will they recognize its importance.

Focused Attention: The Lawyer as Detective

The typical lawyer is barraged with information. Rarely does the successful lawyer have the luxury of handling only one matter or client at a time. Moreover, each case is itself filled with literally thousands of details, each of deceptive importance. Indeed, the most inconsequential shred of evidence can in the right circumstances lay the foundation upon which to build an entire legal argument.

As a result, lawyers—especially litigators—must in many respects act as detectives. In preparing their case, they need to listen attentively to piece together the facts of a case from the information they receive from their clients, other persons whom they interview, and persons from whom they take sworn testimony (called "depositions"). More importantly, they need to use active listening skills to bring out information which these people may not readily volunteer. The attorney can detect this hidden information through listening for subtle nuances in the way the information is stated. Then, the lawyer as detective can follow up with a more pointed inquiry leading to a more complete disclosure.

The task of the lawyer as careful listener, however, does not end with preparatory work. When in the courtroom, the litigator must use his or her listening skills in interpreting judicial instructions, so that he or she can determine the judge's view of the case. Similarly, the attorney must apply active listening skills to interpret the tactics of opposing counsel. Finally, the attorney must listen to detect both the emotional state of witnesses, as well as the degree to which they have either spoken forthrightly or seem to withhold information.

The detective listening skills the lawyer needs, moreover, go beyond the courtroom. Much of an attorney's work deals with client counseling, which Weaver has defined as "talking with clients on subject matters that do not result in law suits, or negotiations with third persons" (p. 12). In such matters, even though the lawyer's task may never involve a third party, the lawyer must listen carefully to advise his or her client properly. To direct the client to follow the best course of action, the lawyer must actively listen to detect whether the client has presented a biased or incomplete description of the facts of the legal problem which the client faces.

Perception: Battling Bias

Even when lawyers have the desire to listen, and do listen with focused attention, they may misunderstand information which is vital to their case because of their own personal bias. Such bias may take two forms: personal and interpretational.

Personal Bias

Lawyers in the course of their work encounter people from all walks of life. As with people in any profession, though, lawyers have personal prejudices. Thus, they may discount a reliable account from a seven-year-old because of a prejudice against the reliability of children. Similarly, they may favor the unreliable testimony of a witness who is comfortable with legal terminology because they are comfortable with legal terminology themselves.

Attorneys may also resist believing what they hear if it runs counter to that which they want to believe. They may be unwilling to listen openly to a person who holds a strong opposing viewpoint or whose personal lifestyle they find offensive. Unlike members of professions who have the option of choosing with whom they will interact, lawyers must remain receptive to the messages of all sorts of people, since—regardless of their views or behavior—they may provide information critical to a full understanding of the legal problem. Also, unlike other professionals, a lawyer may, in fact, be compelled, either by a more senior attorney or a judge, to represent particular clients.

Interpretational Bias

Bias likewise mars perception when attorneys themselves hold too firmly to an interpretation. After investing numerous hours to develop a legal argument or position, lawyers quite naturally may find themselves resisting openly listening to information which undercuts the validity of that argument or position. Indeed, in the situation of unexpected testimony revealed during a trial, the entire direction of a lawyer's argument and legal strategy may have to be reformulated on the spot. If the lawyer clings to his or her prepared position, the case most likely will be lost. Only the lawyer who is receptive to listening to opposing viewpoints can maintain the flexibility needed in such situations to represent clients most effectively.

Interpretation

Lawyers are experts in the law. However, the legal problems which lawyers handle cover every aspect of life, and cannot be handled solely by reference to legal precedents. The lawyer is, therefore, almost always a lay person in all but the particular legal area of a client's case. The banker knows more about banking than the corporate lawyer, the scientific inventor more about science than the patent lawyer, husbands and wives more about their spouses than the divorce lawyer, and so on.

To the extent that the details of such non-legal matters go beyond the expertise or even interest of the lawyer, the issue of interpretation as a component of listening plays a part. To interpret what a client says to an attorney, the attorney must make sense of the communicated message. This poses two listening impediments for the attorney: expertise and personal experience.

Listening Impediments: Expertise

Attorneys are limited by their own background in those areas of expertise which their clients possess. This puts the lawyer in a quandary. He or she must appear knowledgeable enough in the client's field to maintain the client's confidence. Yet at the same time, the lawyer must be honest enough to request clarification when the expertise of the client surpasses what the lawyer knows.

A similar situation can occur when the attorney interacts with persons other than clients. The expertise of expert witnesses and even of opposing counsel in non-legal areas may prove an impediment to the attorney no matter how attentively he or she listens. If attorneys pretend to understand that which is actually too complicated for them given their individual backgrounds in a particular subject, the possibility of a full understanding is greatly reduced. Indeed, attorneys who pretend to have an understanding of material which they are in fact unable to interpret run the risk of failing to elicit key information needed to help their clients resolve their legal problems.

By requesting further clarification, the attorney may garner a greater understanding of a complex or technical situation. Yet such a request for information may also suggest that the information is beyond the attorney's understanding. In such a situation, the opposing side's expert witness may deliberately sidestep revealing pertinent information, knowing that the attorney lacks the expertise necessary to ask for the information directly or even question the bases of the expert's opinion.

Lawyers, therefore, have two tasks in interpretation. First, they must listen to interpret the information which the speaker provides. Second, they must listen to determine what it is they do not understand well enough to interpret on their own.

Listening Impediments: Personal Experience

The second aspect of interpretation as a component of listening skills goes beyond expertise to the lawyer's specific personal experiences. In interpreting a message, people determine the meaning of a message in terms of their own personal experiences. Yet because of the extremely broad scope of the people with whom lawyers must interact, lawyers' personal experiences are likely to represent only a very small range of the experiences of those to whom they listen.

In other words, the personal experiences of lawyers are less adequate as a basis for interpretation than the personal experiences of many other professionals. For example, an engineer's professional experience is largely limited to interaction with other engineers about engineering. The range of behavior among engineers is comparatively small due to similarities of education, income and the nature of the problems they face at work. In this respect, the personal experiences of one engineer are likely to be fairly similar to that of other engineers. The task of interpreting what other engineers say when gauged against any individual engineer's own personal experience is therefore made relatively easier. By contrast, the people with whom lawyers interact are frequently very dissimilar covering a wide range of professions, educational backgrounds, income groups and other variables. The personal experiences of these people are unlikely to overlap with the personal experiences of the lawyer whose job it is to listen to them. The personal experiences of the lawyer, therefore, are less likely to prove as reliable a means of interpretation during listening.

Remembering

The vast amount of material covered in most cases makes reliance on note-taking and transcripts of depositions and trials necessary. Yet the truly effective lawyer must be able to remember, even without written aids or recorded messages, the pertinent issues in what others say. Indeed, it is often insufficient to remember approximately what is said. Rather, it is necessary in fact to be able to remember verbatim the words of key testimony or statements from people central to a legal situation (see chapter 3). The successful lawyer, therefore, must listen to remember.

Responsive Listening and Receptivity: The Counselor as Consoler

The attorney's listening skills are important for more than just detecting and recalling information. To a very large extent, the lawyer is expected to act as an emotional support to his or her client.

Clients frequently approach their attorney in states of great emotional distress over the issue that has led them to contemplate legal action. The attorney must be able to listen for the emotional state of the client and use listening skills as a means of comforting them and directing their emotional distress into active participation in the case and support for the attorney's legal strategy. In short, clients frequently use lawyers as someone to whom they can talk or let off steam and so feel better. In such situations, the lawyer must act as the proverbial hand-holder of the client.

Even when clients are not greatly distressed, the lawyer must be a good listener to appear accessible. Clients must feel comfortable enough with the lawyer to trust him or her with the truth of their situation. If clients feel uncomfortable with a lawyer, they may attempt to present information in a more favorable light. They may discount or even leave out negative events while emphasizing positive ones, leaving the attorney unprepared when opposing counsel reveals and uses the omitted information.

Strengthening Listening Skills

Although lawyers may recognize that increasing their listening skills is needed, they may be unsure of the way in which to develop and strengthen those skills in different situations. Lawyers should examine each of the components of the listening process and work on strengthening each component, so that they can adapt their listening skills to the client or witness with whom they are discussing a case and interpret correctly the nonverbal cues transmitted by the speaker.

First, if an attorney has had little or no training in practical communication skills, he or she should seek out that training, whether by attending a local college or business school program or continuing legal education seminar, or by consulting with a communication specialist. Second, lawyers need to make sure that, whether in conversations with clients or witnesses or in the courtroom, they focus their attention on the information which the other party is providing. Indeed, lawyers should encourage the other party to the conversation to disclose information more completely by asking open–ended questions which do not suggest an answer, such as, "what happened during your meeting with the bank president?" Clients and witnesses are then free to provide a narrative of facts, during which the attorney can exercise his or her listening skills, rather than short answers to narrowly–delineated questions.

Next, attorneys should examine whether their perceptions and personal biases interfere with their listening skills, and if so, recognize that they will have to listen even more carefully and objectively, so that their perceptions and biases do not prevent them from really "hearing" the facts of the legal problem. Likewise, attorneys should recognize and accept their own limitations in specialties and areas about which they have little knowledge or training, so that these limitations do not become a bar to effective listening.

If an attorney has difficulty in remembering facts of the legal problems he or she handles, it may be that he or she is not "listening to remember", and therefore, not picking up on and retaining information which may prove useful at a later stage of the legal problem's resolution. Therefore, lawyers should keep in mind during conversations that they must listen, not only to obtain information at that time, but also to retain it for later purposes. Finally, lawyers should practice accessibility and receptivity as a listener, so that persons feel comfortable in revealing information helpful to the lawyer's strategy decisions.

Summary

As we have discussed, an attorney is only as effective as his or her ability to communicate. Listening, though not central to the attorney's work of interpreting and applying the law, nonetheless represents a much greater share of the lawyer's day-to-day work. Listening not only takes up the most time of any communication skill among experienced lawyers, but arguably affects many aspects of his or her daily tasks. Indeed, the greatest part of an attorney's job, as we have seen, involves his or her ability to listen.

Consequently, the importance of listening as a learned skill is strong in the legal profession. The importance of listening to the legal profession, however, should not be limited to the lawyers themselves. Listening training for the legal profession, possibly in response to the lack of enthusiasm for the subject among lawyers themselves, has long been overlooked by listening specialists and communication professionals. While law schools traditionally provide very little, if any, training in listening as a professional skill, the area of listening training in the legal field is one filled with opportunity. Lawyers who are skilled listeners hold a competitive edge not only in practicing law but in maintaining strong client-counselor relationships and in client development. If the advantages to be derived from good listening skills can be sold to attorneys, the absence of law school or formal training in listening skills can actually provide an advantage to the listening specialist willing to train the legal profession.

Exercises

1. Interview two or more attorneys, preferably one new attorney and one attorney who has been practicing more than 10 years. Ask what role listening plays in the performance of their job and in relations with clients. Have them rank the importance of listening as compared to the other communication skills they use in their profession. Do the answers you received from the new attorney and the more experienced attorney differ? If so, in what way?

2. Interview two people who recently hired lawyers to resolve their legal problems. Ask them:

   • were they pleased with the attention the lawyers paid to their cases?

- did they feel that the lawyers actually listened to them during lawyer–client encounters?

- did they feel that the resolution of their legal problems had been favorable?

- did they believe that the resolution of their legal problems had any relation to the listening skills of their attorney?

3. Divide into small groups. Research a legal problem and its factual background. Have different members of the group act in the roles of lawyer and client. Determine whether listening skills help the lawyer learn the details of the factual situation, counsel and comfort the client, and develop a legal strategy.

4. Observe actual trials or other courtroom proceedings. Listen carefully to lawyers when they question, or cross–examine, the other side's witnesses. Do the attorneys ask questions which relate to statements the witnesses have previously made, or do they follow a prepared set of questions? Do the attorneys who use listening skills seem more flexible and effective than attorneys who do not? What other observations can you make?

References

Cotton, S. M. (December 1986). An assessment of time spent in various communication activities by attorneys. Unpublished Master of Arts Thesis, Auburn University.

Gee, G. E. and Jackson, D. W. (1982). Current studies of legal education: Findings and recommendations. Journal of Legal Education, 32, 471–505.

Stevens, R. (1983). Law School: Legal Education in America from the 1850's to the 1980's. Chapel Hill: The University of North Carolina Press.

Weaver, J. F. (1983). Review of research on legal interviewing. In Ronald J. Matlon and Richard J. Crawford (eds.), Communication Strategies in the Practice of Lawyering. Annandale, Virginia: Speech Communication Association, 126–48.

Chapter 13

LISTENING: A Crucial Competency for Effective Health Care Delivery

Gary L. Kreps, Ellen W. Bonaguro and Jim L. Query, Jr.

Points to be Addressed

- The centrality of listening for health care consumers and providers.
- The role of information in health care.
- Effective listening is an active process.
- The perceptual bases of listening.
- Listening and relational development in health care.
- Listening and health care teams.
- Listening and health care advocacy.
- Helping health care consumers and providers develop effective listening skills.

After passing out at work, Jerry was taken to the Emergency Room (ER) of County Hospital. The attending physician in the ER diagnosed Jerry as suffering from diabetes, and prescribed daily injections of insulin to manage this health problem. Jerry's diabetic condition was subsequently stabilized in the hospital. Prior to being released from the hospital, Jerry received instruction on how to administer daily insulin injections.

At the health education session, a nurse educator told Jerry how important it was to carefully monitor his diet and to make sure insulin was injected at prescribed times each morning and evening. The nurse showed Jerry how to carefully fill the syringe with the correct amount of insulin, how to test the syringe, and how to inject the insulin. Jerry seemed very nervous about the injections. To avoid unnecessary discomfort, the nurse demonstrated the procedure by making injections into an orange. Jerry also practiced filling the syringe and injecting it into an orange. The nurse asked if the procedure was clear and if there were any questions. Jerry found the procedure to be easy and had no questions. He was released from the hospital and sent home with an initial supply of insulin and syringes.

A few days later, Jerry was readmitted to the County Hospital ER in diabetic shock. After stabilizing the condition, the attending physician asked Jerry if the insulin had been taken. Jerry emphatically replied that the medication was injected every morning and evening just as instructed. The doctor was puzzled. Se did not understand how Jerry could have gone into diabetic shock if the medication had been taken correctly. After further questioning, Jerry explained more precisely how the medication had been taken.

Jerry had injected the insulin into the orange and ate the orange every morning and every evening! The doctor explained that this was the wrong way to take the medication and sent Jerry for further instruction prior to being released. When the nurse educator heard about this situation, her response was, "I guess some people just do not listen!"

The Centrality of Listening for Health Care Consumers and Providers

There was a potentially fatal lack of understanding in the insulin-injection, health education session. But, what was the cause of the misunderstanding? Ineffective listening was certainly an important part of this problem. Jerry probably did not listen carefully enough to the nurse educator to learn how to correctly administer the medication. The nurse educator probably did not listen carefully enough to Jerry either to ensure his understanding. The nurse and Jerry could have avoided the return trip to the ER by doing a better job of communicating.

Jerry needed to be encouraged to provide in–depth feedback concerning the health education session before being released from the hospital. The nurse educator could have elicited relevant information by asking Jerry to describe exactly how the medication would be taken. Without seeking relevant information about another person's point of view, we can never be sure about his or her interpretation of the verbal messages and accompanying nonverbal cues (see Edwards & Brilhart, 1981).

Modern health care is a very complex process and it is crucial that both health care consumers and health care providers communicate strategically and effectively (Kreps & Thornton, 1992; Jones & Phillips, 1988). Communication becomes an even more integral part of health care as consumers are channeled into managed care programs that alter the provider–consumer relationship in a variety of ways. Within a managed care program, the consumer may be seen by a number of physicians rather than one. The consumer and physician also confront rigid time constraints due to economic concerns. For instance, the consumer's insurance carrier will not pay for protracted visits unless the charted information justifies longer office visits. Additionally, physicians who consistently do not see a selected number of patients, justifying visit lengths and recommended treatments, are soon removed from the carrier's approved network.

Changes in the health care system provide further evidence for the need for effective communication between provider–consumer, provider–provider, and consumer–significant others. These changes encompass technological advances, treatment modalities, and DRGs to name a few (Geist & Hardesty, 1992). While innovations in each of these areas may ultimately enhance the quality of health care, they also have the potential to become barriers to effective interaction. Individuals already confronting threats to their health are often ill-equipped to cope with and understand novel information such as industry-wide developments.

Encouraging providers and consumers to establish effective listening styles could actually be a cost-saving strategy for health care organizations. In Jerry's case, the high cost of ER may be passed on to his carrier possibly raising his premiums. It is further plausible that Jerry could have to pay for these services out-of-pocket. County Hospital could also reduce its resource costs if Jerry had not used one of its most expensive "doors." Additionally, had effective listening occurred between Jerry and the nurse educator, there would be a much smaller likelihood of malpractice litigation and subsequent legal costs. Emphasis on listening behavior for both the provider and the consumer will result in less misinterpretation. In the opening situation, had the nurse educator been trained in active listening we would have read examples of how providers could elicit additional information to assure understanding. If Jerry had been asked questions about the injection procedure, the nurse educator would have recognized that Jerry misinterpreted the directions, thinking that the orange (which contained the insulin) could be digested to produce the proper results.

Listening skills are essential for health care providers. Table 11.1 offers ideas that could be used to establish a listener friendly environment.

Table 1
Environmental And Interpersonal Strategies For Providers To Facilitate Active Listening

Environmental

- Control distractions and interruptions

- Provide ample ventilation and comfortable room temperature

- Arrange seating so that eye contact can be easily maintained

- Make the surroundings attractive, interesting, and comfortable

Interpersonal

- Encourage the client to speak

- Allow the client to finish responses

- Be attentive to both verbal and nonverbal cues

- Use language that the client can understand

- Elicit feedback from the client to gauge understanding of condition and treatment options/regimen

Wohl (1989) suggests that a primary goal for providers is to try to fully understand what their clients are saying as well as understand their clients' unique "cultural" perspectives. This quest for understanding calls for careful attention to listening (Kreps & Kunimoto, 1994). Yet, health care providers are often taught to make quick decisions and may be more concerned with weighing and evaluating diagnostic information than with really listening to their clients (Jones, Kreps, & Phillips, 1995). Studies show that physicians regularly interrupt clients' descriptions of their symptoms early in diagnostic interviews, and often do most of the talking during these interviews (Cassell, 1985; Katz, 1984; West, 1984). Clearly, it is very difficult to listen when one is doing most of the talking! Health care providers must be encouraged to focus their energy on active listening. The benefits of listening outweigh the costs as the outcome leads to better provide/client relationships, and a greater understanding of information presented and received. Consumers must also be prepared to engage in active listening.

While the time constraints of managed care are unlikely to be eased anytime soon, this communication obstacle also provides a clear impetus for consumers to prepare for office visits. For example, it would facilitate active listening among providers if consumers could demonstrate a "good" working knowledge about their bodies and concisely describe their symptoms. Consumers also need to be able to identify their concerns and ask questions (see Jones, Kreps, & Phillips, 1995). Had Jerry asked appropriate questions, it is unlikely he would have again experienced diabetic shock.

All too frequently, in North American culture, questions directed to authority figures (health care providers for example) are seen as signs of incompetence. Both consumers and health care providers can combat such misperceptions by engaging in timely and sensitive interaction fostered by active listening.

Jones, Kreps, & Phillips (1995) contend that health care consumers should communicate strategically to get the most out of the health care system. They must listen carefully to the advice of their providers, carefully weighing different professional opinions and recommendations to make effective health care decisions. The principle of *informed consent* mandates that health care professionals must provide their clients with full information about health care recommendations so the consumers can make sound choices. Yet, if clients do not listen carefully they are unlikely to understand all the details of complex treatment strategies.

One's motivation and cognitive ability to listen effectively are greatly challenged during times of medical distress. When we are sick, we are not in the best condition to listen carefully. We may be in pain. We may be anxious or preoccupied. We may even be irrational. When receiving a serious, frightening, or perhaps even fatal diagnosis it is not uncommon for consumers to become confused and block out much of what the provider has to say. Table 2 identifies internal listening barriers and suggestions for change.

Due to these barriers to effective listening, consumers must be encouraged to work diligently at focusing their listening skills, and providers need to be sensitive and aware of these barriers to make sure their clients really hear and understand what is being said. Of course, "listening" is not a panacea. There are numerous obstacles in health care contexts that cannot be anticipated or controlled. A key objective should be to lessen their intensity and uncertainty; thereby guiding the journey of providers, consumers, and their families. Improving both provider and consumer listening styles it thus an achievable goal that can lead to more efficient, sensitive, and effective health care delivery.

Table 2
**Potential Barriers To Active Listening Among
Clients And Providers And Ideas For Behavior Changes**

Barriers	*Change Strategies*
• Lack of purpose	• Establish a goal(s) for each listening situation
• Overly critical	• Avoid judgment and listen for important messages
• Uninvolved	• Find meaning in messages and show a sincere interest
• Impatience	• Mentally relax and allow responses to be completed
• Anxiety	• Set aside personal status in order to gain information
• Insecurity	• Recall that the provider's role is help

The Role of Information in Health Care

Information is the most powerful resource health care providers and consumers can possess. When they have relevant health information, they can demystify many of the complexities and ambiguities of illness and health care, enabling them to make knowledgeable (informed) health care decisions. We can all use relevant health information, interpersonal information, and bureaucratic information) in many different ways. It can help us interpret different symptoms of illness to discover the sources of our and others health ailments. It can help us identify appropriate diagnostic and treatment technologies, as well as strategically select the best available treatment options for addressing health ailments. It can help us understand the reasons for and implications of the different health care activities performed by doctors and other health care providers. It can provide a basis for establishing cooperative working relationships with different members of the health care team. Relevant information can also help us negotiate the complex rules, regulations, and procedures that are so often impediments to effective health care in modern health care delivery organizations.

Communication is the primary tool we have for gathering relevant health information. Effective listening is a critical communication strategy for gathering relevant *health information*. Consumers must listen carefully to understand diagnostic and treatment information so they can effectively participate in directing their health care. Providers must listen carefully to the information given by the client in order to fully understand their experiences, symptoms, and concerns. Without effective listening, health care providers and consumers are denied access to the relevant health information they so desperately need to make the best health care decision.

Effective Listening is an Active Process

Effective listening skills do not occur naturally. These skills need to be nurtured and developed carefully, especially in health care contexts. As previously noted, consumers and providers face a formidable array of communication obstacles (e.g., fear, uncertainty, jargon, time constraints, and a wide range of client medical knowledge levels). Listening is thus not a passive process; it is an active process! Ideally, consumers and providers attempt to reduce uncertainty, validate their understanding, and coordinate their activities as they listen. Indeed, we need to think about what we hear. Additionally, we often make active choices about what the messages we hear mean by comparing and contrasting these messages to past meanings we have created. This retrospective sense–making can aid, muddle, and/or hinder the communication process among consumers and providers.

Rosey is a thirty–seven year old female. She has been recently diagnosed as having a large tumor located near her reproductive organs. Her OB/GYN, Dr. Marnie Gibbs, explains that most likely, given the size and location of the growth, this tumor is fibroid and benign. Dr. Gibbs subsequently recommends a hysterectomy.

Rosey then avoids eye contact with the doctor, stutters in her response, and searches for the "right" questions. Dr. Gibbs quickly realizes that Rosey is frightened and unsure of all the implications of such a procedure (e.g., loss of child–bearing ability, hormonal changes, sexuality issues, and self–image doubts). She then gently touches Rosey on the shoulder and says: "You know, several of my patients have undergone this operation successfully. Many have even formed a support group to help others deal with this condition. The meetings are informal, and while everyone's experience is somewhat unique, they really seem to debunk many of the myths surrounding reproductive surgery. Our time is almost up today...why don't I give you their phone number?" Rosey replies: "Yes, I think it would be helpful to listen to others who have been through this." This situation exemplifies how a physician, operating within proscribed time constraints, can help a client take advantage of sense-making vehicles such as support groups (see Query & James, 1989).

Unfortunately, however, these support forums can also muddle interaction between providers and clients by imparting mixed messages. For instance, at her first meeting with the support group, Rosey is simultaneously encouraged and discouraged by the members. Angela Kay is about the same age as Rosey. She shares with Rosey how deep her doubts were; yet, her husband and family were very understanding and supportive. Moreover, she feels so much better now that there are no symptoms. In contrast, Maria, about thirty years old, lambasts all OB/GYNs and this procedure: "These doctors think they are God, and their fees reflect this illusion of themselves. I think I could have gone without the surgery for a long time, but my insurance company insisted that the procedure should be done as soon as possible. They are blood-suckers too, you know!" Rosey is thus faced with conflicting messages and must weigh whom to believe.

Finally, supportive delivery systems, such as support groups, can hinder sensitive and timely interaction among consumers and potential helpers such as family members and health care providers (see Hobfoll & Stevens, 1990; Peters-Golden, 1982; Rook, 1984; Rook & Pietromonaco, 1987). This maladaptation usually is characterized as interaction that: denies reality; promotes passivity and dependence; and/or over-protects the client.

Further hindering sense-making in health care contexts is the widespread myth that hearing and listening are synonymous. The former process is physical involving sound waves, the ear canal, and ear drum. The latter process is cognitive involving recognition of verbal and nonverbal cues, as well as interpretation of messages. Hence, effective listening does not just involve the use of our ears to hear. It involves the use of all of our senses to perceive the wide array of relevant verbal and nonverbal messages that enable us to understand different social situations. We listen with our eyes, our sense of touch, even our sense of smell. We don't just listen to spoken words. We also listen to the way the words are spoken. We pay attention to the nonverbal and contextual cues that surround verbal messages. An excellent example is the film, "The Doctor." The main character, a surgeon played by William Hurt, learns first-hand the importance of active listening and attending to nonverbal cues when he becomes a patient presenting with throat cancer.

Skilled providers and educated consumers are often like detectives seeking clues to appropriate diagnoses and action plans. A key weapon in their repertoire is active listening skills. The fictional detective, Sherlock Holmes, was also a great listener. He paid rapt attention to the wide array of cues available in different situations to gather information that enabled him to make many decisions to solve mysteries. We all can take a good lesson from Sherlock Holmes and actively pay attention to the many verbal and nonverbal messages around us to make sense of the different situations we find ourselves in health care.

Active listening is essential to achieving timely and sensitive interaction in health care contexts. It is a strategy for enhancing the quality of listening by increasing the listener's involvement and participation in perceiving and interpreting communication events. It involves having the listener carefully prepare to hear important information, pay close attention to relevant messages, compare what is heard to what is already known, and apply new ideas to personal goals. By increasing personal involvement in the communication exchange individuals are able to enhance their listening efficiency and recall.

Empathic listening is also imperative in health care situations. This strategy adds another level to active listening by heightening the listener's personal involvement in the communication exchange and increasing personal identification with the speaker or speakers he/she is listening to. This type of listening encourages the listener to focus on the feelings of the client. The empathic listener attempts to understand and relate to the perspective of the individual or individuals they are communicating with. By increasing empathy in interactions the listener enhances his or her ability to understand the point of view of the person they are listening to, and thereby enhance the quality of their understanding of what that person has to say. Empathy is an extremely important process in health care delivery, where there is often a great deal of psychological and cultural differences between providers and consumers (Kreps & Kunimoto, 1994).

The Perceptual Bases of Listening

Due to limited cognitive space and sensory mechanisms available for processing, storing, and perceiving information, we make active choices about what messages we to focus on and how to assign meaning to those cues. This global process is called *selective perception* (see Kreps & Thornton, 1992), and it is comprised of three interrelated sub-processes. The first sub-process, *selective attention*, describes how individuals decide to focus on the most salient messages available in a given moment; especially since we cannot process all of the messages around us. The second sub-process, *habituation*, details how we actively block out extraneous messages that can interfere with making sense of the messages attended to in the selective attention process. The third sub-process, *closure*, captures how we link together the selected messages into a meaningful configuration, allowing also for the influence of assumptions and guesses to fill in the blanks.

Not surprisingly, selective perception is a very fragile and idiosyncratic process, with individuals making different choices during each stage. This highly individualized feature of being helps account for why when different people, even long-time relational partners, are exposed to the same message, they interpret the message in unique and incongruent ways. A common and widespread problem individuals have in interpreting messages is when they make *premature closure* by failing to update the conclusions they reach from any one situation.

Due to the fragile nature of perception, we must be careful to seek feedback and listen carefully for additional information when reaching conclusions. For example, in the case at the beginning of this chapter, both Jerry and the nurse educator reached premature closure. Both the nurse educator and Jerry assumed they were "on the same page." Both perceived that the other fully and correctly understood the insulin injection procedure. It is imperative, then, that individuals seek ample feedback to avoid such pitfalls.

Listening and Relational Development in Health Care

The relationship established between providers and consumers has powerful influences on the exchange of health information and the quality of health care delivery (Kreps & Thornton, 1992). Relationships develop incrementally as relational partners exchange messages and get to know one another. Listening carefully to others is a personal from of communication that demonstrates respect and humanizes interaction in relationship development. When we listen carefully to another person we nonverbally let them know that they are important to us and we are interested in what they have to say. Health care consumers and providers who exhibit active and empathetic listening behaviors help to establish an effective provider/consumer relationship (Kreps & Thornton, 1992).

It is important for health care professionals to use the provider/consumer relationship to encourage and empower their clients to participate actively in the modern health care system (Jones, Kreps, & Phillips, 1995). Due to the systemic power imbalance that exists in modern health care between providers and consumers, many consumers are wary of being assertive and participating fully in health care (Kreps, 1996a; 1996b). Providers can use active and empathic listening to overcome this power imbalance. Peters (1987) emphasizes that empowering involves engaged listening by relational partners. Engaged listening is a critical representation of concern that one person can communicate to others in any setting, but particularly in health care setting. Cogner and Kanugo (1988) explains empowerment as sharing power within a relationship. Health care professionals who carefully listen to their clients and act upon the information they provide empower their consumers as active participants in health care and enhance provider/consumer relationships. When consumers are empowered they feel more willing and able to contribute to decisions. They develop a belief in personal efficacy and a desire to participate in the health care process.

Listening and Health Care Teams

It is very rare that any one health care provider will have all the necessary expertise to treat complex health care problems alone. We depend on a network of interdependent health care providers, especially in modern health care delivery systems, to coordinate efforts in providing health care services. *Health care teams* are an important part of modern health care, where interdependent health care providers and consumers collaborate on directing health care treatment. The effectiveness of these teams, however, is dependent on the quality of interaction between team members and their ability to share relevant information (Kreps & Thornton, 1992). Effective listening is instrumental in enabling team members to share information, coordinate efforts, and engage in true collaboration.

A major problem limiting the effectiveness of many health care teams is a breakdown in *interprofessional relations* among team members (Kreps, 1988a; Kreps & Thornton, 1992). There are often "cultural" barriers that limit the effectiveness of communication between interdependent health care providers based upon differences in these providers' professional training, areas of expertise, and specialized use of language (Kreps & Kunimoto, 1994). Instead of cooperating with one another, different health care specialists are often in competition with one another for control over diagnostic and treatment decisions (the teledrama, Chicago Hope, is an exemplar). These providers need to overcome interprofessional "cultural" barriers to improve listening in health care teams. Increased respect for "cultural" differences between team members will lead to enhanced receptivity to one another's messages, a prerequisite to effective listening in health care teams.

Listening and Health Care Advocacy

Increasingly today, it is important to serve as an advocate within the modern health care system for family members and friends who are seeking treatment. When people are ill, they are not in the best condition to be assertive and pay close attention to details. Often, a family member or a friend offers to assist the consumer in accessing and understanding health care. Advocates serve loved ones well by making sure they receive relevant health information, participate fully in health care decision making, and obtain the best possible care (Jones, Kreps, & Phillips, 1995). A "good" health care advocate listens carefully to gather relevant information. Advocates must be able to listen carefully to the consumers so they can represent their interest well. Also, they must be able to listen to health care providers and staff carefully to understand the diagnostic, treatment, and other information provided. Frequently, it only takes a phone call to a provider to find out what a hospitalized family member's current condition is and to hear about proposed treatment options. "Good" advocates can also seek relevant information from other health care providers, professional organizations (such as the National Cancer Institute, the American Heart Association, National Alzheimer's Association, or the National Library of Medicine), and/or self-help and support groups. Careful listening enables the advocate to gather full and accurate information from these different sources which can be used to help providers and consumers in delivering more effective treatment.

Helping Health Care Consumers and Providers Develop Effective Listening Skills

As we mentioned earlier, effective listening skills do not just happen naturally. These skills need to be taught and nurtured. We strongly recommend in-service training programs on listening skills for practicing health care providers, courses on listening skills for students preparing for careers in the health care professions, and workshops and public school courses on listening skills for consumers of health care.

While the format of such training session would differ somewhat according to several factors (e.g., audience size, room layout, multimedia accessibility, time constraints, and economic constraints), the programs would most likely employ similar teaching strategies. One of the most popular methods is role-playing or simulated interaction. In this method, the "actor" may review a script with background information (e.g., a hypothetical medical history) and cues about his/her style of response (e.g., out-going, reticent, and/or combative). Once familiar with this information, the scenario unfolds and the provider must strive to realize his/her objectives. A variation on this approach occurs when the "actor" models a condition that he/she has actually experienced. Then, the script is only useful in terms of guiding the nature of the "actor's" response. The remainder of the participants may be recruited to help debrief the scenario.

During these experiential exercises, participants often wear special clothing, and use props to better simulate the target client. The props could include cotton in the ears, earphones with accompanying music, wheel chairs, walkers, motorized carts, gurneys, hospital beds, etc. The goal here is to reproduce as much as possible the conditions in which this interaction typically occurs.

Another popular method is the use of videotapes that illustrate the role of listening, or portray the range of listening behaviors across several specially-prepared situations; the latter technique is often referred to as a type of "challenge exam." With either approach, participants are charged with analyzing and critiquing the featured behavior. To facilitate their review, trainers often instruct participants about how to use rating scales previously supplied by the trainer.

Standardized listening tests are also popular as they provide a gauge of one's recall and interpretation skills. Of course, it is best to track the results over-time as one-shot administrations only provide a brief glimpse of what is occurring. A final possibility is an exercise affectionately called the "rumor mill." This simulation unfolds with one student leaving the room. He/she is then given an important message, returns to the classroom, and whispers that message to one other student. The message is passed on using the same procedures until every class member has participated. The typical outcome is that the original message has undergone major revisions. This exercise allows the class to laugh at themselves and "drives home" the complexity of the communication process by focusing on the role of effective listening.

Summary

There is widespread agreement that the health care system in many parts of the world, and in the United States, is in a crisis (see Badgley, 1992; Francis & Francis, 1987; Nichols, Johnson, & Maas, 1994; Pan American Health Organization, 1990), and in desperate need of reform. While many "thorny" issues must be identified and addressed (e.g., universal coverage, rationing, "sin" or self-abuse premiums, insurance carrier administrative policies and obligations, malpractice prevalence and costs, and new ethical standards, etc.), a new public initiative and mindset focusing on prevention and effective communication among key publics must be adopted. As Ratzan (1994) contends, "A vital component of this perspective is that effective communication between participants, advocates, and publics becomes the currency to achieve optimal health" (p. 202).

While effective communication cannot solve all the woes of the health care system, the interdependent parts of the system cannot function effectively in its absence. In this chapter, we have attempted to illustrate the integral role of active listening in effective interaction across health care contexts. As the complexity of the health care system continues to grow, and the shape of the health care delivery systems further evolves, listening skills will become increasingly important. The development of listening skills empowers participants in the modern health care system by enabling them to access relevant health information, use this information to make informed decisions, and thereby obtain the most out of health care.

Exercises

1. The next time you visit your doctor, dentist, or other health care provider observe how he or she listens to you. Does the health care provider look at you while you are speaking. Does the provider give you feedback (verbal and nonverbal) that they have heard and understand what you are saying? Does the provider appear to be interested in what you have to say?

2. The next time you visit your doctor, dentist, or other health care provider observe how well you listen to him or her. Do you look at the health care provider while he or she is speaking? Do you provide the health care professional with nonverbal or verbal feedback that you have heard, and understand what he or she is saying? Do you demonstrate that you are interested in what the health care provider has to say.

3. Obtain permission to accompany a friend or relative on a visit to their doctor or other health care provider. Observe and analyze the listening behaviors the provider and client engage in. Are the behaviors of the provider and client different? If so, how? Which participant do you believe is doing a better job of listening? Why do you think so? Are you aware of any barriers to listening? How could these barriers be removed?

4. Compile a list of medical terms that you think are confusing and might limit a typical consumer's understanding of his or her providers explanations and/or instructions. Write an alternative wording for each of these terms that will be easier for consumers to understand. How can providers be taught to limit their use of jargon and explain health care concepts understandably to their consumers?

5. Rewrite the nurse educator and Jerry story so that it reflects active listening. Write a script that can be used as a role–play exercise. Consider Table 11.1 and 11.2 in developing the activity.

References

Badgley, R. F. (1992). Public health: Trends and challenges. In Pan American Health Organization (Ed.), *The crisis of public health: Reflections for the debate* (pp. 53–67). Washington, DC: World Health Organization.

Cassell, E. J. (1985). *Talking with patients: Volume 1. The theory of doctor-patient communication.* Cambridge, MA: MIT Press.

Conger, J., & Kanungo, R. (1988). The empowerment process: Integration theory and practice. *Academy of Management Review, 13,* 471–482.

Edwards, B. J., & Brilhart, J. K. (1981). *Communication in nursing practice.* St. Louis, MO: C. V. Mosby Company.

Francis, J. G., & Francis, L. P. (1987). Rationing of health care in Britain: An ethical critique of public policy making. In T. Smeeding, M. Battin, L. Francis, and B. Landesman (Eds.), *Should medical care be rationed by age?* (pp. 119–134). Totowa, NJ: Rowman & Littlefield Publishers.

Geist, P. & Hardesty, M. (1992). *Negotiating the crisis of DRGs and the transformation of hospitals.* Hillsdale, NJ: Erlbaum.

Hobfoll, S.E., & Stevens, M.A.P. (1990). Social support during extreme stress: Consequences and intervention. In B. R. Sarason, I. G. Sarason, & G. R. Pierce (Eds.), *Social support: An interactional view* (pp. 454–481). New York: John Wiley and Sons.

Jones, A., Kreps, G.L, & Phillips, G.M. (1995). *Communicating with your doctor: Getting the most out of health care.*
Cresskill, NJ: Hampton Press.

Jones, A., & Phillips, G. (1988). *Communicating with your doctor.* Carbondale, IL: Southern Illinois University Press.

Katz, J. (1984). *The silent world of doctor and patient.* New York: Free Press.

Kreps, G.L. (1996a). Promoting a consumer orientation to health care and health promotion. *Journal of Health Psychology,* schedule for Volume 1, issue 1.

Kreps, G.L. (1996b). Communicating to promote justice in the modern health care system. *Journal of Health Communication,* scheduled for Volume 1, issue 1.

Kreps, G.L., & Kunimoto, E.N. (Eds.). (1994). *Effective communication in multicultural health care settings.*
Thousand Oaks, CA: Sage Publications.

Kreps, G.L., & Thornton, B.C. (1992). *Health communication: Theory and practice* (2nd. ed.). Prospect Heights, IL:Waveland Press.

Nichols, B., Johnson, M., & Maas, M. (1994). Rationing health care: What are the implications? In K. Kelly (Ed.), *Health care rationing: Dilemma and paradox* (pp. 3–10). St. Louis, MO: Mosby.

Pan American Health Organization (1990). *Strategic orientations and program priorities, 1991–1994.* Report prepared for the XXIII Pan American Sanitary Conference, Washington, DC.

Peters, T. (1987). *Thriving on Chaos*. New York: NY: Alfred A. Knopf.
Peters-Golden, H. (1982). Breast cancer: Varied perceptions of social support in the illness experience. *Social Science and Medicine, 16*, 483-491.
Query, J.L., Jr., & James, A.C. (1989). The relationship between interpersonal communication competence and social support among elderly support groups in retirement communities. *Health Communication, 3*, 165-184.
Ratzan, S. (1994). Editor's Introduction: Communication—-The key to a healthier tomorrow. *American Behavioral Scientist, (38)2*, 202-207.
Rook, K.S. (1984). The negative side of social interaction: Impact on psychological well-being. *Journal of Personality and Social Psychology, 46*, 1097-1108.
Rook, K.S., & Pietromonaco, P. (1987). Close relationships: Ties that heal or ties that bind? In W.H. Jones & D. Perlman (Eds.), *Advances in personal relationships* (vol. 1, pp. 1-35). Greenwich, CT: JAI Press.
West, C. (1984). *Routine complications: Troubles with talk between doctors and patients*. Bloomington, IN: Indiana University Press.
Wohl, J. (1989). Integration of cultural awareness into psychotherapy. *American Journal of Psychotherapy, 11* (3), 343-356.

Chapter 14

LISTENING IN JOURNALISM: All the News (We've Heard About) That's Fit to Print

Rob Anderson and George M. Killenberg

Points to be Addressed:

- Journalism as a form of Public Listening

- How Listening Shapes the News

- Institutional, Editorial, and Reportorial Levels of Journalistic Listening.

- Skills of Informational, Discriminative, and Personality Listening for Interviewers

- The Emerging Public Journalism Movement

The brass ring here is producing journalism that's unmistakably written from the citizen's point of view. . . . [I have] insisted that ordinary Americans see issues in a subtler, more sophisticated light than the press and other political "players" do (at least publicly), that they see problems as more interconnected, and that listening to them with greater care and intelligence—greater attentiveness to the whole thing they're trying to say as citizens—has the power to bend and shape

good journalism into something significantly different from what it is
at most newspapers today.

Arthur Charity. *Doing Public Journalism.* (1995, p. 41)

Everyday citizens can't listen to all they want to know—or need
to know—in a society that buries us in new complexities and triviali-
ties each day. Do most of us even comprehend the options?
Hundreds of channels from cable or satellite dishes? Magazines for
every taste and subject? A dozen or more television stations in some
major markets? Virtually instant access to a worldwide network of
computer chat rooms, web sites, databases, electronic publications
and bulletin boards? Out of habit or necessity, we tell ourselves that
the daily monitoring of information trends is beyond us. We entrust
that responsibility to journalists.

Professionals in the news business are usually described as "print
journalists" (working at newspapers and magazines, for example) or
"broadcast journalists" (they—or their words—are found on radio and
television). These classifications are obviously accurate in that journalists do indeed write and speak in their media. But if journalists are
seen primarily as writers or speakers, we acknowledge only a middle
stage of the process by which audiences become informed about
news. Before journalists can report the news, they must become sensitive to the complex social and cultural processes that constitute the
ingredients of news. The writing and delivery of the news depend
upon journalists' abilities to observe, comprehend, interpret, assess,
and perceive—abilities associated with effective listening.

What label better captures the journalist's basic responsibility
than the role of listener? Many working journalists would be surprised to hear it put this way, because so little attention is paid to
listening within the professional education of journalists. Few working reporters or editors would list skillful listening among the tasks
they accomplish every day. Ask journalists to describe their jobs,
apart from time spent at the keyboard or in the studio, and most are
likely to say something like "reporting" or "newsgathering." Like
most people, journalists tend to underestimate the power of receptive
and perceptual skills, and they overestimate the power of their own
expressiveness and autonomy. The newsgathering metaphor is revealing; it suggests that somehow the news already exists in the
environment as well-defined packages waiting to be collected and re-
packaged. Unfortunately, the real world is not that simple. The best
journalists understand that their own definitions of "news"—their
own expectations for what to listen for—influence what ultimately
makes it into a paper, magazine, or newscast.

Although textbook definitions of listening vary, most experts
suggest that a listener   recognizes, receives, interprets, and responds
to messages within a particular interaction context. Relevant contexts

may be psychological (someone is listening while worried about paying a bill, for example), social (listening while trying to be polite at a dinner party), or cultural (listening while trying to decide if the speaker's lack of eye contact is meant as a put-down or if it perhaps reflects a different cultural norm). Communication researchers remind us that no message comes without a history of its own, nor is any message understandable except by reference to some type of surrounding human experience that gives it meaning.

Journalistic listening can be organized into three levels or kinds of experience: the *institutional*, the *editorial*, and the *reportorial*. Listening, in other words, is central to the entire profession, central to the decision-making process that actually creates a front page or an evening newscast, and central to the face-to-face communication of reporters interviewing news "sources." To explain why we divide the field this way, we'll analyze the kinds of challenges and skills that characterize each type of listening. Finally, we will link listening to the "public journalism" movement, whose advocates are challenging the profession to become less obsessed with transmitting an objectively valid reality, less committed to the formal routines of traditional reportage, and more concerned with helping people become engaged as citizens within the democratic process of their communities.

Institutional Listening

Researchers have suggested a number of important reminders about listening. Although they are described more systematically in other chapters of this book, several should be highlighted here. First, listening is enabled by an openness to and curiosity about the environment, along with an essential willingness to be surprised. A listener, in other words, has to be as tuned for receptivity as for expressivity. Second, listening is enabled by a certain kind of preparation. A listener must have the knowledge necessary to decode what is heard and place messages into a realistic context. Third, listening can never be total; all messages are processed selectively. This selectivity is affected by a variety of factors, including the listener's beliefs, attitudes, and values. Just as a reader will read certain news stories because they are "interesting" (which, roughly translated, means that the stories are relevant to personal experience, meet a personal need, or appeal to the person's idiosyncratic sense of humor, etc.), and skip other stories because they are "boring," listeners in conversations will never "get" the whole message. The interest and the boredom are not in the story or the talk but in the person.

Journalism as Surrogate Listening

Although most people believe journalism involves the mass media of writing or broadcasting, its historical connection with everyday conversation has long been noted. Robert Park's (1923) description of "The Natural History of the Newspaper" explains how in the beginning, papers functioned as a community's way of organizing and extending its informal talk and making that talk more coherent and meaningful for a wider audience. Park observed that "the first newspapers were simply devices for organizing gossip and that, to a greater or less extent, they have remained" (p. 277), and that "the work of the newspaper, as a gatherer and interpreter of the news, was but an extension of the function which was otherwise performed spontaneously by the community itself through the medium of personal contact and gossip" (pp. 282-283). Therefore, in a sense, journalism is not a *substitute* for conversation, but in theory an *extension and enhancement* of it that is ideally based upon the same principles, human needs, and interests. Even as journalism moved further away from its original narrative functions and more toward a fact/objectivity model, listening remained central to the news professions because it was central to their audience's daily lives.

Journalism's professional self concept reflects the basic elements of effective listening: receptivity, preparation, and selectivity. First, journalists are paid to be receptive; they monitor the information environment systematically for the new, the interesting, the entertaining, the exciting. They go to the city council meetings or the school board sessions that the rest of us don't have time to attend; they gain special access to the mayor through an interview, and try to ask the questions citizens themselves would like to ask. Listening carefully, they tell us who lost her temper in the courtroom, who insulted the senator, who didn't vote the way he promised he would. Second, journalists—we trust—have prepared themselves factually to understand the nuances and inner workings of the news. We ask journalists to immerse themselves in a wide variety of historical documents or moldy reports so the public won't have to. They listen for context as well as to messages. Finally, journalists have the difficult job of being our gatekeepers; at their best, they winnow out the peripheral and the trivial, presenting—as the famous slogan once claimed too ambitiously—"all the news that's fit to print."

The institution of journalism, of course, encounters many problems when it tries to listen for us. For example, take the knotty problem of how gatekeeping and selectivity are actually decided upon. In his important study of decision-making in journalism, Herbert J. Gans (1979) writes:

> In reporting the news about a nation of over 200 million potential actors in news stories, journalists could, in theory, choose from billions of potential activities. In fact, however, they can learn about only a tiny fraction of actors and activities; and having limited air time and magazine space, they must select an even tinier fraction. More important, they cannot decide anew every day or week how to select the

fraction that will appear on the news; instead, they must routinize their task in order to make it manageable. (p. 78)

Thus, journalism re-enacts on a grander scale the problems of the individual listener: Where to turn? What to listen for? How to filter out the buzzing cacophony of competing voice and sounds, in order to get to the good stuff? How many more complicated decisions need to be made in a busy day? Individuals and news organizations all address these quandaries by what Gans calls "routinizing." Everyone develops listening habits. But at what price?

The British cultural critic Richard Hoggart (1972) cautions that too many journalists short-circuit effective listening by implying that theirs is a profession with mysterious insight and it takes a journalist to know what's important (by definition), without checking much with the audience. Routinization may be inevitable to some extent, but journalism is particularly good at rationalizing it. Journalism adopts habits, says Hoggart, that automatically preordain that some events are newsworthy and others are not. Thus, its decision-makers are tempted to deny that they are in fact choosers and constructors of public sensibility, and not just reporters. In addition, journalism functions as an unwitting censor, because of a potentially limiting view of listening. Whenever a "typical Western journalist" says "I choose by my news sense," or "I simply know what my audience will think an interesting feature," or "I can tell a good TV programme when I see it; that's all," these answers beg the question:

> In my experience, most people who work in those media do not recognize the power of these influences behind their terms of art; they take the terms as absolute statements about universal and objective characteristics of their trade. Not to recognize this cultural colouring or these structural biases is to become an unwitting prisoner of the culture and the structure. Your choices, your rejections and your acceptances, will be forced on you from below and within, even whilst you are thinking yourself a free and easy rider in the medium. You may well be a success, but because you may have a natural sense of what your culture most wants and what the structure will most allow you to exploit. But you will be missing the big opportunities. This is blind censorship, censorship by blind omission. (Hoggart, 1972, p. 91)

This institutional failing of journalism does not develop because people are evil or lazy, but simply because they are people. It reinforces the need for us all to be critics of journalism, not just consumers of its products. It should worry all students of human nature that our journalism is subject to the same problems as our individual listening habits. In a sense, journalism's products aren't just news stories. Its products are certain kinds of citizens. Us.

Counter-Listening Models:
Neutral Conduit, Active Advocate, or Neither?

History has given us several visions of what journalism could be. The earliest journalism, at least in the United States, was a literature of partisanship, and journalists were openly expected to be passionate public spokespersons for particular beliefs or reforms (See Schudson, 1978, on whose analysis this brief survey is based). This gave way to a more "scientific" belief that the world could be described with accuracy if empirical facts were simply gathered carefully and reported fairly. There was relatively little overt concern among these kinds of journalists that interpreting facts involved differing and subjective perceptions and that these perceptions were not the same thing as "reality." Following World War I, journalists experienced a "growing anxiety that facts themselves, or what they had taken to be facts, could not be trusted" (Schudson, pp. 6–7), and experiments in subjectivity–based reporting were encouraged. More recently, some journalists have merged literary styles with traditional news goals, and new genres have emerged that are quite different from so–called "straight" reporting. Of course, as we have seen, the listening tasks of journalism have never been particularly linear.

Underlying these broad stages in American journalism history are two approaches that we could term "counterlistening models," because they seem inconsistent with what researchers have discovered about effective human listening and information processing. We call them the "Journalism as Neutral Conduit" and the "Journalism as Active Advocate" models.

Neutral Conduit?

Objectivity is a God–term among many journalists. By it, they mean that they are not bought–and–paid–for by special interest groups, that their personal opinions don't matter because they only seek to provide information to the public, that their reports are reliable because they've given "both sides" of a story. Although some of them do not use "objective" to imply lack of involvement, but simple fairness, many others do believe that they play no active role in making news. Such journalists still take on critical functions (such as editorial page commentary, for example, or interpretive reporting), but they want readers and viewers to know that such comments are based on careful and neutral weighing of evidence. Most often, the institutional rhetoric of this perspective is "don't blame the messenger," or, in other words, "we're just a conduit or pipeline for the news—we don't make news."

Yet, although these journalists don't believe they "make" or "influence" news, their presence makes and influences talk, and talk is news: "The most valuable and original contributions in journalism today are usually obtained in interviews," writes editor and reporter John Brady (1976, p. 1). We've all been in groups where an unduly cynical or negative member has in effect silenced shy members who might have contributed a great deal otherwise. We've been in groups where a contentious or nit-picking listening attitude has profoundly influenced the speech patterns of other group members, often causing them to become argumentative, too. Journalism can be an objective conduit of information only if we believe—naively—that listening styles and behaviors do not influence other people's topics and ways of speaking.

Active Advocate?

Some journalists, forsaking the neutrality assumptions, have advocated near-complete subjective immersion in the news. They assume that because complete objectivity and neutrality is psychologically impossible, overt individual evaluation is justifiable. Some, who have been called "new journalists," have no qualms about plunking themselves squarely in the middle of the action so that they can write exciting accounts that will make certain social or political changes more likely.

These journalists are right about the inevitability of any observer's involvement in what is perceived, and journalism has a place for their kind of exciting writing and speaking. However, if they go too far they pay a price; active advocates often find themselves shut out of certain stories, or the stories they write are seen as easily dismissed. Effective listeners know that a dogged allegiance to particular viewpoints often come across as merely dogmatic or small-minded. People quit talking if they believe potential listeners have already made up their minds, or that potential listeners are so caught up in themselves that there's no space for any new ideas. In interpersonal or journalistic communication, in other words, dogmatism can fill up the free psychological spaces that would otherwise invite open talk. Active advocates, if they push their own debaterish positions on issues, often filter outside information through a screen of self-interest—and this habit reduces the likelihood of encountering new information that could change one's mind. Advocacy has a place in journalism, but this is hardly a basic listening model by which journalism makes consistently better decisions.

Inquiring Conversationalist?

Obviously, we are not claiming that journalists who try to be neutral or objective in the public clash of issues are doing something wrong, and we are not claiming that journalists shouldn't sometimes take positions. Fairness is a hallmark of an effective democratic journalism, as is the courage to advance certain strong arguments editorially, such as in the realm of social justice. We merely note that, while neutrality (in the sense of basic fairness) may be a goal, it can't be the entire model for journalistic listening. Journalists kid themselves if they think they can listen with thorough neutrality, renouncing their own biases and subjectivities. However, we would also warn that embracing or celebrating that subjectivity by excessive advocacy, if taken as a basic model or mission, skews journalism in the other direction.

Consistent with a view we've presented elsewhere (Anderson, Dardenne, & Killenberg, 1994), we suggest that an effective listening-based model for journalism is that of a well-informed conversation partner. Conversation partners try to be fair, but they try to be true to their own attitudes as well. They renounce neither what the other has to say, nor what they themselves have to say. They start conversations without knowing precisely how they will end. Consistently they invite others to contribute new insights, to say interesting things. Conversationalists expect to be both informed and entertained at the same time—and they model that kind of discourse for others. Conversationalists find themselves changed by the experience, and they can never be certain at the beginning how events will play out, or which positions will ultimately be best. Journalists, in other words, are not merely transcribers of social action, but are in some ways inevitable participants in that action; as participants, however, they accept special responsibilities of fairness and special responsibilities of facilitating the interaction of other citizens. These, to us, are the aspirations of a listening journalism. But institutional aspirations must be reflected in the day-to-day decisionmaking practices of journalism; these practices are enacted in the newsroom, journalist to journalist, and in a wider theater—interviews in the streets, offices, stores, and factories of public life.

Editorial/Newsroom Listening

The quality of listening in a typical newsroom is probably no better or worse than conditions found within other businesses where people work in close proximity, facing interruptions, distractions and impediments that frustrate effective communication. The productivity and success of any collective enterprise depends upon listening well. In any group, mistakes are made, tempers flare, and frustrations rise when listening is poor. Yet there are few organizations where the negative result is distributed so rapidly to the rest of society.

Two major environmental factors appear to influence listening quality in newsrooms: *newsroom design* and *hierarchical work routines*. Each poses its own particular communication problems, and brief discussions of them may suggest that it is impressive than any effective listening gets done at all in newsrooms. They can be among the most chaotic and nerve-wracking environments imaginable for listeners.

Newsroom Design

Stereotypical versions of newsrooms, established for the public by films like "Front Page" and countless television shows like "Lou Grant" or the various incarnations of "Superman," depicted large open spaces filled with rows of reporters behind gunmetal-gray desks, banging away at manual typewriters. Actually, the stereotypes were reasonably accurate (with some concessions to dramatic license); most newsrooms historically have been open and noisy bullpens. Telephones rang, teletype machines clattered, and editors stuck their heads out of glassed-in offices to shout questions at reporters who shouted back just as loudly. Listening was difficult amid the hubbub, but the cacophony forced journalists to pay attention as best they could, and at least reinforced the sense that a news organization is a vigorous, tuned-in, animated team. While in some organizations, workers are unsure of what other workers even do, journalists and editors quickly discover who are the slackers and who are the doers.

Listening in today's newsroom is easier in some ways; certainly the typical newsroom is less raucous. The teletype machines are gone. Computer keyboards click rather than clang like typewriters. There is less shouting, and even ringing phones are muted. Newsroom design still follows the bullpen philosophy, in that they remain somewhat open environments, although noise-absorbing paneled cubicles often separate desks and make it easier to have semi-private conversations. Desks and offices are electronically linked by e-mail, and reporters easily can share developing stories—and even coauthor them—without being in each other's physical presence. These changes subtly affect the listening styles of a newsroom, perhaps encouraging more deliberative listening and expanding the opportunities to verify facts and compare versions of a story. At the same time, the changes encourage less face-to-face communication and the vigorous interchange that physical presence can enhance.

Hierarchical Work Routines

Journalism is now having an argument with itself—an internal conversation concerning the nature of its relationship with the public. Should it be primarily a conduit of accurate information to the public, or should its future role also in part be to serve as a forum by which that public can speak its own mind, opening new avenues for community participation? Currently, journalists readily accept the conduit function, but many have not yet embraced the forum function. Part of that conversation necessarily involves the hierarchical assumptions of how journalism goes about fulfilling its role, because much of journalism's role hierarchy is based upon reporting information accurately. Journalism is self-consciously in the business of information: it tries to get it straight, depict it truly, and avoid errors that would mislead its public. Journalists rightly believe there is little room for error, and therefore, do not—as the saying goes—suffer fools for long. Reporters who are sloppy listeners and get the facts wrong are not around for long. Similarly, reporters who are lone wolves, pursuing only their own agendas without much attention to those of their superiors, are out of work. They are fired by editors, to whom they must listen just as closely as they do to their "sources."

Inaccurate reporters are checked by editors, the decision-makers of journalism. Editors don't just "edit" (revise) stories. They also decide which stories are worth journalism's attention, which reporters are assigned to which stories, which kinds of stories reporters should write, how much space those stories should take, how the stories should be framed and featured in the paper or newscast, and what, if any, follow-up stories are necessary. At every stage, the hierarchical interaction between editors and reporters is pivotal in determining the nature of news. According to one insider, "When editors behind glass sneeze, people out in the newsroom tend to get pneumonia" (Gesaliter, 1995, p. 57). And the rest of us, readers and viewers alike, may need to reach for the Kleenex.

The editor/reporter relationship is complex and multifaceted, but reporters understand that they are hearing the voice of authority when editors talk. Editors can't just listen to people; they must also listen for the nuances of trends, for the development of themes, for the perhaps partly submerged needs of a community. Thus, one crucial aspect of the editorial role is the responsibility of steering the daily journeys of journalism. To do so, they must decide reporters' assignments proactively, and subsequently listen carefully to reporters' discoveries. We would like to think, therefore, that editors are effective listeners. Yet a sizable literature warns that many editors define themselves as persons of decisive action, working with inexorable deadlines only they can fully understand, who have little time to concentrate on listening carefully, little time to engage in contemplative or decision-making conversations.

Too often, conformity is the result, as Gans (1979) found in his study of magazine and broadcast journalism organizations. This conformity, which most journalists do not seem to be aware of (Gans, 1979, p. 98 ff.), makes the "suggestions" of more powerful editors into "thinly veiled orders" (p. 101); most reporters and writers "play only a consulting role in story selection" (p. 101) and, before producing the story, discover what editors want out of it. "Senior editors generally decide how many words a story 'deserves,'" and "offer suggestions about the organization of the story and a possible lead"—and some editors even "virtually dictate the story to the writer" (p. 101).

Not only do such habits limit the editor as an active listener, they also limit the kinds of open listening the reporter might subsequently accomplish in researching the story. Somewhat disturbingly, Powers & Fico (1994) described research showing that "reporters tended to see their roles as filling a need for the city editor, rather than serving the public's need for information," and that "expectations from superiors strongly influenced . . . reporters' work." Such "pressure from superiors" caused stories to "conform to newsroom ideals" (p. 89). While this phenomenon would not be particularly surprising in most organizations, the public expects journalists (and journalists frame themselves) to work not just for a news corporation but for the public as well, as society's trustworthy listeners.

Recent trends in the hierarchy of the newsroom have been more encouraging, however. Some newspaper editors are experimenting with newer strategies that emphasize effective listening. Several are especially noteworthy. First, more news editors are deciding that many stories are well served by forming teams of reporters (perhaps called "pods" or "units"); the differing perspectives generated by such teams can then be compared, contrasted and evaluated in editorial meetings. When journalism professor and former reporter Jan Whitt (1995) recently returned to work as a professional intern at a daily paper, the team approach was one of the bigger changes she encountered after being away from reporting for seventeen years: "Reporters [in the interim] began replacing long-entrenched, individual beats with writing teams," and the concept extended to a thoroughgoing newsroom reorganization as well (p. 89). While this approach would not always be efficient for daily reporting of crises, accidents, or quotes from the courthouse corridors, it is particularly well suited for complex systemic issues that emerge over a long period of time. Listening, clearly, will also be emphasized in other new forms of journalistic cooperation. Her executive editor at the *Boulder Daily Camera* told Whitt that in order to create "a newspaper that thinks like readers," journalism needs to include such "important tools" as "readership research, focus groups, and listening exercises" (p. 90).

The second innovation, promoted by media experts at the Poynter Institute for Media Studies (Clark & Fry, 1992), involves editors' "coaching" or debriefing reporters after they return from investigating an event but before they write the story itself. Instead of just turning thumbs up or thumbs down on a story already written by a reporter, an editor becomes responsible for interviewing the reporter carefully *before* the story is written. Editors ask such questions as "who else was there?", "what might have happened before you got there?", "would you have seen anything different—or talked with different kinds of people—if you'd been standing back in the crowd rather than by the stage?" Editors, whose roles have always included pointing out holes and inconsistencies in stories (see Hausman, 1990, p. 50), become in a new way institutionalized listening consultants. They are able to counteract or soften authoritarian hierarchies and avoid unnecessary conformities by contributing more personally and directly to the development of reporters' work. The resulting stories thus tend to be more thorough and more representative of differing points of view, primarily because of a process that stresses sensitive editorial listening.

Finally, newspapers are opening the *inner sanctum* of newsroom decision-making—the story or news conference, as it is variously called—to more diverse points of view. Until recently, Sigal's (1973) description of the story conference remained fundamentally unchanged. The story conference was a meeting, controlled by the managing editor, at which editors for various sections, such as metro, national, foreign, and business news, pitched their best stories for page one or other prestigious spots in the next day's newspaper. The managing editor typically had the final say, and the editors under him (rarely her) learned what stories would pass muster, and which ones would not. The select group of editors around the conference table, usually white, middle-aged males, listened and learned in a process that seldom was democratic or conducive for open, multiperspectival discussion. The impact of the story conference extended far beyond the content of each day's edition; the prevailing attitude of the managing editor toward news was communicated in word and action by the editors in attendance, reinforcing the conformity that already characterized many newsrooms. Today, though, other voices are being heard, as some newspapers have experimented with diversity, inviting community members and reporters to join the story conference or other decisionmaking meetings. It is not a movement overtaking the profession, but it is another sign of changing listening attitudes and behaviors in journalism.

Reportorial Listening

Someone who wants to go into journalism but doesn't enjoy meeting and listening to people ought to tag along behind a good reporter for a week or two. Although the product of good reporting is well-written stories, the process of reporting—asking, listening, conversing—is what provides the raw materials for the stories.

Interviews: The Essential News Encounter

When reporter and communication researcher Alan Bell (1991) straightforwardly assures us that "the basic stuff of news is what people tell a reporter" (p. 41), he is also implying that the public probably misses many stories because reporters are not skillful enough listeners to encourage the right kinds of telling. Interviews are at the heart of news, and news circulates, like informational lifeblood, when good listeners pay careful attention. But on this crucial front, journalism can do much better. Kristen Gilger, who reports for the *New Orleans Times-Picayune*, describes why: "Most reporters

... are competent enough interviewers to get a story. The problem is missing information, either because the reporter has already made up his mind about what he wants from the interview and closes the interview before the person has had his say or because the reporter lacks the compassion and curiosity to get more than the facts—the description, the details, the 'why' of the story" (Biagi, 1992, pp. 2-3). This view of news obviously places the reporter on the front lines of journalism, and therefore on the front lines of democracy; it doesn't matter whether she works for a suburban giveaway paper or is backed by the high-tech support and millions of dollars CNN can muster. The individual reporter's listening style is always potentially the unavoidably weak link in the chain.

In this brief essay, we cannot explore fully all the listening skills used by effective interviewers; therefore, we will survey only a few of the most important issues for beginning journalists to consider. In *Before the Story: Interviewing and Communication Skills for Journalists* (1989, Ch. 4), we divided reporters' listening in interviews into three interrelated types: *informational listening* (which asks "what happened?"); *discriminative listening* (which asks "what's different?"); and *personality listening* (which asks "who are you?").

Informational Listening

Informational listening is helpful when reporters conduct interviews primarily to discover the facts and ideas necessary to write an accurate story. When listening for facts, reporters are wise to emphasize the following communication habits and styles:

- Remember that listening is not agreement, and disagreement need not be expressed. You should encourage a conversational process for the interview, but unlike other conversations, the interviewee does not need to know—and probably doesn't care about—your personal feelings about the topic. Remember too that you are a listening-representative of others, who will have different attitudes and values than either you or your interviewee.

- Familiarize yourself with the language habits, jargon, and special meanings the interviewee is most likely to use. You'll listen much better if you're not mentally trying to define every other word.

- Listen to repair your ignorance. Journalist James Fallows in his best-selling critique of journalism, *Breaking the News* (1995), contrasts the kinds of questioning lawyers and journalists do: "The rule for lawyers examining a witness . . . is that they must never ask questions whose answers they do not know. The rule for reporters should be something like the reverse. You must sometimes ask questions whose answers you think you know, so as to confirm what you have heard and to compare answers from several sources. But the main work of reporting involves asking questions whose answers you don't know, simultaneously exposing your ignorance but opening up the possibility of learning something new" (p. 143).

- Use "perception checks" as often as possible. Perception checks are those moments when you insert your interpretations tentatively into the conversation in order to verify whether you've heard a statement accurately. For example, say: "Senator, I want to make sure I got that last point right . . . you're saying that you're likely to support Senator Washington only if she changes her stand on education vouchers?"

- Listen to, but also beyond, the details. All good reporters get the essential details, but they don't get buried by them. They listen for larger patterns that tie the details together and the motivations that may underlie the talk. One way to accomplish this is to use what Nichols and Stevens (1957) called "listening spare time"—the difference between the rate of normal speech and the faster rate of verbal thought. Another way to listen past details is to tape record the interview (if this is acceptable to the interviewee) and concentrate on speech and idea patterns; then you can return later to the tape for details you might need for the story.

- Listen not only to statements but to and for silences. Silences can tell a reporter a great deal about what an interviewee thinks and what he or she values—but they can also tell a reporter when to move on to the next point. When someone pauses infrequently, or monopolizes the time, it may be necessary to interrupt. But recognize the dangers. Broadcast interviewers often have time constraints that pressure the conversation, or even encourage the interviewee to filibuster, but most interviewers need not interrupt to stop someone's flow of thought unless your respondent is clearly off the track.

Discriminative Listening

This kind of listening unearths different ways of interpreting events and people. It presumes the listener is much more than a stenographer, because effective reporters carefully analyze the issues during their interviews. Discriminative listening, therefore, builds upon the skills of informational listening but depends upon others too:

• Develop a critical listening attitude. The word "critical" is critical. We do not mean "be cynical." The press has a long and storied history as democracy's watchdog, and many public figures assume that an interview is to some extent a test or trial. Therefore, they may regard reporters either as enemies or, at best, sources of ammunition for their enemies. Your goal as a listener should be to maintain an attitude of basic fairness that is open to a wide variety of interpretations without being gullible. Your comments and questions should show that you understand the nuances of the subject, but have not completely made up your own mind.

• Understand that each of us listens through our theories as well as through our ears. Journalists are often advised by professors and editors to have the story half-written (in their minds) before completing the interviews. While this helps in meeting deadlines, it doesn't help in avoiding the negative effects of shaping stories subtly to confirm your own partly developed expectations. Does this happen often? Stocking and Gross (1989) in their study of how journalists think, describe several ways that journalists "test theories using a theory-confirming strategy"—"seeking out evidence that confirms (rather than disconfirms the theory they currently hold" (p. 27). By choosing to listen only to certain interviewees, by eliciting information from them with preferential questions, by coddling or harassing them unintentionally, and by interpreting even silences and denials through the screen of the theory, journalists often find what they expect to find.

• Listen for examples and metaphors. These can provide good clues to how the interviewee conceptualizes the

issues and problems being discussed. Often when a reporter goes over notes or tapes later, he or she will find
the real message was in the revealing metaphors rather
than in the rational arguments.

• Listen for fallacies, ruptures of logic, and evasions. The
purpose here is not to argue with the interviewee, but
to understand better how this person interprets the ins
and outs of an issue. Remember that as a listener,
you're responsible for recognizing when a respondent
has not answered your previous questions, and responsible for appropriate follow-ups.

• Be suspicious when you think an interviewee is simply
saying "the same old stuff." This is when you may be
most vulnerable into being lulled into listening gloss-
overs. What sounds like the same old rhetoric that the
president or governor has been peddling for years may,
in fact, contain new and carefully planted qualifiers, ca-
veats, and reservations designed to allow for new
flexibility or changes of course. Reporters who listen in
automatic-pilot mode risk missing these clues.

Personality Listening

Listening in order to capture another's personality is an important
journalistic task, especially since personality profiles are increasingly
common. Personality interviews obviously are built upon facts and,
just as obviously, attempt to put into perspective the distinctive
characteristics of the person's life. Therefore, this style of listening
builds upon the other types of listening by adding new responsibilities:

• Avoid premature judgment. Listen carefully to your
inner tendencies to judge or to stereotype certain persons or groups. When you feel a negative reaction
developing, you should understand that this will
probably filter your listening in some way. In *Before the
Story* (1989) we recommended the technique of the
"inner reminder"; when you find yourself responding
in certain ways, give yourself the silent reminders. For
examples:

"I can't believe he's so sexist. " (Inner reminders: "I
wonder about the environment in which he was

raised." "I wonder if I'm oversensitive to that word." "I wonder if he consistently talks this way or if these are unique circumstances.")

"She's so stupid." (Inner reminders: "I wonder how she justifies that stand from her vantage point." "I wonder why I have such a heavy investment in my own attitude.") (p. 113)

Inner reminders are one way to create a kind of empathy in the interview. Empathy is the social process of imagining yourself into the other person's experience, but all the while knowing that you can not actually *be* "over there." You won't know exactly how someone else feels, for example, but you can remind yourself profitably through empathy that others probably could feel very differently than you do. Being empathic is also a way to signal your willingness to be fair to a skeptical interviewee. Most interviewees will not expect a reporter to agree automatically with him or her, but they justifiably respect empathic responses. Empathy and agreement are not the same thing.

• Confirm the other person's statements and experiences aloud, when appropriate. In other words, acknowledge that you understand what they might be trying to communicate (if you indeed do understand). This need not be phony or dishonest; even with someone you dislike, it's not only possible but honest to say at times, "That must have been a very hard time in your life—first a divorce, then losing someone else you love." This simple confirmation could by itself give your interviewee the justification to continue to explore difficult circumstances.

• "Listen" to nonverbal cues, and display appropriate cues of listening. Many otherwise smart people are interpersonally impaired because they fail to understand that communicators can listen to each other's gestures and body movements, vocal qualities, and other nonverbal messages as well as to their words. Often celebrities being interviewed send "mixed messages" that beg for follow-up questions: the statement that one is happy, while wistfully looking out the window into the distance; the vocally unenthusiastic assertion that a candidate is looking forward to the upcoming campaign; the couple who profess mutual love without touching or looking at each other for the entire interview. Effective journalistic interviewers know, too, that their nonverbal cues signal what kind of listening they are doing. For example, many novice reporters believe they don't need to look often at the interviewee in order to listen (they can review past notes, check the time, etc.). This is only physiologically true. In social interaction within Western culture, however, most speakers continue talking only as long as he or she is convinced that good listening is taking place. A good way to get people to stop talking is to display, intentionally or not, signals that you don't care about their talk.

Listening Attitude

Reporters do listen in one fashion or another. But too few recognize—and even fewer appreciate—the fundamental importance of a commitment to listening. Today's journalists often are socially distant from people who most need to be heard, a point made by William Greider (1992) in his book, *Who Will Tell the People?* Recalling his introduction to journalism in the 1950s, he observed:

> For all its shortcomings, the *Cincinnati Post* had one great redeeming quality. Like its reporters, the newspaper was frankly and relentlessly "of the people." (p. 290)

> [L]ike many other similar newspapers in other cities, [it] deliberately cast itself as a representative voice. . . . It unabashedly identified with the people who were least likely to be heard on public issues and those citizens were invited to identify with it. (p. 292)

Good reporters and editors not only accept their responsibilities as society's listeners; they also know that they must position themselves, physically and attitudinally, in settings where they can best hear the public voice.

Conclusion: Stressing Listening Within a More Public Journalism

Journalism finds itself in flux these days. Old newshounds who thought they knew what the profession was all about are seen at conventions and in newsrooms shaking their heads in disbelief. Computers are everywhere, but readership is down. Talk shows demonstrate that people are ready to talk politics, but newspapers and magazines have never seemed more peripheral to public life. Some talk about the brave new world of the *electronic newspaper*, but just as many journalists scoff at that possibility. The lines between information and entertainment blur more each day. Civility in public discourse often seems to be missing in action. Where is journalism going? Who needs it?

One of the most profound controversies debated by both professional journalists and academics is the movement by some toward what has been termed "public," "civic," or "conversational" journalism (Anderson, Dardenne, & Killenberg, 1994; Charity, 1995; Rosen, 1993). Some critics of this movement have argued that public journalists risk sacrificing traditional journalistic values, but most public journalists do not argue that traditional values such as fairness, clarity, timeliness and thoroughness are outmoded. These values simply do not define the whole scope of journalism's public responsibility. Public journalism does not, to be sure, address all the problems we have outlined, but it suggests that journalism in the future must become much more skilled at social listening. Journalism tries to find new ways to become relevant for its various communities, but to do that it must listen for what those communities are, for who lives there, and for the fabric of their everyday talk. To accomplish these goals, writes Charity (1995), it must listen in fundamentally new—and less intrusive—ways:

> . . . [T]he ways in which journalists habitually listen to people do very little to encourage them to sound like good citizens. Polls rarely care about people's thoughtful nuances and doubts. Letters and phone-in lines (particularly when they're responding to editorials, columns, or op-ed pieces) invite narrow-mindedness at least as much as reflection. And reporters out for an interview typically shove people into cubbyholes before they even open their mouths. Crime reporters, seeing people as victims or criminals, ask, "How do you feel?" or "What led him (or her) to do it?" Election reporters, seeing people as voters, ask "Who will you vote for, and why?" Reporters on urban conflict, seeing people as blacks or whites, ask about nearly any problem "Was racism involved?" People duly respond as victims, criminals, voters, and members of a racial group—just as they would respond as consumers to "What's your favorite detergent?" (p. 20)

Thus, we shouldn't be surprised that some people blame the media at least in part for our social turmoil. The easy answer—"don't blame the messenger"—evaporates if we consider the ways that journalism has operated as far more than a messenger for someone else's message. Its routines have helped to create some of the very problems journalism decries.

Now, however, journalism may be getting the message: It is in how we listen to people that we signal their worth, and our own.

Exercises:

1. In a two-person conversation, discuss what kinds of journalists specialize in the following forms of listening:
   - informative listening
   - discriminative listening
   - personality listening

2. Can you think of at least one or two famous journalists, magazines, papers, or shows you'd associate with each form? Should all professional journalists be able to perform all three functions to some extent?

3. Interview at least two reporters about their own strategies for avoiding unnecessary bias when they interview politicians and other public celebrities. What do their answers tell you about their listening habits?

4. Visit a newsroom at a local paper. Take notes on its physical set-up, decor, and equipment. List ways this environment is conducive to effective listening among journalists. Then list factors that might impede effective listening.

5. Check our from a library an autobiography or memoir written by a prominent journalist, such as Barbara Walters, Carl Bernstein, or Larry King. Does this journalist overtly acknowledge how listening habits have affected the quality of his or her work? Or, does the author seem to take listening more or less for granted?

References

Anderson, R., Dardenne, R., & Killenberg, G. M. (1994). *The conversation of journalism: Communication, community, and news.* Westport, CN: Praeger.

Bell, A. (1991). *The language of news media.* Oxford, UK: Blackwell.

Biagi, S. (1992). *Interviews that work: A practical guide for journalists* (2nd ed.). Belmont, CA: Wadsworth.

Brady, J. (1976). *The craft of interviewing.* Cincinnati, OH: Writer's Digest Books.

Charity, A. (1995). *Doing public journalism.* New York: Guilford.

Clark, R. P. & Fry, D. (1992). *Coaching writers: Editors and reporters working together.* New York: St. Martin's Press.

Fallows, J. (1996). *Breaking the news.* New York: Pantheon.

Gans, H. J. (1979). *Deciding what's news: A study of CBS Evening News, NBC Nightly News, Newsweek, and Time.* New York: Pantheon.

Gesaliter, D. (1995). Fresh ink: Behind the scenes of a major metropolitan newspaper. Denton, TX: University of North Texas Press.

Hausman, C. (1990). *The decision-making process in journalism.* Chicago: Nelson-Hall.

Hoggart, R. (1972). *On culture and communication.* New York: Oxford University Press.

Killenberg, G. M., & Anderson, R. (1989). *Before the story: Interviewing and communication skills for journalists.* New York: St. Martin's Press.

Nichols, R. G., & Stevens, L. A. (1957). *Are you listening?* New York: McGraw-Hill.

Park, R. E. (1923). The natural history of the newspaper. *American Journal of Sociology, 29,* 273-289.

Powers, A., & Fico, F. (1994). Influences on use of sources at large U.S. newspapers. *Newspaper Research Journal, 15,* 87-97.

Rosen, J. (1993). *Community connectedness: Passwords for public journalism.* St. Petersburg, FL: Poynter Institute for Media Studies.

Schudson, M. (1978). *Discovering the news: A social history of American newspapers.* New York: Basic Books.

Sigal, L. V. (1973). *Reporters and officials: The organization and politics of newsmaking.* Lexington, MA: D. C. Heath.

Stocking, S. H., & Gross, P. H. (1989). *How do journalists think? A proposal for the study of cognitive bias in newsmaking.* Bloomington, IN: ERIC Clearinghouse on Reading and Communication Skills.

Whitt, J. (1995). Exiting the ivory tower to revisit the newsroom. *Journalism & Mass Communication Educator, 50,* 86-91.

Chapter 15

CONCLUSION: Strengthening Your Listening Skills

Deborah Borisoff and Michael Purdy

Ralph Nichols described the growing import of the role of the professional in the foreword to this book. He referred to the importance of training for professionals and would-be professionals. Seldom, however, is listening taught as part of that training. And yet, as demonstrated by the chapters of this book, listening is central to the success of any professional.

When we first enter the job market we listen to know better what we need to do in specific work situations. We listen to our colleagues, to our superiors or employees, and of course, to our customers, clients, patients, and students. We utilize the five types of listening in the different situations in which we find ourselves, namely, (1) discriminative, (2) comprehensive, (3) critical (evaluative), (4) therapeutic (empathic), and (5) appreciative. We listen so that those we work with—or for—will know we are eager to learn, and will palpably feel our respect for who they are and what they know. We listen so that we may better coordinate with our co-workers.

We do all of this listening because we know it will help us to serve better the needs of those with whom and for whom we work. By listening we can be more efficient and effective at what we do. With practice our listening abilities are enhanced. When we have been in a profession for many years, we come to appreciate the delicate art that listening represents in the subtleties of our daily encounters. Hence, we realize the benefits of listening and know we can never outgrow our need to work at being a better listener.

All of our efforts to be successful in our chosen field begin with the ability to listen. And we should know, as the contributors to this book stress, that what we learn about listening for our career translates into better relationships both at home and in social situations. Listening with our friends, spouses, and children are of equal importance to maintaining a healthy outlook on life and to living a balanced and harmonious existence. Listening is truly required equipment for living.

Varied Approaches to Listening

We, as editors of this book, have chosen a broad definition of listening which include the following seven attributes: (1) volition, (2) focused attention, (3) perception, (4) interpretation, (5) remembering, (6) response, and (7) the human element. These aspects of the listening process encompass all of the extant definitions of listening (including the new definition approved by the International Listening Association and the Speech Communication Association) as articulated by the authors who have contributed to this book. We did not plan it that way, but a general definition of listening meant to address interpersonal listening in all situations also naturally applies to effective listening behavior in diverse professions. And yet each of the professions operating within a subset of life must choose a definition which accurately describes the purposes–including specific needs and concerns—of listening in its own context. So each of the definitions in the chapters represented in this book, having emerged from the experience of the practicing professional will, consequently, vary slightly from one another.

For example, in a traditional managerial position, the emphasis of listening is on the *purposeful and intentional* behavior of the manager. That is, the manager listens to gather information, to establish and maintain relationships with employees, and to effectively *direct* employees in the best interests of both the employee *and* the organization.

In contrast to listening in the managerial context which is goal-directed, a therapeutic model of listening aims at empathic, non-directive, non–judgmental, and supportive listening. It should be stressed that even though the primary aim of listening in organizations may be discriminative, evaluative, and comprehensive, research indicates that the ability of managers to also be effective empathic listeners is critical to the overall performance and morale of employees (Bredin, 1985).

The service model, as explained by Brownell (chapter 10), Victor and Victor (chapter 12), and Kreps, Bonaguro and Query (chapter 13), is probably somewhere between these two types of listening. It is typically non–directive, and focused on understanding the customer. It is important in many service situations to gather information about customers, clients, and patients to serve their needs better. This is often a model of listening where the consumer and provider share the responsibility for helping to define the product or service of the service transaction with the customer, client, or patient. Management of superficial impressions such as looks and voice are critical in service interactions, although they should also be genuine.

Our role as professionals is to discover the definition of listening that works best for ourselves and our organizational setting. Some professional environments work better with a coaching model of management which is closer to the therapeutic model. Here, the manager may work one-to-one, or in small groups with employees or colleagues thereby facilitating interaction and drawing upon their expertise for accomplishing tasks (see Chapter 5 by Johnson and Watson). In other organizations, managers are in roles where a service model of listening is more appropriate. In these instances, employees are treated as customers or clients who, appreciating and responding to the attention, in turn work more productively for the organization.

The educational arena provides another context for a service model of listening. As Coakley and Wolvin emphasize in Chapter 8, the teacher, parent and student must participate fully in the listening process to assure clear communication and to facilitate successful learning.

Chapters 8 through 14 address professional contexts of listening: organizational training, the service industries, the therapeutic relationship, journalism, and the legal and medical professions. Common to these chapters is the notion of role. Each party in the professional transaction has a role to play as speaker and as listener. Success and satisfaction in the communication exchange are connected to how well each party in the interaction plays his or her role.

When we consider factors that affect listening outside the role relationship, it is much more difficult to identify precisely how these factors influence the listening process. Chapters 3, 4 and 5 by Borisoff and Hahn, Thomlison, and Johnson and Watson consider how gender, ethnicity, and the conflict setting affect listening. Borisoff and Hahn contend in their chapter on gender that listening styles of women and men are informed by socialization. Because men and women may learn to listen for different cues and to adopt distinct styles to demonstrate listening behaviors, misunderstandings are likely to occur when each sex displays divergent affective listening behaviors, or interprets listening behavior through the lens of gender.

Essentially, many of the gender-based listening differences are typical of the kind of misunderstandings that occur in intercultural communication–only they are more difficult to detect because ostensibly women and men from the U.S. share the same culture. In intercultural encounters, such cognitive processes as contexting (putting behaviors with a unique context), authority and social conception, language use, and spatial and temporal factors affect communication. As Thomlison explains in Chapter 4, a lack of attention to these processes may contribute to breakdowns in communication between members of different cultures. If members of different cultures are unable to listen fully to each other's cues—that is, to attend to, understand, interpret, and respond appropriately—then effective communication will likely be impeded.

As we increasingly become a global as well as a multi-cultural community, it becomes even more important for individuals to listen accurately to cues not only beyond, but within our borders. A report in *Time* (Henry, 1990) indicates that the U.S. is experiencing "the Browning of America." The. Latino (Latina), African-American, and Asian populations are increasing at such a rapid rate that within the next two decades, the White majority will, in fact, become the minority. As each culture exerts its influence on the communication styles of the country, it becomes increasingly important for each of us to listen fully to our own messages as well as to the messages of others. Carl Rogers (1951, pp.. 50–55), in his seminal work an psychotherapy, maintains that interpersonal relations are strengthened when individuals:

- accept others for *who* they are;

- avoid trying to mold others into who *we* are;

- and, when individuals can see the world from others' *viewpoints*.

While Rogers' observations are intended for U.S. culture, this advice is applicable to any encounter that is informed by difference, be that difference related to gender, ethnicity, or culture.

Finally, as technology—especially the use of computers—has become a prominent part of our personal and professional interaction, the extent to which communication in "virtual reality" influences interaction in real life has attracted considerable attention. Writing about identity in the age of the Internet, Sherry Turkle (1995) raises several issues about the networked community this technology might engender:

> Many of the institutions that used to bring people together—a main street, a union ball, a town meeting—no longer work as before. Many people spend most of their day alone at the screen of a television or a computer. Meanwhile, social beings that we are, we are trying (as Marshall McLuhan said) to re-tribalize. And the computer is playing a central role. We correspond with each other through electronic mail and contribute to electronic groups whose participants include people from all over the world. Our rootedness to place has attenuated. These shifts raise many questions: What will computer-mediated communication do to our commitment to other people? Will it satisfy our needs for connection and social participation, or will it further undermine fragile relationships? What kind of responsi-

bility and accountability will we assume for our virtual actions? (p. 178).

What we mean by listening to one another, as with other aspects of communication, is undoubtedly being affected by the machines we employ to interact with one another. How listening behavior is being transformed is the focus of Chapter 6 by Anderson and Chapter 7 by Gumpert and Drucker. Both of these chapters address some of Turkle's concerns.

Steps to Strengthening Our Listening Skills

The chapters in this book indicate that our ability to listen and to value this behavior is influenced by many sources, among them our family, friends, role models and work associates.. These chapters further contend that effective listening can be learned and enhanced—if this were not true there would be no growth or evolution in relationships, and no possibility for cooperative effort in the workplace.

Summarizing the skills highlighted in the chapters of this book is best done by discussing how we can direct our energies to improving listening regardless of the profession we represent or plan to pursue. To reiterate the steps outlined in each of the chapters would be redundant, but we can articulate an approach applicable to any individual interested in maximizing his/her listening abilities.

First, remember from Chapter 2 that one needs the following skills and attitudes:

- A desire to listen

- A willingness to help

- Patience

- The ability to attend accurately to verbal and nonverbal cues

- The ability to self-monitor behaviors that interfere with good listening

- Respect for others and their expertise in their area of work or life experience

- The ability to provide a non-judgmental response to others

In addition, one needs to:

- Become more self-aware, "know thyself" (become conscious of biases, attitudes, use of language, etc.)

- Look at the values you hold toward self and toward others and how these values affect your listening

- Develop awareness of and empathy for the other (examine your attitudes toward others)

- Examine your attitudes toward the practice of listening itself

- Review the skills you are proficient at, and identify those which need work (i.e., the ability to develop trust, to self-disclose, to use questions effectively, and to build a supportive climate for communication)

- Explore avenues for obtaining mastery of the above values, attitudes, and skills, as well as, knowledge of listening, that are readily available in self-help books, films, college classes, training programs, etc. (Steil's Chapter 9 examines different approaches to listening skills training)

Regardless of the effort you must make, don't ignore your listening training. Do what it takes to become more proficient in the most important human behavior—listening. As John Powell (1969) has stated:

> How beautiful, how grand and liberating this experience is, when people learn to help each other. It is impossible to overemphasize the immense needs humans have to be really listened to, to be taken seriously, to be understood (p. 5).

Powell's words express the importance of listening to others. When individuals believe that others are listening acceptantly to their thoughts and feelings, they are more likely to listen to themselves. However, as stated in Chapter 2, listening to others begins with listening to oneself. Carl Rogers' (1961) words eloquently attest to the power of listening to oneself:

> I find I am more effective when I can listen acceptantly to myself, and can be myself (p. 17).

> As I try to listen to myself and the experiencing going on in me, the more I try to extend that same listening attitude to another person, the more respect I feel for the complex process of life (p. 21).

This book begins and ends with listening to self. Overall, however, it has demonstrated how crucial effective listening is in the many roles we play in our personal and professional lives. All of the contributors have worked diligently to provide you with the key elements for acknowledging, understanding, assessing, and strengthening your listening ability for everyday use. Listening is, after all, a skill for life. Use it well.

Exercises

1. Although there is a homogeneity of outlook to this book there are also some healthy divergences. Compare and contrast the various definitions of listening used by different authors in this textbook.

2. In a similar manner review the different models used in some of the chapters. Why did the authors feel a need to use a different model to describe listening?

3. As you review the range of the chapters in this textbook what viewpoints and applications are missing? For example, list professions that depend strongly on listening.

4. Can you sketch out what might be included for a profession not yet represented? How does this profession differ from other professions represented? How is it the same?

References

Bredin, A. (Dec. 23, 1985). Today's Manager Listens. *The West Side Spirit*, pp. B-9.

Henry, W.A. III. (April 9, 1990). Nation: Beyond the Melting Pot. *Time*, pp. 28-31.

Powell, J. (1969). *why am i afraid to tell you who i am?* Niles, IL: Argus.

Rogers, C.R. (1961). *On Becoming a Person*. Boston, MA: Houghton Mifflin.

Turkle, S. (1995). *Life on the Screen: Identity in the Age of the Internet*. NY: Simon & Schuster.

About the Contributors

Rob Anderson (Ph.D., University of Missouri) is Professor and Director of Graduate Studies in the Department of Communication at Saint Louis University, where his teaching merges interpersonal communication, rhetoric, and media studies. His writing on listening has appeared in *Journalism Educator, Journal of Mass Media Ethics,* and the *Journal of the International Listening Association,* as well as in numerous other journals, texts and scholarly books. He is the author, coauthor, or coeditor of six books, the most recent of which are *The Reach of Dialogue* (Hampton Press), *Questions of Communication* (St. Martin's Press), and *The Conversation of Journalism* (Praeger Publishers). Currently, he is investigating the philosophical and practical problems of public dialogue.

William E. Arnold (Ph.D., Pennsylvania State University), is a Professor of Communication at Arizona State University. Dr. Arnold has presented over 120 papers at national and international conferences, written over 40 articles and six books on various aspects of communication and listening, including *Urban Communication, Crisis Communication,* and *Communication Training and Development.* He has served as the President of the Association for Communication Administration and the International Listening Association. He is currently the Editor of the International Listening Association Journal.

Deborah Borisoff (Ph.D., New York University) is Associate Professor and Director of Speech and Interpersonal Communication at New York University. She has developed several training programs for individuals and groups in corporations and government agencies and educational systems in the area of listening as well as other aspects of communication (e.g., conflict management, intercultural communication, presentation skills, speaking to the media, and conducting effective meetings). Recent articles on listening include "Listening Skills for Lawyers" (with Lisa Merrill, *The Champion,* 1987), "Listening in the Conflict Management Cycle: A Cultural Perspective on the Decoding Behavior of Women's and Men's Listening" (*Speech Communication Annual,* Vol. 4, Spring 1990) and "Interrelationships Between Gender and Listening in Intimate Relationships" (with Dan Hahn, *Journal of the International Listening Association,* Vol. 6, Fall 1992). She has co-authored and co-edited the following books in the field of communication: *Conflict Management: A Communication Skills Approach* (with David Victor, Simon and Shuster, 1989); *The Power to Communicate: Gender Differences as Barriers* (with Lisa Merrill; Waveland Press, 1992); and *Women and Men Communicating: Challenges and Changes* (with Laurie Arliss, Harcourt Brace, 1993).

Judi Brownell (Ph.D. Syracuse University) is a Professor of Managerial Communication and Director for Graduate Studies in the School of Hotel Administration at Cornell University. She teaches both undergraduate and graduate managerial communication courses and conducts seminars in the School's executive education programs. She is an active trainer and consultant on managerial listening, organizational communication, strategic communication planning, customer service, and human relations skills. Her publications include books on listening (*Listening: Attitudes, Principles, and Skills*, Allyn & Bacon, 1996) and organizational communication (*Organizational Communication and Behavior*, Holt Rinehart, & Winston, 1989), as well as numerous articles in business, communication, management, and hospitality journals. She has served as an executive officer in the Southern Tier Chapter of the American Society for Training and Development, the New York State Speech Communication Association, and the International Listening Association.

Ellen Bonaguro (Ph.D. Ohio University) is Assistant Professor of Speech Communication at Ithaca College. She has held previous academic appointments at Northern Illinois University and Ohio University. Her areas of expertise include health communication, health education, and health promotion. She has worked in the health care field as the Director of a Community Health Care Center. She has also conducted research and training programs on HIV/AIDS education and prevention for elementary, secondary and college students, and has designed a national AIDS training program that has been presented throughout the United States.

Carolyn Coakley (M.A. University of Maryland) is co-author with Andrew D. Wolvin of the widely-used text, Listening, now in its 5th edition (Brown & Benchmark, 1996), and Listening Instruction (SCA/ERIC, 1979). Additionally, she and Wolvin are co-editors of Experiential Listening: Tools for Teachers and Trainers (Spectra, 1989) and Perspectives on Listening (Ablex, 1993). Coakley is the sole author of Teaching Effective Listening, Volume 1 (Spectra, 1993) and Volume 2 (self-published, 1996), both of which are practical guides for listening instructors. She is past president of the International Listening Association (ILA), recipient of four ILA Research Awards, and inductee into the ILA Listening Hall of Fame. Currently, she and Wolvin are collaborating on a parent/teen listening book. In addition to being an author, Carolyn is a college listening instructor and a corporate listening trainer.

Susan J. Drucker (J.D., St. John's University) is an attorney and Associate Professor of Speech Communication and Rhetorical Studies at the School of Communication, Hofstra University. She is the co-editor (with Robert Cathcart) of *American Heroes in a Media Age* and co-editor (with Gary Gumpert) of *Voices in the Street: Gender, Media and Public Space*. Her primary interests include media law and the impact of laws on social interaction and public space. Her work has appeared in *The New York State Bar Journal, Communi-*

cation Theory, Communication Quarterly, Critical Studies in Mass Communication and *Journal of Communication.*

Gary Gumpert (Ph.D., Wayne State University) is Professor Emeritus of Communication Arts and Sciences at Queens College, City University of New York. He is the author of *Talking Tombstones and Other Tales of the Media Age* and co-editor (with Robert Cathcart) of three editions of *Inter/Media: Interpersonal Communication in a Media World*. He is the co-editor, with Sandra Fish *of Talking to Strangers: Mediated Therapeutic Communication* and (with Susan Drucker) co-editor of *Voices in the Street: Gender, Media and Public Space*. Numerous articles have appeared in *The Quarterly Journal of Speech, Critical Studies in Mass Communication, Journal of Communication* and *Communication Theory.*

Dan F. Hahn (Ph.D., University of Arizona) is Professor Emeritus at Queens College. He teaches both undergraduate and graduate courses in rhetoric, political communication and communication theory. He has developed programs both here and abroad on how we listen, with a major focus on presidential communication and its impact on society. The co-author of two books on presidential communication (*Listening for a President* and *Presidential Communication*) and the author of *Introduction to Political Communication* , he has published nearly 80 journal articles and book chapters, including 7 co-authored works on gender and communication.

Patrice M. Johnson (M.A. Tulane University) is a member of the adjunct faculty of University College, Tulane University, where she teaches human resource management. After 15 years of university experience designing and teaching technical and business writing courses, Ms. Johnson spent ten years in industry, including key communication positions with the U.S. Department of Energy and Mobil Oil Corporation. She is currently Director, SPECTRA, Inc., where she specializes in conflict management, leadership skills coaching, facilitation skills training, and business writing workshops. A regular contributor to human resource journals and presenter at International Listening Association conferences, Ms. Johnson is particularly interested in the role of listening in organizational development.

George M. Killenberg (Ph.D., Southern Illinois University) is Professor in the School of Mass Communications at the University of South Florida at St. Petersburg and a journalist with extensive experience as reporter and editor for several major daily newspapers. He is author or coauthor of three books, *Public Affairs Reporting: Covering the News in the Information Age* (St. Martin's Press), *The Conversation of Journalism* (Praeger), and *Before the Story: Interviewing and Communication Skills for Journalists* (St. Martin's Press). His articles on listening have appeared in *Journalism Educator, Journal of Mass Media Ethics*, and the *Journal of the International Listening Association*. He is currently interested in investigating cultural influences on reporters and their methods.

Gary L. Kreps (Ph.D., University of Southern California) is Professor and Executive Director of the Greenspun School of Communication at the University of Nevada, Las Vegas. Before moving to UNLV he was a faculty member at Northern Illinois University, Rutgers University, Indiana University at Indianapolis, and Purdue University Calumet. He has expertise in organizational communication; health promotion; interpersonal/group interaction; multicultural relations; communication theory; leadership and empowerment; conflict management and research methods. He has written many well received books, chapters, and scholarly articles concerning communication, management, education, and health care. He is the editor of two Hampton Press book series: "Communication and Social Organization" and "Health Communication," was the founding editor of the SCA "Applied Communication Publication" series, and edited special issues of the *American Behavioral Scientist* and the *Journal of Health Psychology*.

Ralph G. Nichols (Ph.D., University of Iowa) is Professor Emeritus and retired Head of the Rhetoric Department at the University of Minnesota. He has authored or co-authored 24 books concerning human communication, and has developed listening training programs used in both industry and education. Scores of his articles have appeared in professional journals and such popular magazines as *Reader's Digest, Nation's Business, Colliers*, and *Harvard Business Review*. He has given special lecture series at five universities, is a founding member of the International Listening Association, and is a past president of both the International Listening Association and the Speech (Communication) Association of America.

Michael W. Purdy (Ph.D., Ohio University) is currently University Professor and academic coordinator of the Communications Programs at Governors State University. He has published articles and/or presented papers on listening/interpersonal communication, communication philosophy, qualitative research, and communication technology; he is managing editor of *Integrative Explorations: Journal of Culture and Consciousness*, and he lectures and conducts workshops for business, government, religious, and service organizations on listening, management communication, and customer service. He is an inductee into the International Listening Association Listening Hall of Fame. He is currently working on another book or two on listening. Listening seems to be an obsession at this point in his life.

Jim L. Query, Jr., (Ph.D., Ohio University, 1990) is an Assistant Professor of Communication at Loyola University Chicago. He was President of the Alzheimer's Association of Tulsa, Oklahoma from 1991 to 1994. In addition to being a summer research fellow and consultant with the National Cancer Institute, he has worked and taught at the Indiana University School of Nursing and the Ohio University College of Osteopathic Medicine. The bulk of his research examines the communication of social support during major life events such as retirement, caregiving during Alzheimer's, returning to higher education, and living with AIDS. His other research interests include organizational communication. His articles appear in the following journals: *Health Communication, Journal of Applied Communication Research*, and *Health*

Psychology. His chapters are found in the following edited books: *Essays to commemorate the 75th anniversary of the Speech Communication Association; Interdisciplinary casebook of geriatric communication; Qualitative research: Applications in organizational communication; A lifetime of relationships; and HIV infection and social interaction*. A forthcoming chapter focuses on the history of health communication. Dr. Query also serves on several editorial boards.

Dean Thomlison (Ph.D. southern Illinois University) is Professor of Communication at the University of Evansville, Indiana. He is co-author of *Toward Interpersonal Dialogue*, a textbook on interpersonal communication, and he has written numerous articles on listening and communication. When not teaching, Dean serves as a communication consultant for communities and corporations on dispute resolution, decision-making, customer relations, intercultural training, and listening. Throughout his three year Kellogg National Fellowship he has had the opportunity to travel the world examining intercultural education environments. Dean served as a member of the executive board of the International Listening Association for the past two years.

Lyman K. (Manny) Steil (Ph.D. Wayne State University), CSP, CPAE, is President of Communication Development, Inc., a St. Paul, Minnesota Consulting and Training Company. He is former Chairman of the Speech Communication Division, Department of Rhetoric, University of Minnesota. Professionally trained in business administration, psychology, speech communication, and organizational communication, Dr. Steil is an experienced businessman, educator, consultant, researcher, and worldwide lecturer. He is the author of numerous articles and educational materials, including the videocassette series "Effective Listening: Developing Your Ear-Q!" He is also author and co-author of four books, *Effective Listening Key to Your Success, Listening . . . It Can change Your Life, Secondary Teachers Listening Resource Unit*, and *Listening, Training and Development: Guidelines for Human Resource Professionals*. Dr. Steil was the founder, first President and past Executive Director of the International Listening Association. In addition, Dr. Steil is an inductee into the Listening Hall of Fame, and a recipient of the National Speakers Association's prestigious CPAE Award which honors professional speaking excellence.

David A. Victor (Ph.D., University of Michigan) is Associate Professor of Management in the Eastern Michigan University College of Business in Ypsilanti. He teaches courses in business communication and management at both the graduate and undergraduate level, and has acted a consultant for companies in the United States, Canada, and Europe. Dr. Victor has published several articles on business communication and is the co-author with Deborah Borisoff of *Conflict Management: A Communication Skills Approach*.

Cindy Rhodes Victor (J. D., University of Michigan Law School) is a partner practicing law in the firm of Howard and Howard in Bloomfield Hills,

Michigan. She has authored numerous articles on legal issues including AIDS in the workplace and sexual harassment.

Kittie W. Watson (Ph.D. Louisiana State University) is Associate Professor and former Chair of the Department of Communication at Tulane University and one of the top 25 most prolific women scholars in communication. She has authored or co-authored numerous books, book chapters, and articles on listening, intrapersonal, nonverbal, small group, and organizational communication. With Larry L. Barker, she developed the Watson-Barker Listening Test, one of the most widely tested listening assessment instruments currently available. Dr. Watson is past president of the International Listening Association, a member of the Listening Hall of Fame, and Associate Director of the Institute for the Study of Intrapersonal Processes. As Executive Vice President of SPECTRA, Inc., she is a sought-after speaker, consultant, and trainer.

Andrew D. Wolvin (Ph.D. Purdue University) is Professor and Chair of the new Department of Speech Communication at the University of Maryland, College Park. He and Carolyn Coakley are co-authors of the widely-used texts *Listening* (William C. Brown Company), *Listening Instruction* (ERIC), and *Experiential Listening* (Spectra). Andy is a founding member, Hall Of Fame inductee, and past president of the International Listening Association. He serves as a listening consultant and trainer to a number of federal agencies, private corporations, and educational institutions.